JEWISH IDENTITY

JEWISH IDENTITY

**EDITED BY
DAVID THEO GOLDBERG AND
MICHAEL KRAUSZ**

Temple University Press
Philadelphia

TEMPLE UNIVERSITY PRESS
Philadelphia 19122
Copyright © 1993 by Temple University. All rights reserved
Published 1993
Printed in the United States of America

The paper used in this publication meets the minimum
requirements of American National Standard for
Information Sciences—Permanence of Paper for Printed
Library Materials, ANSI Z39.48-1984 ∞

LIBRARY OF CONGRESS CATALOGING-IN-PUBLICATION DATA
Jewish identity / edited by David Theo Goldberg
and Michael Krausz.
p.   cm.
Includes bibliographical references and index.
ISBN 1-56639-039-7 (cloth). — ISBN 1-56639-040-0 (pbk.)
1. Jews—Identity.   I. Goldberg, David Theo.   II. Krausz, Michael.
DS143.J456   1993
305.892'4—dc20
92-31754

For my father, Isidore Goldberg,
and for my father's father, Solomon.
D.T.G.

To the memories of my grandparents,
Simon and Franciska Krausz, who perished in Auschwitz,
and to the memories of my father, Laszlo Krausz,
and my brother, Peter Krausz.
M.K.

CONTENTS

PREFACE

Jewish Identity is a collection of philosophical essays revealing how being Jewish raises questions about what it means for persons to have a cultural identity, to identify with a culture, and to be identified in terms of cultural membership. The concept of Jewishness raises philosophical issues faced by all cultures concerning cultural definition: Can a single or unifying identity be attributed to Jewish culture, and if so what are its identifying features; and is there a Jewish self, or only many persons that are Jewish? The contributors address these issues within the context of the philosophical debates about the changing conceptions and significance of personal and cultural identity in late modernity and postmodernity. This in turn raises related ethical issues faced in the volume: First, do moral obligations and rights derive from general rules universally applicable that are simply embodied in or expressed by the likes of Jewish culture, or are the force and enforceability of moral rules strictly bound by and to a particular community and its historically specific traditions? Second, is there a duty for members of a culture to perpetuate their traditions, especially where the traditions are rich and long-standing but which modernization and cultural interchange seem to be transforming beyond recognition?

We wish to thank Barbara Lammi, a graduate student, and Kay Korman of the School of Justice Studies, Arizona State University, for their generous assistance in preparing the manuscript. Our thanks, too, to Fran Mularski of the Auxiliary Resource Center of the College of Public Programs for putting it all together, Pietro Toggia for help compiling the Index, and Debby Stuart for seeing the book through the production process.

JEWISH IDENTITY

INTRODUCTION

The Culture of Identity

David Theo Goldberg and Michael Krausz

SOCIAL identities are not just givens, they are not simply established facts. What one is—the slipping tangle of what one takes oneself and is taken to be—is produced and reproduced against a complex of social, political, cultural, technological, and economic conditions. In being reproduced from one moment to the next, from one social setting to another, one's identity is often transformed by the push and pull of political economy and ideology, by the identities of others with whom one interacts, by what one does and says and reads. In short, whether one is Jew, Muslim, or Christian, Hindu or Buddhist, proletarian or capitalist, black or white or Arab, gay or straight is in large part a product of the conditions in which social subjects find and in terms of which they make themselves.[1] This production is, short of death, never complete, always in process (and after death is often carried on by others, in one's name).

By contrast, philosophical analysis of identity has been preoccupied with the nature of persons and selves. In this philosophical debate, some distinguish between the self as proper object of metaphysical analysis and the person or subject as what comes to be socially constituted on the basis of the metaphysical posit. But because we are concerned here with cultural identity, we use "persons" and "selves" interchangeably.

The philosophical literature addresses such questions as the existence of a single or of many selves. One's commitments on this issue, in turn, raise further questions: If single, can the self be divided? If many, is there any identity between the different selves? What, for example, are the relations between my present and my future self? Clearly, responses to metaphysical questions of this sort have implications for ethical issues. Whether a person has duties and rights that persist from one time to another presupposes an answer to whether there is a self, a core identity to the person that persists over time. A central concern here is whether there is any reason to be self-interested, especially about the future. In contemplating present actions, is it in my self-interest to take seriously its long-term effects, especially the consequences for future generations? And if there is no single identity to a self that persists over time, what are the implications for compensating persons in the future for a culpable harm they suffered in the past?

The question of personal identity in the Lockean tradition (the features of a person that underlie all changes across time), as Cora Diamond points out in "Sahibs and Jews," seems little concerned with the issue of who one is, of what sociocultural identification amounts to. But the question of cultural identity and the moral and sociopolitical issues it raises has only recently been taken up in a general and vigorous way as a pressing concern of philosophical discourse.

So, the metaphysical conception of personhood has largely failed to address seriously, if at all, the cultural conception of the person. Yet the latter may have important implications for an analysis of the fundamental metaphysical questions. Persons, on this wider conception, are taken to be culturally defined, acquiring identity and being identifiable in cultural terms. Culture is understood, as Bernard Berofsky understands it in "The Identity of Cultural and Personal Identity," to invest persons with identity, to sustain their identity, and more generally to furnish grounds for identity between persons.

One possible defense by the metaphysicians of personal identity against the critical thrust of cultural theorists is this: There must be some conception of the self that is the bearer of culture. So, a conception of personal identity must be presupposed by any conception of cultural identity. The general philosophical question here, then, is whether there is anything to persons qua persons other than their cultural definition. Stated in wider terms, we can ask what implications an analysis of cultural identity has for issues central to the debate over personal identity. This generates questions about what it is to have a culture, to be a member of a culture, to identify with and be identified as a member of a culture.

A primary concern underlying Diamond's distinguishing between the Lockean metaphysics of personhood and the analysis of cultural identity is that the concepts of identity central to each sort of theoretical discourse differ in meaning. The issues here are difficult. One strategy in trying to get at them is to look at the way some particular culture structures persons and imputes identity to its members. Jewish culture is rich and varied. There is a strong commitment by its members to Jewish cultural and self-definition. This is reflected especially in the common (self-)reference to Jewish identity. But Jews now are seldom if ever just Jews. They hail, and virtually throughout their history have hailed, from different countries, speak different languages, occupy different class positions, and in some ways practice different religions—if they practice at all. Jews then raise in an especially acute way the general question of what it means for one to have an identity, to identify with a culture, and to be identified in terms of cultural membership. This concern with the identity of culture, with identity through culture and its commitments, and so with the culture of identity, has assumed increasing importance as a response to the spreading alienation and anonymity that is so often taken to mark interpersonal relations in late modernity.

It may be that culture is a necessary way of living out personhood and, as Garry Brodsky argues in "A Way of Being a Jew; a Way of Being a Person," that Jewishness is one culturally defined way among others of living it out. Yet the concept of Jewishness also raises problems concerning cultural definition: Can a single or unifying identity be attributed to Jewish culture? Is there a Jewish self, or only many persons that are Jewish? What are the implications—metaphysical, social, political, and moral—for any attribution or identification as Jewish? As Alan Montefiore suggests in "Structures of Personal Identity and Cultural Identity," Jewishness seems to offer fertile ground for a general analysis of the intersection of personal and cultural identity.

Many of the essays collected here address themselves to the reconciliation of personal and cultural identity from postmodernist or postfoundationalist assumptions. They do so by focusing on the case of Jewish identity, recognizing that the analysis may well be replicable, with appropriate adjustments, in the cases of other cultural groups. Meditation on the theoretical concerns raised by cultural identity are pursued in many essays here through personal narratives. Autobiographical narrative is seen to be suited to, because necessarily reflective of, the radically contingent constitution of the self. In "Next Year in Jerusalem?" Richard Shusterman offers the rationale for this sort of "bio-philosophy." There are deep links between action, narrative, and personal identity. The self is seen to be formed through (self-)narration, revealing through narrative who one is or may be. Because different narratives can be articulated, no single identity, no one true self can be said to exhaust all personal and cultural constructions. The postmodern dissolution of the self finds itself reflected in and through narrative fragmentation of the culturally defined subject.

In any study of this sort, different conceptions of identity and identification need to be distinguished. In "Identification and Identity," Nathan Rotenstreich reminds us that the logical concept of identity—that something is itself and not another thing—is presupposed, and so taken for granted. This is to be distinguished from the sum features of a thing that enable us to pick it out, to recognize it as a thing of a given kind, to individuate or re-identify it. As Diamond points out, these senses differ again from determining a person's identity, from establishing what the person identifies *with,* what values a person adheres or is loyal to, what sorts of collectivities the person is aligned with and in terms of which may be comprehended.

Now it may be objected that if you take away a person's identity in this latter sense, what remains is precisely personal identity in the metaphysical sense of Locke. For reasons obviated by Berofsky, this identity cannot simply consist in the body, though Rotenstreich is surely correct in insisting that the body plays some role in setting the span of the subject. Berofsky's candidate is memory, which has some appeal in this context. But the point that needs to be stressed, as Berofsky does, is that even if memory plays only a less than complete part in setting the parameters of personal identity, that it plays any part at all necessitates the centrality of culture in defining personal identity. Witness the importance of names to the establishment of a personal identity. That David Theo Goldberg is the same person now as the twelve-year-old child who attended a Hebrew day school in South Africa may have in part to do with the actual causal relations linking the body now going by that name to the body then going by it. But this causal continuity, including the psychological, is meaningful—and not just epistemologically—only in the light of the present memories (Goldberg's own and perhaps others') of those events as attached to this body. And this body of memories, in turn, assumes continuity as Goldberg's in terms of his "I," the public signification of which is carried by the proper name "David Theo Goldberg."

The history of this sort of name, the history of experiences of those bearing such a name, in part structures expectations others have of the bearer, of who he is, and by extension of the bearer's self-conception. One's handwritten signature perhaps captures this duality of the personal and cultural knot that constitutes the self. The signature is in a particular alphabet, if not quite a given language; it is the public mark of culturally inscribed naming; but it is also and equally one's expressed individuation. In this, the signature is the outward sign of who one takes oneself and who one is taken to be.

Diamond draws our attention to the example of concealing one's identity by using a "false" name, a name by which one is not known. Equally, one might be driven to conceal one's culture by changing one's name, and by changing one's name to conceal—*to transform?*—who one is. There have been times nevertheless when, in spite of themselves, people have been identified with some culture, with "who they really are." Names of course often play a large part in this, but not the whole part. For the Nazis it was not just the "Jewishness" of the name itself. It was especially the experience of the name, what one was taken as in terms of the name, what place one came to stand in by virtue of bearing and being identified by the name. Historically, then, the name for Jews has played a role not dissimilar to skin color for blacks. In "Characterizing the Evil of American Slavery and the Holocaust," Laurence Thomas articulates the implications for contemporary black and Jewish identity, respectively, of the significance and significantly different experiences of slavery and the Holocaust. There are obvious differences between the name and skin color: one does not wear one's name as one does one's skin color. But once known, significance may be attached to the name in something like the way it has been and continues to be attached to skin color. So a "Jewish name" may serve to identify one as Jewish or of being of Jewish cultural background in much the way skin color identifies a person as "black." The analogy extends to "passing." One may have difficulty determining that the bearer of a specific name is Jewish (how can one know just by looking at the table of contents which of the contributors to this volume is Jewish?) just as one might establishing whether someone of a particular hue is black (why in either case would one want to?).

These various ways in which the personal and the cultural are knotted together—they are perhaps just the same phenomena viewed from different perspectives—raise the question of what is meant by culture. To have a culture, in Diana Meyers's minimal sense articulated in "Cultural Diversity," is to share a system of beliefs, values, *and* practices basic to human existence through which members are able to make sense of themselves and their world. Viable cultures in this sense are necessarily more or less open and elastic, porous at their boundaries, to some degree pragmatic in relation to other cultures, and transforming.

What then, one may ask, gives distinction or "identity" to a culture, to Jewishness, say? The passage Berofsky cites from Yoram Kaniuk's *Rocking Horse,* like so many passages one might cite from various sources of culturally located literatures, expresses directly—culturally, to risk circularity— what it is so difficult to identify theoretically as unique about the culture. It is caught up in a feeling, the particular nuance of sensibility, the shade of humor, the mode and manner of expression, the turn of phrase. To say that some are clearly identifiable as Jewish in this cultural sense is perhaps to say that they assume something of this tradition of expression as their own, that they identify *with* it, identify themselves *through* it. And this identity, this identification, as Berofsky suggests, can be sustained only by a wealth of knowledge of particular experiences and their accompanying feelings, that is, by the lived experiences of the person in question. Thus, to make sense of the personal identity of anyone presupposes that we recognize the "psychosocial context" in which the individual's experiences are embedded, against the background of which they are to be read.

As several contributors point out, one can distinguish between membership of a collectivity in virtue, on one hand, of satisfying some assent-independent criterion like matrilineal descent and, on the other hand, of consensual identification with the collectivity. To *be Jewish* simply by way of descent will differ from assuming a Jewish identity, from *affirming one's Jewishness* as a matter of choice. As Asa Kasher and Michael Krausz both make clear, Jewish identity—as collective identity in general—differs from the criterial imposition of Jewish identification (at the extreme of which stands the yellow star). In contrast to satisfying the criteria (whatever they are) for "being a Jew," taking on Jewishness as one's cultural identity presupposes the conjunction of self *and* other ascription, of what Meyers defines as attestation and social affirmation. So, it may not be sufficient, though it is necessary, only to consider oneself so. In these terms, then, both Krausz and Berofsky remind us that one can be identified as Jewish, one can literally *be* a Jew without ever knowing it; but it would make no sense to say of one that she has assumed a Jewish identity but knows it not.

It may be thought in the light of this that conversion is necessarily consent based. Yet, at least in the case of Judaism, this would be misleading because incomplete. Krausz makes it clear in "On Being Jewish" that converting to Judaism is centered not on assuming or denying some set of credal beliefs but on embracing law-defined practices. So at most one could say that Jewish converts are consenting to direct their practices in terms of an established set of laws. And taking oneself as Jewish presupposes having beliefs about oneself in relation to others "of the same kind." Central to Judaism, but not to Jewishness, then, is a set of law-defined practices; while central to Jewishness, but only at most in part and by extension to the religion of Judaism, is the question of group history. This distinction raises in an acute way the question of the place Judaism as a religion occupies in Jewish cultural identity, for the Old Testament, Hilary Putnam reminds us in "Judaism and Jewish Identity," serves also as the basic historical document of the Jews.

Many of the contributors to this volume concur that to be Jewish is not just, in Diamond's terms, to identify with or share others' values, aims, interests, or feelings. It is moreover to have a sense of belonging, to share a history with others (which one does precisely as a member of a group), or to participate in the group's forms of life. Denying this common past is tantamount to denying a shared culture. There is some question about what or how much identification with a people's past one can deny, or how much of it one can be ignorant of and still claim belonging. Diamond, for one, insists that to deny the place of Israel in the historical memory of Judaism and thus to deny attachment to Israel is to deny one's Jewishness. But others are not so sure. There is disagreement among the contributors about the centrality of Israel in the definition of their Jewishness. For Shusterman, the myth of return seems a necessary condition for being Jewish. One must hold out the perennial possibility of "next year in Jerusalem." But in "Going and Resting," Israel plays only a contingent historical role for Gabriel Josipovici's self-identification as Jewish and identity with Jewishness. Here the condition of being a Jew is not one of exile from the promised land but of "going and resting," of a sort of sojourn and moving on or having to move on and settling for a time elsewhere. This nomadic quest across the ceaseless duration of history has become so set in the historical consciousness of Jews that Israel becomes just one more resting place. Jews, then, epitomize the peripatetic condition of the postmodern person.

In "Structures of Personal Identity and Cultural Identity," Alan Montefiore properly insists that this nomadic condition differs both from that of rootlessness, for which Jews have so often been criticized, and from the state of being uprooted. A cultural condition of wandering, both physical and psychological, likely promotes fierce independence. This independence manifests in both geographical and political terms. Israel is an "imagined community" reinvented in the consciousness of European Jewry quite recently; it flourished only briefly—as long as it took for the myth of place to lose its brilliance, to be sullied by the realpolitik of dominance and subjugation. Restless but not rootless, Josipovici reminds us that the Jew as wanderer needs no home to which he or she longs to return, no place of be-longing, no homeland. Wandering is at once suffered as a curse (the injunction, as Diamond puts it, to "live the life of the natives" is at once the imperative to assimilate, to abrogate one's Jewish being) and lived as a blessing (the imperative to serve as the world's conscience, to be the guardian of historical memory, to be true only to the Moral Law).

If this is right, and Josipovici's basic insight strikes us as a compelling one, it opens up the possibilities of reading into Jewishness, if not defining it in terms of, a range of competing and conflicting thematics. It is this existential conflict of paradoxical principles, of what Berel Lang in "The

Phenomenal-Noumenal Jew" calls antinomies, that perhaps best articulates the density of a properly contested cultural identity; of what it is to be Jewish, of Jewishness as both curse and blessing.

In a dominant intellectual culture that is universalist in thrust and articulation, commitment to any particular cultural content appears contrived, narrow, and irrational, if not premodern. This is a point Gordon Lafer makes clear in "Universalism and Particularism in Jewish Law." Montefiore in turn suggests that this tension is more deeply generalized as basic to the contemporary human condition. It plays itself out as the pull between seeing ourselves on one hand as generically and inclusively human, as connected to and concerned with the well-being of all other human beings, while on the other hand taking ourselves to have particular natures bound by space and time. While we may engage in discourse with "man" at large, Montefiore points out that a precondition for the possibility of discourse is that it be conducted by persons with particular commitments, with identities that are necessarily localized, and which by that token tend to be exclusionary. What then, asks Lafer, are Jews: citizens of the world or tribal members? This question is especially poignant in the case of Jewishness, for here we find articulated a general outline of universalist moral obligations hand in hand with a fierce clannishness, cultural separation, and the exclusivity of a particularist ethnic ethic.

This tension in the constitution of identity between universality and particularity may be overdrawn. For abstract universal characterizations of human beings can be lived out only in the particular circumstances and conditions of daily life, of cultural and social and political context, in terms—as Putnam among others puts it—of a way of life. It is this way of life, Jewishness in the case at hand, that furnishes the conventional background against which particular actions and events, projects and ends make sense. Putnam contends that this knowledge of tradition is not so much constraining as it widens the sense of the possible for cultural adherents. From the point of view of liberal universalism, all claims are treated from the impossible, the irresolvable standpoint of equal urgency. Difference is ignored. From the standpoint of the cultural community, by contrast, claims are interpreted in light of the relations of responsibility people have to one another. Difference is valued and to be respected. The primary difference, however, between premodern forms of communitarianism and contemporary ones—between "primitive communitarianism" and "communitarianism proper," as a Marxist might put it—is that where once a subject might have been fully defined by a single membership, memberships now tend mostly to be multiple and identities accordingly complex.

As Lafer points out, these differences rest on an underlying conflict in conceptions of rationality. For universalism, rationality consists in deriving general principles from a priori axioms and then constraining particular circumstances to fit the general principles. Rationality in the Jewish tradition, by contrast, consists in comparing particular cases with each other against general background conventions constructed out of the long history of experience.

There are implications here too for the metaphysical characterization of values. For the rational universalist, values are given by inherent nature. Inherent nature by definition is unchanging, and so values are deemed objective and essential, general and atemporal. Those committed to the particularism of lived culture, by contrast, take values to be deeply historical and slowly transforming, socially constituted and reaffirmed (without being reified) across the long waves of time. As Krausz suggests, identities here are constituted as intersections in specifically located human bodies of historically defined discourses.[2] While those like Leon Goldstein, in "Thoughts on Jewish Identity," continue to insist on a single, unified construal of Jewishness, on the picture articulated here there is no essential, singular conception of Jewish nature, only people situated in positions contingently and perhaps contentiously identifiable as Jewish. Even under the rubric of Lang's postmodernist "pastiche" of culture, there may be limits on how far the multiplication of Jewishness(es) may extend. There may be some general parameters determining what can count as part of the culture and what not. Yet this need not presuppose some unified, idealized, nominal construal. Rather, the general rules may be developed, in a sense inductively, through the comparison of family resemblances among particular instances. As Brodsky insists, the fact that there is no Jewishness as such, no overarching set of beliefs, implies that no one general theory or metanarrative of the (set of) cultural condition(s) will suffice as an account. Lafer furnishes the reason: There is no extracultural place from which to construct such a grand theory and no generic social setting in which to apply it.

Accordingly, the standard view of contemporary diasporic Jewry as cosmopolitan, largely assimilated, adrift from their cultural roots, alienated and at a spiritual loss seems limited and one-sided. The sense that emerges from this volume is that the picture of postmodern Jewish identity, and by extension of cultural identity in general, is significantly richer and more complex, that personal-and-cultural identity is usually more porous, more fraught with tension and ambiguity than the standard picture is able to admit. It also suggests a commitment expressed by many in this volume to views critical of methodological individualism: Jews are, qua group, *a* people, not just a collection of individual persons, to use Thomas's useful distinction. The differences between conceiving cultural identity as flat and superficial, on one hand, and as perspectivally complex and nuanced, on the other, reflect deep differences in attitude and social commitments between the modernist and postmodernist. For the former, the prevailing question came to be, "Why assume a cultural identity, a community commitment at all?" and in particular, "Why be a Jew, say?" For the latter, by contrast, the questions have come instead to be, "What significance does cultural commitment have for social relations at large?" and "How are such identities constituted in the context of contemporary social conditions?" What, then, does it mean at the close of the second millennium to be, and to choose still to be, a Jew?

It is in the context of this latter set of concerns that the politically fraught question of the obligation to perpetuate one's culture assumes pertinence. A culture, Eddy Zemach argues in "Custodians," is what renders one human. The greater the culture the more, and the more diverse, the ways it furnishes its members to flourish. This suggests two reasons why resistance to domination is so often first and foremost cultural. First, the production, expression, and appeal of culture cannot be so easily controlled as material resources. And second, to wrest control over one's culture is at once to pry loose the hold over naming and (self-)representation. This is the first step to self-determination, and it is a necessary condition for taking command of the power to rationalize actions, conditions, and relations. The great value of a culture, then, is intrinsic. But Zemach insists also that the greater the culture—and great cultures are few—the more fragile it is. So cultures need nurturing, and the most capable cultural stewards will obviously be those whose culture it is. Thus Zemach thinks there is a duty—a duty by kinship, he calls it—for cultural members to sustain their culture. The source of the duty is the great evil of cultural death, what Krausz calls "cultural suicide," that would inevitably follow were one to fail in this obligation.

It follows that the grounds of Zemach's duty by kinship have to do in part with relations of descent and in part with denying success to the cultural exterminator. Appealing to unqualified relations of descent as grounds of a moral duty strikes us as a form of the naturalistic fallacy: A moral conclusion is deduced from nonmoral premises. The obligation a person has to look after aging parents surely is not biologically based, for to oblige an abused child later to take care of the abusive parent seems almost as egregious as the abuse itself. One cannot be said to owe allegiance to a culture—a drug culture, say, or a racist one—merely because one is a child of it. Cultural obligation, if it pertains at all, arises in virtue of the values embedded in the historical relations, the forms of cohabitation, and the sense of cultural belonging and sharing a history that emerges. As Diamond points out, the denial of this history, of one's ancestry and what one's ancestors stood for, is to deny one's cultural belonging, to obliterate one's sense of cultural self. And as Putnam maintains, there is no raw obligation to acknowledge one's Jewishness. The concern instead is whether in Jewish culture there is something culturally enriching that would be unavailable to those who reject the culture.

So, if there is a duty to perpetuate one's culture, it must more likely rest in the responsibility to maintain a good that is intrinsically valuable, and by extension to deny success to those who would obliterate it. As Lionel Rubinoff concludes in "Jewish Identity and the Challenge of Auschwitz," Jews, then, would have an obligation to deny Hitler posthumous victory by committing themselves to sustain the rich tradition of Jewish culture. From the twentieth century on, accordingly, the Holocaust has come to occupy for Jews the role of a defining experience, what Rubinoff, quoting Emil Fackenheim, calls a "root experience," much as Thomas points out by analogy that American slavery has become for American blacks. But it is an experience *against* which Jews, like blacks, are to define themselves, for they are to refuse domination or annihilation. That Jews and blacks have different experiences of racist domination supports the conclusions drawn elsewhere that the faces of racism are many, that the injustices racisms thus involve may differ from one case to another, that their influences upon and affects for identities may be various, and that the resistant response they call forth should not be singular and limited.[3]

Yet as Diamond observes, a negative commitment not to deny one's Jewishness fails in and of itself to specify more positively what the responsibility of Jewishness amounts to in any context. In the autobiographical narrative "Talking to Myself," Joseph Margolis (like Thomas) insists that there is no principled reason to assign the suffering of the Jews that culminated in the Holocaust, or any other suffering for that matter, a privileged position over all others, to elevate it to the paradigm case of human suffering. The assumption of a collective identity is based necessarily on a principle of exclusion. Recognition only of the suffering of one's own group is to privilege the history of one's own identity, to exclude the experience of others, and by extension ironically to invite one's own continued exclusion. Like Marx, Margolis challenges the Jew to bear witness to the suffering of all, not just his own, to be the eyes of justice. Poised uneasily between "an impossible adherence to the letter of the law" and the "ever-tempting embrace of assimilation" (Josipovici), Jews seem as well placed as any not just to be Brodsky's liberal pragmatist, but to assume Rubinoff's injunction to "feed the hungry," "clothe the naked," and (above all) "fight against oppression."

Yet as we noted earlier, to be Jewish is now necessarily to have some relation to Israel, to Israel as imagined community, as home to the Jewish displaced. But Israel is not home to those displaced for whom there can be none. For Israel also is a real state, one that for all its deep value to Jews the world over was founded on the violence of a profound displacement, a blessing and a curse. Israel, then, in its very proclamation—to borrow Josipovici's eloquence—is a coming in and a going out, homeland and state of homelessness. And in that it continues to represent Jewish history.

If we are to take seriously the conceptions of contributors to this volume of Jewishness as witness to oppression, it is one's own oppressiveness that one must first acknowledge and critique. Israel may be imagined at once as the haven to which many could flee from the cruel hand of power, as the hand that assumed and cultivated power, and as the fierce expression of power over others. Those once excluded now exclude, those imposed upon impose themselves. These sets of political condition are assumed, and they become constitutively integral to contemporary Jewish identity in the filial identification with Israel. It is an identity to be resisted only by unapologetically recalling the central place of wandering in the Jewish imagination. It is, perhaps paradoxically, only from this space of "in-betweenness," of "going and resting" and going again that the moral burden of the Jew as witness to oppression can be satisfactorily borne. And this diasporic condition of Jewishness, split between reflection of past belonging and future commitments, may serve in turn as symbolic of the increasingly cosmopolitan and nomadic condition of postmodernity's personal-as-cultural identity.[4]

NOTES

1. See Stuart Hall, "Cultural Identity and Diaspora," in *Identity: Community, Culture, Difference,* edited by Jonathan Rutherford (London: Lawrence and Wishart, 1990), 222–37.

2. See David Theo Goldberg, "The Social Formation of Racist Discourse," in *Anatomy of Racism,* edited by D. T. Goldberg (Minneapolis: University of Minnesota Press, 1991), 295–318.

3. David Theo Goldberg, *Racist Culture: Philosophy and the Politics of Meaning* (Oxford: Basil Blackwell, 1993), especially chap. 4.

4. See Hall, "Cultural Identity," especially 235–36.

I

CULTURE AND THE IDEA
OF IDENTITY

1

CULTURAL DIVERSITY

Rights, Goals, and Competing Values

Diana Tietjens Meyers

THE STRUGGLES of peoples to preserve their own cultures against the onslaughts of alien cultures number among the constants of human history, and cultural perpetuation persists today as an issue in various forms. Israel has denied automatic immigration rights to Jews who believe in Christ. The People's Republic of China makes it a matter of policy whether to sell decadent Western products, and much of the Islamic world is actively engaged in expelling Western social and political practices. The French Academy worries about Americanisms creeping into colloquial French. And members of U.S. society with histories as different as those of Hassidic Jews, Native Americans, and refugee Cubans are striving to keep their cultures from being overwhelmed. This essay addresses the problem of cultural perpetuation in culturally pluralistic societies, leaving aside the complications of international relations but stressing moral and political concerns.

Before considering whether there is some sort of moral warrant for cultural perpetuation, I briefly examine the nature and function of culture as well as the value of cultural diversity. Then I turn to the question of how moral and political theory might seek to realize that value. Though I urge that there is neither an individually held right to perpetuate one's culture nor a right held by cultural groups to perpetuate their cultures, I argue that in culturally pluralistic societies cultural diversity should be regarded as a social goal.

CULTURE AND CULTURAL PERPETUATION

The accounts of culture advanced by anthropologists vary in their emphasis.[1] Some stress conduct—a way of life—while others focus on experience—a set of rules for interpreting the world. But wherever the accent falls, the account lands us in a tangled nexus of ideas and activities. Transmitted to each new member of sundry social groups, these intricate ideational-behavioral systems enable fellow cultural initiates to recognize one another and endow them with a powerful social bond.

Yet cultural identification is not a straightforward matter of credentials similar to nationality. Cultural markers are sometimes definite and obvious, but they are commonly subtle and distinguished by degrees. Different cultural groups may speak wholly different languages, or they may speak dialects of a single linguistic stock. Characteristic comportment may be codified in rules that are taught to children, but children also assimilate certain cultural proprieties unconsciously as they grow up. Furthermore, these countless elements, some overt and others submerged, do not stand alone but rather mesh to form complex, evolving patterns.

The subtlety, mutability, and diversity of cultural traditions and cultural groups explain why the mechanisms and institutions of cultural affiliation resist schematization into a few paradigmatic modes. The concept of a culture compasses both the idea of a group of interconnected individuals and the idea of a heritage that unites them. Moreover, all cultures must supply solutions for the basic problems confronting human beings—how to obtain nourishment and shelter, how to interact with other persons, how to procreate, how to dispose of corpses, and the like. Still, this universal cultural function does not entail a universal infrastructure for all cultures. It is doubtful, then, that any one set of categories can comprehend the elements of all cultures and that any one ordering of these categories can represent the relations among these elements in all cultures. Consequently, little more can be said about cultures in general than that they consist of shared systems of beliefs and practices that handle, but are not limited to handling, the inescapable problems of human existence.

One consequence of understanding culture this way is that the borders between cultures are acknowledged to be somewhat indeterminate. The claim that cultures are delineated by the sharing of beliefs and practices makes cultural membership a matter of individual attestation matched by social confirmation. Since there can be disparities between self-perception and group perception, controversy is bound to arise over the precise limits of cultural groups, as in my example of Israel's need to reach a decision about the status of Jews for Jesus. Likewise, since there can be disagreements about the orthodoxy of some individuals' beliefs and practices, controversy is bound to arise over the contents of cultures. Some Jews regard turning on electric lights on the Sabbath as permissible; others do not. This indefiniteness seems appropriate, however, under conditions of cultural pluralism where cultures may come to overlap and where there may be a national heritage that members of otherwise distinct cultural groups nevertheless have in common.[2]

Cultures are not sharply demarcated, nor are they static. Succeeding generations face new circumstances and adjust their culture to meet unanticipated personal and collective needs. Whereas women were once restricted to the balconies of synagogues, the Reform branch now permits women in the main auditorium. If cultures were not sufficiently pliable to admit intracultural innovation in response to changing circumstances, cultural groups would be obliged to abandon their heritages so often that cultural continuity would be a rare phenomenon, lasting a few decades at most, and new cultures would spring up at every historical turn. Similarly, cultural fixity would entail that no culture could survive borrowings resulting from intercultural contact, regardless of how beneficial they might be. To avoid multiplying cultures fantastically while acknowledging that cultures can be enriched from within and without, cultures must be viewed as evolving systems.

Since cultures are at once plastic and vulnerable, it is necessary to distinguish between cultural evolution and cultural destruction in order to grasp cultural perpetuation. The autonomy of a cultural group and the survival of its original stock of beliefs and practices are both germane to the question of cultural perpetuation. Yet neither of these considerations is decisive.

Here it is important to realize that cultural isolation or other protection from alien intervention does not guarantee cultural autonomy. Just as senility is an autogenous form of personal debilitation that compromises the individual sufferer's capacity for self-direction, such events as a stunning technical breakthrough within a cultural group or a disastrous military campaign initiated by the group can precipitate development too rapid and profound for the culture to absorb. Convulsive cultural change can originate within a culture and impair the cultural group's autonomy. Furthermore, a cultural group's autonomy does not guarantee the integrity of its culture. If a cultural group were to decide unanimously and freely to discard its traditional beliefs and practices in order to adopt an altogether new system of beliefs and practices, no one would claim that the original culture had evolved into its replacement. Evidently, neither a cultural group's freedom from external direction nor its control over its course is a sufficient condition for cultural evolution.[3]

If the dynamics of cultural groups cannot account for cultural perpetuation, it seems the question of whether cultural change is evolutionary or destructive can be settled only by its extent. To assess the amount of cultural change taking place, criteria tailored to individual cultural systems and capable of gauging departures from customary beliefs and practices are needed. One way to generate such criteria would be to extract from the culture a controlling idea (or set of ideas) constituting the culture's worldview. Once a culture's worldview has been established, any changes in shared beliefs and practices compatible with this worldview could be styled evolutionary, and any changes implying another worldview could be tagged destructive. But extrapolating from particular beliefs and practices to overarching worldviews is hardly a mechanical or uncontroversial process.

Trouble arises because worldviews can be formulated with more or less specificity. A culture might, for example, be said to regard the West Bank as its ancestral homeland, in which case it would fit Jewish culture as well as Palestinian culture. Or this belief could be described as a biblically based belief in a divine promise of this homeland, in which case it would pertain exclusively to religious Zionists. In short, accounts of worldviews can be so detailed that no two people, let alone cultures, would share the same worldview, or so general that many ostensibly different cultures would share the same one. But since the level of generality at which accounts of cultural worldviews are pitched will determine whether a given change counts as evolutionary or destructive, it is critical that choices among worldview formulations be well grounded. Unfortunately, arbitrariness is inevitable in the absence of independent criteria of cultural evolution.

Evidence that a cultural group's autonomy has not been compromised or that changes in a culture are neither pervasive nor profound lend support to the claim that the culture is evolving. Nevertheless, neither type of evidence suffices to show that a culture is evolving, nor would evidence to the contrary by itself warrant the conclusion that the culture is defunct. Cultures are not reducible to sets of beliefs and practices from which departures can be quantified, and they are not reducible to the insular operations of self-regulating organizations whose symptoms of derangement can be diagnosed.

The weakness of both cultural autonomy and cultural cogency as indicators of cultural evolution is their insensitivity to the social dimension of culture. Beliefs and practices, it should be stressed, must be shared or must once have been shared by the members of a cultural unit to qualify as elements of a culture. Because the two criteria I have been considering abstract changes in cultures from collective adherence to a cultural heritage, these criteria illuminate the mechanics of cultural change without distinguishing evolutionary from destructive results. Giving the requirement that adherents share a culture's beliefs and practices its proper weight suggests that cultural change would count as evolutionary provided that it did not impair the culture's ability to sustain a cultural group—that is, provided that the culture's adherents were not prevented from recognizing one another and also provided that they continued to understand themselves as participants in a tradition that preceded them and that would survive them.[4]

Questions about this sort of viability can be answered only through field research on particular cultures. Cultures must be stable, and cultural change must be within the ken of the members of the cultural group. Otherwise, these individuals would experience no cultural bonds linking them to one another and would lack any awareness of cultural continuity over extended periods. Still, questions about which changes, how much change, and what rate of change a cultural group can tolerate are answerable only through documentation and analysis of actual cultural developments, for cultures differ in their adaptive capabilities, as well as in the content of their beliefs and practices.

What is clear, however, is that cultural evolution is highly unlikely to issue in cultural homogeneity. Cultures are distinguished not only by their current beliefs and practices but also by their histories. A culture's history serves to inspire respect for its traditions, and, by furnishing interpretations of novel events and options for coming to grips with such events, it guides the course of future development. For two cultures to merge, their distinct histories must recede so far into the past as to be beyond recovery. Of course, the line between evolution and destruction, that is, between cultural interaction and assimilation, is not always easy to discern since destruction can proceed glacially through the cumulative free choices of adherents. Nevertheless, cultural evolution underpins cultural diversity.

WHY CULTURES ARE WORTH PRESERVING

An often-voiced instrumental justification for cultural perpetuation is precautionary self-defense. Peoples that have been colonized or otherwise persecuted may come to believe that integration with the dominant culture is always superficial and never rules out the possibility of future attacks. If this is so, assimilation only induces a false sense of security—such as that of many German Jews during Hitler's rise to power—whereas cultural unity maintains social structures that can be adapted to purposes of self-defense should circumstances require it. The recent resurgence of neo-Nazi groups in Germany and anti-Semitic groups in Russia lends force to this position.

One advantage of this reasoning is that it does not rule out cultural pluralism. Each of a society's constituent cultural groups can consistently adopt the view that it must ensure that it is able to protect its members without proceeding to claim that it must achieve superiority over other cultural groups. Various cultural groups, each of which is sufficiently organized for purposes of self-defense, can coexist, balancing one another's strengths.[5] Nevertheless, justifying cultural perpetuation as a defense strategy is unsatisfying both because this justification presupposes inalterably bellicose relations among cultural groups and also because it fails to pinpoint anything about cultures *qua* cultures that should not be destroyed.

Here the support cultures lend to personal identity might be adduced to explain their value. Having been molded by their cultural milieus as children, adults cannot make sense of themselves without reflecting on this aspect of their upbringing in conjunction with their present cultural expectations and roles. Though one's place in a culture accounts only partially for personal identity, its contribution is substantial. Accordingly, it can be argued that cultures ought to be preserved, for they help to make people intelligible to themselves.

Unfortunately, this justification argues convincingly for the maintenance of some culture but not necessarily for the perpetuation of existing cultures. Consistent with this view, a campaign to consolidate all cultures could be deemed warranted, despite the deracination of a few transitional generations. After all, the unification of peoples thereby achieved would rid the world of a powerful and tenacious source of antagonism, and a unified culture would sustain personal identity just as well. While conceding a culture to be necessary, this position condemns cultural diversity. Accordingly, if opposition to cultural homogenization is to be defended, claims about the roots of personal identity in culture must be supplemented with an account of the value of each culture or the value of cultural pluralism.

To justify their defiance of assimilationist forces, traditionalist cultural adherents commonly advert to religious beliefs. When a religion assigns special temporal duties or a singular supernatural destiny to a cultural group, cultural perpetuation may seem self-evidently good. But this view of the matter runs into difficulties when cultures with competing beliefs and practices intermingle. In these situations it becomes evident that religions sanction the preservation of the culture (or cultures) that espouse them without endorsing cultural perpetuation in general. Indeed, this ethnocentrism explains why intercultural rivalries often have degenerated into campaigns to subjugate weak cultural groups and to repress their errant beliefs and practices, such as the Spanish Inquisition's demand that Jews renounce their faith.

Yet appeals to a culture's divine mission or privileged access to occult wisdom are attractive reasons for cultural perpetuation, because they feature elements of cultures that make them worth preserving. If any religious precepts about how to live or doctrines about the nature of reality are true, it surely would be lamentable if the culture embodying them perished. In the interest of reducing transcendental risk, then, we might consider ourselves well-advised to secure the perpetuation of as many cultures as possible, since we do not know which, if any, of their ostensible revelations are genuine.

To some extent this line of thought echoes John Stuart Mill's *On Liberty*, which defends free expression as a means of making social progress and discovering the truth. On Mill's model, cultural groups might be seen as laboratories testing alternative systems of beliefs and practices. But whereas Mill pictured a debate in which the best ideas and arrangements would gain ascendancy, I do not envision a cross-cultural free-for-all in which less attractive cultures would be marginalized, if not eliminated. Nevertheless, since Mill insists that inquiry and experimentation should never cease, his view requires making provision for some form of diversity within society.

It might be thought, however, that ad hoc groups that would form and dissolve at the pleasure of their membership could take the place of cultural groups in sustaining the testing process. While it is clear that voluntarist groups play an important role in social experimentation and change, this suggestion overlooks the richness of cultural traditions as sources of fresh understanding and direction. Indeed, it overlooks the fact that voluntarist groups are to some extent parasitic on unacknowledged cultural traditions. If these cultures disappeared, I suspect that the insight and imagination of these ad hoc groups would dry up.

Various instrumental considerations argue more or less convincingly for cultural perpetuation. Yet cultural diversity seems to exert an intuitive appeal that is not reducible to any culture's role in self-defense, personal identity formation, or social progress. The loss of a culture, it seems to me, would be a misfortune even if these other goods could be secured without it.

Paradoxically, a satisfactory account of the intrinsic good of cultural perpetuation cannot rest on whatever intrinsic goods are to be found in each culture. The trouble with this approach is that it implicitly bestows on every culture a title to precedence that either obviates mutual accommodation or invites evaluation of the relative worth of the intrinsic goods different cultures embody. By locating the good of cultural perpetuation at the level of the spectrum of cultures rather than at the level of individual cultures, these difficulties can be avoided, and the residual, noninstrumental appeal of cultural perpetuation can be captured.

Cultural diversity is, I believe, the social counterpart of the uniqueness we attribute to each person, and the value attaching to cultural diversity mirrors the value of personal uniqueness. Individual diversity is the upshot of freeing people to express themselves. Likewise, if each cultural group is composed of a singular combination of participants who collaborate to create and develop a shared system of beliefs and practices—a system answering to their distinctive collective genius, as well as to their particular historical circumstances—the result is cultural diversity. Just as we value individual diversity because we regard the unique individual as precious, we have reason to value cultural diversity since it is the prime manifestation of unique human collectivities.

Now, it might be objected that, since many cultures drastically curb individual expression, the desideratum of individual expression cannot account for the value of perpetuating diverse cultures, if those include repressive ones. This objection raises an important issue that is addressed in the next section—that is, whether for the sake of cultural diversity people are obligated to uphold cultures that they find uncongenial. However, as a critique of the account of the value of cultural diversity I propose, this argument mistakes analogical reasoning for instrumental reasoning. Cultural diversity is valuable, not because or insofar as it secures opportunities for personal expression, but because cultural uniformity would bespeak societies of interchangeable individuals living in indistinguishable environments and interacting in identical ways. In contrast, cultural diversity is emblematic of the uniqueness of human collectivities and is valuable for this reason.

PERSONAL MORALITY AND CULTURAL PERPETUATION

It might seem that the next step must be to propound a duty incumbent on each individual to uphold the culture of his or her birth. If cultural diversity is good, and if people ought to promote the good, it appears to follow that people are morally bound to perpetuate their respective cultures. What better way could there be to ensure that a multiplicity of cultures survives? And yet, what could be more stultifying for individuals who conscientiously dissent from fundamental tenets of their cultural heritage than a duty to uphold their cultures?

A duty to uphold the culture of one's birth would either be redundant or egregiously confining. To the extent that people cannot help exhibiting indelible cultural traits acquired during childhood, no one could fail to discharge this duty. However, to the extent that this duty prescribes participation in practices from which persons are capable of abstaining, it comes into conflict with basic personal liberties. If people are entitled to decide whom to befriend, where to live, what work to do, whether to believe in a religion, and the like, they cannot be duty-bound to perpetuate their cultures, since this duty would supersede these rights. Though there are circumstances in which people may be obligated by ties of solidarity not to abandon their culture, there is no natural duty contravening personal liberties to conform to cultural norms.

Rejecting a duty to perpetuate one's culture raises the question of whether cultural perpetuation is morally accidental. In one sense it clearly must be. If upholding one's culture is not usually morally compulsory, it is just happenstance that enough individuals from different cultures have chosen traditional observance to maintain a variety of cultures. Still, as a compromise between moral indifference to cultural perpetuation and moral enforcement of it, a right of cultural perpetuation might register moral approval of cultural perpetuation and thus underwrite cultural diversity. In exploring this proposal, it is necessary to consider both who would possess this right and what guarantees it would afford.

To see that a right of cultural perpetuation cannot be held by individuals, it is necessary to ask whether persons, taken singly, are the agents of cultural perpetuation. Consider an individual who is the sole surviving adherent of a culture and who continues to engage in its prescribed practices. If this individual possesses a right of cultural perpetuation, this behavior must be an instance of exercising this right affirmatively—this individual must be perpetuating a nearly defunct culture. It is not clear, however, that this lone individual's activity should count as perpetuating a culture. Obviously, she is trying to perpetuate her culture, but presumably she will fail in the long run for lack of committed fellows. Can she, then, be exercising a right to perpetuate her culture?

Of course, it might be objected that there is no more mystery here than there is in the right to assemble. Just as one person cannot assemble, one person cannot perpetuate a culture. Nevertheless, we acknowledge an individually held right to organize a meeting and to meet, and we would think a person entitled to publicize a gathering even if it could be reliably predicted that no one would attend. Similarly, a right of cultural perpetuation could be exercised unavailingly, and this would show nothing about the intelligibility of this right.

I believe, however, that this reasoning overlooks a crucial difference between organizing an assembly and perpetuating a culture. Whereas organizational activities are recognizable as such whether or not the intended meeting ever convenes, cultural perpetuation is irreducibly social. The main ground for allowing that a lone cultural exponent can perpetuate her culture is that she is a bona fide recipient of her cultural group's continuously transmitted body of doctrine and regulation and, consequently, some of her beliefs and actions must surely be authentic instantiations of her heritage. Still, the fact that this individual has ceased to share her culture's beliefs and practices with anyone else provides grounds for doubting that she is engaged in cultural perpetuation.

Although her credentials as an interpreter and practitioner of her culture are not suspect, her isolation conflates what she does because of her personal propensities with what she does because of her cultural background. If culture were not shared by individuals who mutually recognize one another as cohorts, culture would collapse into personality. Because a single remaining adherent of a dying culture does not share it with anyone else, it is impossible to separate culture from personality in her case. Without the distinction between culture and personality, no one's conduct can qualify as cultural perpetuation.

Now, it might be urged that this problem could be handled by independently documenting the culture's beliefs and practices. If a dispute arose over whether the individual was engaged in cultural perpetuation or merely doing what she wanted, expert anthropologists could be called in to make a determination. But, of course, this solution commits the cultural exponent to the cultural practices that prevailed whenever the culture was last accepted by a cultural group and thus bars cultural evolution. If a stagnant culture is a dead culture, it follows that cultural perpetuation would not be possible under this arrangement.

Needless to say, a lone cultural adherent should be free to pursue her chosen course—basic personal liberties entitle her to do so, and the worst that can be said of it is that it is futile. Still, such a person's liberty is not predicated on any special prerogatives arising in connection with cultural perpetuation. Unless she has the cooperation of others, a person cannot perpetuate her culture and cannot claim a right to do so. Consequently, any right to perpetuate cultures over and above basic personal liberties must be ascribed to cultural groups.

COLLECTIVE RIGHTS OF CULTURAL PERPETUATION

On one interpretation, a collectively held right of cultural perpetuation would be a right of noninterference endowing each cultural group with a liberty to uphold its shared beliefs and practices and imposing a reciprocal obligation not to intervene in the internal affairs of any other cultural group. This version of the right of cultural perpetuation is attractive in part because its implementation would allow each cultural group to devote its resources to shared cultural purposes and also because it does not conflict with cultural adherents' personal liberties. Unfortunately, this right squares better with a politics of cultural nationalism—that is, a political order in which cultural groups are self-sufficient and self-governing—than it does with a politics of cultural pluralism—that is, a political order in which cultural groups interact amicably under the auspices of a central authority.[6]

One problem with a group right of cultural perpetuation is that it would run afoul of the personal liberties of cultural strangers. Within broad limits, people are entitled to form and act on their own convictions without regard to their ancestral cultures. For example, cultural initiates may reject religious doctrine altogether or convert to a religion other than the culturally sanctioned one.[7] A cultural right of noninterference would not impinge on such liberties, but, if this right is to have any force, it would presumably bar missionary work. Yet representatives of alien religions are entitled to speak freely and to practice their religions, some of which command them to save heathens. Why should the liberties of cultural adherents constrain their cultural group's rights while cultural rights of noninterference govern the personal liberties of strangers?

The explanation of this asymmetry must be either that the limitations on strangers' rights are relatively unimportant or that the religious convert does not but the missionary does sabotage a viable culture. The former reasoning is unconvincing since it assumes that choosing to embrace a religion is momentously important but that practicing it is not. In defense of the latter line of thought, it might be argued that the impact of an individual's apostasy is confined to that single person's violation of cultural norms, whereas a missionary has designs on the entire community. But this argument rests on the implausible assumption that the choices of independent converts are harmless from the standpoint of cultural perpetuation. Yet it is evident that the cumulative effect of unsolicited individual conversions could be just as pernicious for a culture as the worst consequences of missionary zeal. Thus a cultural right of noninterference would arbitrarily favor the liberties of cultural adherents over the comparable rights of strangers.

Equally serious, it is not clear what protections a cultural right of noninterference would afford. Granted that cultural evolution is compatible with intercultural borrowing and that different cultures are supple and rigid in different ways and to different degrees, it is impossible to distinguish generically between destructive extracultural initiatives and felicific ones. Some cultures have been able to accommodate religious dissent and have embraced the value of religious tolerance, while others have dissolved in the wake of mass rejection of religious tradition. Similarly, whether exporting industrial technology or donating medical services to a cultural group unaccustomed to these benefits will prove benign is by no means apparent in advance.

In contrast, core violations of such well-established rights to noninterference as the right to life can be specified. This right prohibits, among other things, shooting, knifing, bludgeoning, and poisoning right-holders, for all people are vulnerable to being killed in these ways. Though some people are exceptionally at risk—for example, people who are allergic to penicillin—human vulnerabilities are sufficiently uniform that people generally know what they must refrain from doing in order to respect the right to life. But predicting an extracultural initiative's eventual effects is hazardous guesswork, and cultural destruction is often detectable only after it has been irreversibly set in motion. If it is not possible to distinguish extraculturally animated evolution from sinister alien manipulation, it is impossible to respect the proposed right of cultural perpetuation without altogether abstaining from intercultural contact. But choking off intercultural overtures, thus rendering cultural pluralism sterile, hardly seems a satisfactory solution.

Two ways to circumvent this impasse suggest themselves. One would be to model cultural exercise of a right of noninterference on individual exercise of an unrestricted right to liberty that permits virtually any form of intervention in the right-holder's life once the right-holder has consented. Wielding this right, cultural groups could entertain proposals for intercultural projects and control extracultural penetration. The other would be to shift away from a right to noninterference and to recognize a cultural right to aid modeled on the individual right to satisfaction of basic needs.

An umbrella right compassing subsidiary rights to various kinds of government support, the cultural right to aid could mitigate the deleterious effects of cultural interaction through government programs designed to maintain the attractiveness of traditional cultures.[8] The idea would be to ensure that any disadvantages attaching to cultural adherence, such as missed opportunities in the mainstream economy or fulfillment of onerous cultural duties, would not render this option ineligible. Policies ranging from enforcement of fair employment practices to bilingual services and subsidies for traditional economies could undercut assimilationist pressures.

Initially, a right of cultural perpetuation requiring strangers to obtain permission before penetrating a culture or requiring governments to make support available to constituent cultures seems admirably suited to the end in view. Whereas a right of cultural perpetuation stressing noninterference on the model of the right to life relies on strangers to anticipate and to desist from actions that would be destructive, this new version lodges responsibility for cultural survival with cultural groups themselves. To forestall cultural destruction, cultural groups would be expected to ascertain their needs and apprise other groups or government agencies of them. Furthermore, it is clear enough what would respect and what would violate these rights. In the first case, seeking approval for intercultural involvement before embarking on it would respect the right, and proceeding without prior consultation or despite being refused permission would violate it. In the second case, government funding of reasonable aid applications would respect the right, and refusal of such requests would violate it. Yet these rights pose other sorts of problems, for they rest on analogies between individuals and cultures that do not hold. The problem of how a cultural group's right to noninterference or government support could be asserted highlights these disanalogies.

An indispensable assumption underlying the attribution to persons of basic liberties and subsistence rights is that these individuals have a permanent interest in their own survival and freedom. Though they may rationally choose to risk their lives or their liberty when pressed by terrible and irremediable circumstances, there is a formidable presumption that people prefer life and self-direction over death and coercion. However, no comparable presumption is warranted with respect to cultures. A culture may be declining as a result of being traumatized by extracultural incursions or as a result of members' disenchantment with and desertion of anachronistic beliefs and practices. Cultures, to be blunt, can be backward and repressive, and cultural adherents can come to realize that their cultures thwart their aspirations. When people freely abandon a culture en masse, cultural devolution signals a legitimate exercise of individual autonomy, and no residual cultural interest remains to ground a countervailing right of cultural perpetuation. Indeed, what might have been taken for a collective interest in cultural perpetuation stands exposed as the sum of its adherents' interests in sustaining their culture, interests that need not be abiding.

Nevertheless, internally motivated cultural destruction is typically a piecemeal process pitting partisans against cultural loyalists. During such transitional periods, some individuals continue to share an interest in cultural perpetuation, and recognition of a right to noninterference or aid could not be decried as an affront to individual choice or as a vain attempt to revive a defunct culture.

Now the crucial question for a right of cultural perpetuation becomes who should exercise this right. Under the envisaged circumstances, cultures would harbor a range of opinion and practice. But surely each subculture could not be entitled to demand noninterference or aid geared to its particular conception of the culture. When a cultural group is engaged in modifying its beliefs or practices to the alarm of some members, enforced insularity or aid at the behest of a few disgruntled traditionalists would amount to alien obstruction of cultural evolution. Conversely, if a splinter group of activists could obtain government support for modernization projects abhorred by most members of the cultural group, the government would again improperly intervene, this time to impose change. In according every cultural subgroup the status of a cultural representative, this interpretation of the right of cultural perpetuation would invite these factions to prosecute their causes with the authority and power of the state, thereby politicizing cultural variegation and aggravating cultural fragmentation.

If a right of cultural perpetuation is not ascribed to every cultural exponent with a following, it must be ascribed to whole cultural units. But, unlike individuals, the contours of cultural groups in culturally pluralistic societies are often subject to dispute. Nevertheless, a right of cultural perpetuation would oblige cultural groups to settle their boundaries, possibly preempting evolution in progress and freezing distinct groupings that might otherwise have been temporary into permanent independent units. Moreover, cultural groups in culturally pluralistic societies seldom have centralized decision mechanisms and frequently lack a unified will. Thus the rights-based approach to cultural diversity would oblige many cultural groups either to invent institutions through which to exercise their rights or to forfeit the guarantees of these rights. The effect of this arrangement would be to give a survival advantage to cultural groups with affinities for existing government institutions, for they would be able to equip themselves institutionally to claim their rights without betraying their own traditions. However, this arrangement would disadvantage cultures with very different institutional histories, for they could not exercise this right in a manner consonant with their heritage. Again, a right to cultural perpetuation that itself disrupts cultural evolution hardly seems a satisfactory solution to the problem of maintaining cultural diversity.

In authorizing custodial tampering with the process of cultural evolution, a right to cultural perpetuation creates an unintended trap for rightholding cultures. Of course, denying a right of cultural perpetuation does not ensure that all cultures will remain supple and vigorous. Still, the artificiality of cultural rights to noninterference and aid in the fluid setting of cultural pluralism defeats their serviceability as vehicles of cultural perpetuation.

THE GOAL OF CULTURAL DIVERSITY

It may seem paradoxical to claim that cultural diversity is good but that there is no individual duty or responsibility, or any individual or group right to perpetuate cultures. If cultural perpetuation is good, it seems it ought to have some sort of moral standing. I would like to conclude by suggesting that Ronald Dworkin's notion of a social goal can help to supply the missing moral support for cultural diversity, but that applying his distinction between a right and a social goal to this issue reveals that the sphere of rights is not as sharply demarcated from that of goals as he sometimes maintains.[9]

The category of social goals compasses a variety of aims, such as prosperity, clean air, scientific progress, preservation of historical landmarks, and national defense. Like rights, social goals concern goods that are sensitive to government policy; however, social goals differ from rights inasmuch as the failure to realize a social goal is not morally appalling, as violating a basic right is. Attainment of social goals is problematic, since no hierarchy of goals is ever lasting and since programs contrived to achieve social goals are rarely, if ever, assured of success.

Social goals are constantly in competition with one another and can be ranked only tentatively. When it is discovered that one social goal has been unduly slighted, remedial action may be taken at the expense of some other goal until yet another commands political attention—prosperity is often at odds with ecological concerns, and recently the conflict between prosperity and the defense budget has come to the fore. Rights, of course, do not admit such ongoing byplay. Though vexing questions about relations between rights do arise, these often concern peripheral matters, and, whether or not controversy is confined to the periphery of the right, the solutions adopted should be enduring, if not permanent. Whereas the politics of rights is a judicial exercise in discriminating among cases and applying principles, the politics of social goals is an inconclusive politics of shifting coalitions and endlessly debatable priorities.

Since social goals are never immune to redefinition and reappraisal in the light of transient interests, it is not surprising that experts sharply disagree about what constitutes attainment of various goals—some arms strategists think we need the Stealth bomber for an adequate national defense; others oppose this program—but it is also not surprising that experts disagree about how social goals can best be achieved—some economists think prosperity will be best served by keeping interest rates low; others recommend moving them up. In the absence of any stable consensus regarding these diverse aims, officials responsible for pursuing them must proceed by trial and error. Implementing rights, in contrast, is not a flexible enterprise. Because the core of the protections that a basic right secures is clearly specified and also because failure to respect basic rights seriously wrongs the right-holder, policy regarding rights can and should be firm. But social goals resist unwavering pursuit. Sighted on the overarching end of the good society but granting that the ideal will always elude us, the politics of social goals affords officials maximum discretion with respect to the means used to promote them, as well as with respect to the urgency with which they are pursued. More fungible than rights, social goals can be adduced to defend policies, but they never secure unassailable backing for any policy.

Now, cultural diversity is not a good that any society ought to pursue regardless of costs. While cultural perpetuation is good, so is integration. But these two goods are in tension, and the best outcome that can be hoped for is that a balance will be struck between them. Furthermore, cultural perpetuation is not a good that can be guaranteed in any straightforward way. Not only does cultural viability ultimately depend on the unpredictable decisions of countless individuals, but also well-intentioned public policies may fail to preserve foundering cultures and may even hasten their demise. Sustaining cultural diversity is bound to remain a continuing experiment. Since cultural homogeneity is not morally calamitous, though cultural diversity is good, cultural diversity is best classified as a social goal.

Still, it seems that this goal has some bearing on rights. Consider the case of freedom of religion—a two-pronged right that empowers individuals to worship as they please and that forbids the state to endorse a particular religion. In the public schools of the United States, the doctrine of the separation of church and state has come to be associated with the ban on prayer. In the public schools of France, however, this doctrine has been interpreted more strictly. There, the separation of church and state is understood to prohibit students from wearing clothing that has religious significance. Not only is the state barred from imposing religious beliefs on public school students, but also these students are barred from introducing tokens of their religious beliefs into the classroom setting.[10] Needless to say, there are historical reasons that explain the difference between the U.S. and the French conception of freedom of religion. But I would like to examine the difference from the standpoint of the values that are at stake.

Though free exercise of religion and the separation of church and state both support freedom of conscience in religious matters, the rationales for these doctrines are disparate and do not always lead to congruent conclusions. Separation of church and state is anchored in assumptions about the need to protect religion from politics and politics from religion—political concerns degrade spiritual ones, and religious passions, especially hatred for unenlightened rivals, contaminate political debate. In contrast, free exercise of religion focuses on the individual—religious conviction is definitive of an individual's identity, and religious persecution attacks the individual's integrity. Plainly, however, politics often impinges on religious territory, and, when it does, free exercise authorizes individuals to advocate religiously grounded positions. Moreover, the effects of political neutrality are not necessarily neutral and can limit the free exercise of religion. Thus, these two principles call for compromise.

Returning now to the contrast between the French conception of state neutrality as the exclusion of religion from state institutions and the U.S. conception of neutrality as not taking sides, it is clear that in France disestablishment takes precedence over free exercise, whereas in the United States free exercise tempers disestablishment. Moreover, part of what is at issue is a pair of competing social goals: on one hand, the survival of minority cultures and, on the other hand, the autonomy of the political process. The French interpretation of neutrality tends to suppress adherence to religious practices that are at variance with the dominant Christian ones (e.g., three Islamic girls who wear *hijabs,* that is, traditional head scarves, being barred from classrooms and confined to the library of a French elementary school), whereas the U.S. conception allows diverse practices to flourish. But whereas the U.S. interpretation invites the participation of religious groups in public institutions (e.g., the demands of fundamentalist sects that creationism be taught alongside evolutionary theory), the French interpretation insulates these institutions from religious opinion. Still, in light of the oscillating politics of social goals, it is necessary to ask whether cultural diversity or the autonomy of the political process can properly be brought to bear on the question of the contours of the right to free exercise of religion.

Each of these goals is associated with a fundamental individual right: the goal of the autonomy of the political process with the right not to be involuntarily subject to religious belief or morality; the goal of cultural diversity with the right to practice one's religion with minimal restraint. These pairings, however, are not symmetrical. Advancement of the goal of cultural diversity is a likely consequence of respect for the right to free exercise of religion, but implementation of the right is independent of real-ization of the goal. In contrast, achievement of the goal of the autonomy of the political process is a precondition for respecting the right not to be involuntarily subject to religious belief or morality.[11] Now, it might seem that people must have a right to whatever is necessary to implement their rights. Thus it would follow that people have a right to a secular state, but not a right to cultural diversity.

That this proposed right would decisively vindicate the French position on religious dress in the public schools reveals, I think, that it would only trade one form of repression for another. As a way of preserving a goal-free sphere of rights, then, elevating social goals necessary for the implemen-tation of rights to the status of rights seems misguided. Rights cannot be delimited without recourse to social goals; however, the goals that rights depend on ought generally to be given greater weight in such deliberations than others. Still, these rights-supporting goals are not invariably disposi-tive. On the assumption that there are expressions of cultural difference that are innocuous and that cannot reasonably be construed as invidious institutionalization of religious beliefs or practices, it seems possible that the goal of cultural diversity could legitimately be invoked to defend some erosion of the secular state.

Though the social goal of cultural diversity is a relatively weak con-sideration, it represents an enduring value, and it can provide moral re-inforcement for personal liberties when individuals are exercising them to uphold beleaguered cultures. After all, however bad it is that people's lib-erties must sometimes be constrained, the disappearance of a culture surely counts as an ancillary evil. Governments of culturally pluralistic societies have a responsibility to avoid subverting cultural diversity and to under-write cultural heterogeneity when doing so will not violate basic rights or interfere with more compelling goals. To neglect this responsibility is, finally, to exhibit contempt for the uniqueness of human collectivities.

NOTES

Acknowledgments: I want to thank David Theo Goldberg, Len Krimmerman, Joel Kupperman, Jerry Shaffer, and Sam Wheeler for their helpful comments on earlier drafts of this essay.

1. An excellent compendium of accounts of culture has been compiled by A. L. Kroeber and Clyde Kluckhohn, in *Culture: A Critical Review of Concepts and Definitions* (Cambridge, Mass.: Peabody Museum of American Archaeology, 1952).

2. John Rawls offers helpful discussion of how a system of recognized personal liberties can serve as a common political culture—an "overlapping consensus," as he calls it—for otherwise profoundly different cultural groups in "The Priority of Right and Ideas of the Good," *Philosophy and Public Affairs* 17 (1988): 267–68, 274.

3. It might be argued that, if one had independent criteria marking cultural boundaries, one could devise worldviews that would preserve these distinctions. We have seen, however, that cultural boundaries cannot be marked definitively, and, in the present context, it becomes apparent that to attempt to do so could needlessly block cultural evolution. Moreover, this proposed strategy would involve carving out worldviews that would define cultures more in opposition to one another than in terms of the substantive beliefs and practices of each.

4. Since cultural cohesion requires not only the persistence of the bonds among the present members of a cultural group but also the maintenance of their ties with their ancestry, cultural cohesion is not vulnerable to the same sorts of objections as is cultural autonomy. Although a collective decision to replace one system of beliefs and practices with another could be compatible with a cultural group's autonomy, it would violate cultural cohesion.

5. Sara Ruddick provides useful insight into the failings of the balance-of-power approach to mutual coexistence in "Remarks on the Sexual Politics of Reason," *Women and Moral Theory*, edited by Eva Feder Kittay and Diana T. Meyers (Totowa, N.J.: Rowman and Littlefield, 1987), 248–55.

6. Under cultural nationalism, of course, the right of cultural perpetuation would coincide with the right of nation states to nonintervention.

7. In this discussion, I will use the example of religious liberty; however, it should be noted that any conflict between cultural norms and individual conduct authorized by basic personal liberties would raise the same problem.

8. For discussion of this possibility, see Michael McDonald's use of the concept of group rights to account for public funding of religious schools in Canada: "Respect for Individuals Versus Respect for Groups: Public Aid for Confessional Schools in the United States and Canada," in *Philosophical Dimensions of the Con-*

stitution, edited by Diana T. Meyers and Kenneth Kipnis (Boulder, Colo.: Westview Press, 1988), 184–86.

9. For extended discussion of the distinction between rights and social goals, see Ronald Dworkin, *Taking Rights Seriously* (Cambridge, Mass.: Harvard University Press, 1977), 90–94, 274.

10. This issue also has come up in U.S. courts, where religious practice has met a more favorable reception. For example, in *Menora v. Illinois High School Association,* 683 F.2d 1030 (1982), it was decided that male Jewish basketball players could wear yarmulkes during play provided that they devised a secure way to prevent them from falling off and endangering other players. However, in *Bitterman v. Secretary of Defense,* 553 F. Supp. 719 (1982), the military's claims of military effectiveness prevailed, and a captain in the air force was refused permission to wear a yarmulke while in uniform and on active duty.

11. Another example of a social goal that is a precondition for the implementation of rights is public order. For discussion of the relation between this goal and the rights to moral liberty and freedom of thought, see John Rawls, *A Theory of Justice* (Cambridge, Mass.: Harvard University Press, 1972), 212–15. Moreover, anyone who thinks there is a right to satisfaction of basic needs must agree that prosperity is among the preeminent social goals. Of course, none of this implies that a society must maximize these objectives. Rather, societies must attain them to a degree sufficient to implement the right.

2

THE IDENTITY OF CULTURAL AND PERSONAL IDENTITY

Bernard Berofsky

PHILOSOPHERS who think about personal identity are fond of observing that the young child who has no sense of identity, the adolescent who struggles to find his or her identity, the young adult with a settled lifestyle, and the older adult who has just become born again are all one and the same person. So the philosopher's concept is different from the more familiar variety to be found in psychological and generally exoteric literature. Thus, the psychoanalyst Eric Erikson is criticized by the philosopher Alan Donagan for failing to acknowledge the philosopher's task.[1] In permitting only the notion of identity embodied in the adolescent's search for or loss of identity, Erikson ignores the more fundamental idea of a single person, currently in the adolescent phase, who is evidently self-identical despite deep psychological concerns about his or her place in the scheme of things.

The philosopher takes himself to be addressing a metaphysical question, whereas others, like Erikson, are really concerned about a normative matter. For an ordinary mortal to be concerned about his identity is not obviously for him to be worried that he is not who he is; indeed such a worry is either pathological or incoherent—one cannot be worried about that! Similarly one cannot fail to have an identity in the philosopher's sense whereas, in the ordinary sense, one can "lose" or "fail to have discovered" one's identity. So the philosopher characterizes the ordinary sense as a normative one: One wants to have a *meaningful* role, an *important* (in some sense) place in the scheme of things. If I am a night watchman and a pianist, I can identify myself as a pianist only because my personal ideal is fulfilled through the pursuit of music and not through my nightly rounds in the office building. Although it is a *fact* that this is my ideal, labeling it as such introduces the normative component because ideals are activities or outcomes we place a positive *value* on. Or, less portentously, one might simply identify with a role one feels comfortable with, with a life that feels natural and free of inhibitions and hang-ups.

We are reminded by the philosopher that, irrespective of this ordinary sense, there must be another, more basic one; for there has to be a sub-ject of predication for the changes and losses of identity undergone by that subject. So no matter how many personal crises and radical "rebirths" *I* undergo, I do persist through all the transformations, and the philosopher wants to know what precisely makes up that "I" which can sustain so much in the way of change. But a few thoughts first about the ordinary sense.

The cultural dimension of the ordinary concept of identity appears in several forms, one of which concerns the source of the ideals that define our identity; for they are chosen from what Joseph Raz calls "social forms."[2] Even efforts to forge novel forms of identity rest on available forms in that they are variants upon, reactions to, or experiments with them.

Our bondage to these social forms is intensified by the linguistic ac-culturation in which we all participate. For we are practically required to formulate our ideals, even in private musings, in our native public lan-guage. We thereby take on the trappings of the forms we contemplate. To weigh the merits of a career in the law is to ponder the consequences of par-ticipation in an institution possessed of an antecedent structure, including the practices, attitudes, expectations, and behavioral forms appropriate to the participants in and those affected by the institution. Thus, social prac-tices and attitudes will determine the significance of a career in the law. If this is our goal, it is evidently derived from the common culture, from the extant social forms. But the culture plays a crucial role even when one attempts to transcend this form as happens when one adopts a life-style at variance with the received stereotype or when one limits one's legal ac-tivities to helping the poor or even when one undermines the role of the law, for example, by promoting anarchism. American Jews, for example, often "find their identity" in anti-Jewish or anti-Zionist activities. Their lives take on *positive* meaning through reaction to cultural givens assigned *negative* meanings.

The cultural dimension is, of course, ubiquitous; one enters a world and a variety of important relations, to family, neighborhood, social class, eco-nomic level, religion, prior to the possession of a self-concept. So it is a truism that our self-concept is necessarily shaped by this web of relations.

We seem to have saddled ourself with two, often inconsistent, senses of "ordinary" identity. For the self that emerges from the acculturation pro-cess is in part a reflective one and, as such, will not uncommonly regret or prefer to change identities—we are often unhappy with ourselves. Now, earlier, we identified the nature of the self with those ideals that may not be exemplified in one's actual life, which may regrettably not now form a part of one's actual identity. But we have just seen that it would be a mistake to limit the ordinary concept of identity to ideals; for, in finding one's identity uncomfortable, one is forced to confront not just the fact that there is a discrepancy between what one is and what one would like to be, but also the fact that one *is not* as one's ideals dictate. The truth is that there are really two notions between which, depending on mood, we often shift. Sometimes I *am* the weak, frightened soul, burdened with a desperate need to please; at other times I *am* the strong, fearless, and independent soul. I *behave* like the former and *identify* with the latter. The Jew for Jesus realizes he is a Jew; but insofar as he urgently wishes to be otherwise, he does not or at least does not try to countenance his Jewishness as part of his identity.

We do not, in other words, contrary to the opinions of some philoso-phers, unambiguously identify ourselves with our ideals. The facticity of our nature is of too enormous a moment to discount in a personal meta-physic. For better or worse, we are what we are.

There is a third dimension to consider. Besides our actual nature and our personal ideals, there is a moral form of evaluation. We judge ourselves from a moral point of view, and it is not always noticed that this mode of evaluation is different from one in which we rank ourselves in terms of our proximity to *personal* ideals. I may conclude that my life as a gambler is wasted because I am not doing anything really important, that is, of "real" value. The judgment is moral in that the perspective from which it is made is impersonal. I am implying that others who live as I do are leading equally worthless lives. Yet it does not follow that I am not embodying my ego ideal. I may have to acknowledge that I am extraordinarily attracted to all facets of gambling: the thrill, the anxiety, the ancillary way of life, the people one meets, the sights, the sounds. It is not just that I *am* this way; it is the way I like to see myself and have others see me. I am pleased when others learn about my eccentric and picturesque way of life. I wish it had some redeeming features so that I could recommend it from a moral perspective. The problem is not that I am hurting others; for I may not be. And it is my ideal except that it falls short in failing to provide me with personal worth. (To those philosophers who find this last sentence inco-herent, I would recommend that they direct their attention to real people, including ones who, though sane, cannot formulate the overriding "life plan" that is supposed to give their existence meaning, and others who are pleased to make it through the day even if they cannot characterize the worth of their lives or that single "project" whose failure would require them, on these doctrines originating in the ivory tower, to commit suicide.)

Thus, I can identify with a life-style, one that incorporates little in the way of other-regarding sentiments, consider that I am fulfilling my personal ideal, yet deem my life basically worthless (beyond whatever worth there is in my having fulfilled my goals and consequently not feeling frustrated). Here again, facticity overwhelms. The total engagement of so many facets of my being elevates a life acknowledged to be of little worth to the rank of an ideal. The classic disharmony of moral temptation is tempered by a harmonious coincidence of the actual and the ideal. *Moral* condemnation coexists alongside *personal* realization.

Think of the enormously complex feelings that must be experienced by many a career officer of the Israeli Defense Forces serving on the West Bank or Gaza. He may have grave misgivings about some of the actions he is called on to perform. Yet he may deem that, in carrying out orders he also acknowledges to be important to national survival, his actions express his personal ideals. It is not just that there is a moral conflict, for example, between the obligation of a citizen to his or her country (or of a soldier to his or her superiors) and the obligation of a human being to other human beings. It is not just that the officer sometimes wants to do what he thinks he should not do, for example, disobey an order to blow up an Arab house. It is also that, when pressed, the officer would judge his life as a fulfillment of his ideals, even if his own conscience has serious reservations about those ideals.

THE PHILOSOPHER FEELS FREE THEN to ignore cultural notions of identity in pursuing an investigation into the conditions of what he or she calls personal identity, that is, the conditions that must obtain if a persisting entity is to be regarded as the life of a single person. Again, since one and the same person can undergo radical cultural discontinuities, the particular cultural matrix is but a contingent state of a being whose identity must be determined by a more indelible mark.

Parenthetically, it is interesting to note that the concept of Jewish identity, interpreted strictly as the halakhic concept of Jewishness, has a curious affinity with the philosophical concept of identity. For both are permanent traits, eradicated only when the person is. No matter what changes *I* undergo, it is I who undergoes them and one of these cannot be a change of mother. So I remain me and I remain my mother's child, that is, Jewish, so long as I exist. But, of course, this concept of Jewish identity is not a species of a cultural concept. The cultural concept requires a psychological condition, that of identification with the Jewish people in one of a variety of possible forms. The halakhic concept imposes no such demand: one can be Jewish and never know it, that is, never identify or even have knowledge of the Jewish people.

As is well-known among students of philosophy, there are three candidates that vie for the status of *the* criterion of personal identity: identity of soul, continuity of body, and psychological continuity.

Most philosophers shy away from the first proposal. The notion of a soul is deemed obscure and anyway unhelpful. If we cannot tell whether we have the same person before us, how can we ever hope to determine if we have the same soul? Besides, if the soul is some sort of thing "inside" us, of what great importance is it to us unless it is intimately linked to our psychological traits? When we turn inward, we confront an arena of variegated mental happenings, conscious states access to which puts us in as close a contact with the core of our being as is possible. Yes, there may even be hidden psychological components that are very important to our conception of ourselves; but they are of the same sort, desires, and feelings, for example, as the elements available to consciousness. If there is a soul functioning as a kind of seat or principle of unity for these phenomena, it must receive its significance indirectly from the prior, intimate attachment to consciousness. Indeed, one should say that a soul counts as mine because it sustains *my* psychological goings on. But if our "psyche," that is, the stream of conscious events, is what really matters to our identity, why not turn to that directly?

Before we do, we must dismiss the bodily criterion, and that is not easy to do. It has many respectable advocates and has been argued for in highly persuasive ways. Although philosophers often dismiss bodily continuity as insufficient for personal identity, a strong case can be made that the person cannot survive the loss of her body and that the idea of persons switching bodies is unintelligible. So even if there is more to the idea of a person than a living human body, there is but one person for each living human body who persists only so long as the body lives.

We saw that a problem for the advocate of souls is that the importance of souls is grounded in their relation to the psyche; that is, my soul is important to me (is me?) because it is the seat of my thoughts, feelings, memories, desires, and ideals. If a powerful creature were to start tampering with my psyche, to change arbitrarily my thoughts and emotions, I would fear for my sanity, for my continued sense of self. I would dread such tampering for I would suspect that my very identity is at stake. I need to know that my psyche has some continuity and stability if I am to feel confident that I am persisting. If, on the other hand, I am told that my soul stuff is to be removed (or perhaps exchanged with another person) with no effect on my conscious life, no effect on my thoughts, feelings, dreams, and so on, I would be indifferent.

Well, then, if this is true, does not the same moral pertain to the bodily criterion? Even if I need a body and can have only one, its importance to me is that it is the seat of *my* thoughts, feelings, sensations, and desires. If *I* feel pain when Bush damages his hand, and *I* want to eat when Bush goes without food for six hours and *I* have visual experiences of the Oval Office when Bush opens his eyes in that office and *I* think of Manuel Noriega when Bush's eyes scan a report on Noriega's trial arrangements, I will begin to lay claim to Bush's body. My body, in other words, is whatever body is related to *my* psyche. Again, the idea most intimately connected to me is the idea of my psychological states and actions. The status of anything else is derivative in that it becomes "mine" only insofar as it stands in the right relation to *my* psyche. The body that is mine is the body intimately connected to my thoughts, sensations, and emotions. The soul that is mine, if there is such a thing, is the soul that houses my thoughts, sensations, and emotions. Thus, as some philosophers have urged, when I worry about my survival, I worry about the continuity of my psychological life. To hope for personal survival after death is to hope that there will be someone with my memories and thoughts after the decay of my body. It is of no great moment to me to learn that my body can be frozen indefinitely if my psyche is lost forever.

Perhaps we tend to overemphasize the role of the body for it is the most obvious way one person decides the identity of another person. I recognize my friend by recognizing features of his body. But that the continuity of a body is helpful for third-party identification is a weak reason to elevate bodily continuity to the criterion of personal identity. Fingerprints are helpful too; but no one regards himself as extinguished in virtue of a badly burned hand; my identity is not lost because I no longer have fingerprints.

A strong case can be made, therefore, that the concept of personal identity is not as remote from the concept of cultural identity as might initially be thought. The psychological dimension is central to both.

If we pursue this line, we get the idea that personal identity is a more general kind of cultural identity. Whereas I may undergo drastic changes of cultural identity, I remain the same person insofar as key psychological components remain unchanged. I can change my religion, my ideals, my values, my life-style, my allegiances, but I am still me because I have not changed whatever it is that psychologically ties this bundle together, whatever it is that enables me to speak of *changes* within me rather than literal *replacement* of me by a totally different person. What might that be?

Memory is the most prominent answer. When Harry changes from an upright Mormon to a Zen monk to a leader in the Satmar Hassidic sect, it is Harry who remembers his drastic transformations and who speaks of his "former self." Memory is the thread without which we would lack a sense of identity. Some demand additional conditions such as continuity of character on the grounds that drastic and sudden changes of personality and character are as devastating to the idea of one continuing person as loss of memory. But memory is at the core of the position of champions of psychological continuity, and we will look at the idea in its stripped-down version.

In rejecting the identification of a person with a unitary principle like a soul, advocates of psychological continuity think of a person rather as a complex, built up out of a multiplicity of psychological states linked by the memory relation. Just as one football game can be thought of as four quarters of play, linked in certain ways, most conspicuously, spatio-temporally, or a family can be construed as individuals related biologically, so a person is really a bundle of experiences. The individual experiences of a person are as distinct from one another as the sand grains of a beach. When individual sand grains happen to share neighboring space-time points near the ocean, we have a beach; when individual experiences happen to enter memory relations, we have a person. There are problems, to be sure, the most obvious being that I can forget an experience that nonetheless remains mine, albeit unclaimed. So complications are introduced into the doctrine to handle these and other difficulties. But the idea that a person emerges out of more fundamental units, individual psychological states, is basic to the position. In the simplest sort of case, there is a desire, say a desire to study medicine, and there is a different experience, a recall of that desire, such that, if Pam is designated as the owner of one of these experiences, she automatically becomes the owner of the other. In theory, then, an experience can be the experience of no particular person should it fail to stand in the right memory relations to other experiences, just as a grain of sand would fail to be part of any beach if it is contiguous to no other sand grains. So the doctrine is committed to the idea that it is at least theoretically possible to describe experiences without incorporating a reference to the person or the web of experiences we normally suppose an experience is a part of. We are usually not purists in this way. Our descriptions, including our recollections, tend to mention their owners as well as other persons and objects, and usually spill over onto other experiences and related phenomena. Consider the following recollection of Yoram Kaniuk in *Rocking Horse*:[3]

> On Shabbat eve I go to see her. Walking among the Yemenite shanties. Seeing Shabbat candles on empty paraffin drums covered with colored tablecloths. They sing chants to Queen Shabbat. The bakery is still. The hallas with poppy seeds, buttered, are laid out in my honor. Grandfather in the bathroom is grooming himself for Shabbat. . . . Then he comes out and pinches me on the cheek. Nu, Aminke, will we go to the synagogue? . . . On Friday night when I go to bed and close my eyes I wait. . . . Father appears in my room, walking on tiptoe. He looks at me for a long while, I hold my breath, he's in his soft slippers and it's hard to hear him. . . . The light from the corridor shines on me and he stands there mute. And then he steals into the kitchen and opens the breadbox and bites into the hallah. . . . And he chews at the hallah and then at the cookies and his face is aglow, he looks as if he's praying, and then he gathers up the crumbs and leaves the marble beside the sink clean and spotless and puts the hallah and the cookies back in the breadbox and comes back to look at me. And I'm already back in bed, pretending to sleep. I peep at him, as if snoring, but I don't snore. He snores. I'm a child, children don't snore, I snore like a child snores. And he looks at me. He smiles, maybe he doesn't smile, maybe he feels a great remorse and goes back to bed. To Jean Paul or Schiller, and he falls asleep with seven pillows and a high feather bed, with a radio beside the bed to hear the news at five in the morning, to know what has happened in this dead world. But to admit that the cookies are marvelous, that the hallah is beautiful, that he won't do.

Like most memories, this is intermingled with narrative not based strictly on pure recollection of the specific events being recalled. That is, Kaniuk incorporates into his recollections elements of an enormous store of factual knowledge pertaining to the episode. For example, the fact that children don't snore is evidently not a component of this incident, nor perhaps is the intention with which the radio has been placed beside the bed, to wit, to hear the 5:00 A.M. news.

Yet if we try to purge the description of these extraneous components in order to arrive at a pure recollection of the events, we discover a crucial, often unnoticed category of depiction. Some examples:

> "Grandfather . . . is grooming himself for Shabbat."
> "He feels a great remorse."
> "To admit that the cookies are marvelous, that the hallah is beautiful, that he won't do."

To those who view memory on the model of a cinematic experience, these elements are difficult to assimilate for one does not strictly see, even if one can be said to see one's own mental images, another's feeling of remorse or his failure to pay a compliment or make a concession. To be sure, a visual experience can contain enough clues to warrant these reports; but it is preposterous to suppose that our visual recall is always as rich as would be required to ground all such interpretations. So a natural move is to treat these constituents of memory as akin to "Children don't snore." They are instances of factual memory superimposed upon memory of events.

This is a mistake. One must first see that the theory that motivates this move cannot anyway be sustained. Memory is not an internal movie. Many people have very poor capacities for imaging, but do not necessarily suffer from poor memories. Moreover, there are many personal facts we recall that cannot possibly be based on visual data. Consider:

> "I go to see her."
> "I hold my breath."
> "It's hard to hear him."
> "I'm pretending to sleep."

We recall a great deal about our own responses to events and these responses are given in judgments obviously not based on visual data provided by an internal screen. Thus, the underlying theory of memory is faulty to begin with.

Moreover, there is a crucial difference between the knowledge of facts superimposed upon the memory of events and the memory of nonvisual or even nonsensuous components of event memory. Kaniuk does not *remember* that children don't snore; he knows that and mentions it in his report of memory. Perhaps it is also true that he knows that grandfather has the radio next to the bed so that he can listen to the 5:00 A.M. news. But Kaniuk does *remember* that the shanties are Yemenite, that songs are chanted to Queen Shabbat, that it's hard to hear his grandfather, that he pretends to sleep. These facts are recalled, just as much as purely visual facts, such as the placement of the hallah and cookies back in the breadbox.

Recall now what the advocate of psychological continuity says. A grain of sand belongs to Jones Beach because of its spatial relations to the rest of the sand that makes up Jones Beach; it can be relocated without adverse consequences to its nature to Paradise Beach. A photograph belongs to grandmother's photo album because it is pasted onto one of the pages in grandmother's photo album; it, too, can become a part of something else— grandfather's photo album—by simple relocation. These are the models for the relation between Kaniuk and his memory experiences. They are his because of their external relations to other facts about Kaniuk. They are theoretically transposable; with the right relations, they might have been the memories of Saddam Hussein or Clytemnestra.

It might be protested that I am ignoring the fact that Hussein or Clytemnestra cannot recall such events because they never happened to either of them. We must be careful. The theory says that in principle events are assigned to owners in virtue of memory relations. Let us collectively call the experiences depicted in Kaniuk's recollection E. We do not want to assign E to Clytemnestra even if she produces an honest report just like Kaniuk. We would conclude instead that she is deluded or mad. So we must say that Clytemnestra is not *really* remembering E just because she produces this report with the conviction that she is indeed recalling E. Now the advocate of psychological continuity would have to concede defeat if he had no way of explaining this fact for he cannot just *assume* that Clytemnestra is different from Kaniuk. In other words, if we have two honestly offered, identical memory reports and can decide that one is genuine, the other illusory, we must be basing our judgments of personal identity not on memory.

The only way out of this for the theorist is to say that we *are* invoking memory to explain the difference between genuine memory and delusion. For genuine memory includes a causal component we have not yet taken into account. We must appeal to the fact that E can cause only Kaniuk to have this recollection. Clytemnestra must have gotten this information in some other way. So even if one believes one is engaged in recall, the memory is only apparent unless it is caused in the right way, in the normal case via a brain trace emanating from the original event. Since Clytemnestra did not acquire, store, and activate an original brain trace of the experiences recounted in the quotation, she is not remembering those experiences.

So we now have the following idea. According to the advocates of psychological continuity, a memory of some original experience E belongs to the same person undergoing E only if the memory arises in the standard way, only if it is properly caused by that experience. Whereas two grains of sand belong to the same beach if they are spatially proximate, and two drops of water belong to the same drink if they are located simultaneously in the same glass, so two experiences are experiences of the same person if they are causally related in the right way. In theory, then, we can be given an experience and a memory of it as discrete entities, and determine whether or not they belong to the same person by undertaking a causal inquiry. The atomism of the original doctrine is preserved. The concept of the individual person is subordinate to the more basic notion of (ownerless) individual experiences. As Bertrand Russell once said, the concept of the self is a logical construction from experiences. The concept of an experience is fundamental and does not presuppose the idea of a self undergoing that experience. It is theoretically intelligible, therefore, to imagine a specific experience of Will's as having been had by Selma; one just imagines it as entering different causal pathways from the ones actually entered. One imagines that, instead of leaving a trace on one brain, it leaves it on another. Why should this be any more difficult than imagining that grain of sand being relocated to another beach? Perhaps highly sophisticated neurological techniques will someday be devised to divert the neural path of a trace from one brain to the brain of a different human being. (Of course, should this happen, the experience will not be Will's, but Selma's.)

If experiences are not essentially owned, then how do we deal with the fact that, in memory, experiences are disclosed *as belonging to the person remembering?* Kaniuk remembers that *he* goes to see her, holds his breath, pretends to sleep. To be sure, he remembers facts about others as well. But states and activities are presented as owned. Kaniuk does not first remember that someone pretends to sleep and then undertakes a separate inquiry to determine who that party is.[4] The memory is *of himself* pretending to sleep. The advocate of psychological continuity, appealing to the fact that we misremember and that it is possible that Kaniuk only *seems to* remember that he pretends to sleep, will insist that, no matter how the experience appears to the person, the actual determinant of ownership is the set of relevant causal facts. Clytemnestra is not Kaniuk even if she reports remembering that *she* pretends to sleep, because she is not related in the right causal way to E. That Clytemnestra takes herself to have experienced E has to do with her (erroneous) beliefs and that she actually experienced some event has to do with causal relations between that event and her current psychological state.

So although the memory experience has phenomenologically a first-person character, presenting itself as something undergone by the one engaged in recall, the actual identity of the person is a separate matter. Indeed, Napoleon-like cases aside, we occasionally have recollections whose veridical character we come to question. Did that really happen to me or am I making it up? These are not, to be sure, the norm; but their existence indicates that the first-person character of the memory *experience* is different from the *belief* of the person that he or she had the experience being recalled. We have then a trichotomy. My experiencing a past event as having been undergone by me is different from my believing that it was undergone by me is different from its actually having been undergone by me.

These facts might be taken to support the psychological-continuity approach according to which identity is determined by a (causal) relation between experiences whose intrinsic character has nothing directly to do with identity. For if my actual identity is not grounded in phenomenology, I should be able to come to realize this and may then come to believe in a particular case that there is a discrepancy between appearance and reality. So I am not the person I would appear to myself to be. I feel that it was I who attended the ball ten years ago; I so clearly remember dancing with Wanda and chatting with the clarinetist in the band. But since all the indications point to the contrary, I must be imagining—I guess I never did attend the ball. I guess the origin of that apparent memory is not a trace left in my brain by an experience of me at the ball.

To test the thesis that experiences are theoretically transferable, that ownership derives from connections between experiences, we will suppose that Kaniuk's recollection is experienced by Helen of Troy. But, as Marya Schechtman argues convincingly about a different case,[5] the supposition is impossible—it is difficult to see, to put it mildly, how Helen can have recollections of her boyhood, Shabbat, hallah, father falling asleep on a high feather bed and with a radio at his bedside, and so on. Only the view of memory as the passive awareness of visual images, a view already judged seriously deficient, can sustain such an implausible conjecture. We can, that is, imagine both Kaniuk and Helen watching the same movie, one depicting the episodes described in Kaniuk's memory. But we forget that, in order for this episode to be a memory of Helen's, in order for her to understand this as a possible past installment of her life, she must place this purely visual experience into a vast context of associations, beliefs, and feelings. She must remember the special feeling associated with the onset of Shabbat, the significance of Shabbat candles, who the Yemenites are, the role of the hallah in ceremonies such as Shabbat eve, the special character of Jewish prayer, the charming way Grandpa would gently prod by saying, "Nu, Aminke, ..." the withdrawal and embitterment of some Jewish men, and so on. We must remember, in other words, that our linguistic and interpretive capacities permit us to recall just about any sort of fact about a past episode, not just those that can be gleaned from an internal screen. But how can a beautiful pagan woman, knowing nothing of Jews and their world, take on such an experience as *hers* without taking on perhaps the whole psyche of Kaniuk, in which case we do not have a case of *Helen* with Kaniuk's memory, but rather a magical transformation of Helen's body into the body of the male person, Kaniuk?

Earlier, we acknowledged the possibility of experiences that have the character of memories (in that they seem to be recollections of events one did participate in), but which, due to independent evidence, one recognizes not to be such. But these cases are isolated and cannot become the norm. More important, if Helen had a memory anything like Kaniuk's, she would *have* to construe it as a delusion for it would be so terribly alien. To assimilate it as a normal memory, Helen would not be able to remain Helen, and that is precisely what the psychological-continuity theorist denies. He insists that experiences, like candy bars, can be transferred without the wrappers. He fails to see that many memories are so rich that the very experience implicates a vast network of associations inseparable from the memory. They cannot be separated from their owners. The atomistic construal of experience breaks down and, with it, the psychological-continuity theory.

Now if the self is not a construction from discrete units of experience, but is rather an essential component of experience, are we then disagreeing with Hume, who denied that a subject can be aware of both an experience and its owner, the subject? No, for the moral to be drawn from the above point is that even an individual memory, as an awareness of a past state, presupposes a network of psychological connections in which the remembered event is enmeshed. This doctrine in no way implies a metaphysical subject of experience, a soul, or a Lockian X I know not what. It implies rather that individuals are necessarily embedded in a psychosocial context. Just as the *meaning* of an individual psychological state cannot be specified in the absence of a personal context, so we are advancing the less obvious thesis that the very state itself cannot be so specified.

The upshot is that the most plausible approach to the *philosophical* or *metaphysical* concept of identity is to reduce it to the so-called ordinary concept. In essence, then, the self is culturally defined and the philosopher's quest for an underlying nonsocial self fails. The familiar observation that the self is defined by its social interactions turns out to go deeper than we might have supposed. The philosophical pursuit of an underlying principle of unity fails.

Well, then, how *do* we trace a person throughout all the stages of his or her career, through all the massive changes of life-style, ideology, nationality, religion, occupation, friends and associates, ideals and ambitions some individuals undergo? If a person is essentially embedded in a social and cultural context, no matter how broadly it is conceived, we should be able to suppose that *one* person moves from one such context to another, in which case the person is not defined by the particular context he or she happens temporarily to be a part of. Who is Harry, the Satmar Hassidic leader and former Zen monk and, earlier, upright Mormon?

One might, as some have done, deny that there is any single person running through changes that are so epic, especially if all psychological connections of memory and character between very early phases and the current phase are lost.[6] But I would prefer to highlight the very unlikely character in any real case of such drastic corollaries. Harry is not an amnesiac; even if he remembers his Mormon phase with a sense of alienation, even disgust, in recalling that it was he who passed through this stage, he lays claim to a host of associations that played a role in a personal evolution whose outcome is the present stage. He does not think of his childhood the way he thinks of the childhood of a Hassidic Jew in his group. Yes, our childhood can appear very remote to us, but we must remember that even when the conscious associations are more or less lost, the intimacy of the connection can be grounded in the powerful causal relations between past and future. As drastic as Harry's psychological evolution has been, the psyche that emerged from childhood played an essential role in this volatile personal history and that psyche's nature was then and is now intimately embedded in a cultural milieu, even one that is itself changing all the time, sometimes radically.

Yes, if Harry is an amnesiac, if, through brain surgery and psychoanalysis, he now has a personality both entirely different from and in no way dependent upon childhood experiences, "Harry" is not the name of a single person. In these very special cases, we will have to revert to the bodily criterion and interpret our use of one name as the name of one living human being. But a case like this is very rare indeed. Most living human beings are single, *evolving* persons, inextricable from the cultural context that determines their existence as persons and the very existence of the psychological states that make up their history.

NOTES

1. Eric Erikson, "Growth and Crisis of the 'Healthy Personality,' " in *Personality in Nature, Society, and Culture*, 2d. ed., edited by Clyde Kluckhohn and Henry A. Murray (New York: Knopf, 1956). Alan Donagan, "How Much Neurosis Should We Bear?" in *Mental Health: Philosophical Perspectives*, edited by Tristam Engelhardt, Jr., and Stuart Spicker (Dordrecht: Reidel, 1978).

2. Joseph Raz, *The Morality of Freedom* (Oxford: Clarendon Press, 1986), 311–18.

3. Yoram Kaniuk, *Rocking Horse* (New York: Harper and Row, 1977), 324.

4. Sydney Shoemaker, *Self-Knowledge and Self-Identity* (Ithaca, N.Y.: Cornell University Press, 1967), 135.

5. Marya Schechtman, "Personhood and Personal Identity," *Journal of Philosophy* 87 (1990): 71–92.

6. Derek Parfit, *Reasons and Persons* (Oxford: Clarendon Press, 1984).

3

IDENTIFICATION AND IDENTITY

Nathan Rotenstreich

I

Let us start with some comments on the two terms. The first, identification, has two meanings: It is the cognitive activity of making certain features or qualities of an object prominent—as we identify an individual human person or just an object as being a stone or a table. Identification also connotes one's acceptance of a certain loyalty or adherence to certain norms. In this sense identification sometimes amounts to absorption of certain modes of response or behavior—as is the case with one's identification with other human beings or one's internalization of modes of behavior, customs, and so on. One's loyalty to a culture is sometimes described as identification.

Identity has two meanings as well: the logical meaning in the formal sense expressed as A = A, and the profile of an object referred to that carries some features that are specific to that object that enable one to become acquainted with it or recognize it when returning to it. Here, too, identity connotes a profile of the object referred to. Within the human scope we speak about the identity of the person, assuming that every person or individual, by being different from another person or individual, carries within himself or herself an identity that can be recognized.

Within the individual human sphere, identity cannot be separated from the bodily existence of the individual. Each individual is a corporeal entity delineated by that body and thus separated and distinguished from the body of another individual. It has to be observed that already the classical term *physiognomy* points to the physics of the person and to his or her gnomia, that is to say, cognition or recognition. The person can be made known by his or her face because of the specificity of that which makes it unique and concurrently distinguishable from the face of another individual.

Within the activity of identifying, eventually expressed in identity, we may distinguish a certain permanent structure. Thus, in the sphere of logic, for instance, we distinguish between the genus to which the particular object belongs and the specific differential features of that object, as in the very simple presentation that the table is a piece of furniture. Within the human scope, the duality of the genus and specificity become prominent in the duality or correlation of the family name and the proper name, though that duality became common only rather late. Plato is Plato and Aristotle is Aristotle without any family context. But Maimonides is Moses the son of Maimon; that is, the specification of one's descendance, pointing to the Hebrew saying "high tree," is an indication of that correlation, though it has as its correlate the proper name of the father and not the name of the family. Even when a people changes their names, they still retain the duality indicated above.

Within the personal scope, we have to add that awareness of one's course in life eventually becomes part of one's identity, though that identity cannot be recognized by fellow persons, but is only part of one's self-consciousness. Because of that self-consciousness that accompanies the organic infrastructure of the person, a person refers to himself or herself as a *me* and not only as an *I*.

In the sphere of the individual, we may say that within that scope, to point to the identity of the individual, we distinguish between that which is specific and that which is the context. In identity as such, the particularity is embodied, but that particularity cannot be made known even to the individual himself without the broader context, which, when expanded, can be characterized as universality. Universality is both ontologically essential and methodologically necessary for the identification of the individual. More specifically, we can say that identity contains in itself a certain equilibrium between the personal aspect and the social; the personal aspect cannot be separated from the social while the social, by being manifest in different individuals, is not necessarily connected with this or that individual.

II

Yet, identity as it became commonly known is applied as a concept or term, not only to individuals, but also to collective entities. This application is certainly problematic because the collective entities do not contain in themselves the component of body in the verbal sense, though we use the expression "body politic." Hence, there is no given infrastructure when we refer to collective entities that can be conceived as carrying the different features of identity. In addition, the collective entity does not contain self-consciousness as do individuals, because there is no consciousness to collectivity. Consciousness can be related to individuals who are characterized by their own consciousness, which in collectivity corresponds, at least in its content and focus, to the consciousness of other individuals. To be sure, we refer in the collective sphere to historical consciousness, that is to say, to the awareness of individuals in a given era or period, to their belonging to a line of historical descendance, though different from the biological one that makes them related to ancestors, to a founding period in history and so on. Because of the lack of the two dualities, that of the corporeal existence and that of consciousness, different as they are, it becomes clear that any reference to a collective identity is to a very large extent dependent upon the personal existence and its features. When a certain individual disassociates himself from belonging to a collectivity, clearly, the collectivity does not cease to exist. But if many individuals would do that, or transfer their awareness of belonging to another entity, the collective entity would cease to exist.

Within the collective sphere one component is of a collective essence and not of an individual one, namely, language. Language, though activized by individuals, as a resource or reservoir, is not the attribute or property of individuals as it is not the expression of an instantaneous situation. Language as a resource is transferred to individuals. To be sure, when individuals cease to speak a language, that language becomes a dead one, though as dead, it can be *langue* and not *parlance* and thus contained in documents and even studied as a subject matter of research. In addition, the collective entity establishes institutions that are permanent or semipermanent and thus transpersonal. In many cases, these are transferred from the past to the present, though the behavior in the actual sense is of individuals, but the pattern of behavior is of the collectivity.

III

These comments are a prelude to some comments on the problem of Jewish identity in the contemporary era. In order to place the aspect of that identity in context, it is mandatory to refer to the profile of Jewish identity during the generations before the modern era. Obviously we point to the Jewish identity in the situation of the exile, because the exile by definition lacks the territorial infrastructure that as part of space could be considered analogous to the body of the individual. The exile and the Jews living in it did not relate to a particular part of the space as a territorial basis of their collective existence. They even moved from one part of the space to another and still maintained with all the disassociations, by and large, their collective identity. This was made possible by an interrelation between two basic components: the normative religious pattern and the modes of day-to-day existence prescribed by that pattern. One of the characteristic qualities of the Jewish religion has been that quality of commanding the behavior in the everyday sense of that term. The religious commandments did not refer only to feelings or to the attitude of piety. They referred to the given and visible reality and demanded its formation. Hence there existed a community of people behaving as individuals in a similar way, which as such has not been grounded in their individual preferences but in their response to the commandments.

In addition, the Jewish religion referred to the collective entity, as has been so strongly emphasized about the Middle Ages by Yehuda HaLevi. Thus the collective entity, with all the problematic aspects mentioned before, has been the receiver of the revelation and, as such, the mediator between the revelation and individual human beings. Because of that collective character of the reception of the revelation, the Jewish religion is inherently a dialectical conception. It refers to the universe at large and to humankind at large and is still a religion of a certain delineated people. Here we find one of the anchors of the difference and the clash between Judaism and Christianity. The Hebrew language ceased to be the spoken language of the Jews but, to a very large extent, remained the medium of what is called "questions and responses" and thus the language of the rabbinic literature.

IV

We just cannot be oblivious to the fundamental change that occurred in all these aspects in the modern era, even when we grant, at least for the sake of argument, that the awareness of the diachronic belonging is maintained. The experience of anti-Semitism's years of hostilities toward Jews gradually transformed their collective cohesion. Jews ceased to shape their day-to-day existence by the norms grounded in the religious commandments. They became emancipated individuals and, consequently, isolated individuals. The community is not present in their existence, but preceding them and at most has been established and has to be reestablished day by day by their own decisions. Religion, to a large extent, became a conviction and not a conjuncture of faith and modes of behavior. Identity ceased to accompany the existence of Jewish individuals and, if at all, is a remnant in the consciousness of individuals but not a pattern of behavior accompanying the existence of individuals and even preceding it. Without going into the details of that topic, Zionism is a response to that situation in its attempt to establish a collective identity of Jews relating to a territorial basis and embraced by the institution of the state as well as by the renascence of the Hebrew language as a spoken language and not only as the medium of expression of the Scriptures.

What is characteristic of Jewish identity in the modern era is, if at all, the internalization of identity or the ongoing erosion of the semi-objective components of that identity. It is not by chance that Jews in the Western world, and mainly in the United States, are looking for foci of identification, that is to say, for centers of their belonging, beyond the scope of their day-to-day existence. These foci are present in the collective entity in the state of Israel, and, in this sense, the collective entity in the existing sense is a surrogate of the collective entity, which does not exist within the boundaries of the Jews of the West. The Jews in the West are looking for an additional center of belonging. They have formed it in the predicament of Soviet Jewry, whereby a predicament evokes identification parallel to the identification with the state of Israel. Yet these modes of identification possibly are expressed in deeds of support, but they are mainly of a sentimental character. The feeling of solidarity becomes the substitute for the consciousness of identity, or one could say sentimental identification becomes the substitute for the identity expressed, at least partially, in some "tangible," concrete attributes of existence.

Strangely enough, there is now a discrepancy between the rhythms of the modern scientific and technological civilization and the mode of existence of the Jews. The modern civilization in its manifestation in science and technology is a manifest civilization expressed in instruments, in modes of communication, in existence shaped by innovations, and so on. The Jewish existence becomes more and more internalized. Being sentimental, it cannot keep pace with reality. Since the reality surrounding the Jews in the West is more and more of a universal character, the particularity of Jewish existence becomes more and more contracted and, perhaps vis-à-vis the pattern of universality and particularity, the pattern of universality proper and individuality will be retained. This is, broadly speaking, the situation of the Jewish identity in the present era. The correlation between identification and identity diminishes, and we may wonder what would reestablish the Jewish identity except the immersion in the collective existence of the Jews inherent in the state of Israel.

This does not mean to imply that there are no problems of Jewish identity within the state of Israel, mainly between the metaphysical character of

Jewish religion and the nonmetaphysical orientation of the modern era, or between attributes of collectivity related to the present and those brought in from the past. But that problematic situation is still transparent within the collective existence as it is. Hence, that existence does not allow any more for the traditional difference or distinction between being a Jew and being a human being. Changes are not identical with uprooting. We face the changes within the Israeli situation and the danger of uprooting in the Diaspora situation.[1]

We are not suggesting that the direction toward uprooting was caused by the Jews. The impact of the climate of opinion is strong to such an extent and degree that it becomes an objective situation. To maintain the identity within that climate of opinion is to maintain it against it. To achieve this position's active internal forces, whose strength does not exist precisely because of that climate of opinion, is no longer of the character of externality. When and where decision directed to a defined pool is missing, inertia may still operate; herein exists a physical notion of the "power of inertia."

NOTES

1. On the various ideological interpretations of Jewish identities since 1945, consult Josef Gorny, *The Quest for Collective Identity* (in Hebrew) (Tel Aviv, 1990). The book is due to be published in English.

4

JEWISH COLLECTIVE IDENTITY

Asa Kasher

To the memory of my son,
Yehoraz, my son,
1966–1991

I

Usually, each of us is a member of various groups: One plays a role in a family, is a member of some community, and is a citizen of a certain state, to mention just a few examples.

In common parlance, views and actions, will and power are ascribed not only to individual human beings but also to groups these individuals belong to: families, communities, and states, as well as councils, institutions, and religious denominations. Thus, a royal family may be said to have resented criticism, a community to have overcome a problem it experienced, a religious denomination to have a boundless will to enforce its norms, and a court to have an authority, exercised when the court reaches a decision and defends it in the opinions.

What, actually, do we mean when we make such ascriptions? In other words, how do we defend ascriptions of a view to a family, of an action to a community, of a will to a religious denomination, or power to an institution?

The required defense sometimes rests on the instituting rules of the collective under discussion. The law institutes courts and determines their powers. The constitution of a university may infix its will to enhance knowledge and wisdom by exercising academic freedom. When the pope speaks ex cathedra on questions of faith, his decrees count as the view of the Catholic Church, by an authority lodged with the Bishop of Rome by a decree of the Ecumenical Council Vatican I, which in turn based itself "upon the decisions of numerous other councils."

On other occasions, predicating views or actions of a collective are defended by alluding to views held or actions performed by the individuals who constitute the collective under discussion or by almost all of them. A royal family may be described as having resented criticism if every member of it, or almost every member, has resented criticism. A claim that a certain community has moved from one region to another would be defended by showing that every member or almost every member has thus moved. The required defense of such a statement about a collective rests on a sufficiently clear notion of the nature of the collective under discussion, including an adequate delineation of the set of individuals that constitute it.

On occasions of still another type, however, a statement about a certain collective is made though there seems to be no unequivocal conception of this collective at the background of the statement. Such an apparently wanting background may lack even a decent delineation of the related set of individuals. Most conspicuous among examples of statements that are often made under such circumstances are those that seem to refer to a people or a religion, or to predicate a national or a religious character. Consider, for instance, some remarks made by Wittgenstein: "I believe that one of the things Christianity says is that sound doctrines are all useless. That you have to change your *life*." [1] "Tragedy is something un-Jewish." [2]

Indeed, these remarks were not made and similar remarks have not been defended on the background of any given system of rules instituting Christianity or instituting what is Jewish, or of any perspicuous delineation of the related sets of individuals, the Christians or the Jews. How, then, should one find out whether Christianity does say or does not say that sound doctrines are all useless? What should count as a successful defense and what should count as unsuccessful defense of a claim to the effect that something, say tragedy, is un-Jewish? To be sure, the same problems arise even when the remark under consideration is of an apparently simpler form, such as: "It is typical for a Jewish mind to understand someone else's work better than he understands it himself." [3]

Such remarks appear to be quite puzzling. On one hand, it is not clear how one should go about pursuit of defense of such remarks, but on the other hand, one finds oneself under an impression that these remarks are meaningful, perhaps even deeply so. This is a genuine puzzle: It creates a distinct impression that it does not rest on some simple confusion. Such puzzles, one is inclined to assume, hide either a precious insight or a pernicious confusion.

My purpose is to make a step toward relief of this philosophical tension. First I outline a general theory of collective identity. Such a theory enables me to delineate the set of individuals related to a collective of a national, religious, or cultural nature and shows how it contributes to a solution of that philosophical problem. I then apply my theory to the particular cases of Jewish identity.

This indirect way of tackling problems that have arisen within a Jewish context, namely, by developing a general theory and then applying it to a particular Jewish case, is to my mind the most natural way of making a *philosophical* remark on any Jewish affair.

II

The neutral recursive theory of collective identity, the first part of my general theory of collective identity, provides us with a method of responding to such questions as: Who are the Jews? Who are the Christians? Who are the blacks? Who are the Sikhs? Who are the Europeans? by outlining delineations of the sets of individuals related to such collectives of a national, religious, cultural, or similar nature.[4]

There is, of course, an abundance of significantly different answers to each of these questions. Such a diversity of answers to the same question usually rests on some deep conceptual or ideological differences. My purpose is not to offer some new grounds for taking sides in such disputes but to put forward a free theory of collective identity. It is a free theory because it is *neutral:* The offered method of responding to a Who are the . . . ? question about a collective will be free of any commitment to some partisan view of the nature of the collective. This method will, however, be even freer: Its application to the case of a certain collective may well result in an utterly new delineation of the related set of individuals, one that has so far been proposed, endorsed, or defended by no party to a dispute about the nature of this collective.

Why should we be interested in a neutral theory of collective identity? A possible answer is that on some occasions we are interested in a neutral, particular theory that rests on general grounds. In other words, one might be interested in having a theory that is (*a*) a neutral view of the identity of a particular collective, for instance, the Jews or the Sikhs, but is also (*b*) an instance of a general view of collective identity, a view independent of any special assumption about Jews or Sikhs.

Why should one be interested in having a *neutral* theory of a *particular* collective? Are those who are interested in theories about a particular collective identity not usually interested in taking sides in the debate on the identity of this collective? Are they not actually interested in eventually forming a view about Who are the . . . ? by constructing or adopting some partisan answer to this question while rejecting the other ones?

If we imagine an educated, ultra-orthodox Jew who has an answer to the question Who are the Jews? then, indeed, we must assume that he is seldom if ever interested in a *neutral* view of Jewish collective identity. Imagine, however, a Sikh anthropologist who would like to know Who are the Jews? or a Jewish anthropologist who would like to know Who are the Sikhs? Should they take sides in such remote disputes, or, instead, should they try to use some neutral views of their subject matter?

Consider also the hypothetical case of an alien person who has been given the task of charting a just constitution for a future state in which the Sikhs will exercise their collective right for democratic self-determination. Assume she has already realized that there are several incompatible answers to the question Who are the Sikhs?[5] Had she been given the task of drafting a partisan constitution for a future province, in which a certain Sikh group, say, the Khalsa, will establish and run their own religious dominion, she would have been interested in the partisan, Khalsa characterization of the Sikh collective identity. Because her charge is to draft a *just* constitution, however, it would be only natural for her to avoid taking sides in an ongoing, long-lasting, and bitter struggle and choose a neutral view of the Sikh collective identity, a neutral answer to the question Who are the Sikhs?[6] Indeed, similar considerations apply to the actual case of the task of charting a just constitution for the state in which the Jews do already exercise their collective right for self-determination.

The theory of collective identity I propose is *recursive* in the ordinary sense of recursive specification. It outlines a process for delineating a set of individuals, be it the Jews, the Christians, the blacks, the Sikhs, the Europeans, or any other group. The process starts at a certain initial approximation and continues by successive improvements of it. At each stage of this process I outline a set of individuals, related to the collective under consideration.

Assume, then, that a certain collective is under consideration. Call it "the Collected." The Christians, the Europeans, the Jews, the Sikhs, the blacks have been our examples of such collectives so far. The problem of characterizing the collective identity of the Collected takes the form of the problem of answering the question Who are the Collected? The proposed theory of collective identity outlines the following process for answering such questions.

First, we consider the *incontrovertible core* of the Collected, that is, the set of those individuals who are unquestionably Collected. Naturally, one is unquestionably Collected when:

1. one considers oneself to be a Collected, and

2. one is considered by the others to be a Collected.

Thus, the incontrovertible core of the Christians includes a person—say, Adam—if he is considered by himself and by the others to be a Christian. The incontrovertible core of the Jews does not include a person—say, Belinda—if she does not consider herself to be a Jew, and it does not include a person—say, Charles—if some of the others do not consider him to be a Jew. Adam is unquestionably a Christian, and therefore he is a member of the incontrovertible core of the Christians, whereas Belinda and Charles are not unquestionably Jews, and therefore they are not members of the incontrovertible core of the Jews. Let us turn, now, to a clarification of conditions 1 and 2.

First, what does it take to consider oneself to be a member of a collective? We assume that if one does not have the faintest notion of who are the Collected, then one does not consider oneself to be a Collected and thereby does not satisfy condition 1. Consequently, a person who has no view of the Collected does not belong to the incontrovertible core of the Collected. If one does have a notion of who are the Collected, whether an articulate notion, fully and clearly expressed and defended, or a notion that is only vaguely or implicitly held, we assume that one is in a position to tell whether one does or does not consider oneself to be a Collected, that is, whether one believes oneself to be a Collected according to one's own notion of who are the Collected. Hence, about whether condition 1 obtains, for a certain person, with respect to a certain collective, there seems always to be a definitive answer.

Second, what does it take for a person, such as Adam, to be considered by "the others" one of the Collected, one of the Christians, in the case of Adam? We distinguish all the other persons who do have a notion of who are the Collected from those who do not have such a notion. The latter need not be considered. Among the former we consider, first, those who know Adam to the extent that they are willing to apply to his case their notion of who are the Collected. In other words, we consider first those who have, in a sense, a ready answer to the question of whether Adam is a Christian. If these ready answers are not all in the affirmative, then condition 2 does not obtain. If Adam is in the incontrovertible core of the

Christians, condition 2 is satisfied, that is, all these ready answers are in the affirmative.

Assume, then, that every person who has a notion of who are the Christians and knows Adam takes him to be one of the Christians. We still have to consider the views of those persons who have their notions of who are the Christians but do not know Adam. If all these persons did know Adam, would they all take him to be one of the Christians? Or, put more specifically, would it be true, for any one of these persons—say, Doris—that if she did know about Adam whatever could have enabled her to apply to Adam her notion of who are the Christians, then she would have taken Adam to be one of the Christians?[7] If some of the answers to these questions are in the negative, condition 2 does not obtain. If Adam is in the incontrovertible core of the Christians, it means condition 2 is satisfied, that is, the answers to these questions as well are all in the affirmative.

Hence, there also seems always to be a definitive answer to the question of whether condition 2 obtains, for a certain person, with respect to a certain collective. Furthermore, since the question of whether both condition 1 and condition 2 obtain, for a certain person, with respect to a certain collective, could thus always be properly answered, the question of whether a certain person is or is not a member of the incontrovertible core of a certain collective can also be thus answered. The notion of the incontrovertible core (of a collective) seems, therefore, to be well defined.

Notice that the incontrovertible core of any collective is a *neutrally* defined set. When the incontrovertible core of the Protestants, for example, is delineated, any view of the Protestants is treated the same way as any other view of the collective of Protestants. One belongs to the incontrovertible core of the Protestants when one is considered a Protestant on every account of this collective: One is regarded as a Protestant by oneself and by the others, whatever one's or their views are of who is a Protestant.

Our characterization of the incontrovertible core bears some noticeable results when we apply it to intriguing collectives. The incontrovertible core of the Jews does not include a person—say, Bruno—who, though admittedly of the same ethnic origin as many persons who are considered by themselves and by the others to be Jews, does not consider himself to be one of the Jews. He does not satisfy our condition 1. Similarly, the incontrovertible core of the Jews does not include a person—say, Daniel—who considers himself to be one of the Jews, who is of the same ethnic origin of many persons who are considered by themselves and by the others to be Jews, but who is also considered by many Israelis not to be a Jew, because he has converted to Christianity. He does not satisfy our condition 2.

Consequently, the incontrovertible core of the Jews, our initial approximation to the Jewish collective, delineates a set of Jews that is narrower than the set of individuals delineated by the strict Orthodox notion of "who are the Jews." Bruno and Daniel may well be considered Jews according to that Orthodox notion, but nevertheless, since their cases are not indubitable, they do not belong to the incontrovertible core of the Jews, the incontrovertible core of the Jewish collective.

Similarly, the incontrovertible core of the Catholics does not include a person—say, Bertrand—who has published a book entitled *Why I Am Not a Christian,* in which he explains why he does not consider himself to be a Christian of any denomination. Nor will it include another person—say, Franz—whose "Old Catholic" community repudiated communion with and obedience to the See of Rome. Those who do not consider the members of the Orthodox churches of the East to be Catholics will not consider Franz to be one either. For similar reasons it does not include another person—say, Joseph—according to whose early Mormon views Adam of Genesis is the supreme ruler of all beings, while Christ, Mohammed, and some of Joseph's contemporaries, including himself, just partake of divinity. Those who do not deem Christian a person who rejects the deity of Christ and excludes any worship of him, will not deem Joseph a Christian.

Similarly, the incontrovertible core of the Sikhs does not include a person—say, Khatri—who considers himself to be not a Sikh but a Hindu. Nor will it include another person—say, Namdhari—since some persons, who happen to consider themselves to be strictly orthodox Sikhs, place outside the circle of Sikhs everyone whose faith involves acknowledgment of a continuing line of gurus, which Namdhari's faith does. For a similar reason, it does not include still another person—say, Nirankari—whose denomination not only exalts their leader as guru but, moreover, has its own system of scriptures, an extension of what is regarded as sacred scriptures by many other people who consider themselves to be Sikhs. Some of the latter place outside the circle of the Sikhs Nirankari and everyone else whose faith involves scriptures not included in their own compiled *Adi Granth.*

III

We turn now from the *incontrovertible core* of a collective, which is an initial approximation to it, to what we call *the union* of the same collective, which is an improved approximation.

A person belongs to the union (of a collective) when he or she is considered to be a member of the collective, according to views held by some members of the incontrovertible core of this collective.

The major intent of this proximate characterization of a collective is clear and simple. The above-mentioned Daniel, who considers himself to be one of the Jews, is not a member of the incontrovertible core of the Jews, because he is not unquestionably a Jew. Although he is of the same ethnic origin of many members of the incontrovertible core of the Jews, some of them do not consider him to be a Jew, because he has converted to Christianity. Other members of the incontrovertible core of the Jews do, however, consider Daniel to be a Jew. According to the view of Orthodox Jews,[8] Daniel is a Jew because of his presumed maternal descent, and hence, no matter what Daniel does, as long as his presumed maternal descent is left intact, so is his status as a Jew, to their mind. Consequently, Daniel is a member of the *union* of the Jews, though he is not a member of the incontrovertible core of the Jewish collective.

Unlike Daniel, some persons who consider themselves to be Jews are members of neither the incontrovertible core nor the union of the Jews. Consider a person—say, Gideon—whose only grounds for regarding himself as a Jew are that years ago, in a dream, an angel told him he is a descendant of the lost tribe of Dan. Taking it for granted that all members of the incontrovertible core of the Jews do not view such reports about dreams and angels as sufficient grounds for holding someone to be a Jew, it is clear Gideon belongs to neither the incontrovertible core nor the union of the Jews.[9]

Understanding the nature of the union of a collective is not tantamount to grasping reasons for introducing it as part of a theory of collective identity. Why should a broader union of some collective be viewed better than its narrower incontrovertible core?

Recall our examples of reasons for pursuit of a *neutral* theory of collective identity: first, the cases of a Sikh anthropologist who would like to know who are the Jews or a Jewish anthropologist who would like to know who are the Sikhs, and second, an alien person who has to chart a just constitution for a future state in which, say, the Sikhs will exercise their collective right for democratic self-determination, given that there are several incompatible answers to the question Who are the Sikhs?

Our alien anthropologist will soon realize that by delineating the incontrovertible core of the collective under consideration, she depicts just the tip of the collective iceberg. For example, a person—say, Singh—is a member of the incontrovertible core of the Sikhs not because of some coincidental, collective whim, as if her capricious self-portrayal as a Sikh serendipitously matches the equally capricious portrayals of Singh as a Sikh by the others. Singh is a member of the incontrovertible core of the Sikhs because she is a Sikh according to her own view of who is a Sikh and according to the others' conceptions of the Sikh collective. Membership in the incontrovertible core of the Sikhs, our anthropologist will have to admit, rests on overlapping *views* of who is a Sikh. Our anthropologist should, then, reach the conclusion that conceptions of the collective of the Sikhs, held by members of the incontrovertible core of the Sikhs, are indispensable elements of one's understanding of the collective of the Sikhs.

Now, if from the anthropologist's point of view, the different views of who is a Sikh, as held by members of the Sikh collective, are part of the subject matter of his project of understanding the Sikh collective identity, the resulting anthropological delineation of the collective of the Sikhs should reflect it. The incontrovertible core of the Sikhs takes all these views into account, because membership in it depends on all the views of who is a Sikh. What it does not reflect is a salient fact of prime importance: Members of it do not share their views of who is a Sikh. There are many significantly different views of who is a Sikh held by persons who are unquestionably Sikh. As long as an anthropological portrayal of the collective of the Sikhs fails to reflect this fundamental fact, it is considerably flawed. The idea of the union is meant to be a correction.

A view of who is a Sikh is now taken seriously in a new way. Whereas the incontrovertible core of the Sikhs reflected such a view only to the extent that it is in agreement with all the other views of who is a Sikh, the union of the Sikhs reflects the same view, even where it is significantly at variance with the other views. If two persons—say, Ratan and Mehar—are Sikhs on all accounts, that is, members of the incontrovertible core of the Sikhs, then whoever is a Sikh according to Ratan's view of who is a Sikh is a member of the union of the Sikhs, whatever Mehar's view of it happens to be; and whoever is a Sikh according to Mehar's view of who is a Sikh is a member of the union of the Sikhs, whatever Ratan's view of it happens to be. Whereas the incontrovertible core of the Sikhs takes Ratan's and Mehar's views seriously only where they are compatible with each other, the union of the Sikhs takes these views seriously, whether they are compatible with each other or not.

The union of the Sikhs, like the union of any collective, is a *neutrally* defined set. Different members of a union—say, Ratan and Mehar in the case of the Sikhs—play exactly parallel roles in delineating it. If some members of an incontrovertible core of a collective consider a person to be a member of the same collective, then whoever they are and whoever that person is, the former have successfully introduced the latter into the union of their collective.

Our characterization of the union seems to yield some significant results, when certain familiar collectives are considered. The union of the Christians, for example, will include members of several denominations that are, in a sense, "controversial." The history, creed, or practices of some religious groups has often given rise to a controversy over whether members of these groups should be regarded as Christians. Since some persons, who are even unquestionably Christians, do not consider, say, Unitarians, Mormons, or Quakers to be Christians, ordinary members of these denominations do not belong to the incontrovertible core of the Christians. However, since some persons who are unquestionably Christians do hold ordinary members of these denominations to be Christians, the latter all belong to the union of the Christians. Indeed, an anthropological delineation of the collective of Christians that excludes ordinary members of these denominations is obviously flawed. Clearly, the union of the Christians fares better than their incontrovertible core, from the present, deliberately neutral point of view.

Similarly, the union of the Sikhs includes all ordinary members of the Nirankaris and the Namdharis. They do not belong to the incontrovertible core, because some orthodox Sikhs of the Khalsa do not consider them fellow Sikhs. Since some members of the incontrovertible core of the Sikhs do consider them to be Sikhs, however, the ordinary Nirankaris and Namdharis are members of the union of the Sikhs. Again, any anthropological portrayal of the Sikhs that disregards these groups would be manifestly inadequate. The union of the Sikhs too fares better than their incontrovertible core, from our present point of view.

We analyze the union of the Jews elsewhere.[10] We will assume that, as a matter of fact, the union of the Jews forms an adequately proximate characterization of the collective of Jews, from a neutral point of view.

IV

The proposed neutral recursive theory of collective identity is intended to provide a method of delineating collectives of a religious, national, or cultural nature, *taking it for granted that a "diversity condition" holds*, namely, that for each common collective of such a nature, the question

Who is a . . . ? has a variety of significantly different answers, held by members of different groups, even within the collective itself. There is no consensus on the collective identity of the Christians or the Sikhs, and clearly no consensus could be reached on who are the Jews. If this diversity condition does in fact hold for such collectives, it seems any general theory of collective identity is inadequate as long as it does not provide one with an explanation of this fundamental, intriguing fact. We turn, then, to an outline of such an explanation.

Collectives of a religious, national, or cultural nature share two general traits: Each of them involves a rich conceptual realm and has its own rich history. We will try to show why a collective of a rich conceptual realm and a rich history is bound to give rise to a whole gamut of significantly different solutions of the problem of its collective identity.

Familiar collectives of a religious nature have each a rich conceptual realm. If a religion has a creed, then the conceptual realm of the related collective includes the major concepts of the creed. Thus, the conceptual realms of the Christian, Muslim, and Sikh collectives include concepts of deity. Underlying each notion of deity, be it a Christian notion of "Trinity," a Muslim notion of "Allah," or a Sikh notion of "Akal Purakh," is a whole system of concepts, such as the Christian concepts of God the Father, the Lord, and the Holy Spirit; the Muslim concepts of God's magnificent attributes; or the Sikh concepts of the "Timeless One." These systems of concepts are also included in the conceptual realms of the respective religious collectives.

If a religion has rituals, then the conceptual realm of the related collective includes the major concepts of the prescribed rites. Thus, the conceptual realms of numerous religions underlie rituals related to certain dates, places, persons, and actions: During certain periods, certain people should go to certain places and perform certain actions. Again, whole systems of concepts underlie the related notions, such as "high holidays," "temple," "pilgrim," "priest," "altar," or "benediction." And again, each of these conceptual systems belongs to the conceptual realm of the respective religious collective.[11]

Similarly, other features of religion also introduce a variety of conceptual families into the conceptual realm of the related collectives. If a religion has scriptures, these texts involve both a general concept underlying the notion of a "holy writ" as well as the particular concepts used in the texts themselves. If a religion venerates certain persons—say, prophets, saints, or gurus—then once again, the conceptual realm of the related collective includes both general concepts that underlie the notions of "prophet," "saint," or "guru," as well as the particular concepts that these revered persons are believed to use during their lives.

The conceptual realm of a national collective is similarly rich. Among the possible ingredients of any prevalent sense of national identity, one finds notions of shared ethnicity and language, culture and religion, history and homeland. Such features of national identity could not play a significant role in the life of a national collective, without the underlying conceptual families forming part of its conceptual realm.[12]

Enter History. In a newly established religion, for example, different major parts of the underlying conceptual realm could, perhaps, all be taken by members of the related collective to be of equal value and importance. In the eyes of these persons, the new creed might be as important as the new rituals, each clause in the creed as important as any other clause of it, and each ritual as important as any other ritual.[13]

Under various circumstances, however, members of a collective would be prone to draw distinctions between different major parts of the conceptual realm of their collective and deem certain parts more important than others. Members of one religious denomination who are being persecuted on grounds of their persistent performance of certain rituals could react by enhancing their persistence and convincing themselves that at least temporarily the endangered rituals are more important than other ones. If persecution continues for quite a while, then a new generation of members of the same collective might grow up in whose eyes the same rituals are *ordinarily* considered to be of greater importance. The status of these rituals and the underlying parts of the conceptual realm has thus been changed. Other members of the same religious denomination, however, or members of another one, might adopt an utterly different policy when being persecuted because of their insistence on observing certain practices. They might convince themselves that at least temporarily these practices are less important than other ones and could therefore be ignored. Again, if persecution goes on for a decade or so, then a new generation of members of the same collective might emerge in whose eyes the same practices are *ordinarily* ignored. Again, the status of these practices and the underlying parts of the conceptual realm have thus been changed significantly. Hence, when external pressure is being exerted on a collective, its reaction might involve the introduction of a new structure into its conceptual realm, some parts of it becoming more central than others or more peripheral than others.

Such internal modifications of the conceptual realm are not confined to cases of external oppression. Other kinds of external influence might also result in a structural modification of the conceptual realm. For example, when members of a collective are continually exposed to an alien way of life, they might import into their conceptual realm seemingly innocuous elements of the alien conceptual realm and adapt them for their own purposes. For instance, members of a religion that, at a certain stage, does not have a written systematic code of practice might draw a lesson from a successful attempt that members of another religion made at introducing a written systematic code of practice and introduce a code of their own practices. If this code turns out to be successful, it might eventually play a central role within the conceptual realm of the collective, because it renders the collective a highly important service: For the first time in the history of the collective, written answers to a vast number of questions are readily available and even easily accessible. Generally speaking, religious and cultural interface could cause structural modifications within the conceptual realm of a collective.

Furthermore, such modifications can be the effects of internal processes, rather than external pressures or influences. Members of a collective sometimes face problems they are unable to solve under the constraints imposed by their conceptual realm in its current form. Consider, for instance, members of a religious collective whose code of practice requires them to act in a certain way. The related practical precepts of the code were introduced into it, by a due process, to solve some problem when certain conditions prevailed. These conditions no longer prevail, however, and the practical precepts are far from providing an appropriate solution to the same problem, under the new conditions. If the code of practice is conservative, to the extent that it does not allow the replacement of one of its practices by a new one, then members of the collective are unable to solve their problem. Under such conditions, some members might make daring suggestions, set up new principles, and apply them to the problem at hand. For instance, a suggested principle might render all practices hypothetical: A practice is a solution to a problem under certain conditions, and it is a living part of the code as long as these conditions obtain; if they do not, another solution may be sought and instituted, replacing the previous one. Of course, the moment such a principle is incorporated into a conceptual realm of a religious collective, the whole structure of this realm may well undergo a radical modification.

The history of a collective is, therefore, an arena of modification; and the richer the history of this collective is, that is, the more internal and external problems its members encounter, tackle, and solve, the more significant are the modifications its conceptual realm sustains. In the history of any living collective, members of the collective, whether all of them at once, most of them, or just some of them first, are bound to view the conceptual realm of their collective as highly structured, some of its parts being conspicuously considered more central than others.

Such a stage in the life of a collective does not bring to an end all processes of structural modification of its conceptual realm. First, new pressures, whether external or internal, as well as additional periods of intercollective interface might result in new modifications. Second, and no less interesting, a collective of a long and rich history will naturally develop a viable sense of a *tradition*, directly related to the underlying conceptual realm. A sense of tradition makes a member of the collective believe and feel that the role one plays in the life of the collective at the present stage is parallel to the role played by members of previous generations of the same collective, under parallel circumstances. For instance, within a tradition of pilgrimage, present-day pilgrims will consider themselves not only to be observing the practice of pilgrimage but also to be following their fathers and forefathers, who observed the same practice in the same way.

Within a long tradition one often knows what one's forefathers did, but seldom does one know why they did what they did. One may assume that they held their activities to be meaningful and that meanings were couched in terms of the underlying conceptual realm, but the precise meaning itself may still remain unexaminable. Meaning, therefore, is going to be sought by concerned members of a collective, for obscure elements of their tradition. If possible, meanings will be couched in terms of the conceptual realm, in its present form, but if this turns out to be impossible, a modification of that conceptual realm might take place in order to save the obscure elements of the tradition by rendering them meaningful. Such a structural modification could be of a *local* nature, being confined to a few elements of the conceptual realm. Moreover, the longer a tradition is alive, the more obscure some of its elements might appear, and the more elements of it might appear obscure. Local modifications might be ineffective, leaving still meaningless a significant share of the tradition. This is how recurrent processes of *global* modification might emerge in the life of a collective, processes, that is, of *self-reinterpretation* of one's whole collective life, tradition, and conceptual realm.[14]

Reinterpretations are at the root of the views members of a collective have of who is a member of the collective. Many different reinterpretations of a rich tradition are indeed possible, and it comes as no surprise to find numerous reinterpretations emerge during the history of a familiar collective.

A view of who is a Jew, for example, can emanate as a personal one, put forward by a member of the collective, endorsed by few, disregarded or rejected by others, but under appropriate conditions it might form the official view of an organized group within the collective, or at least crystallize as the dominant view among members of some circles. Further developments might involve not only additional structural modifications of the conceptual realm but also the eventual emergence of different conceptual realms, ones that are distinct from one another in both substance and structure. For instance, a view of who is a Jew that rests on Aristotelian philosophy will share a significant part of its underlying conceptual realm with a mystical view of who is a Jew, but the two views do not share with each other much, perhaps most, of their conceptual foundations. Consequently, since the emergence of such disparate views of who is a Jew, the collective of the Jews has not had a unique conceptual realm anymore, underlying its rituals, liturgy, and scriptures as well as other elements of its tradition. The emergence of different traditions within the confines of a single collective is a natural ensuing result.

A collective of an original rich conceptual realm and of a rich history could, then, resist any attempt at capturing its nature in terms of some conditions shared by all its members and none but them.[15] To use an apt, celebrated notion, a collective of an original rich conceptual realm and of a rich history is a *family* of groups, subcollectives, each with its own view of who is a member of the collective, its own sense of tradition and its own underlying conceptual realm, but each bearing some *resemblance* to the other ones.[16] Members of a certain group within such a family could share with one another their view of who is a member of the collective, their sense of tradition, and their underlying conceptual realm, but they share with members of other groups only parts of their view of who is a member of the collective, sense of tradition, and conceptual realm.

A full portrayal of such a family of groups will include a specification of family *features*. Features are shared by different members of the collective, though not by all of them, and play an essential role in characterizing groups within the collective. For example, the conception of the Trinity is a feature of the collective of Christians: It is shared by many Christians, though not by all of them, and it is an essential element of the characterization of several groups within the Christian collective. The practices of refraining from cutting one's hair and from smoking are features of the collective of the Sikhs: They are observed by many Sikhs, though not by all of them, and they are essential elements of the characterization of certain groups within the Sikh collective.

The project of specifying the features of a collective that consists of a family of groups is, however, only the final stage of a general project of portraying such a collective. It could not be carried out without a preceding delineation of the set of members of the collective. The application of the proposed neutral recursive theory will, therefore, serve as the starting point of such a portrayal project. An outlined delineation of the set of members of the collective will be an intermediate product, to be used in the ensuing project of specifying the features of the collective.

This is an outline of our explanation of the fact that the diversity condition holds for familiar collectives, the fundamental fact that for each common collective of such a nature, the question Who is a member of the collective? has a variety of significantly different answers, held by members of different groups, even within the collective itself. The familiar collectives are each a family of groups, which have emerged and evolved during a significant period of time—millennia—or at least are at the root of the ubiquitous diversity of collective identities.

V

The time has come for drawing from our discussion some lessons specifically pertaining to the collective of the Jews. In conclusion, we outline two applications of the proposed theory of collective identity to issues that have drawn much attention in the life of the Jewish collective.

The first issue is the nature of puzzling remarks about the collective of the Jews, such as those we quoted from Wittgenstein, in the first section of this essay, or as:

(F1) To be Jewish is to be honest, idealist, and ambitious.

(F2) The Jewish people is arrogant, condescending, and stubborn.

(F3) The Jews form a religion, not a nation.

How should one interpret such remarks? The proposed theory of collective identity provides us with several alternative directions:

1. One possible direction is that of the incontrovertible core of the collective: A remark about a collective could be interpreted as one about its incontrovertible core, about its members, the incontrovertibles, or about their properties. (F1) would, thus, be interpreted as:

(F1.1) A person who is incontrovertibly a Jew is also an honest, idealistic, and ambitious person.

2. Another possible direction is related to the best delineation of the collective, say, its union: A remark about a collective could be interpreted as one about its union, about its members, or about their properties. Remark (F2) could now be interpreted as:

(F2.2) The group of persons who are considered Jews by some persons who are incontrovertibly Jews is arrogant, condescending, and stubborn.

Or perhaps as

(F2.2') A person who is considered a Jew by some persons who are incontrovertibly Jews is also an arrogant, condescending, and stubborn person.[17]

3. A different possible direction is related to the features of the collective: A remark about a collective could be interpreted as a remark about the set of features of the collective, about one of them, its nature, history, or value. Accordingly, remark (F3) could be interpreted as

(F3.3) The features of the collective of the Jews are features of a religion, not features of a nation.

4. Finally, there is a possible direction of interpreting a remark about a collective as a suggestion that a reinterpretation be introduced, of the collective or of some of its facets. Remarks (F1)–(F3) could here be taken to mean:

(F1.4) The tradition of some groups of Jews should be reinterpreted as one that has fostered, above all, honesty, idealism, and ambition.

(F2.4) The history of all Jewish groups should be reinterpreted as one that nurtured mainly arrogance, condescendence, and stubbornness.

(F3.4) The conceptual realm of almost all Jewish groups, whether of religious, national, or cultural self-identity, should be reinterpreted as one that consists of mostly religious rather than national elements.

It seems we are now in a position to understand why remarks such as (F1), (F2), and (F3), or Wittgenstein's (W1) "Tragedy is something un-Jewish"; and (W2) "It is typical for a Jewish mind to understand someone else's work better than he understands it himself" seem to be puzzling. On one hand, if one tries to take them seriously and interpret them as pertaining to the collective of the Jews, then one often encounters either falsehoods, such as (F1.1) and (F2.2'), which are obviously untrue, or (F3.3), which is less blatantly so, or obscurities, such as (F2.2), which seem to be readily interpretable only in terms of some glaring falsehood such as (F2.2'). On the other hand, all these remarks could be read as suggestions rather than as assertions. Each of them suggests that the Jewish collective or some of its elements be reinterpreted in a certain way. Still, suggestions are not more self-evident than assertions. Why should one adopt, say, any of the suggestions made in (F1.4), (F2.4), or (F3.4)?[18] If we do not see any reason for following any of these suggestions, we simply do not follow them. And here is where the puzzle starts emerging: Not following a suggestion is not tantamount to rejecting it. Sometimes a suggestion for reinterpretation seems to be neither obviously worthwhile nor plainly worthless, and we are inclined to choose a middle course of neither following it nor rejecting it but instead pondering it.

This is, then, why remarks about the Jews (or any other familiar collective) seem to be puzzling. Whether they are read as assertions about the collective or suggestions for reinterpreting it, there seems to be no reason for accepting them. But rejecting offhand what could be read as a suggested reinterpretation might also seem to be unwarranted. Such a combination of attitudes seems puzzling, because these attitudes seem to be in conflict, but actually they are not. By putting a suggestion to thorough scrutiny still without following it, we express both of the attitudes.

Notice that we have said nothing about motivations persons may have had for making remarks such as (W1) and (W2), (F1) or (F2), (F3), or numerous similar ones. We are not interested in hidden agendas or ulterior motives. We have shown how one could try taking such remarks seriously, without resort to any practice of marking their authors as anti-Semites, as Jewish self-aggrandizers, or as anything in between.

Two pleas seem warranted at this stage. One is a plea for *restraint in interpreting remarks* about the Jews as straightforward truths or falsehoods. More often than not, such remarks are related to features of the Jewish collective rather than to every single Jew or group of Jews. An important insight is sometimes gained by properly understanding a remark that is not most general in nature. Similarly, quite often remarks about the Jews are related to suggested reinterpretations of the Jewish collective, or elements thereof; and again, insights into the nature of some facets of the Jewish collective could be acquired through a scrutiny of such a suggestion, even if it is not followed, even if it eventually turns out not to be defensible.

Our second plea is for *restraint in making remarks* about the Jews. Simple remarks about the Jews are likely to be overly simple, "in a nutshell" claims about the Jews do not hold much water. It is very difficult to make a *general and accurate* observation about a collective as conceptually rich and historically rich as that of the Jews. It is impossible to make a *simple,* general, and accurate comment about it. Moreover, more often than not, what is presented by some Jew or Jewish group as a general statement about the Jews is in fact just one view in vain disguise, futilely struggling for unachievable hegemony, as if major modifications of conceptual realms, alternative traditions, and articulate views of who is a Jew could simply be vanquished by pretentiously disregarding their very existence. Finally, suggestions for reinterpreting the collective of the Jews, or any of its facets, also should not be disguised as innocent aphorisms of the descriptive mode, as if it does not take more than a twinkle of one's eye to introduce a new perspective and show that new light could be shed from it on conceptually and historically rich facets of the collective of the Jews.

The last issue to be briefly addressed in this essay, by way of applying the proposed theory of collective identity to some current affairs, is the problem of who is a Jew as tackled in the State of Israel.

We take it for granted that a constitution of a state is unjust if it introduces discrimination against citizens of the state on grounds of their views. All the more so, if citizens are discriminated against on grounds of their fundamental views of their own identity, whether personal or collective. Hence, a just constitution of a state that counts among its citizens persons who hold extremely different views of religion in general or of some denominations in particular, does not introduce a discrimination either against staunch atheists or against ardent theists, on grounds of their views, nor, indeed, against anyone else in between.[19]

We also take it for granted that the State of Israel is the state of the Jews, in the following *minimal* sense:

1. It has been proclaimed and internationally recognized as the state in which the Jews exercise their collective right of sovereignty in their homeland.

2. A vast majority of its citizens are Jews.

3. Jews who are persecuted because they are Jewish are entitled to residence in it.

To be sure, this minimal sense, in which Israel is the state of the Jews, is clearly compatible with a sigificant number, though still a minority, of its citizens being non-Jews, and more generally, with its ability to have a truly democratic regime.[20]

Within this framework, the problem of who is a Jew is of major significance. The two most fundamental elements of the nature of the State of Israel are that it is meant to be a democracy and that it is meant to be the state of the Jews. Who, then, are those referred to as "the Jews" in the expression "the state of the Jews," which plays such a major role in the rationale of the state and its collective self-image?

The sporadic political struggles for adoption of a more orthodox answer to this question, within the framework of Israel's Law of Return, indicate a divergence of views, a lasting dispute, a permanent disunity. No partisan view of who is a Jew, as held by numerous citizens of Israel, could be used in the fundamental Law of Return, without thereby rendering that view constitutionally superior to all the other partisan views of who is a Jew, also held by numerous citizens of the state. In other words, a strictly Orthodox view of who is a Jew, or any other similarly partisan view, could not be formally adopted by the State of Israel, even for the sake of a single fundamental law, as long as the State of Israel does not introduce into its constitutional foundations a fundamental discrimination, a blatant violation of the most basic principle of justice and democracy, and commits thereby a flagrant desertion of one of the two most fundamental elements of its intended nature.

Under circumstances of a permanent variance of views on fundamental issues, constitutional decisions should be made from a *neutral* point of view.[21] Therefore, under the lasting conditions of disunity, the just constitutional delineation of the Jews that the State of Israel should use for its Law of Return, is a delineation drawn from a neutral point of view. Our proposed general process of delineating a collective is a neutral one, as we argued earlier, and it can provide us with the required just constitutional delineation of the Jews. We suggest that what we called *the union* of the Jews be used as the constitutional delineation of the Jews, within the framework of the Law of Return.[22]

Accordingly, the State of Israel would be the state of those who are incontrovertibly Jews, but also, and to exactly the same extent, of all those who are held to be Jews by some, though perhaps not by all, incontrovertible Jews. Hence, Israel is also the state of the Ethiopian Jews, of the persons who went through Reform or Conservative procedures and rituals of conversion, of the persons who used to be considered incontrovertible Jews but converted into Christianity, Islam, or another non-Jewish religion, as well as of the spouses and offsprings of incontrovertible Jews who have joined an incontrovertible community of Jews without going through any ritual of conversion at all. Thus delineated, the State of Israel will be the state of all those who are held to be Jews by some incontrovertible Jews.

NOTES

Acknowledgments: Most of the work on this essay was done during long visits to the Department of Philosophy at UCLA and a short one to the Department of Philosophy at Stanford University. I am grateful to Marilyn Adams, Robert Adams, Michael Bratman, Keith Donnellan, Julius Moravcsik, and Marleen Rozemond for many illuminating remarks.

1. Ludwig Wittgenstein, *Culture and Value,* ed. G. H. von Wright, in collaboration with Heikki Nyman (Oxford: Basil Blackwell, 1980), 53e.

2. Ibid., 1e.

3. Ibid., 19e.

4. For illuminating background discussions of such delineation problems outside the Jewish context, see F. James Davis, *Who Is Black?* (University Park: Pennsylvania State University Press, 1991), and W. H. McLeod, *Who Is a Sikh?* (Oxford: Clarendon Press, 1989). The same theory seems to be applicable to collectives of different types as well, including professions, for example. We will not discuss such applications here, however.

5. See, for example, McLeod, *Who Is a Sikh?*

6. A similar hypothetical case involves a hypothetical constitution of the state in which the Jews exercise their collective right for democratic self-determination. We will return to this case later on.

7. What information about one person, say Emil, would enable another person to answer the question of whether Emil is one of the Collected depends, of course, on the latter's notion of who they are. One person would need information about Emil's views, a second person's answer might depend on information about Emil's behavior, and a third person's criterion of being a Collected might require information about Emil's mother.

8. Strictly speaking, at this point we need to assume that the incontrovertible core of the Jews "includes" some Orthodox persons. We see no reason for casting any doubt on this assumption.

9. The union of a collective, such as the Jews, is for many collectives broader and for no collective narrower than the preceding incontrovertible core. This follows from the definitions of these two classes.

10. So far, three ingredients of the proposed neutral recursive theory of collective identity have been presented: (*a*) a characterization of the incontrovertible core of any collective, (*b*) a characterization of the union of any collective, and (*c*) a defensible claim to the effect that, from a neutral point of view, the neutrally delin-

eated union is a better approximation to its collective than the neutrally delineated incontrovertible core. Other ingredients of this theory are developed and defended in Asa Kasher, "Collective Identity" (manuscript on file with author). This essay outlines replies to several likely objections to the theory, as presented so far.

Objection One: "The proposed process of approximation seems to start with the incontrovertible core and end with the union. Why stop at the union rather than go on and improve it by introducing some new classes?"

Objection Two: "Assuming that the approximation process has been extended, perhaps even indefinitely many times, where would you stop? How could one justify a decision to stop at one point and not at another? Wouldn't it be rather an arbitrary decision to stop proximating, say, the collective of the Sikhs, at its union, rather than later?"

Objection Three: "How do we know that the incontrovertible core of a collective is never actually an end point, too? Isn't it possible that the incontrovertible core of a collective would be simply empty, no person being considered a member of it both by oneself and by the others?"

Objection Four: "How do we know that the incontrovertible core of a collective is never an end point, too, not because it is empty, but for other reasons? Isn't it possible that the union of a collective is the same as its incontrovertible core?"

Objection Five: "Finally, even if the rules of the theory provide us with a pregnant starting point—a nonempty incontrovertible core, which gives rise to a broader union—couldn't the whole approximation process be rendered trivial by eventually reaching a class that includes every person?"

11. On the conceptual background of rituals, see Leo Apostel, "Mysticism, Ritual and Atheism," in *Religious Atheism?* edited by L. Apostel et al. (Ghent: E. Story-Scientia, 1982), 7–54; and Asa Kasher, "Ritual," in *The Philosophy of Leo Apostel: Descriptive and Critical Essays,* edited by Fernand Vandamme and Rik Pinxten, (Ghent: Communication & Cognition, 1989), 191–210.

12. The same holds for cultural collectives, which involve systems of meaning, attitude, and value.

13. A newly established nation is a much less common phenomenon than a newly established religion or religious denomination. However, one may assume that in the eyes of the citizens of a new nation-state, the constitution that governs their internal civil affairs and the organs of sovereignty that govern their foreign affairs are of exactly the same importance.

14. On the process of reinterpretation, see Asa Kasher, "Philosophical Reinterpretation of Scripture," in *Interpretation in Religion,* edited by Shlomo Biderman and Ben-Ami Scharfstein (Leiden: E. J. Brill, 1992), 9–37.

15. By "original" we do not mean at the historical stage of inception of the collective but rather at any historical stage in the history of the collective that serves as a starting point of the outlined development.

16. On the notion of "family resemblance," commonly associated with Wittgenstein's later philosophy, see G. P. Baker and P.M.S. Hacker, *Wittgenstein, Understanding and Meaning* (Oxford: Basil Blackwell, 1980), 320–43.

17. It is not our view that when a human property, such as being arrogant, is ascribed to a human collective it is meant to be applied to each member of that collective. On some occasions, however, this is exactly what is being implied.

18. Notice that before one starts evaluating the merits or demerits of (F1.4), (F2.4), or (F3.4), one has to clarify the reference to "groups of Jews" or "Jewish groups" in terms of some appropriate class of the Jews, such as their union.

19. Where a state, such as Israel, does not have a constitution, but only laws of some fundamental status, what we have just assumed about the just constitution of a state would be assumed about its fundamental laws. In the sequel, we use the notion of "constitution" in this broad sense.

20. On the seeming paradox of a nation-state that has a significant national minority and its solution in terms of affirmative action in international relationships, see Asa Kasher, "Justice and Affirmative Action," *Israel Yearbook on Human Rights* 15 (1985): 101–12.

21. For the most elaborated philosophical presentation of this position, see John Rawls, *A Theory of Justice* (Cambridge, Mass.: Harvard University Press, 1971).

22. We take it that union of the Jews is an adequate approximation of the Jews, from a neutral point of view. See Kasher, "Collective Identity."

5

THOUGHTS ON JEWISH IDENTITY

Leon J. Goldstein

In memoriam: Pinchas Hacohen Peli

I SUPPOSE that those who conceived the project that is this book know that the task we contributors have collectively undertaken is quite impossible to realize. There is no simple, or even moderately complex, way to determine what Jewish identity is and how it affects those who are Jews. I know of a man, though I do not know him personally, who is black and identifies himself as such. Yet his mother was a Polish Jewish woman. I do not know if she converted to Christianity when she married his father; but whether or not she did, *halakhah,* traditional Jewish law, does not recognize such conversions and so takes it that her children, including the person I have in mind, are Jewish. Since he is the son of a Jewish woman, halakhicly Jewish, concerning whose Jewishness there can be no question, I take it that the man I have in mind is certainly Jewish himself. I dare say that this would be quite surprising to him.

Then there is Jean Améry, son of a Jewish father and an unconverted non-Jewish mother, a man who certainly would not undergo religious conversion since he was without religious belief—Jewish or otherwise. From the point of view of *halakhah,* he certainly was not a Jew. Yet being a Jew was a central part of his self-identity, though he did not consider Judaism to be an option for himself.[1] Since he was raised a Catholic, one may suppose that Améry did not experience his Jewishness bodily as is customary for Jewish males on the eighth day of their lives, but it is not only *halakhah* that has its definition of Jewishness. There is also the conception of Jewishness that is to be found in the Nuremberg laws, and its conception was very much experienced by Améry on his body, as characterized in the essay called "Torture" in his book *At the Mind's Limit.* The Nazis were unambiguous in defining him as a Jew, a definition he accepted without qualification.

Sidney Hook, in an interview shortly before his death and published not long after it, observed the following:

> Some people ask, What makes you a Jew? I say, a Jew is anyone who calls himself such or is called such and lives in a community which acts on the distinction between Jew and non-Jew. That's a purely nominal definition, but it's the only one that does justice to the way the term "Jew" is used throughout the world. People who have given up their Judaism are still called Jews, people who have no belief at all. A Jewish atheist, is that an oxymoron? It's not, because he's still Jewish. Well, that's my view.[2]

Three individual human beings, different in all manner of ways, yet each, in his own way, a Jew. Obviously, when I speak of "his own way" I am not speaking of his own chosen way. It is not clear that choice is appropriate to the characterization of the Jewishness of any of the three, and, as we have seen, it is quite likely that the first of the three doesn't even know that there is a criterion of Jewishness that he satisfies completely. Satisfies completely, though it is not in the least a subjective aspect of his being. That, I suppose, is worth pondering, for most Jews are aware of themselves as Jews even if some of them may wish that they were not. In the well-known Brother Daniel case, in which a Jew by birth who had converted to Catholicism and joined a religious order claimed Israeli citizenship under the Law of Return, Haim Cohn, a member of the Israel supreme court and former attorney general, took the view that a Jew is one who regards himself as such, though the court decided that Jewish identity is not compatible with choosing conversion.[3] Is Brother Daniel a Jew or not? The court ruled that he wasn't. Had he appealed to a rabbinic court, which, I suppose, would have been difficult for a Catholic, he would likely have been vindicated inasmuch as such a court would not have recognized his conversion. (My colleague Professor Samuel Morell thinks not, pointing out that rabbinic courts have denied converts privileges that would otherwise have accrued to them as Jews.)

The question is quite muddled. Yet in a sense it isn't. It isn't for each of the parties cited. It isn't for the rabbinical court: its halakhic standards make the answer unambiguous. Nor is it for Judge Cohn. Given his standard, the answer is likewise unambiguous. (Though what would he say of someone not born of a Jewish mother, not part of any organized Jewish institution—religious or other—who simply pronounced himself a Jew?

What does he think of the claim made by the so-called black Hebrews, American blacks illegally domiciled in Israel who pronounce themselves the original Jews? I suspect, without actually knowing, that Judge Cohn's standard works only for cases like that of Brother Daniel.) I imagine that the black who descends from the Polish Jewish woman would have no doubt about his not being a Jew. What seems a muddle is the total picture with its variety of perspectives, though for each individual the issue and its outcome seem clear enough.

And yet it is not obvious that this points us in the direction of a solution. Perhaps we would like to say—in the spirit of an open-handed tolerance— that each may choose for himself or herself. Yet there is a sense in which that cannot be correct. There is no being a Jew for an individual if there is no such thing as a Jewish collectivity—however that turns out to be defined. One does not reject being a Jew, opt out of the Jewish people or a Jewish identity, without there being a something one is rejecting. If being a Jew were a characteristic of persons and if such determination were simply a matter of individual determination or subjective decision, what would the rejecter reject? I am not a chemist, but I do not go about rejecting such an identity. But, you might say, this really has no relevance since by and large non-Jews do not go around denying that they are Jews.[4] Thus, you might continue, being a Jew is precisely like being a chemist, and chemists do, in the end, have a collective identity that is manifested in membership in organizations of chemists, membership in departments of chemistry, and employment in chemical companies. Yet, it is really not the same. I doubt if anyone was ever troubled by being identified as a chemist, and I doubt if anyone was ever a chemist against his or her will. Even those who would wish not to be Jews are, from some point of view, Jewish nevertheless. Surely, no one was ever a chemist who chose not to be, and the being of a chemist never penetrates to the core of one's being human.

Chemists are individual human beings, and superficially, it might seem possible to define the chemist in individual terms. Some may have their private laboratories, and those who teach their subject confront their classes quite by themselves. Yet they are chemists because they participate in a common discipline, and without the discipline—which, in a way, defines the activity of a collectivity of some sort—there are no chemists. An individual chooses to be a chemist—we need not bother about reasons or motives—but the realization must inevitably involve the chooser in some form of group participation, indeed group identity. What needs to be explicated is the character of the individual-group relation.

(Let me say at this point, that I am not trying to suggest that every such choice and its realization must involve the individual with a collectivity. One may choose to be a poet. And poetic creativity is a form of activity that is capable of being defined or characterized. There are poets in the world, and that suggests a collective entity. Yet it is not obvious to me that being a poet involves participation in a collective entity, and it may well be that in the world of poets it is, indeed, each for himself. There is no purpose of this essay to be served by exploring this. The chemist example suits my need here, and I want only to say that this is in no way affected by the possibility that some choices and their realization need not involve an individual's participation in a collectivity.)

It is possible to specify in terms of what some individual is a chemist. I do not say that this is absolutely simple. There are varieties of chemists, different kinds of specialties that result in chemists doing different things, yet, I think there is a kind of core identity that can be pointed to and characterized. The organic chemist and the materials chemist don't define themselves in opposition to one another, nor do the rest of us, external observers or behavioral scientists studying the institutions of the chemists' world, see any point to proposing radical distinctions among the tribes and sects of the chemists. But perhaps the focus upon chemists is not to the point. I have never understood the rationality of having cultural anthropologists and physical anthropologists in the same department. To be sure, both study *anthropoi*, but no more so than psychologists and sociologists, political scientists and economists, who manage to have departments of their own. Cultural anthropologists and physical anthropologists do not do the same sort of theory, yet it is clear to any regular reader of *The Anthropological Newsletter* that there is a certain passion about keeping the field of anthropology united and not allowing it to spin off into its specializations. The "field" seems, to some degree, to be defined by a historically shaped tradition, and whatever rationalization or justification might be offered by defenders of unity, one may well wonder about the effect of that historically shaped tradition in influencing those intent upon preserving the unity of the discipline.

Without being clear about the consequence, one thing seems to emerge from the discussion in the immediately preceding paragraphs, namely, that being a Jew is more like being an anthropologist than being a chemist. Why do Jews who have little in common *qua* Jews still concern themselves about the unity of the Jewish people. There is a wide variety in the attitudes Jews have with respect to *halakhah,* yet there are Jews, even among those who do not share the orthodox point of view, who are fearful lest a loosening of the practice with respect to the laws of divorce results in the shattering of the unity of the Jewish people into groups among which intermarriage would be impossible. Why, one may wonder, should anybody care? There is very little—if any—interaction between those for whom strict adherence to the *halakhah* on divorce is a matter of importance and those to whom it is not, so why worry about it? Yet it is something that at least some Jews worry about, and central to the worry is not the legitimacy of this or that method of divorce, but, rather, the unity of that collectivity—whatever its nature proves to be—which is the Jewish people.

Recognition—and experience of—the unity and identity of the Jewish people is present even in individuals who are not otherwise participant in Jewish life. There are those who think of Judaism in terms of their own conceptions of social morality, not infrequently grounding that view in a rather one-sided and selective reading of the Hebrew Bible in which the focus of attention is on certain prophetic texts and little else. Why think of those values as Judaism? Why not identify with organizations that exist to further those purposes and which consist of members drawn from all segments of the population? Surely, a rational effort to further such values would seem to require that sort of approach. In addition, all of us know that not infrequently Jews who think of their Judaism in terms of social morality take a dim view of the conservative politics of increasing numbers of ultra-orthodox Jews almost to the extent of disassociating themselves from them. Given the life-style and character of the commitment of the ultra-orthodox, no one questions or could question that they are Jews. How can those who are not observant in any serious way and who identify Judaism with a liberal social commitment think of that as defining Judaism? I suspect that what we have here is a sense of an historically grounded continuity and identity that transcends the explicit commitments just referred to. Again, more like anthropologists than chemists. It is not hard to doubt that a visitor from outer space examining the matters we have been discussing—as well as others that could be added—would conclude that there is no such thing as a Jewish people even if a number of different groups choose to call themselves by that term.[5]

In spite of its seeming reasonableness, the visitor's conception is clearly mistaken. There is a Jewish identity, and, in spite of the difficulties we have been encountering, it has some kind of unity shaped by its history.[6] But given its unquestioned historical reality, why does it appear to be so difficult to characterize? Other peoples have—or have had—ongoing historical identities and continuities, but it doesn't seem, in the typical case, that the attempt to state what they are is as difficult as in the case in hand. I am, of course, thinking of straightforward historical thinking about such matters, not ideologically self-serving attempts to define one's own group as racially superior to others or superior in some other sort of way. No doubt, a major contributor to the ease—at least comparatively speaking— with which this may be done is the fact of continuous occupation of a given territory, which is patently not the case for the Jews. There are other groups, however, that are defined without reference, or total reference, to territory—one thinks of the Armenians and the Gypsies—and others that do, indeed, have a large component of territoriality in their identities, yet that is not exhaustive. Think of how Americans of Irish or Italian origin, though completely assimilated to American ways and culture, continue to think of themselves—and are thought of by others—as Irish and Italian. Being myself neither Irish nor Italian, I may incline to see them as unities in ways that people who actually possess those identities do not. I have no desire to examine the matter in a scholarly way, but I did once know an Italian woman who came from Milan and who seemed to distinguish between herself and most Italian-Americans whose ancestors came from the southern part of Italy. She certainly inclined to make fun of them with reference to cultural ways she did not share.

If we have achieved anything to this point, it is an awareness that de-fining the Jew and defining Jewishness is rather elusive, if only that. To be sure, this would be denied by some, particularly by those who adhere to the halakhic point of view. For them, there is no ambiguity about who is a Jew, nor is there any doubt that Jewishness is the content of the divine reve-lation to the people of Israel, through the instrumentality of Moses, which prescribes the way of life that is Judaism. But, clearly, we are trying to look at the question from a perspective—perhaps a historical perspective—that takes seriously what we find in the Jewish world on its own terms, and that requires a perspective that transcends the particular ideological standpoint of any particular group of Jews.

We seem to be dealing with two sorts of entities, Jews as particular human beings of determinate sort and the Jewishness they share. And that may seem to suggest that old controversy over the nature of the concepts used in the social sciences, whether they may be analyzed without re-mainder in terms of the dispositions and other characteristics of individual human beings or whether there is some essential sociocultural remainder that cannot be reduced to individuals. Perhaps it doesn't suggest that at all, but only seems so to me because I participated in that debate,[7] and while, in the end, I don't think that the discussion as it was then understood, cer-tainly as then understood by me, will resolve our present difficulties, I do think it useful to speak briefly about it in order to see why it is not the case.

I do not really wish to review the details of that old debate, and I will limit myself to making some general observations. On the one hand there were those who argued that there was nothing more to social reality than the sum of the individuals who make up the group, and that there are no irreducible social properties or social concepts beyond the dispositions and the like of individuals. We need not deal with reasons for such a view— adherence to a radical empiricism that precludes the acceptance of what isn't given to the senses or fear of the political consequences of acceptance of nonindividual entities[8]—but will be satisfied to note that such a position exists. The opposing view takes it that there are irreducible social concepts. There are variations on this view. Thus it has been claimed that the concepts used in theory and theoretical *explanation* in point of logic cannot be reduced. And it has been claimed that social situations could not be *described if* social scientists did not have available concepts that are strictly social: Only if social concepts are available to the observer can he distinguish between genuine interactions and accidental juxtaposings.[9]

In large measure, philosophical discussions of such things include the discussion of simple examples invented for the purpose of illustrating the point of view the writer is trying to defend. In consequence, they are rarely realistic. Simple instances of social or cultural being—or of individual existence—designed to function in the way the writer intends without getting in the way of his presentation is what we often find in the literature. What we never find is anything as complex as the character of Jewish being that I have sketched in my opening paragraphs, and even that is rather more abstract than concrete and doesn't begin to convey the actuality to which it purports to point. If we want to take seriously the claim of the individualists, then the conceptions we have of Jewish collectivity ought to be constructable out of Jewish individuality and analyzable into Jewish individuality.

But how would we go about it? If we want to construct the Jewishness of Jewish individuality—if such a project is the least bit intelligible, though we must suppose it to be so in the view of the individualists—we would have to be able to identify such individuals, but that is not possible without our having some sense of Jewish collectivity. It is only as part of the collective that the individual has its being. I know, and it has already been indicated, that the collective is not easy to define and may well be impossible to define, and that some individuals may be excluded or included according to one's sense of the nature of the collective; yet it seems to me there is an intuited reality with its own appropriate kind of being, which is, in the end, pointed to by all of our accounts and discussions, exclusionary or inclusionary. Jean Améry may have recognized himself as Jewish and no doubt could have told us why, and an interpreter of *halakhah* could have denied that Améry was Jewish and could have told us why, too. They would each have had a different "why." Perhaps, one might think, this opens the way to the solution. Different "why's" suggest different senses of the collective, different Jewishnesses; we have a collection of collectivities. This seems to suggest a genuinely philosophical approach to the issue: who better than philosophers at making distinctions. But it will not work. There may be a multiplicity of "why's," but there is only one Jewishness. David Vital speaks of something as having "accelerated the . . . breakup of Jewry into even less coherent communities, each imbued with a distinct culture and language, each subject to specific influences and needs and so, inevitably, each intent on social purposes of its own definition." [10] He is, of course, right. That sort of thing happens. For all that, there is only one Jewishness. It has a wide stretch, and it is interesting to observe how the Jews of Ethiopia are being absorbed into the Jewish world—the religious Jewish world—in Israel though their own tradition involves only a fraction of the Hebrew Bible and no Talmud at all. But while it has a wide stretch, its stretch is not unlimited: It unambiguously excludes Karaites and Samaritans, and in spite of what its adherents may claim, a Jewish Christian is a contradiction in terms. [11]

In a recent edition of his column "Report from Israel," Carl Alpert tells of a stage performance in which four totally diverse characters appear. [12] "The four were a black-coated rabbi from Mea Shearim, an Egged bus driver, a new immigrant from France and a wealthy American tourist." Each character is completely unlike the others in every describable way, yet each is Jewish and is recognizable as such to himself and to those who witness the performance. Alpert reports that the performance was stimulating and lacked only the failure of the characters to confront one another, a patent impossibility since each character was performed by the same man, a rabbi who, no doubt, had his own message to impart. Alpert has interesting things to say about the performance he describes and the ways in which the varieties of Jews who have seen its performance—in Israel, the United States, England "and even Moscow"—reacted to it, but the question his account evokes for me in our present context concerns what this shared Jewishness is, and how, on the individualist view, we may construct it out of the multiplicity of Jewish types—the four presented in the performance and many others as well. [13]

I have been trying to say, with reference to that old controversy that

John O'Neill collected, that any attempt to understand or construe the idea of Jewishness from the point of view of the methodological individualists is a nonstarter. How would we make the first move in the attempt at that sort of analysis? And, surely, no one could claim to be able to abstract the common Jewishness from the varieties of Jewish types that we discover historically and by encounter. Because Plato could not find a common, abstractable quality that all virtuous acts share, he concluded that virtue cannot be taught, yet inasmuch as it was clearly known he was led to essential forms and the theory of recollection. I am sure that readers will not suppose that this is the appropriate direction for us to take with respect to the idea of Jewishness. Yet, surely, some will wonder whether or not the nonindividualist position that I defended during that old controversy will prove to be useful in resolving our problem.

I tend not to be overly sanguine about that possibility. In those days I think I took a concept's givenness for granted and was simply concerned with how it was to be analyzed. I do not think that I had come across Gottlob Frege's saying that a "concept that is not sharply defined is wrongly termed a concept,"[14] but I don't think that it would have bothered me.[15] The point I tried to argue is that there was no way to reduce the concepts used in social science *theory* to the dispositions and other qualities of individuals, but I agree, as well, with those whose attention was focused on the terms used in social *description* and who wanted to claim with respect to them that the individualist reduction was also impossible.[16]

The old debate was not over the nature of concepts as such nor how to analyze them. The issue was over the kinds of element that had to go into the analysis of certain concepts, namely, those used in the social sciences. The outcome of analysis, regardless of how you stood on the point at issue, would be an account of the conditions necessary and sufficient for the application of the concepts that interested us. The inquiries that produced the accounts were presumed, I believe, to be entirely systematic, and not in the least historical. We wanted to know what the concept means, not how it came to be as it is or what the factors were that gave it the shape it has. And is that not what we want here? What is a Jew? What does the term "Jew" mean? What are the conditions necessary and sufficient for the application of the term to particular individuals?

There is no way to provide answers to these questions. That is why the brief selections of approaches to this issue with which the essay began seemed so perplexing. I venture to suggest that the only solution to the problem of Jewish identity—a solution in the sense that we could approach an understanding of why there is such difference and why there seems to be no way to characterize conceptually what Jewish identity is, though, for the most part, we identify the same people as Jewish and have strong intuition that there is something shared by this diversity of individuals—is to come to see why it is that these questions have no answers.

According to F. S. C. Northrop, science has to do with two kinds of concept: concepts by intuition and concepts by postulation.[17] The former kind are concepts the meanings of which are exhausted by our sense experience. Thus, if we speak of "blue" we refer to a determinate color content, and there is no remainder beyond that content. The latter kind, on the contrary, have no reference to sense at all, and their entire meaning is provided by the theoretical context in which they function. Thus we are not able to ask "What does 'atom' mean?" because outside of a determinate theoretical context it means nothing at all. Rather one can inquire only into the meaning of "atom" in Democritus' philosophy or in Newton's physics. The theories are different, hence the term functions differently—means different things—in the different theories. One consequence of this is that there can be no history of atomism, and that is because there isn't one thing—atomism—that has persisted over time.

Northrop's point is that each use of "atom" as we find it in different theories names a different concept the full meaning of which is exhausted by the sense it gets from the theory in which it functions. But let us consider a different kind of example—an essay written on the theme "The role of Parliament in the government of England"—the point being to produce an explication of the concept named by the word "Parliament." The essay is written in 1550, 1650, 1750, 1850, and 1950. We have then not one but five essays, but do we have five concepts or one? The character of Parliament in each of the five years is quite different from what it is in each of the other four: Its function and powers are different, the way it fits into the political culture of England is different, and likewise different are the ways it relates to the powers of the sovereign and its relationship to those who are its constituents. One could argue that in each of the five essays the concept of Parliament is different, that it gets its meaning from the context of the essay, which, I suppose, may be said to articulate the sociopolitical culture of England in the year it was written. Thus we have five concepts of Parliament, not one, and we are left with a situation analogous to that with respect to theoretical concepts according to Northrop's analysis. But that would seem to require us to say that there is no history of Parliament, that the idea of it in each of the essays is self-contained. How can we take seriously a conclusion of this kind? There is a history of Parliament; it begins—many historians tell us—about 1290 and continues on to our own day.[18] There is, surely, a connection of some sort between the Parliament of the 1550 essay and that of the 1650 essay, and so on.

Let me pursue the direction I am taking by considering one more example, the history of freedom. I am not particularly knowledgeable about that, so I shall make use of Hegel's lectures on the subject, which present a conceptual and institutional account of the history of freedom.[19] To be sure, such a work by someone who died in 1831 cannot possibly be the last word on the subject, but with all of its limitations as far as historical accuracy is concerned, it suits my purpose. Hegel seems to think that the territory from China to Western Europe is a unit that has a history, and the course that he describes in the lectures encompasses the entire area. He begins with ancient China, characterizes what freedom was then and there, and locates Chinese freedom within the sociocultural framework of Chinese life.[20] This is followed by a similar account of freedom in India, Persia, ancient Israel, Greece and Rome, medieval Europe, and the Germanic peoples, by which he means Western Europe in his modernity. In every case freedom is understood within the framework of the sociocultural system within which it appears, and its features are understood as expressions of the spirit of a people. On the face of it, Hegel's account seems reminiscent of the successive accounts of parliamentary government. There is, however, one important difference, a difference that entirely precludes the similarity I suggest above in regard to the use of "Parliament" and that of "atom": Hegel presents the ways in which the successive kinds of freedom are related historically.

The point is that Hegel does not simply present us with a sequence of ideas of freedom. The history—conceptual and institutional—of freedom begins in ancient China, where its character is shaped by the elements of Chinese culture—Hegel calls it "state," but this is distinguished from the strictly political state.[21] This is not simply followed by Indian freedom. The concept of freedom as that which had emerged in China is reshaped by the conditions—sociocultural—of India. The same concept has undergone change, and Hegel specifies the elements of culture that are relevant to the new shape the concept takes. If Frege were right, and concepts must be sharply defined, what I have just said would make no sense.[22] Northrop, at least tacitly, accepts the Frege dictum and so can have only a succession of sharply defined concepts of "atom," each defined by its theoretical context and not capable of being changed or reshaped. It is often said that Hegelian dialectic is an internal process with each stage generating its successor from within, and Hegel says as much in the account of his method he offers in the introduction to his *Lectures on the History of Philosophy*. But that is not the way Hegel actually works. A point reached does not change until it is affected by something from without, something logically contingent with respect to the point reached. That contingency changes the context within which the concept functions, brings about a conceptual tension— what many writers call a contradiction, to my mind an unfortunate term— and leads to a reshaping of the concept.[23]

I am not prepared to offer an account of the concept of Jewish identity and, thus, resolve the confusion that the variations of Jewishness with which I begin this essay seem to suggest. It may well be that no one possesses the detailed knowledge necessary for the tracing out of the various kinds of Jewishness that there are in the world. But it does seem to me that we can now understand how such variation is possible. I do believe that most of us in philosophy and science and most forms of intellectual life assume—at least tacitly—that Frege is right, and, thus, the presence of what seems so radically inconsistent disconcerts us. As we become increasingly serious about conceptual openness, we may become more relaxed about it. We have seen that concepts change over time, not because of internal movement but because they are affected by external factors that result in their being reshaped. When we realize how dispersed over natural and social space the Jewish people is, how differently Jews are affected by social, cultural, and intellectual elements, the variability in their conceptions of themselves is hardly to be wondered at. Even within the same highly complex societies, different Jews are affected by different sets of circumstances, and so a variety of different kinds of reshaping constantly occurs. There is, to be sure, a sense of awareness, the recognition that, for better or for worse, all are Jews, yet the idea of what that is, as we have seen, is so variable as to be dazzling. And yet, I should now wish to say, it is the most reasonable thing in the world.

NOTES

1. See Jean Améry, *At the Mind's Limit* (Bloomington, Ind.: Indiana University Press, 1980); see also, my review in *International Studies in Philosophy* 18, no. 1 (1986): 65.

2. Sidney Hook, "On Being a Jew," *Commentary*, October 1989, 34.

3. See A. F. Landau's review of *Haim Cohen, Supreme Court Judge: Talks with*

Michael Shahan, in *Jerusalem Post International Edition,* November 25, 1989, 16.

4. Though, to be sure, there may be occasional confusion, which may lead to such a denial. Surely, for the most part, the problem of non-Jewish identity does not exist for non-Jews.

5. Perhaps analogous to the way in which there is no such social entity as humanity but only human groups or peoples of determinate sort—Greek, French, Hopi, and Zulu—even though all of these may refer to themselves as human.

6. It is unfortunate that more than sixty years after it was first published, what remains one of the best, if not the best, attempts to deal with this question— Yehezkel Kaufman, *Golah ve-Nekhar* (Exile and alienage), 2 vols. (Tel Aviv: Dvir, 1930)—remains unavailable to those who cannot read Hebrew. The two volumes run to a thousand pages, but, given the author's long-winded style, it should be possible to produce a much-abridged translation.

7. The main contributions to the debate as it was manifested in the 1950s and 1960s were collected in John O'Neill, ed., *Modes of Individualism and Collectiveness* (London: Heinemann, 1973). My essays are on pp. 264–86.

8. Actually this latter is more clearly expressed in J. O. Wisdom's essay, "Situational Individualism and Emergent Group Properties," in *Explanation in the Behavioral Sciences,* edited by Robert Borger and Frank Cioffi (Cambridge: Cambridge University Press, 1970), 271–96, than in any of the essays in O'Neill's collection.

9. Cf. Orvis Collins and June M. Collins, *Interaction and Social Structure* (The Hague: Mouton, 1973).

10. David Vital, "Power, Powerlessness and the Jews," *Commentary,* January 1990, 27.

11. There have been several court cases that have established that Jewish Christians are not admissible under the Law of Return, although, of course, they may seek citizenship in Israel as any Gentile immigrant might.

12. Carl Alpert, *Jewish Week,* January 19, 1990, 23.

13. Once I started to work on this essay, I began finding relevant examples in all manner of Jewish periodicals I read regularly: *Commentary, Midstream, Jewish Week,* and *Jerusalem Post, International Edition.* I can not keep up with it all, and I certainly cannot refer to it all. But let me note Andre A. Aciman, "Gardens and Ghettos," *Commentary,* January 1990, 55–59. Its point of departure is the appearance of Vivian B. Mann, ed., *Gardens and Ghettos: The Art of Jewish Life in Italy* (Berkeley and Los Angeles: University of California Press, 1989), a book that indicates the varieties of Italian Jewishness and suggests "that regardless of the degree to which Italian Jews were, or tried to be, completely assimilated, they continued to exhibit aesthetic and intellectual tendencies *indissolubly* linked to their Jewish origins" (59, emphasis added). His immediate observation about "the inevitable reinterpretation of the meaning of Jewish experience" that has followed "in the wake of the Holocaust" is interesting.

14. Quoted in Morris Weitz, *The Opening Mind* (Chicago: University of Chicago Press, 1977), xi.

15. Now, of course, I think it is entirely mistaken; see my "Reflections on Con-

ceptual Openness and Conceptual Tension," in *Essays in Honor of John Watkins*, edited by Fred D'Agostino and I. C. Jarvie (Dordrecht, Boston, London: Kluwer Academic Publishers, 1989), 87–110.

16. See Maurice Mandelbaum's essays in O'Neill, *Individualism and Collectiveness*, 221–47; and Collins and Collins, *Interaction*; see, also, my "Reflections on Conceptual Openness," 105–7.

17. F.S.C. Northrop, *The Logic of the Sciences and the Humanities* (New York: Macmillan, 1947), chaps. 3 and 4.

18. But, *pace* Northrop, there is a history of atomism, too.

19. The work is called *Lectures on the Philosophy of History;* but once we are past the introduction, there is precious little said about history, and the book is largely about the history of freedom.

20. See my "The Meaning of 'State' in Hegel's *Philosophy of History*," *Philosophical Quarterly* 12 no. 1 (1962): 60–72.

21. The evidence for this is presented in ibid.

22. See my "Reflections on Conceptual Openness."

23. See my "Dialectic and Necessity in Hegel's *Philosophy of History*," in *Substance and Form in History,* edited by L. Pompa and W. H. Dray (Edinburgh: University of Edinburgh Press, 1981), 42–57; and "Force and the Inverted World in Dialectical Retrospection," *International Studies in Philosophy* 20, no. 3 (1988): 13–28.

6

SAHIBS AND JEWS

Cora Diamond

"But I am to pray to Bibi Miriam and I am a Sahib. . . . No; I am
Kim. This is the great world and I am only Kim. Who is Kim?"
He considered his own identity, a thing he had never done before,
till his head swam. [Rudyard Kipling, *Kim*, chap. 7]

A very few white people, but many Asiatics, can throw themselves into a mazement as it were by repeating their own names
over and over again to themselves, letting the mind go free upon
speculation as to what is called personal identity. . . . "Who is
Kim-m-Kim-m-Kim?" [chap. 11]

"I am Kim. I am Kim. And what is Kim?" His soul repeated
it again and again. [chap. 15]

FROM KIM'S IDENTITY TO JEWISH IDENTITY

Kim's question about his personal identity arises for him as a Sahib, the son
of Sahibs, who has lived as natives live, who has seen the life led by Sahibs
only from the outside.[1] It is not his life. The question he asks about his
identity—"Who is Kim?"—is not separable from what it means or what it
is to mean for him to be a Sahib. Being a Jew in America is not quite like
being a Sahib in British India; except in the minds of the more demented
anti-Semites, the Jews do not run America. But, just as Kim was comfortable in the clothes and in the skin and in the language of the natives, but
had questions about who he was, what he was, questions inseparable from
the strangely weighty fact of his having been born to two Sahibs, so may
a Jew comfortable in the clothes and skin and language of the present-day
natives of America have questions about who he is or who she is, tied to
the facts, of uncertain weight, of ancestry. I choose to write about Jewish
identity by starting with Kim's identity.

Kim's Question and the Lockean Tradition

What did Kim want to know? What is it for which Kipling uses the expressions "identity" and "personal identity"? Kim knows that he is Kimball O'Hara, the son of Kimball O'Hara, a British soldier dead since Kim was very little. He knows, has always known, that he is the son of a Sahib. There are facts about himself that he does not know or does not understand (e.g., concerning specifically Irish ancestry), but there is not some fact that he is ignorant of and seeks to know and that would give him the answer to "Who am I?" He is not like the heroes or heroines of some fairy tales, brought up by peasants and unaware of their being princes or princesses, unaware in that sense of their identity, of who they are.

The novel *Kim* is about Kim's quest to find out who he is; it is about personal identity; but it is not about personal identity in the sense in which personal identity is a question for the philosophical tradition going back to Locke. That tradition is concerned with what is or what we believe to be "involved in our own continued existence, or what it is that makes us now and ourselves next year the same people."[2] The question Kim asks has as part of its background the continued existence of one person, but it is a distinct question. Kim does not want to know, for example, whether the schoolboy O'Hara in the Lucknow school is the same person as the brown-skinned boy in the dress of a lama's disciple, chased by a policeman off the steps of Lucknow station. "Who is Kim?" asks who this boy is, this continuing being, the Sahib schoolboy, the brown disciple chattering away in Hindi.

The question Kim asks is hardly visible to the philosophical tradition. The questions Locke asks about personal identity arise in connection with his general discussion of relations; he wants to argue that the identity of substances, that of animals and that of persons are *different* relations. From Locke's point of view, "Kim is a Sahib" is also a relational statement (although on the surface it may not seem to be; see Locke's treatment of *European* and *Englishman* as relations),[3] but the relation is not any kind of Lockean identity. To be a Sahib is to be the child of Sahibs. The relation expressed in "Kim is a Sahib" has no special relevance to questions about Lockean identity, for those questions deal with someone's identity *with* a person named or described in some other way. And yet for Kim the question Kipling speaks of as a question of personal identity *is* tied, but in ways that are dark, to Kim's being a Sahib.

There are characters in *Kim* who meet Kim but do not know *who he is* and who find out; but what they find out he (for the most part) already knows. The knowledge in question is largely that of Lockean relations, including Lockean identities, but it is not Lockean knowledge that is sought by Kim. He uses the language, the interrogative sentences, that may be used by someone seeking Lockean knowledge, the sentences that might be used by Bennett and Father Victor, the two regimental chaplains who want to find out who this boy is, but he is after something else. But before discussing what Kim wants to know, it will be useful to look further at what they are after.

The Chaplains' Question

Bennett and Father Victor, in wanting to know who this boy is, want to place him in relation to other things they know. To know that this boy is Kimball O'Hara, a Sahib, the son of a Sahib, that his parents are dead, that his father was in this regiment, the Mavericks, and was a Mason, is to be able to fit the boy's existence into the system of other things known and to be able to act appropriately. In the background of their kind of wish for knowledge is the fact that the appropriateness of certain actions, the inappropriateness of others, depend on precisely those Lockean relations, including Lockean identities, that they seek. (One might note that the information they want could be used in filling out a form, should Kim be entered at the Punjab Masonic Orphanage or the Military Orphanage, two possibilities the men have in mind for him.)

The two men can be said to wonder *about the identity* of the boy in front of them, and then to establish his identity (as Kimball O'Hara, son of Kimball O'Hara of the Mavericks). This use of "identity" is not usually considered in philosophy. (And my reason for considering it here is that it is a way of talking about identity related to talk about "one's identity as a Jew" and so on.) When philosophers distinguish different ways of talking about identity, they sometimes tell us that there are two ways of using "identity" and "identification"[4]: We may be said to "identify" a thing when we individuate it, pick it out from other things as this particular thing of such-and-such kind, "that man in the corner" (say), or when we pick out the particular someone else is referring to; and we may be said to identify a thing when we *re*identify it, that is, recognize it as the same as such-and-such thing picked out at some earlier time. To these ways of using "identify," a philosopher might add the establishing of any proposition of the form of an identity, such as, "The man in the corner is the only man in the room wearing green socks"; "The murderer of A is the person who sent him the chocolates." Bennett and Father Victor do not have a problem about individuating the boy in front of them; and each knows which boy the other is speaking of. When I ask who the man in the corner is, or try to identify the plant in front of me, what I want presupposes success in individuating the thing whose identity I want to know. But it is not the case that I want to reidentify the thing; to be told that the plant is the same as the one I picked two minutes ago, or that the man in the corner is the same man as the man whom I saw arrive at a quarter to eight, is not to be told what I want. Bennett and Father Victor know that the boy in front of them is the boy who earlier kicked Bennett in the stomach; but that is not to know his identity: to reidentify a thing is not necessarily to *know its identity.*[5] And, when Bennett and Father Victor do establish the identity of the boy, they do not find out that he is the same as something picked out at some earlier time. Their knowledge can be put in the form of statements of identity, but it is not in general the case that knowing some identity-statements about a thing is knowing its identity, knowing who or what it is.

As I have suggested, to have identified a thing, in the sense in which Bennett and Father Victor do this, is to have information about it that enables one to fit it into a body of information one already has. And *proper names* play a central role in this.[6] The notion of identity that I use when I say that Bennett and Father Victor establish the identity of the boy in front of them has ties to a group of uses of names: names of people, places, species of things, kinds of artifact, types of aircraft, and so on. (The connection may be seen, for example, in the relation between *concealing* one's identity and using a false name.) It is a quite striking fact about philosophy that although it produces millions of words about identity, it has very little to say about what we are doing when we produce a little card, always including our name (or the name we are claiming is ours) in response to a request to prove our identity. Philosophical discussion of identity tells us that there is individuation, there is a hearer's picking out the thing the speaker is referring to, there is reidentification and there is what Frege said about the morning star and the evening star; it is concerned with whether indiscernible things need be identical and vice versa; and it looks steadfastly away from what we are doing with those little cards, or what we are doing with a bird-identification book.[7]

I am not saying that knowledge of someone's *name* is all we want when we want to identify the person, although it may be. I am suggesting that, depending on the context, certain kinds of information will be relevant to establishing his or her identity, and other kinds (perfectly capable of serving in sentences that individuate the person or reidentify him or her) are quite irrelevant. That this boy is the son of Kimball O'Hara of the Mavericks is profoundly relevant to *who he is,* if "Who is he?" is the question of Bennett and Father Victor; that he is the disciple of the Tibetan lama outside, on the other hand, deepens the mystery of who he is. It specifies further the person *whose* identity is in question but does not help *answer* the question.

Kim's Question and the Chaplains' Question

I have discussed the question "Who is this boy?" as it arises for the regimental chaplains, because Kim's own questions are significantly related to it.

1. As I said, Kim's questions are in form like theirs, but theirs does and his does not have as background a desire to relate the existence of this particular boy to a system of things already known, with further connected ways of judging the appropriateness of actions. Far from there being a system of knowledge and of connected ways of acting into which he can fit his being a Sahib, the fact that he is a Sahib (which he has not so far bothered much about) suddenly raises the question *what* systematic way of taking in facts, relating them to one another and judging the appropriateness of actions, he can use in all his day-to-day thought about what he encounters and what he does. There is for him no fixed context into which this fact about this boy—I, Kim—can be slotted. This fact, that he is a Sahib, in its strange and puzzling relation to *all* the structures by which he grasps what happens, how to behave, what he takes to be ridiculous or funny or reasonable or contemptible, confronts him with questions utterly unlike those that *he* poses for Bennett and Father Victor.

2. Although Kim's question about his identity differs from that of Bennett and Father Victor in not assuming some structured ways of thinking into which Kim's existence can be fitted, it is like theirs in its distance from philosophical questions about how he may be picked out in speech or thought or how he may be reidentified. Thus, for example, for Bennett and Father Victor, his being a Sahib is a central point in who the boy is, and for Kim himself his being, like it or not, a Sahib is central in *his* consideration of who he is. If we say that the book is about Kim's quest for his identity, what we see at the end of the quest is what he makes of being a Sahib in relation to both the British Raj and the lama whose disciple, whose "chela" he is. But, for most of the traditional philosophical questions about identity, a fact like one's *being by birth a Sahib* has no special relevance. There are recent discussions of the question whether anyone at all would be the same person as so-and-so if the world had gone differently in certain ways, for example, if the particular sperm and egg from whose

union he grew had never got together. Apart from that question, though, birth and the facts connected with it have little to do with philosophical discussion of identity; whereas *what we are by our birth* has great bearing on what it is for someone else to know who or what we are,[8] and knowing that by birth one is a Sahib or that by birth one is a Jew is exactly the sort of thing that can be central in one's wondering about one's own identity, if one does wonder about it.

(Those things that are relevant to one's identity are not all relevant to it in the same way. I do not want to suggest that "being a Jew" and "being a Sahib" are relevant in the same way; and, indeed, if we turn away from *Kim,* and towards the questions of identity with which an American Jew may be concerned, we can see that "being an American" and "being a Jew," although both are relevant to *who one is,* are not relevant in the same way, as is illustrated by the fact that assimilation into American life is not, for the Jew, an option analogous to expatriation.)

It might be asked whether Kim's question who he is and the question of the regimental chaplains who he is have any more than a *verbal* similarity. Are they merely two distinct questions about identity, both of them distinct from what philosophy attends to? I do not think it is possible to make sense of Kim's question except in relation to the kind of question they ask.

Kim has known all his life that the sort of people who ask who he is—"missionaries and white men of serious aspect"—are people likely to make trouble, and are to be avoided. But he has not, until the events of the novel, come to see them as having a view of the world that he needs to take into account. But suddenly for him *who Kim is* has to be related to how people—not all people, but certainly some—answer the question who Kim is and fit the existence of Kim into their world. What brings Kim to the question who he is is the sudden tension between *his* world—the great and wonderful world, teeming with life and ever new—and what he is in *their* world, the world of Sahibs like Bennett and Father Victor. The tension is already present at the opening of the novel: "He sat, in defiance of municipal orders, astride the gun Zam-Zammah": the municipal orders are part of the orderliness imposed on the teeming life of India by Sahib rule, and Kim's free life is in violation of that rule. How he sees life, his life, and how he is seen: Kim cannot go on paying no attention to the relation between the two; and his question about who he is expresses his need to understand that relation. Although it is not the question asked by Bennett and Father Victor, it is tied to it; and the similarity of verbal form is no accident.

Kim's Question and Jewish Identity

I have argued that Kim's question about his identity arises in a context with these two features:

1. For others he counts as a Sahib. Their way of answering the question "Who is he?" and fitting him into their way of looking at the world and dealing with things in it impinges seriously on his life.

2. He has lived the life of a native; he thinks and dresses like a native, talks like one, laughs at Sahibs for what natives laugh at them for. "But actually I am a Sahib" is no longer a little fact that can be accommodated in a corner of his life; it comes into his consciousness now from those who mean to take seriously that *he is not a native* and to detach him from his old life. He can no longer rest unself-consciously in his world's being that of the native and must understand "being a Sahib" in some new way.

There is an analogy between Kim's situation and the situation of Jews in western Europe after the French Revolution. (See Isaiah Berlin's description of the latter in "Benjamin Disraeli, Karl Marx and the Search for Identity" and "The Life and Opinions of Moses Hess.")[9] It became possible—or seemed to—for Jews to live the lives of the natives, to think like them, dress and eat as they did, read the same books, find the same things ridiculous, make themselves at home in the world as they did. As in Kim's case, what gives rise to the question about identity is not the fact that one is not actually one of the natives—for there is nothing in the fact itself that makes it weighty, that makes it not a fact that can be kept in a corner of the mind. ("[U]ntil precisely those months [during which the Italian Fascists began promoting the idea of racial purity] it had not meant much to me that I was a Jew: within myself, and in my contacts with my Christian friends, I had always considered my origin as an almost negligible but curious fact, a small amusing anomaly, like having a crooked nose or freckles; a Jew is somebody who at Christmas does not have a tree, who should not eat salami but eats it all the same, who has learned a bit of Hebrew at thirteen and then has forgotten it.")[10]

What makes Kim ask who he is is that his Sahibhood has been *made* to count by others for whom it is a central thing in his identity, in who he is and what is to be done with him. Here there is a partial disanalogy with the situation of Jews. For when Kim's Sahibhood is made to impinge on him and thus to raise for him the question about his identity it is not the natives who do this. Whereas, for the Jew who, in nineteenth-century Europe, lived as the natives do, the identification that threatens his place in the world comes, at any rate in the first instance, from the natives.[11] (But, as Berlin makes clear, by the middle of the nineteenth century, the moral pressure on Western Jews to question whether they had any business living the lives of the natives was beginning to come also from such Jews as Moses Hess.)[12] The disanalogy goes deeper. In Kim's case, there is nothing in the mode of thought and life of the natives that will, as it were, say to Kim: "This is not *your* life, for you are a Sahib"; the pressure to work out what it can mean that he is a Sahib comes entirely from outside the non-Sahib life he has led. Whereas, for the Jew in the West, living the life of the natives, the more inward he is in that life and culture, the more it may seem to him that, despite its being *his* mode of life and culture, it is in important ways *not* his. Here is an example, from the literary culture of the natives. A Jew, reading Matthew Arnold with (as he takes it) the eyes, the mode of thought, of the natives, finds Arnold writing that the superiority of Chaucer's poetry over romance poetry lies in part in the superiority of substance, "given by his large, free, simple, clear yet kindly view of human life," his ability "to survey the world from a central, a truly human point of view." To convey a sense of the charm of Chaucer's verse, Arnold then quotes the retelling in *The Prioress's Tale* of the blood libel, the Christian child describing his own murder by the Jew: "My throte is cut unto my nekke bone," and so on. The charm of the verse, Arnold tells us, is gone in Wordsworth's version of the poem.[13] The charm of it! The clear yet kindly view! A truly human point of view! All this by a humane and decent Englishman, with great respect for and interest in not only ancient Israel but also the Jewish thought and literature of his time. My point here is not that the Jew comes across anti-Semites, but that there is in the culture that he takes to be his own a willingness to see the Jew as not seriously a person but (in this case) a part of the fourteenth-century landscape, as it were. Arnold does not say, "I am not writing for you, you Jew," but he writes as one participating in a culture that is not yours, you Jew.

My interest in this section has been in the question "Who am I?", "What am I?"; I have tried to show something of the kinds of context in which it is not a demand for information about one's birth or ancestry or nationality or place in some fixed scheme. Kim can ask that question; so can a Jew living a life just like that of the natives.

IDENTIFYING WITH THE JEWS, IDENTIFYING WITH THE SAHIBS

In discussions of Jewish identity, or of "cultural identity" more generally, we find talk not only of identity but of "identification *with*." (A good example is Berlin's "Benjamin Disraeli, Karl Marx and the Search for Identity," the first section of which is about the general human need to identify oneself with some group [community, nation, people, race, religious denomination, etc.], and the particular wish of many Jews in the nineteenth century in the West to identify themselves with the dominant group, the majority, in the countries in which they lived.) There are really here two distinct notions: to *identify with* some group and to *have a sense of belonging to* some group are different. I may identify with a group to which I do not belong; if I read about the Persian Wars, I may identify with the Greeks and be glad about the defeat of the Persians at Marathon. To identify with them is, in this case, to share their feelings. In imagination I cheer them on; I am on their side. In cases like this, when one speaks of someone's identifying with some group, what is meant is the sharing of such things as feelings or aims or values or interests, the sorts of things one can share without being a member of the group.[14] There are, however, cases in which, when we speak of someone's identifying with a group, we mean that he takes himself to share such things as a history, things shared precisely *as* a member of the group. Here identifying oneself with the group and having a sense of belonging to it are not separable. And there is at least one other kind of case, in which identifying oneself with a group means living a life of the sort they lead or actually participating in the life lived by the group as a group. Again, this is something that someone who is not a member of the group, who does not have a sense of belonging to it, can do. If we bear in mind that identifying oneself with a group in the sense of sharing its projects, values, or feelings, or in the sense of participating in its life, is not the same as identifying oneself with the group, if that means having a sense of belonging to it, we can see that there is a question whether someone, a German, say, might have a sense of belonging to a group (the Germans, with *their* history), a sense of being rooted there, without sharing what he takes to be the interests, aims, or feelings of the group. In the case of Jewish identity, the point seems occasionally to be ignored. The refusal of a Jew to identify with the values, aims, or interests of some or other Jewish community may be taken to be the same as the absence of any identification with Jews as the group to which he belongs, and thus to be the same as the denial of identity as a Jew. I now turn to the question what, if anything, justifies the move from the claim about a Jew that he or she does not share aims or values taken to be those of Jews as a group (or does not cheer the side on in its projects, or does not participate in some Jewish form of life) to the claim that he or she does not identify with Jews as the group to which he or she belongs and is denying his or her identity as a Jew. The unexamined slide between these notions seems to go back at least as far as Moses Hess, for whom it appeared impossible to accept, as in honor one had to, that one belonged to this "unfortunate, slandered, despised and dispersed people" without accepting also its ancestral values and its attachment to Palestine as its land.[15]

To examine the issues here I turn back to *Kim*.

Kim is described as rejecting almost everything one can think of as characteristic of the life, mode of thinking, and values of Sahibs. Kipling provides an enormous amount of detail to make clear not just the differences between Kim's life and that of Sahibs but the weight of those differences. Some of the central features of Sahib life as Kim sees it from the outside are embodied in the character of Bennett, the Anglican chaplain, with his easy contempt for the spiritual life of India and his easy assumption that life in general may be channeled in the directions into which a bureaucracy chooses to send it. "You will be what you are told to be," said Bennett; "and you should be grateful that we're going to help you." [16] How could one identify with that awful complacent Sahib "we"?

But the novel is, as I said, about Kim's quest for his identity. And in the end there is no denial of Kim's Sahibhood; but neither is he detached from Indian life, detached as are such Sahibs as Bennett. In fact his attachment to that life and his inwardness with it deepens. There is no going back on Kim's rejection of what Sahibhood means in men like Bennett; what Kim finds is that there are things that it means or can mean to be a Sahib, other than integration in Bennett's world, on its terms, a world whose vices include its wilful ignorance of the wonderful life of India. (That there are such possibilities is clear from the beginning of the novel, with the character, based on Kipling's father, of the curator of the Lahore museum.)

When the lama whose disciple he is says, "To abstain from action is well—except to acquire merit," Kim replies that what they taught him at the Sahib school was that to abstain from action is unbefitting a Sahib, and he is a Sahib.[17]

The story of Kim's relation with the lama is the story of the lama's dependence "in the body" on Kim, and of what Kim receives from the lama. The security of India from foreign tyranny and crude exploitation depends on a peculiar type of Sahib, on Sahibs who are thoroughly familiar with, inside, understanding of, Indian life and language, whose protection of India has in it an appreciation of what it is they are protecting.

The relation between Kim and the lama, between India and the sort of Sahibhood that protects it, depends on what is good on each of the sides of the relation. The capacity to act when that is necessary and good, the capacity to see abstention from action as a goal—*both* are important, as is also the capacity, on each side, to see the good that comes to it from the other. That is Kipling's picture of an ideal relation;[18] what is important is his conception of *action* and of *responsibility* in the resolution of Kim's quest for his identity. There is, one might say, a teleological notion of Sahibhood. For Kim to take Sahibhood up into his identity is not at all for him to go and join some group of Sahibs and share their life; and, although *action* is important in this identity, what is meant is not Kim's acting as Sahibs tend to act. What is meant is rather the using of his capacities for action in the service of responsibilities he the young Sahib has to the lama and to India. To belong to this people—Sahibs—is for him to take on these responsibilities and to acquit himself as best he can.

I want now to turn back to Jewish identity. I have emphasized that, for Kim, his understanding of his own identity as that of a Sahib, his not denying his Sahibhood, does not mean identifying with the Sahib community and its values or modes of thought. It is tied rather to his understanding of responsibilities he bears as Sahib, and the way in which those responsibilities can be exercised in the great world that India is, the place where, for him, the currents of life flow. (The streams of life are dammed up, stagnant, in the Sahib community precisely because of its isolation from Indian life.) Let me consider here the remark of Moses Hess's, a part of which I quoted earlier. Hess wrote, of the effect on him of the Damascus affair of 1840 (an accusation of ritual murder): "It dawned on me for the first time, in the midst of my socialist activities, that I belonged to my unfortunate, slandered, despised and dispersed people."[19] Hess later connected with the notion of belonging to that people a very particular responsibility, as comes out in his account of why Moses was not allowed into the promised land and why Joseph's bones were brought in. According to rabbinic lore, Moses concealed his Jewishness from the man whose daughter he wished to marry; that is, he presented himself as not a member of his unfortunate enslaved people. He let himself be taken for an Egyptian; whereas Joseph acknowledged who he was. As Isaiah Berlin puts it in the account of Hess's writings on which I am drawing, "One moment of weakness deprived Moses of his right to burial in the land of the ancestors whom he had by his silence denied . . ."[20] By our silence we may deny our ancestors. And the responsibility we acknowledge, if we take ourselves to belong to this "unfortunate, slandered, despised and dispersed people" is that of not denying our ancestors; at any rate, that is at the heart of Hess's view. If he also thought that we could not deny attachment to Palestine, or the values of our ancestors, that was because he took the severing of connections to the traditional values, and to Palestine, to be tantamount to disowning one's Jewishness. Living the life of the natives, sharing their values, was as much a way of saying to them, "I have no connection with that despised people" as would be an explicit lie about one's ancestors, or silence in the face of anti-Semitism in a context in which one's own Jewishness was not known.

But that equation need not be made. Take the case of Wittgenstein's felt need (in 1937) to confess that he had allowed people he knew to continue under the misapprehension that he had had only one Jewish grandparent, when in fact three of his grandparents were Jews. If we read Fania Pascal's description of Wittgenstein's confession to her, we can see that she shares his understanding of the shame a Jew may feel about not having come out with the fact of one's Jewishness when the anti-Semitism of one's friends or acquaintances had surfaced or was about to.[21] The memories of such failures, she knew, could be searing. The point I wish to make is that the painful shame here of having by silence denied one's membership in the despised people has nothing whatever to do with distancing oneself from the shared life of the Jewish community or from any of the traditional values of Jews (except for the value given to not denying one's Jewishness).

There is here implicitly a denial of Hess's view that there is no owning, no acknowledging, one's membership in the despised people consistent with living the kind of life Wittgenstein led, outside the Jewish community. Wittgenstein did not need, as he saw it, to have joined a synagogue, or become a Zionist, but simply to have said, "I am one of them." My point is not that in *any* context that is all that may be called for,[22] but simply that to speak of the responsibility of not denying one's Jewishness is not yet to say what it will come to in any context to take that responsibility seriously.

Let me go back here to *Kim*. One thing that Kim learned in the Sahib school was that it is unbefitting a Sahib to abstain from action; and that notion of the value of action (as contrasted with the value of abstention from action) is important in his understanding of what it means to take on the responsibilities of a Sahib. One may take the responsibility of the Jew as Jew to be that of not denying his ties to his people; the value that is connected to that notion of responsibility (as the value of action is connected to the responsibilities of Sahibhood) is that of memory. Here are the opening sentences of Berlin's piece on Disraeli, Marx, and the search for identity: "All Jews who are at all conscious of their identity as Jews are steeped in history. They have longer memories, they are aware of a longer continuity as a community than any other which has survived."[23]

They have longer memories, Berlin says. But (as is clear elsewhere in his discussion) the length of the memory—the awareness of that long continuity—is combined with a sense of the great significance of more recent history. (In my childhood, the relation between the old past, the immediate past, and the present was symbolized for us by the replacement of hanging Haman, in the children's game at Purim, by hanging first Hitler and later Ernest Bevin.)

That historical memory, alive in action, thought, feeling, language: *That* is essential to the responsibility of the Jew as Jew. It is alive in Hess's description of the people to whom he came to recognize that he belonged and in Berlin's account of Hess's life and thought; it is alive in the sense of shame that Mrs. Pascal and Wittgenstein shared; it is the spirit that animated Zionism and is also in Jewish responses to the persecution of members of other races. It may be seen in the extraordinary fusion achieved by the word "baptism," as Primo Levi uses it to describe the tattooing on his arm, on his arrival at Auschwitz, of the number 174517.[24] The transformation of Primo Levi to *Häftling* 174517 is thus linked to centuries of Christian anti-Semitism and the will to baptize Jews and the "Jewish problem" into nonexistence. That historical memory may also be alive in the sense that the word *araberrein* is one of the most poisonous words of the German language, alive in the sense that in that word there is the suppression of memory, the evasion of responsibility.

I mean to suggest that what counts as the livingness of memory is not obvious, is disputable. But we may learn a corresponding thing from *Kim*. *Kim* leaves itself open to question. Is the idea of Sahib responsibility in the book (to India, to Indian life) a self-deceptive myth? It is no part of my essay to answer that question or to deny that it is a question. And any attempt to understand what it means for someone living the life of the natives to take himself to be a Jew, to take himself to belong to his despised people, may be open to the same question.

NOTES

Acknowledgments: I am indebted to A. D. Woozley and to James Conant for helpful suggestions.

1. In referring to Kim, I use the word "native" as Kipling does, as Sahibs did. Thus Kim, born in India, is describable as "native-born" but not as a native.

2. Derek Parfit, *Reasons and Persons* (Oxford: Clarendon Press, 1984), 200.

3. John Locke, *Essay Concerning Human Understanding*, bk. 2, chap. 25.

4. See, for example, Terence Penelhum, "Personal Identity," in *Encyclopaedia of Philosophy* (New York: Macmillan, 1967), 6:95; P. F. Strawson, *Individuals* (London: Methuen, 1959), chap. 1, especially p. 31.

5. Success in reidentifying a person may make it possible to discover his or her identity, as in Oscar Wilde's *The Importance of Being Earnest*. Because Miss Prism and Lady Bracknell are able to reidentify Jack Worthing—*he* was the baby Miss Prism misplaced—he and they are able to establish *who he is*.

6. Again, compare *The Importance of Being Earnest*.

7. J. L. Austin must be mentioned as an exception. On the relation between knowing *what a thing is* and knowing the name for it, see "Other Minds," *Proceedings of the Aristotelian Society,* supp. vol. 20, p. 155. In a letter to A. D. Woozley (December 2, 1957), he explained what he had had in mind in a passage (which I have not been able to identify) about which Woozley had raised a question: "Suppose I hold out some strange object in my hand for yr inspection, as say in some quiz on the Radio; you maynt be able to identify it,—don't know what it is in the sense Sir M. Wheeler knows what it is (or *would* know *if* it were presented for *his* inspection). Yet surely there is a sense in which *you know what the thing in my hand is* and Sir M. Wheeler (who hasnt inspected it) does *not* know what it is? This was all I meant by the sense of 'know what' in wh it amounts only to 'has the opportunity to identify.' Perhaps weak?"

8. And not just for someone else. See again *The Importance of Being Earnest*. Jack Worthing's discovery of his identity is the discovery of who he is by his birth.

9. Both essays are reprinted in Isaiah Berlin, *Against the Current* (Harmondsworth: Penguin Books, 1982).

10. Primo Levi, *The Periodic Table* (New York: Schocken Books, 1984), 35–36.

11. Compare also the case of the anglicized Indian, Harry Coomer/Hari Kumar, in Paul Scott's *The Jewel in the Crown*. He has no language, no mode of life, in which he can be at home other than that of an educated Englishman; and so, on his return to India, it is the refusal of the English to allow him, despite or even because of his voice and manner, to be one of them—their incapacity, looking at him, to see anything but another indistinguishable brown face—that leads to his recognition that, as it were, no identity is available to him: "I am nothing, nothing."

12. Berlin, "The Life and Opinions of Moses Hess," sections 2 and 3.

13. Matthew Arnold, "The Study of Poetry," in *Four Essays on Life and Letters,* edited by E. K. Brown (New York: Appleton-Century-Crofts, 1947), 76–78.

14. Compare also the present use in the United States of "I can really identify with that," where the "that" is not a group of people but an expression of someone's, or some group's, views or aims or values. James Conant drew my attention to this sort of case; he pointed out that one could in such cases speak of *recognizing oneself* in that about which one says one identifies with it.

15. Berlin, "The Life and Opinions of Moses Hess," sections 2 and 3.

16. *Kim,* chap. 5.

17. Ibid., chap. 12. Cf. also Matthew Arnold on the characteristic virtue of the English: "this energy driving at practice, this paramount sense of the obligation of duty, self-control and work, this earnestness in going manfully with the best light we have," in *Culture and Anarchy,* chap. 4.

18. It may be contrasted with Matthew Arnold on the relation of Hebraism and Hellenism. To say that Kipling simply substitutes Buddhism for Hellenism would

be oversimple, but see his "The Miracle of Purun Bhagat" (in *The Jungle Books*) and Angus Wilson, "*Kim* and the Stories," in Wilson's *The Strange Ride of Rudyard Kipling* (New York: Viking, 1978).

19. Berlin, "The Life and Opinions of Moses Hess," 235.

20. Ibid., 236.

21. Fania Pascal, "Wittgenstein: A Personal Memoir"; originally in *Encounter* 41 (1973), reprinted with revisions in C. G. Luckhardt, ed., *Wittgenstein: Sources and Perspectives* (Ithaca, N.Y.: Cornell University Press, 1979), and in Rush Rhees, ed., *Recollections of Wittgenstein* (Oxford: Oxford University Press, 1984).

22. I do not want to suggest, either, that it is always called for; see "The Story of Avrom," in Primo Levi, *Moments of Reprieve* (New York: Summit Books, 1986).

23. Berlin, *Against the Current*, 252.

24. Primo Levi, *If This Is a Man* (published with *The Truce*) (Harmondsworth: Penguin Books, 1979), 33.

7

JUDAISM AND JEWISH IDENTITY

Hilary Putnam

A CERTAIN ambiguity hovers around the very topic of "Jewish identity." "Judaism" is the name of a religion, but a "Jew" is someone who, by birth or by conversion, is affiliated with an ancient tribe. Of course, for secular Jews, being "connected with the Jewish religion" might seem not to be a relevant sense of "Jewish." In Chapter 6, Cora Diamond speaks of Jewish identity in the sense of Jewish responsibility, but she does not mention the Jewish religion. Yet I doubt that things are so simple. Indeed, it is precisely for the secular Jew, and especially for the intellectual secular Jew, that the question of a relationship to the Jewish religion is likely to be an *issue*.

This may not have been so for most intellectual secular Jews when Nazism was at its height. (Wittgenstein in 1937 is Cora Diamond's main example of someone for whom acknowledging a relation to the Jewish people became an issue.) Today, however, the Jews are likely to be in the newspapers because of events in Israel, and some of those events involve a revival of Jewish fundamentalism. Fundamentalism is rightly a concern of all who support the cause of liberal democracy, and the rise of fundamentalism naturally provokes a response (one that, unfortunately, does not always distinguish between fundamentalism and religion as such). The Jewish liberal intellectual (secular or not) is, thus, likely to be aware of (and concerned to combat) Jewish fundamentalism at this time. But even this problem, important and timely as it is, is not the main reason for the concern with the Jewish religion. The Jewish religion is a special concern if one is a Jew simply and obviously because for so many thousands of years to be a Jew and to be a member of the Jewish religious community were virtually the same thing. Moreover, the Jewish Bible is not just the religious scripture; it also contains the historical documents of the Jewish people, including the story of their kings, their conquests, their defeats and humiliations, and their moral and political aspirations. One cannot simply identify with "the Jews" as a historical people without relating oneself, positively or negatively, to that history and those aspirations. As soon as one takes seriously Cora Diamond's injunction to "remember the past" (and, as she points out, in the Jewish tradition, memory and study are closely linked), the Jewish religion rears its head—beautiful to some and ugly to others.

If one is the sort of person to whom all religion is just "outmoded irrationality," then one will redefine "Judaism" so as to marginalize the religion, if one does not exclude it from one's conception of living Jewishness altogether. And if one is the sort of person to whom Cora Diamond's injunction to remember and to study does not speak, one will not even have a conception of living Jewishness. These remarks are not addressed to this last sort of person; but I do wish to address them to Jews of the first sort, as well as to Jews who are (as I am) observant. I wish to reflect on what a Jew should see as of lasting value in the Jewish tradition.

The liberal Catholic theologian David Tracy has pointed out correctly that both the Jewish Bible and the New Testament show internal theological tensions.[1] There are not only liberals and conservatives, reinterpreters and literalists, and so on, today; there were all those sorts of thinkers two thousand and more years ago, and their voices are to be heard in the scriptures themselves. One of these tensions in the Jewish tradition itself has been brilliantly described by David Hartman in his *Judaism: A Living Covenant*.[2] One strain in Judaism is universalistic, messianic, and (potentially) triumphalistic. This strain, Hartman points out, to a large extent has inspired Christianity, Islam, and perhaps Marxism; whenever a Jewish principle is universalized, it seems that the Jews are among the victims! But there is another, equally old and at least equally vital strain. This strain, which I think one can also find in Islam and in Hinduism, sees traditional Jewishness as literally a *way of life*. In this strain, praying for the Messiah was less an expression of a genuine hope than a ritualization of an idea that had no living relevance; what had living relevance was rather the performance of *mitzvot*, the carrying out of religious and ethical obligations (the two were not separated) that filled the smallest details of life—washing one's hands before a meal, for example—with a sense of the sacred. I have heard an Indian philosopher of my acquaintance talk movingly of the way in which traditional Hinduism does exactly this. This sense of the sacred was connected with one's obligations to others (above all the obligation to "love one's neighbor as oneself," as expressed in acts of *tzedakah* and in plain neighborliness) and with one's obligations to animals and with one's sense of an obligation to the fruit trees and the land.

A CORRECTIVE TO "HUMANISM"

The point just made seems important enough to justify what may look like a digression. The alternative to a religious orientation is often described as "humanism," and in its cruder formulations humanism holds that the *sole* source of value is humanity—in some versions humanity is said to "create" value (whatever that means), while in others it is held that human "needs," and *only* human needs, determine what is valuable. Unfortunately, even sophisticated philosophers sometimes subscribe to these views. In most of the religions I know of, by contrast—even in religions that do not involve belief in a personal God—human needs are seen as *a* matter of concern, but so are the needs of other living things. I do not, of course, mean to suggest that the needs of other living things are *not* of concern to humanists; what I mean to challenge is the reason that hard-core humanists give as a justification of that concern. On the hard-core position, it is our *needs*—presumably our need to feel a certain way about how we treat animals—or our "understanding of ourselves" that are the basis, and the only basis, for animal rights. This view is well expressed in a passage in Bernard Williams's *Ethics and the Limits of Philosophy*.

> A concern for nonhuman animals is indeed a proper part of human life, but we can acquire it, cultivate it, and teach it only in terms of our understanding of ourselves. Human beings both have that understanding and are the objects of it, and this is one of the basic respects in which our ethical relations to each other must always be different from our ethical relations to other animals. Before one gets to the question of how animals are to be treated, there is the fundamental point that this is the only question there can be: how they are to be treated. The choice can only be whether animals benefit from our practices or are harmed by them. This is why speciesism is falsely modeled on racism and sexism which really are prejudices. To suppose that there is an ineliminable white or male understanding of the world, and to think that the only choice is whether blacks or women should benefit from "our" (white, male) practices or be harmed by them;

this is already to be prejudiced. But in the case of human relations to animals, the analogues to such thoughts are simply correct."[3]

It is of course the case that each of us is the object of his or her own understanding of himself, and animals are not the object of my or your understanding of myself or yourself; but very little follows from that fact. If it *did* turn out, for example, that there is an ineliminable male (or female) "understanding of the world" (e.g., if Carol Gilligan turns out to be right!),[4] it would not at all follow that (a form of) sexism had turned out to be justified, as Williams suggests. Indeed, Williams's tone here is in contradiction to his tone elsewhere in the book; for the talk of "our" understanding of the world suggests that there is such a thing as the *human* understanding of the world, while the thrust of Williams's whole book is that very little is common to all human understandings outside of the exact sciences; in ethics, according to Williams, there are only the understandings of "some social world or other."[5] (If Williams had been consistent, he would have said that animals [women, blacks] have rights only from the "perspective" of certain social worlds.) The very language of "understandings of the world" serves to raise a false issue. What the philosopher who believes that animals have objective rights is saying is just that; he is not committed to the further claims that we (humans, or Americans, or Jews, or whatever) can have a conception of those rights that is not a *human* conception; an "absolute" conception, to use Williams's own jargon. The question is not whether we can know how things are "from the universe's point of view" in ethics or anywhere else; the question, to repeat, is whether the *basis* for respecting the rights of animals is conceived to be "our understanding of ourselves" or *their* welfare.

An opposite mistake to Williams's is made by those who claim that *only* from the perspective of some form or other of theism can one reject the sort of "humanism" I have just criticized. I am not making that claim; I am simply pointing out that one of the virtues of the Jewish religion in particular, with its prohibitions against cruelty to animals[6] (prohibitions that, regrettably, were not taken over by ancient and medieval Christianity), is that it reminds us that humanism can degenerate into speciesism—and, *pace* Williams, speciesism *is* a form of prejudice. (But to say this is not to endorse the error of supposing that humans do not have a right to be *specially concerned* with human welfare.)

"TRADITIONAL" JUDAISM AND ITS VALUES

Before my digression on humanism and speciesism, I was saying that there was a strain in Judaism, a strain that dominated Jewish life for centuries, that was not triumphalistic or messianic, but was characterized by a sense of fulfillment in the here and now (even under terribly hard conditions), a sense of the sacredness of the small details of everyday life, and a sense that while we may be God's stewards over Nature, we are not its creators, and it has its own value that we should respect and seek to enhance, not abuse and despoil.

I want to emphasize once again that I am talking about values that Jews who are atheists should also, however they may wish to restate them, recognize to *be* values. My purpose is not to say "look what religious Jews have that nonreligious Jews don't." At the same time, I do want to say that precisely because modernity has been characterized by what Max Weber called "purposive rationality," we have for a long time emphasized hustle and bustle, "getting things done," and for that reason premodern understandings of the world are likely to surprise us with their quietism, their "fatalism," and their search for a serenity that does not depend on having a "practicable" goal and being able to find efficient means to it. Our fathers and mothers, understandably, found quietism, fatalism, and a concern with serenity as evasions; they were eager to get on with the task of enlightenment. But today even we who value enlightenment can see that there is more to enlightenment than purposive rationality (as Jürgen Habermas recently has emphasized).[7] One good reason for not despising tradition is that after three or four centuries of "modern is better," we have reached a position in which we can find that a knowledge of the tradition offers us not a straightjacket but a widening of our sense of what is possible.

In particular, what has been seen as "quietism" or "fatalism" in traditional Judaism is not at all a sense that things can never be improved. Rabbi Tarphon's great saying that "It is not up to you to finish the work, but neither are you free not to take it up" expresses beautifully the sense that one can do one's best without needing a guarantee that the reign of justice will come in the foreseeable future.[8] This is a sense that all mankind—not just the Jews—need if our various passionate commitments to our different conceptions of the reign of justice are to be kept within bounds, as they must be if we are not to destroy ourselves in a nuclear war or imprison ourselves in a totalitarian system of one sort or another. It is true that this is a sense that it is easier for a religious person to have, since religion is above all an expression of fundamental trust, but there are also secular worldviews that can find room for such a sense.

The aim of the traditional Jew was to be the Lord's *eved,* or servant. This aim was to be realized in two ways: through study and through the performance of *mitzvot.* Both ways have been misunderstood. Those who are unacquainted with the way in which Talmud is traditionally studied are likely to imagine something like rote learning. Nothing could be farther from the truth. The way in which one studies Talmud is by *arguing* about it. This freedom to argue is protected by the Talmud itself; one of its rulings is that a rabbi is free to say that he disagrees with the received view of the *halakhah* (the Jewish law), and to teach his dissident opinion, provided he conforms his practice to the received interpretation until such time as he may succeed in convincing the rest of the rabbinate to change it.[9] While it would take more space than I have available to give even a sketch of what a page of Talmud looks like that would make sense to someone not acquainted with it, this much also has to be known to appreciate the notion of "Talmud study": the Talmud is a record of the arguments of the sages, and the record contains the opinions of those who lost out on any given question as well as of those whose views carried the day. (In this respect it is very different from the sacred writings of the Christian church, for example.) And a good student of the Talmud is supposed to spend as much care and attention on the views and arguments that did not become *halakhah* as on the views and arguments that did. And "care and attention" include raising difficulties; the best Talmud student is generally the one who can raise the most and the deepest difficulties.

The second way, the performance of *mitzvot,* has been *worse* than misunderstood: St. Paul distinguished Christianity from Judaism in large part by characterizing (and caricaturing) the Jewish concept of *mitzvot* as empty legalism. (I wonder how many Jewish intellectuals have employed the adjective "Pharisaical" without realizing that it is anti-Semitic?) The fact is that the elaboration of *mitzvot* was precisely the way in which the smallest details of daily life were invested with sacred significance. My friend Deanna Mirski has remarked that "the best-kept secret" of Judaism is that it contains a spiritual discipline fully as elaborate (and as mystical and as rich) as any. That discipline is the system of *mitzvot.*

The *mitzvot* are not all equally detailed however. They include broad ethical and social injunctions (care for the poor of the community, for example) as well as detailed instructions for preparing the home for Passover, and "keeping kosher." And the evidence we have is that prior to the Enlightenment, there was a great deal of variation from one Jewish community to another, concerning both the interpretation of specific *mitzvot* and concerning the emphasis given to one or another strain within the tradition. The very word "tradition" acquired the connotation of something fixed once and for all and not subject to question in the writings of Durkheim, Weber, and of post-Weberian sociologists: but in that sense, Judaism was never "traditional."

Once the Enlightenment began to seriously compete with rabbinic Judaism, Judaism began to splinter, however. The currently dominant *haredi* version of "Orthodox" Judaism was as much a reaction to the Enlightenment as was Reform Judaism.[10] (Conservative Judaism is a much more recent phenomenon.) Part of our misunderstanding of the tradition comes from accepting uncritically the self-description of the leaders of Orthodox Judaism as the simple continuers of the tradition. Both the social morality that is the heart of Reform teaching and the emphasis on rigorous observance of *mitzvot* that is the heart of Orthodox teaching are "traditional" and neither exhausts the tradition.

WHAT ALL THIS HAS TO DO WITH "JEWISH IDENTITY"

In one sense, there is no mystery about "Jewish identity." Anyone who considers himself or herself Jewish has, in that sense, a Jewish identity. Nor can I get seriously excited about the question, Does a Jew have an *obligation* to consider himself or herself Jewish in any serious sense? It may be a moral failing to conceal one's Jewishness under certain circumstances (this is what Wittgenstein accused himself of), but if the only reason for having a Jewish identity is that Jews are still persecuted in some places, this would seem to be too "thin" a reason to keep anyone from assimilating in a country in which Jews are not persecuted. And it is hard to see how one could justify a collection of essays on *that* topic.

The very use of the term "identity" invites one to think of philosophical discussions of "personal identity," and Cora Diamond explains very well why those discussions have little or nothing to do with our topic. But I don't find the issue of Kim's identity as a Sahib quite the right model either. It is not wholly the *wrong* model, for one of the things Kim is thinking about is what in his Sahib background is better than mere stuffiness and baseless feelings of superiority, what is *worth* his feeling "responsibility" to; and I too have been urging that to have a Jewish "identity" one has to be able to find something in the Jewish past that one will feel is *worth* appropriating. But Professor Diamond undercuts her own analogy by suggesting that this may all be a species of self-deception; and to make that suggestion is to distance oneself from the very thing that one is trying to appropriate. Her starting point in Wittgenstein's problem (the problem of someone whose forefathers had been very devout Christians for several generations, even if they were of "Jewish descent") prevents her from encountering what, for me, is *the* problem: whether there is something in Judaism that is spiritually enriching, something such that if a Jew rejects or ignores it, he or she is the loser, and not the Jewish people. I have been arguing that there indeed is, and that what it asks of each Jewish man or woman is not slavish adherence, but reinterpretation—for all genuine appropriation of a tradition involves continual reinterpretation, and a tradition that is not constantly reappropriated and reinterpreted becomes fossilized.

NOTES

1. David Tracy, "Creativity in the Interpretation of Religion: The Question of Radical Pluralism," *New Literary History* 15, no. 2 (Winter 1984): 289–310.

2. David Hartman, *Judaism: A Living Covenant* (New York: Free Press, 1988).

3. Bernard Williams, *Ethics and the Limits of Philosophy* (Cambridge, Mass.: Harvard University Press, 1985), 118–19.

4. See Carol Gilligan, *In a Different Voice* (Cambridge, Mass.: Harvard University Press, 1982).

5. In the exact sciences, according to Williams, we can attain to a view that can be shared by all humans because it is really "absolute"—that is, not dependent on our human perspective(s) at all. For a criticism of Williams's position, see my "Objectivity and the Science/Ethics Distinction," in my *Realism with a Human Face* (Cambridge, Mass.: Harvard University Press, 1990).

6. Cf. *Babylonian Talmud*, Mishnah Sanhedrin, chap. 11.2.

7. See Jürgen Habermas, *The Theory of Communicative Action* (Boston: Beacon Press, 1988), especially vol. I, chap. 2.

8. Rabbi Tarphon, *Pirke Avot*, chap. 2.21.

9. *Baba Metziah*, 32b.

10. This claim is, of course, not new. It was argued convincingly by Rabbi Saul Berman (who is himself Orthodox) in a symposium, "On the Frontiers of Religious Diversity," at a CLAL Critical Issues Conference (May 8–10, 1988); this is contained in "Materials from the Critical Issues Conference II" and may be obtained from CLAL, The National Jewish Center for Learning and Leadership, 47 W. 34th St., 2nd fl., New York, NY 10001.

II

CULTURAL IDENTITY AND MORALITY

8

CUSTODIANS

Eddy M. Zemach

A N AMERICAN student of mine by the name of Cohen once asked me the following question. Jews, he knew, do not celebrate Sunday; so what day of the week is their Sabbath? He was not sure. A Jewish colleague at a large university in the eastern United States remarked during a conversation that the Bible was written in Greek; when I said that this is not entirely true, he replied that he knew that the original language of the Old Testament was Aramaic. In the Church of Santa Maria la Blanca (in it there is a synagogue that dates from 1203, one of the only two synagogues left standing in Spain after the expulsion of the Jews in 1492), I met a Canadian woman who later told me she is Jewish. Hearing that only two synagogues from the Middle Ages are left in Spain, she remarked, "So Jewish religion was not popular in Spain, was it?" A Jewish man in Boston asked me whether the Arab Jews in Israel support the Arabs or the Jews in the current conflict. A Dutch man of Jewish extraction on a visit to Israel wanted me to show him "the remnants of the Hassidic sect," those, he said, who "in the old days used Christian blood for Passover" (he was sure, though, that this custom has been discontinued). A fellow philosopher of Jewish parentage said to me that however reprehensible the Nazi treatment of Jews during World War II was, it was not worse than the way Native Americans were treated by the U.S. government.

I must confess that on a number of these occasions I have lost my temper, and, to make a further confession, I do not think I would have been quite so upset had it not been Jews who said those things to me. Now I do not think that Jewish people are or should be more informed, better educated, or less unreasonable than other people. Why, then, am I so distressed to find out that a Canadian woman knows nothing about the Jewish civilization in Spain? Why should she care about all those poets, craftsmen, philosophers, physicians, astronomers, rhetoricians, talmudic scholars, military men, winegrowers, courtiers, and hundreds of thousands of ordinary Jews who had been, most of them, physically destroyed and their culture eradicated? What if these people happened to be her forefathers? Why should a philosopher who happens to be Jewish be more morally sensitive, and hence more guilty of moral blindness, than a non-Jew who utters the same abomination about the United States government being no better than the Nazis? What if it was his own relatives, his own people, that were murdered by the Germans whom they had never harmed in any way whatsoever? Most Bostonians know very little about foreign nations and peoples; why then should a Jewish one be special and not show utter ignorance of Jewish history and present reality by using the absurd phrase, "Arab Jew"? Why should he know that there is no one in Israel who would describe himself or herself in that way?

Personal freedom of choice in matters cultural is one of our most important values, perhaps the most important of them all. People have an inalienable right to intellectual freedom, which includes the right to be inspired by, and associate oneself with, a tradition of one's choice. You will not blame an offspring of dentists (I am one) who does not carry on their tradition (I didn't). Why should the cultural tradition of one's parents be treated differently than their vocation? Why should an ethnic group have a right that we would deny to most other groups, that is, a right to have their progeny follow in their footsteps, continue their way of life, identify with and be inspired by their history, and feel responsible for other members of their group? Such a claim sounds reactionary and repressive.

Yet I think that a modified version of that claim is valid: There is a right here that cannot be easily abrogated even though it infringes upon one's right to absolute cultural freedom. That right can be described as a duty that stems from kinship and is not based on one's having contracted to assume it. If all moral duties are contractual, and no one can incur an obligation except through an informed, rationally considered, and free consent to enter a compact or accept a responsibility, then indeed my claim is preposterous. Such autonomism, however, is false. Your duty to save a drowning man or a victim of a car accident does in no way depend on your having contracted to save that person, or any other person (say, provided that you obtain some benefits, for example, a right to be treated in the same manner). No such compact exists; it is a sheer fiction, an ad hoc contraption dreamed up by philosophers to avoid the glaring counter-intuitive consequences of their view. One may explicitly refuse to enter any compact, decline to join any mutual-insurance society with others, and yet be held morally responsible for not rendering help when one happens to be in a position to do so. The source of your obligation in such cases is the evil that results if you fail to act appropriately, and the goodness that results if you do so act, being accidentally placed in a fortuitous position that enables you to do good without incurring undue hardship. It is *being there* (e.g., physical proximity) that puts you under the obligation to act in a certain way. Even though it was not your intention to be there and you regret or deplore being there, even though your being there is a totally random happenstance, it is your unambiguous duty, just because you *are* there, to do what is necessary to avert the ensuing evil.

Let me call such a duty *"duty by kinship."* It is not what one does, but where one is, that places one under the obligation: The thing has to be done, and one is kindred to it. There are many kinds of kinship and what counts as "being kindred" can be different in different cases: It may be plain physical proximity, as in the case of the drowning man, or physical proximity plus some acquaintance, as in the case of the duty to help a neighbor, or biological kinship. All duty by kinship is conventional, but the goal the convention serves is not; hence the "why me" objection is powerless with respect to it. A duty by kinship obligates not because one tacitly or explicitly accepts it, but because it is the best way to get the right thing done.

Take, for example, one's duty to one's old and infirm parents. Where does it come from? No contract has been signed by the child when it came into the world, or at any later time, to care for its parents when they are old; most parents do not make undertaking this obligation a condition for providing for their children. Some philosophers think that this obligation is an obligation of friendship, inherent in the relations between members of the same family, but that too seems wrong, for there may be no love or friendship in the family; children may feel cold or even hostile to their parents. Yet that matters not at all; it is still the children's obligation to care for their parents. One's feeling notwithstanding, a decent person is expected to rise to the occasion and do the right thing. Even if there is friendship in the family, what is expected of a son or a daughter much exceeds what can be reasonably expected of friends. Fair-weather friends are not morally repugnant; we do not condemn a person who severs relations with a friend if that friend becomes dull or when the relationship is no longer mutually beneficial; but severing relations with one's parents when one can no longer benefit from it is morally reprehensible. I therefore say that duty to one's parents is duty by kinship. It is a duty by default: Old people need to be taken care of, and the next of kin fall heir to that duty by conventional default. Feelings have nothing to do with it: The duty is there whether you love your parents or not. Of course, like any other duty, that duty is not absolute: It may be overridden by other duties that conflict with it. The point, however, is that such prima facie duties *exist*. When something precious is in jeopardy, the obligation to save it falls to those who are in one way or another kindred to it. The convention that regulates who must assume the duty is not arbitrary: It relies on advantageous placing. It may single out those who are physically near the object of mandated care, or those who know better how to satisfy the need, or those who started doing it, or those who can most easily or painlessly assume it. Such conventions for designating who is obligated are not to be confused with the obligation itself; it obligates even when the circumstances are atypical. The "why me" excuse fails to apply not because there are perfect reasons why it is I, rather than anyone else, who has to do it, but for general, rule-utilitarian reasons. Indeed, there is no reason why precisely I must do it, but that is true for everyone else, too. If everyone can use the "why me" plea, what should be done would not be done. Thus, even though the kind of obligating kinship is semi-arbitrary, its binding force is undiminished.

Some liberals maintain that one can incur an obligation only by obligating oneself, that to have a duty one must freely (for example, by contract) assume that duty. That, however, is certainly wrong; a murderer who shuns all compacts with others is no less vile for his openness and deserves moral blame, because what he does is objectively wrong. The metaphysical ground of such liberalism is also dubious. We treat the agent as if it were the selfsame atom at almost all times, but that assumption is surely not true, for people change in time. By what right, then, do we ignore these differences and treat the present subject as identical with the past one? Why is my past self allowed to bond my present self and use it as collateral security? Why not let the present be free from the tyranny of the past? The obvious answer is the great good generated by our policy: Social life is impossible without that form of bondage. Thus the very principle of moral autonomy (*only consent obligates*) is itself based on the consequentialist principle of maximizing the good.

A culture is the most valuable thing we have. Neither angels nor beasts, we exist in society; society is a vehicle of a culture; an aggregate of people that lack common culture is no society. It is being a part of a living culture that makes one human. At the peril of repeating well-known platitudes, let me say that a culture gives one ideals and defines one's desires and aspirations, shows a way to lead one's daily life, provides one with a home in time, historical roots, a style of thought and feeling, or an object of ultimate concern. It generates language and concepts, it makes possible science, art, and religion. One cannot refuse ingression into a culture without ceasing to be human. The question is not whether one is to accept a culture; it is what culture, and what group that incorporates it, with which one chooses to associate oneself. That decision is most significant: Choosing not to align oneself with a group, say, not to join the local Jewish community, shapes the community's destiny, for one makes it an even smaller minority. That decision may determine the life of the said community, for if due to lack of interest the community disbands, the culture it embodied will no longer be an option for one's own children and for others in the future: It will not be there anymore. Cultures can die.

A culture is the most elaborate and complex thing that the human race has created; it takes hundreds or thousands of years for it to evolve, but only one or two generations to die out; a culture is therefore a most fragile and delicate thing. Some theorists claimed that in modern society traditional communities lose their affective role, but that is a mere euphemism for saying that in our society some people lead alienated, cold lives. There is probably no issue on which Marxism has been proven so wrong as on the importance to the individual of communal, ethnic, and national identity. It is false that the proletariat has no homeland and no people: Cultural affiliations lie much closer to the core of human identity than the economical destiny Marxists have tried to place there. Neither family nor ethnic and national groups became obsolete under socialism. Even in Yuppiedom, the most individualistic of all societies, roots are sought and artificially implanted in the empty internal space of the liberated and postmodern Yuppie to prevent catastrophic implosion that even the most fashionable of therapists would be unable to deconstruct.

Cultures are many and come in all shapes and sizes, but major cultural traditions are very few; cultures that reached a high degree of richness, complexity, and sophistication can be counted on the fingers of two hands. A highly developed culture is one that has a sufficient number of ways for human beings to flourish in. It is a language, great ideas, a philosophy, an ethics, a religion, a literature, great stories, traditional music and dances, food, dresses; it is a chain of metaphors that can structure a human life, a myth that gives rise to institutions, a wide network of meanings to interpret birth and death, suffering and hope, nature and art. Cultures, however, are mortal: Think of the ancient Egyptian, for instance. A great culture is therefore the object of duty by kinship: It places its members and their progeny under an obligation to keep it alive.

I think of the remnants, the pitifully few remnants, of the once vibrant and creative Jewish culture in America. In some ways, tracing Jewish life in America is like walking through a bombed-out city, where skeletons of buildings mutely bear witness to the life that once thrived there. In a way, the tragedy is even greater for the destruction is self-inflicted, and those who deserted it do not lament the eradication of that rich cultural world. I will not speak of defunct Hebrew and Yiddish theaters, political parties, social organizations, newspapers, publishing houses. These stories of self-annihilation and decline are too well known. Instead, let me mention a phenomenon that some may think trivial, but I find tragic. I have met in America grandchildren and other close relatives of eminent Jewish figures—poets whose work I admire, innovative talmudic scholars, social thinkers, leaders of people; in most cases these young Americans were utterly ignorant of the achievements of their relatives. Some did not even know who they were; others knew that that uncle, or grandfather, had written some things that they could not read, and did not care about anyway, for they were irrelevant to their lives. I think one can find such estrangement in no other ethnic group in America except blacks and Native Americans, where the family was violated and sundered by force. It is probably improper and sacrilegious to speak of cultural "genocide," but barbarization and loss of cultural pride on such a scale makes one wonder. It is as if Nazi murder, Communist oppression, and American freedom have all conspired to erase Jewish culture from under the sun.

But are we not better off when cultures die? What is wrong with having only one culture in the world? Do we really need a post-tower-of-Babylon proliferation of many different traditions, languages, literatures, ethnic identities, interpretations of the past complete with distinct holidays and dates of mourning, old hopes, old grudges, old pride, and conflicting ambitions? Is war not the inevitable fruit of that plethora of cultures? Why not have one culture, one living tradition, and consign the others to ethnological museums for future historians and archaeologists? There are, I think, three reasons why neither the process leading to such cultural uniformity, nor the outcome, is a good thing.

First, such *Gleichschaltung* or *Nivellierung* (for obvious reasons the German terms are more suggestive than the English ones), a leveling of all cultural variety, even if desirable, is unlikely to occur peacefully. Societies are loathe to disband and disappear. People do not willingly abjure the right to shape their progeny in their image so that they can understand and respect their parents. A people would not consent to leave its cultural home, to lead a secondhand life in the straightjacket of a foreign culture, to see all that it held dear neglected and scoffed at by its children. Mass assimilation did occur in the past (many Jewish communities underwent it) but always under duress. It happens when a very long foreign occupation or exile leads to slow decline and loss of self-respect, when the natural desire to retain one's heritage and pass it on breaks down. In general, cultural imperialism is resisted by those whose culture is sentenced to die, for it reduces sophisticated adults to the status of small children trained in the elements of culture; it erodes the adults' position in the family and hence the family as such. The need to assimilate breeds frustration and despair, and when it is forced, hatred and bloodshed. It is our duty to fight oppression and loss of human dignity, so we must respect cultural identity and help endangered cultures survive.

Second, cultural uniformity is undesirable. Even if one could bulldoze all civilizations save one, it would be wrong to do so. A plurality of civilizations saves us from parochialism and the ignorant tyranny of one paradigm; it lets us see that there is more than one way to be human and that experience may be codified in many ways. If all cultures except, say, the Chinese, are wiped out, most works of art will be experientially lost: One could not appreciate literary works such as the Bible, Dante, Shakespeare, or Tolstoy; Bach, Beethoven, and Rembrandt, too, would look alien; they would say nothing to those who were not brought up in the relevant tradition. A cultural product cannot enrich human lives if the values it excels in are not one's own values. Those exclusively immersed in the Chinese culture, great as it is, could not empathize or in any deep sense understand any of the great figures of the Western tradition. Cultural genocide even if due to best intentions is evil; it pauperizes mankind.

The third reason is that even a benevolent elimination of a civilization is likely to be unjust. The natural candidates for planned oblivion are the least populous cultures. But they (e.g., the Jewish) came to be so not because they have failed in the open market, where all traditions could freely compete. The reason for paucity of attendance may be (as in the case of the Jews) brutal suppression of the culture by its enemies, including a periodic physical annihilation of those who practiced it. Thus, the cultures destined to perish will be those that were mostly wronged against in the past; those whose people were forcibly kept from flourishing as long as they adhered to the culture. Before the great rebellion (66–74), the Jewish people was once one of the largest in the world, about five million strong. It did not grow in number until the nineteenth century, not because the Jews freely chose to abandon it, but because they were systematically decimated, and subjected to relentless persecution wherever they lived. The Hebrew language was once spoken by many nations from Carthage in the west to Moab in the east. It lost its peoples (though, contrary to common belief, neither literary creation in it nor its use as a spoken language has ever ceased in four thousand years) due to forced obliteration, oppression, war, exile, and the need to survive in the world of the victors. A planned phasing out of minority cultures by liberals would thus be an outrageous injustice. Wrongdoers get the big prize, their culture becomes the universal culture, and those who in the past were persecuted are further punished by having their culture summarily euthanized.

That brings me back to the clash between values: personal freedom on the one hand, responsibility on the other. Suppose that at a time of great cultural decline, when classical painting is at best ridiculed, at worst entirely forgotten, you fall heir to some large canvases, say, some Titians, Klees, and Picassos. You live—as everybody does at that period—in a small cubicle in a teeming city of billions, where living space is extremely scarce. The pictures take a great deal of room that you could otherwise use for your own convenience. You yourself know the value of the paintings, but those around you do not. Perhaps you hope that your children will live in a better world, could enjoy art, and be thankful to you for having kept the paintings for them. Yet you cannot be sure of that; it is quite possible that your children will curse you for having bequeathed that burden to them, for their world will be even harsher, more ignorant, more inhospitable to art, than yours. Do you have an obligation to keep the paintings? Is it your duty, as a de facto custodian of the last of European art, to keep it, whether it is convenient or not? You have no obligation, I think, to volunteer for the job; but that is not the point; you did not volunteer. The paintings were entrusted to you by your parents. You can throw them out; that unvalued yet priceless treasure is to you a burden, a cross on your back. Do you have a moral duty to keep the paintings no one wants? I think so. Suppose that in previous generations all art was systematically destroyed by the government, and those who hid artistic heirlooms were put to death or sent to concentration camps. The neobarbarians are no more in power: You may keep your pictures now, if you wish. But due to past persecutions most people (yourself included) cannot understand why anyone has ever cared for such pictures. Knowing that those who burned the museums were evil, knowing the depravity of those who made people (yourself included) blind to artistic values, may you discard the last art that you were made a custodian of? I think you may not. Tossing the last Rembrandt to the dump heap will make you an ally of those you hate, the neobarbarians who enslaved the world and made it the dreary artless place it is.

I therefore think that the very fact that there has been a Hadrian and a

Hitler, that the crusaders destroyed a vast number of Jewish communities, that in Massada, and in York, and in the Warsaw Ghetto, Jews made a desperate heroic stand against their exterminators, fighting till they all died, defines an ethical space in which we find ourselves today and in which we have to act. It makes us responsible for what has happened. Had our forefathers been free to live in peace, or at least not hounded by all nations, universally hated for no fault of their own, had Israel, the land of the Jews, been as prosperous and as secure as the land of the French, not surrounded by hundreds of millions of mortal enemies, we could do with our heritage as we please. But that is not where we are now; we are in immediate proximity to a culture in danger of imminent drowning. History defines the parameters within which freedom of the individual is limited by ethical obligations; we are not free not to right those wrongs that history has put in our lap.

Let me change my parable and take music instead of visual art. Suppose the barbarians were not after painting; it was music they hated. Suppose that music making was often a capital crime, and at "liberal" intervals those who practiced it were "merely" confined in ghettoes, denied access to most occupations, not allowed (as Jews were most of the time in most of Europe) to own land, and subject to constant harassment and humiliation. Suppose, as before, that now the barbarians are no more in control; music making is allowed, but there are very few who can appreciate it anymore. Now you happen to be born to musicians who taught you to play the violin. Sure, you are no great artist: You can barely keep up with the notes, and many works, perhaps most of the violin repertoire, are beyond your ken. Yet you can appreciate the beauty of music, you can play simple pieces, and you can surmise, albeit darkly, what a real string quartet may sound like (hearing one is an unrealistic prospect since most other people cannot tell a cello from a power drill). Now you have children of your own; should you teach them how to play the violin? Should you insist on their practicing every day? What if they do not like it and do not share your reasons? Yet are you at liberty *not* to teach them? Suppose they think it is silly to grate strings in order to make funny noises when all other kids are out enjoying wholesome sports or learning something profitable, such as the use of recent model supercomputers. Is it your right, given the value of what you have been entrusted, being the last custodian of music for the violin, to make your children study it? I think it is; it is not only your right; it is your duty.

To be quite candid, I know that I am asking Americans to do a lot more than Israelis have to do. An Israeli kid does not have to go to a special school to learn that Passover is not another name for hopscotch, that Yom Kippur is not a kind of sushi. In their own backyard Israeli kids find traces of biblical events that shaped the destiny of their people, and through the Jewish calendar, by which they live, they connect with holidays that encapsulate the history and philosophy of traditional Judaism. Not so in America. To be able to receive their Jewish heritage in a meaningful way, they have to learn a language, a different kind of tradition, another history. Consider prayer. An Israeli atheist can enjoy the Hebrew liturgy, which contains an anthology of hundreds of years of literature, channeled through the religious sentiment. The *siddur* alternates between biblical and Mishnaic texts, which are up to a thousand years apart and have different grammars and vocabularies; it uses early poems written in Palestine in the sixth century and the mature poetic expression of Jews who lived in Spain or Germany five hundred years later. One need not use the Jewish prayer book to supplicate a personal deity any more than one must use Bach's great Mass only to affirm the dogmas of the church. Yet a historical-cultural attitude toward the liturgy depends on a knowledge of Hebrew and is entirely lost when the prayers are read in translation. In English translation one gets, instead of fine poetry and live history, only a bland porridge of dull formulae cast in the same artificially pious, sugar-coated, uniform, phony, twentieth-century imitation King James English. Those prayers are mannequin texts: lifeless, genderless, ageless, pretty face and no character. There is no shortcut solution to that problem: using a guitar and a catching tune may somewhat enliven the service, but it further erodes the reason for attending it in the first place. The only honest way is to learn the language and the history of the Jews and make the culture come alive in one's life.

That is difficult. Impossible, however, it is not. Many ordinary people are bicultural, and they are not worse off for the effort. Small nations have always educated their children so that they could be at home in more than one culture. Canadians are doing it and so have some minorities in America. Perhaps, with Europe unified, it will become a necessity for all Europeans; a monocultural person will find it hard to find work in Europe. Judaism need not be watered down: The comic-strip instant version of Jewish culture concocted for consumption by Jewish kids in America (the minority that does get some Jewish education) is indeed not very appetizing. The children pick up the attitude of their parents and teachers, that the whole thing is an exercise in futility; they are not expected really to learn anything. It need not be that way; Americans of Jewish parentage are not inherently dumber than Canadians or Europeans. Jewish men and women who have it in their hearts can make their culture live. It can happen. But, truth to tell, I doubt that it will. Perhaps the process has gone too far, and most American Jews have already lost the will to retain their culture. If that is so, it is a true calamity: for other Jews (who once again, for the second time this century, will have lost the greatest and most advanced part of their people), for America, who will as a result be culturally poorer, and, above all, for humanity.

9

JEWISH IDENTITY AND THE CHALLENGE
OF AUSCHWITZ

Lionel Rubinoff

APOCALYPSE AND JEWISH TRADITION

Apocalypse is nothing new to Judaism. It is, if anything, a Jewish invention. What is important about the Jewish experience of apocalypse, however, is the attitude that Judaism has come to adopt toward it. A central theme in Jewish literature and scholarship is the refusal of the Jewish people to surrender to the crippling sense of powerlessness to which the experience of apocalypse would normally give rise. As Robert Alter points out in his essay "The Apocalyptic Temper of Our Time," the response of Judaism to apocalypse has been both prophetic and messianic, a continuous affirmation of the belief in the redemptive power of the communicated word to help us change ourselves and our history.[1] To exist in this way, Alter explains, is an affirmation as well of the faith that by "carefully attending to the bewildering human particularities of this world, with the assumption that they can and must be coped with, we may make it somewhat more likely that we can grab hold of history before it goes skidding off to that awaited end";[2] whether that end be the result of human-produced catastrophes, brought about by the destruction of ecology, or the unleashing of the weapons of apocalyptic destruction, or, whether it will come about naturally through the inevitable working out of the Second Law of Thermodynamics, which, in the fullness of time, will culminate in the vast, fiery death of the solar system in which we reside.

Notwithstanding such prospects and potential ordeals, enough to test the courage and will to survival of any people for all eternity, the greatest challenge to Jewish survival was and continues to be the experience of the Holocaust. For it was not until the gas chambers of Auschwitz that the Jewish people were forced to confront the possibility that God had finally abandoned His chosen people. That the Jewish people survived even this ordeal, unprecedented in the history of mankind let alone in the history of the Jews, should not distract us from confronting the terrible consequences that even survival has had on Jewish faith. For whereas in former times Jewish survival could be interpreted as resulting from partnership with God, thus affirming His presence in history,[3] Auschwitz was, if anything, an experience of God's retreat from history. If Jews survived it was in spite of, not because of, God's help. The degree of despair over God's apparent betrayal of the divine human covenant is expressed by the story told by Elie Wiesel of a small group of Jews who were gathered together to pray in a little synagogue in Nazi-occupied Europe. As the service went on, suddenly a pious Jew who was slightly mad—for all pious Jews were by then slightly mad—burst in through the door. Slowly he said: "Shh, Jews! Do not pray so loud! God will hear you. Then He will know that there are still some Jews left alive in Europe."[4]

But even if Auschwitz tested the Jewish people's faith in God, it did not destroy their will to survive as a people. The Jewish response to Auschwitz was a renewed dedication to the newly created State of Israel. Once again, faced with the threat of apocalyptic destruction, Jews reached into their orphic depths and responded creatively. Indeed, for many Jews the return to "*eretz* Israel" is likened to the Exodus; which is why the celebration of Passover each year is an occasion of special significance.

Yet because of Auschwitz the Jew's attitude to Israel, to himself, and to the future of World Jewry, is charged with ambiguity. What is at stake is not simply the Jew's traditional belief in God's presence in history, but the belief of all Jews, secular and religious alike, of the continued existence of Jews as a people. As Emil Fackenheim puts it, the challenge of Auschwitz presents itself in the form of a question: "Dare a Jew of today continue to obey the God of history—and thus expose to the danger of a second Auschwitz, himself, his children, and his children's children? Never, within or without Jewish history, have men anywhere had such a dreadful, such a horrifying, reason for turning their backs on the God of history."[5] Norman Podhoretz speaks for many Jews when he confronts this question and responds: "Will this madness in which we are all caught never find a resting place? Is there never to be an end to it? In thinking about the Jews I have wondered whether their survival as a distinct group was worth one single hair on the head of a single infant. Did the Jews have to survive so that six million innocent people should one day be burned in the ovens of Auschwitz?"[6]

Of course it is not unreasonable for a group of people who have suffered as have the Jews to emerge from an experience such as Auschwitz with the temptation to question the very basis of their historic existence. Boris Pasternak confronts precisely this issue in his novel *Dr. Zhivago*. Here the Jewish problem is presented as a question. What is the sense of being a Jew in a non-Jewish world? Why should there be Jews at all? Typical of the astonishment that perennially plagues the non-Jew is the exclamation by Zhivago's mistress, Lara: "It is strange that these people, who once liberated mankind from the yoke of idolatry, and so many of whom devote themselves to its liberation from injustice, should be incapable of liberating themselves from their loyalty to an obsolete identity that has lost all meaning; that they should not rise above themselves and dissolve among the rest whose religion they have founded and who would be so close to them if they knew them better." [7]

When this attitude is internalized by the Jew himself, the result is the surrender to self-hate as represented by Pasternak's Mischa Gordon. How is it, Gordon asks himself, "that a human being with arms and legs, like everyone else, and with a language and way of life common to all the rest, could be so different—a being liked by so few and loved by no one? He could not understand how it was that if you were worse than other people you could not improve yourself by trying. What did it mean to be a Jew? What was the purpose of it? What was the reward or the justification of this unarmed challenge that brought nothing but grief?" [8]

To the question, Why be a Jew? Gordon could find no answer. For him assimilation would seem the only rational response. Gordon has decided that to remain a Jew is as irrational as are the cruelties perpetrated upon him, as irrational even as the traits attributed to him in order to condone the malice and sadism under which he suffers. Gordon thus represents the generation of exhausted Jewry no longer able to grapple with the historic mission of the Jew. Whereas the Jew has never been unaware of the absurdity of Jewish existence, he has for the most part resisted the temptation to escape absurdity by renouncing his tradition. Of course we have yet to see what it means to affirm tradition in the face of Auschwitz.

In the pre-Auschwitz world the Jewish record of transcendence was truly exemplary. Nevertheless, the temptation to surrender is perennial. "Oh let me hear no more of Jews and Judaism and of myself as a Jew," exclaims Alexandre Mordekhai Benillouche, the hero of Albert Memmi's autobiographical novel *The Pillar of Salt*. [9] For Memmi it appears that it is only because of their refusal to give up their separateness that Jews suffer in this world. And as long as they persist in clinging to their traditions Jews must pay for it with voluntary martyrdom. In short, to be a Jew is to suffer an unbearable burden: "The Jewish fate . . . is first of all one of misfortune. . . . Are there no happy Jews? I am tempted to answer: no. But let me be prudent and make myself clear: no, not *as Jews*. No, in truth, I know scarcely any Jew who rejoices in being one. There are Jews who, perhaps, are happy in spite of their Judaism. But because of it, in relation to it—no! Adjusting to it, eluding it, forgetting it, if one can. The moment you face it, the moment it arises, it inevitably becomes a strain, another shock, an honorary obligation if you insist, but in every way a burden." [10]

But why be that invalid called a Jew when you can be a man? This is the question that torments writers like Podhoretz, Memmi, and Pasternak. "Why," Memmi exclaims, "forsake so many splendid adventures to remain vanquished among the vanquished?" [11] It is in a similar spirit of self-hate that Mischa Gordon declares in a burst of near rage:

> Their national idea has forced them century after century to be a people and nothing but a people. . . . But in whose interests is this voluntary martyrdom? Who stands to gain by keeping it going? So that all these innocent old men and women and children, all these clever, kind, humane people should go on being mocked and beaten up throughout the centuries? . . . Why don't the intellectual leaders of the Jewish people ever get beyond facile Weltschmerz and irony? Why don't they . . . dismiss this army which is for ever . . . being massacred nobody knows for what? Why don't they say to them: "That's enough, stop now. Don't hold on to your identity, don't all get together in a crowd. Disperse. Be with all the rest"? [12]

THE CHALLENGE OF AUSCHWITZ

It is clear that for Jews who are concerned about their identity Auschwitz is the most decisive of all historical events. Like Nietzsche's death of God, "there never was a greater event," and on account of it "all who are born after it belong to a different history." But unlike Nietzsche's event, which ushered in the possibility of a higher history for humanity in general, Auschwitz appears as the eclipse of history—particularly for Jews, who were the victims not in spite of but because of the fact that they were Jews. After Auschwitz how is it possible to avoid the question, What does it mean to be a Jew? What is the meaning of Jewish history and tradition?

Emil Fackenheim reminds us in *Quest for Past and Future* that the essence of midrashic Judaism lies neither in an unchanging dogmatic universality imposed by tradition, nor in the unique immediacy of the individual construed as the sole measure.[13] It lies rather in an openness that listens and responds, works and waits, in a posture of receptiveness to the uniqueness of revelation experienced within the context of immediacy defined by tradition.

Of course Jews are free to seek their identities elsewhere than in revelation if they so choose. And such choices might well result from the very openness prescribed by the midrashic interpretation. To be a Jew is and remains the outcome of choice, which may be the choice to assume an essence as defined by revelation and tradition or else the choice to reject essences altogether. But even for those who choose their essence and identity in revelation and tradition, midrashic receptiveness or listening remains the source of its structure. Is this perhaps what Goethe meant when he wrote: "What from your fathers you receive as heir, earn in order to possess it"?[14]

Thus, if I understand Fackenheim and the midrashic interpretation correctly, that a Jew "listens" to his contemporary situation and predicament from within the context of an eighteenth-century ghetto in Eastern Europe, or from within the context of a twentieth-century post-Auschwitz world of suburban America, is the source of *uniqueness*. That Jews listen in their post-Auschwitz context of immediacy, as self-chosen descendants of those who have traveled the route from Mount Sinai to Auschwitz, is the source of *tradition*. The essence of Judaism thus emerges dialectically from the tension between immediacy and tradition—a resolution to be achieved in action as well as in thought.

How can such tensions be resolved? In any genuine resolution it must be possible to establish a measure of internal coherence. But what continuity, if any, can be found between the secular world of American Judaism, on the one hand, and tradition, on the other; or, between Auschwitz and tradition? In the course of confronting this challenge, Fackenheim addresses three specific questions:

1. Why a commitment to any religious truth?

2. Why a commitment to Judaism? and

3. How do Jews respond Jewishly in the here and now?

Or, to put it more specifically, How carry on the midrashic tradition into the twentieth century?

The gist of Fackenheim's response to the first two questions is that the very raising of the question is itself an event of Jewish significance. For, whether the questioner is explicitly aware of it or not, he raises his questions as a Jew questioning the grounds of his Jewish commitment. In short, the mere fact that such questions are taken seriously at all amounts to an affirmation of one's Jewishness.

The third question is in many respects the most challenging. Indeed, as Fackenheim puts it, the characteristic feature of the midrashic tradition, the tradition through which the Jew responds Jewishly to the here and now, is that Jewish thought, however firmly rooted in past revelatory events, has always remained open to present and future, and this openness includes vulnerability to radical surprise. He writes: "The Torah was given at Sinai, yet it is given whenever a man receives it, and a man must often hear the old commandments in new ways. There are times in history when evil can be explained as deserved punishment, others when no such explanation is possible—when divine power is, 'as it were,' suspended, and God himself suffers in exile. Such openness is necessary if history is to be serious." [15]

The test of this capacity for openness, according to Fackenheim, is nowhere greater than in the challenge of Auschwitz. Auschwitz is the scandal of evil for evil's sake, and Jews were the singled-out victims. The vulnerability to radical surprise that characterizes Jewish theology and Jewish existence lies precisely in the fact that Jews seeking their identity in tradition must be prepared to confront such dread events as Auschwitz.

What does it mean for a Jew to respond Jewishly to an event like Auschwitz? According to Fackenheim, the midrashic Jewish response takes the form not only of memory but of witness as well. For Jews who are committed to the midrashic interpretation, and who freely choose to inherit an obligation to the victims, not to remember would be a blasphemy; not to be a witness would be a betrayal.[16] At the same time, for a Jew to respond through memory and witness is to commit oneself to survival *as a Jew*—the full meaning of which must be determined through a *critical confrontation* with tradition.

But finally, to dedicate oneself to survival as a Jew in the age of Auschwitz is a *monumental act of faith,* not only in the messianic covenant, but in the rationality of history and the promise of reason to overcome evil. To be a Jew after Auschwitz is thus to confront the demons of Auschwitz and to bear witness against them in all their guises. It is to assert, as the basis of one's beliefs, the conviction that evil will not prevail and that human reason will play a role in ensuring its overthrow.

Auschwitz thus remembered can therefore be regarded, Fackenheim tells us, as nothing short of revelation. Through that revelation the Jew is commanded to survive as a Jew through memory and witness in order that Hitler may not be permitted a posthumous victory. Jews are forbidden also to despair of God and of the world as the domain of God lest the world be handed over to the forces of Auschwitz. For a Jew to break this commandment would be to do the unthinkable—to respond to Hitler by doing his work.[17]

The question remains, however, concerning what precisely it means to survive as a Jew. For Michael Lerner, the editor of *Tikkun,* what he hears when he listens to the Jewish tradition, whether before or after Auschwitz, is embodied in the Shema prayer: "Hear O Israel, YHVH (the force in the universe that makes possible human liberation and a breaking of the bonds of all the various forms of slavery) is Eloheynu (the creator of the universe, the organizer of the processes of nature), YHVH is one (that is, the totality of all being and all reality)." The governing force of the universe, writes Lerner, is the force that makes for the possibility of human liberation.

Moreover, because we have benefited from the workings of that power in history (that is, because we have gone from slavery in Egypt to self-governing freedom), we are under an obligation to testify to the possibility of human liberation from every form of slavery. Our religion embodies the memory of that struggle and witnesses the possibility of liberation. The weekly observance of Shabbat, the seasonal holidays, the prayers are all built around retelling the story and reminding us of its lessons.[18]

The most noble words in the Jewish tradition, Lerner continues, are spoken when most Jews are in synagogue: just before Yizkor (the memorial service for the dead) on Yom Kippur. On that occasion we read the chapter of the book of Isaiah in which the prophet denounces the Jews assembled for their own Yom Kippur feast, and reminds them what it means for Jews to bear witness. " 'Is this not the fast that I have chosen' thunders Isaiah in the voice of God, 'to feed the hungry, clothe the naked, or fight against oppression?' "[19]

To bear witness in this way would indeed result in denying Hitler a posthumous victory; although for Fackenheim more than this would be required if the full meaning of his midrashic openness to revelation after Auschwitz is to be considered. And for Fackenheim, this something more is the obligation to survive *as Jews* in order that the messianic promise of God to man be fulfilled.

IDENTITY AS THE OUTCOME OF IMMEDIACY AFTER REFLECTION

Fackenheim and Lerner are in agreement that whatever the response to Auschwitz it must, following Jewish tradition, take the form of a stubborn persistence in our Jewishness, and not an attempt to abandon or escape from it. But Fackenheim would argue that Lerner's emphasis on secular and human values—which is similar to what we find in the writings of George Steiner—does not succeed in capturing the paradox of God's presence in history and cannot, therefore, capture the essence of the meaning of Auschwitz. Nevertheless, Fackenheim can respect and enter into dialogue with the humanistic emphasis. What he will not attempt, however, is a dialogue with unauthentic Jews who use Auschwitz as an excuse for abandoning their commitments to Judaism. This does not mean that he expects authentic Jews to be totally unshaken in their faith. On the contrary, according to Fackenheim, the real test of faith in the post-Holocaust world comes only when the Jew risks self-exposure to secularism and secular-nihilism. Religious immediacy must expose itself to both the threat of the critical reflections of positivism (which reduces history to natural law and religious experience to psychology, thus dissipating God's historical presence in history) and historical nihilism (which uses Auschwitz as evidence of the futility of belief). For the authentic Jew, tradition and commitment can be affirmed only by stepping outside that tradition and commitment, thus calling it into question. Such a stance of faith was called by Kierkegaard "immediacy after reflection."

According to the dialectic implicit in "immediacy after reflection," as Fackenheim interprets it, the believer exposes his faith to criticism and brings himself into the midst of doubt and despair with respect to his formerly held beliefs. He then steps back once again and becomes critical of his criticism, with the result that he transcends immediacy only to be returned to his original beliefs transformed. Having suffered through the dialectic of criticism, the believer continues to participate in tradition and in the recovery of the primordial root experiences upon which Judaism is founded, but no longer in a religious immediacy that has never risked the consequences of stepping outside the traditional framework.

The dialectic of "immediacy after reflection" is thus not simply a stance of pure critical reflection that stands outside only and merely looks on. To expose oneself to immediacy after reflection is to risk the possibility of a *desacralization* of history and a total dissipation of belief in a divine presence, while yet remaining open to the possibility of a renewed commitment to whatever meaning and obligations are entailed by a critically inspired *resacralization* of history.[20] Auschwitz, even more so than the logic of scientific-secular rationalism, constitutes such a challenge to religious immediacy.

THE LOGIC OF MIDRASHIC JUDAISM

For Fackenheim the tradition from which Jews begin and to which they return following their encounter with immediacy after reflection is the tradition of the Midrash. The midrashic tradition takes the form of a stubborn persistence of Jewishness and not an attempt to abandon or escape from it.[21] The question to be faced is, "How is it possible and indeed necessary for the Jew of today to be a witness to the world?"[22] To this question the midrashic tradition provides at least the outline of an answer, an answer that takes the form of an affirmation of God's presence in history. But not only does the Midrash affirm God's presence in history, it suffers as well the contradictions inherent in that presence.

The essence of the midrashic tradition lies in the notion of what Fackenheim calls "the root experience," which is a direct experience of God's presence in history; an experience that may be compared with Hegel's notion of experiencing the "Real (or rational) in the Actual." Contrary to the midrashic affirmation, however, modern thought seems compelled to deny that presence. The study of nature reveals not God but blind natural laws, while the study of history reveals man at the mercy of his passions. In the words of the historian Carl Becker:

> Edit and interpret the conclusions of modern science as tenderly as we like, it is still quite impossible for us to regard man as the child of God for whom the earth was created as a temporary habitation. Rather must we regard him as little more than a chance deposit on the surface of the world, carelessly thrown up between two ice ages by the same forces that rust iron and ripen corn. . . . What is man that the electron should be mindful of him! Man is but a foundling in the cosmos, abandoned by the forces that created him. Unparented, unassisted, and undirected by omniscient or benevolent authority, he must fend for himself, and with the aid of his own limited intelligence find his way about in an indifferent universe.[23]

Since from the standpoint of secular humanism God must be expelled from history just as He is expelled from nature, the contemporary historian—to the extent that he seeks to rescue God from oblivion—would thus seem to have no option but to affirm at most the Providence of a God *transcending* both nature and history; a God who may somehow use nature and humanity in history, but who is Himself absent from history. In short, neither contemporary science nor theology seems able to assimilate the contradictions inherent in any serious attempt to affirm God's presence in history.

As we already have acknowledged, the most challenging of these contradictions is the Holocaust, whose symbol is Auschwitz. If it is difficult to comprehend the possibility of a midrashic encounter with the ordinary history of evil, it seems virtually incomprehensible how there could be "immediacy after reflection" on Auschwitz, unless we are to regard Auschwitz as not simply a challenge to such root experiences as the revelation at Sinai and the Exodus but as itself a root experience. This is precisely what Fackenheim proposes. Following Elie Wiesel's suggestion that the Holocaust may be compared with Sinai in revelatory significance, Fackenheim, with a boldness and daring unparalleled, I suggest, in the history of recent theology, turns his ear to the Holocaust and listens. And what he hears, through the reenactment of that root experience in accordance with midrashic tradition, is what he refers to as "the Commanding Voice of Auschwitz." Thus is revealed the 614th commandment, according to which the authentic Jew of today is forbidden to hand Hitler yet another posthumous victory.

> Jews are forbidden to hand Hitler posthumous victories. They are commanded to survive as Jews, lest the Jewish people perish. They are commanded to remember the victims of Auschwitz lest their memory perish. They are forbidden to despair of man and his world, and to escape into either cynicism or otherworldliness, lest they cooperate in delivering the world over to the forces of Auschwitz. Finally, they are forbidden to despair of the God of Israel, lest Judaism perish. A secularist Jew cannot make himself believe by a mere act of will, nor can he be commanded to do so.... And a religious Jew who has stayed with his God may be forced into new, possibly revolutionary relationships with Him. One possibility, however, is wholly unthinkable. A Jew may not respond to Hitler's attempt to destroy Judaism by himself cooperating in its destruction.[24]

It may appear that Fackenheim's conception of the revelatory significance of Auschwitz may be compared with Hegel's conception of History as "the slaughter-bench at which the happiness of peoples, the wisdom of States, and the virtue of individuals have been victimized"; which for Hegel provokes the question, "To what principle, to what final aim have these enormous sacrifices been offered?"[25] The difference, of course, between Hegel's "cunning of reason" and Fackenheim's conception of the revelatory significance of Auschwitz is that, whereas for Hegel there is a final purpose at the end of history, whose realization in history is fully rational, Fackenheim's Auschwitz reveals no such rationality. And yet, Fackenheim argues, notwithstanding the absence of rationality and purposefulness in this dread event, Jews are commanded not to abandon their faith in either human reason as an instrument of salvation or God's presence in history as a condition of rediscovering tradition.

But how is such a commandment to be obeyed in a post-Auschwitz world? If the astonishment that accompanies the revelation at Sinai is difficult to bear, what can be said of the astonishment that accompanies the revelation at Auschwitz? The astonishment is made all the greater by the fact that whereas at Sinai the Jew hears the commanding voice of a God who is present, at Auschwitz he hears—contrary to Hegel—the commanding voice of a God who is not present. That is to say, at Auschwitz he hears a commanding voice at the same time that he experiences the absence of God. The commanding voice of God at Auschwitz is the voice of a God in exile. Is such a notion merely the result of madness, the madness of a midrashic tradition tortured by paradox after paradox until it finally breaks down altogether? Is this perhaps the real legacy of Auschwitz, that in their attempt to preserve the authenticity of midrashic tradition the best minds of our generation have been destroyed by madness?

Perhaps it is a madness of sorts to think this way, and to suggest the possibility that even in Auschwitz there is revelation. But if so, perhaps it is a madness without which we humans cannot continue to be human. As the Enlightenment philosopher and poet Gotthold Ephraim Lessing once put it, "He who does not lose his mind over some things has no mind to lose." Paradoxical as it may seem, the fact remains that never have Jews been so aware of what it means to be Jewish than when they humble themselves before the commanding voice of Auschwitz. For by heeding that commandment, in the only way it can be heeded, with imagination, courage, and creativity, we Jews who come after not only preserve the memory of the dead, and honor the presence of those who survived, but we dignify and consecrate that death in the most sublime manner possible; by providing future generations with abiding astonishment at the manner in which we have listened to and have heeded that commandment. And what is affirmed through the memory of Auschwitz is not the demonic madness that produced it, but the divine madness of our response to it.

Whenever one attempts to meditate along such difficult paths there is always a temptation to seek out parables. In this connection I am reminded of a story by Philip Roth that in its own way expresses the madness of midrashic stubbornness in the face of absurdity. It is called "Eli the Fanatic."[26]

The story takes place in the middle-class community of Woodenton, typical of so many American suburbs, and outstanding for the fact that Jews and Gentiles live side by side in harmonious togetherness. But the day arrives when the Jewish community is suddenly confronted by the specter of its past—symbolized by the opening of a Yeshiva for displaced children whose parents had perished in Hitler's gas chambers. The most disturbing spectacle of all was the sight of a bearded Hassidic Jew, dressed in a black suit and wearing a black hat, walking down the main street of Woodenton. The more "responsible" members of the community, who regard themselves as the vanguard of the newly assimilated American Jew, engage a lawyer, Eli Peck, and instruct him to secure the immediate and total removal of the Yeshiva, and especially the man with the hat. The hat and the suit soon become the primary symbol of the whole problem. Among the complaints, the following seemed particularly disturbing: "Someday," warns Harry Shaw, "it's going to be a hundred little kids with little *yarmulkehs* chanting their Hebrew lessons on Coach House Road." "Goddam fanatics," exclaims another irate member of the community. "This is the twentieth century, Eli. Now it's the guy with the hat. Pretty soon all the little Yeshiva boys'll be spilling down into town. Next thing they'll be after our daughters." And finally, Eli Peck says to himself, as he tries to make sense of the whole business, "if that Guy would take off that crazy hat . . . I know it's what eats them. If he'd just take off that crazy hat everything would be all right."[27]

Eli tries to persuade the Yeshiva to relocate, but without success. When it becomes clear that the Yeshiva cannot be moved—a symbol of the historic fact that Jews have refused to be exterminated—the officials decide to be "tolerant" and "liberal," and they extend an invitation to the director of the Yeshiva to assimilate. The conditions under which their continued presence will be tolerated are stated in a letter that Eli presents to Mr. Tzuref, the director of the Yeshiva, on behalf of the assimilated community of Woodenton. The letter reads in part as follows:

> Dear Mr. Tzuref:
> Our meeting this evening seems to me inconclusive. I don't think there's any reason for us not to be able to come up with some sort of compromise that will satisfy the Jewish community of Woodenton and the Yeshiva and yourself. It seems to me that what most disturbs my neighbours are the visits to town

by the gentleman in the black hat, suit, etc. Woodenton is a progressive suburban community whose members, both Jewish and Gentile, are anxious that their families live in comfort and beauty and serenity. This is, after all, the twentieth century, and we do not think it too much to ask that the members of our community dress in a manner appropriate to the time and place.

Woodenton, as you may not know, has long been the home of well to do Protestants. It is only since the war that Jews have been able to buy property here, and for Jews and Gentiles to live beside each other in amity. For this adjustment to be made, both Jews and Gentiles alike have had to give up some of their more extreme practices in order not to threaten or offend the other. Certainly such amity is to be desired. Perhaps if such conditions had existed in prewar Europe, the persecution of the Jewish people, of which you and those 18 children have been victims, could not have been carried out with such success—in fact, might not have been carried out at all.[28]

The rest of the letter states the conditions under which the Yeshiva will be allowed to remain in Woodenton without further complaints from the Jewish community. Two days after delivering his letter Eli received his reply; in one sentence, which sums up the whole matter and speaks for itself without the need for further comment.

Dear Mr. Peck:
The suit the gentleman wears is all he's got.
Sincerely,
Leo Tzuref.[29]

Fackenheim's 614th commandment and Leo Tzuref's reply to Eli Peck are in keeping with the traditional midrashic obligation for Jews to survive in order that the messianic promise of God to man will be fulfilled. It commands that Jews survive not simply by following tradition blindly and passively but by critically reenacting the root experiences of Judaism in the context of the Jew's contemporary situation—which for us is a post-Auschwitz world. It is also in keeping with the messianic obligation to survive through creativity. The essence of this dimension of messianism is contained, I suggest, in Martin Buber's interpretation of the teachings of the B'al Shem Tov, the founder of Hassidism. According to Buber, the Ba'al Shem Tov explained the meaning of man's being created in the image of God this way: "The Man of true piety takes unto himself the quality of fervour, for he is hallowed and become like the Holy one, blessed be He, when He created His world."[30] Responding to this passage, Buber writes: "It was then that I experienced the Hassidic soul. The primarily Jewish reality opened to me, flowering to newly conscious expression in the darkness of exile: man's being created in the image of God I grasped as deed, as becoming, as task. And primarily Jewish reality was a primal human reality: the content of human religiousness opened to me there."[31]

From Hassidism, then, Buber learned to find the essence of religion in creativity. As God made man so man must remake the world as well as himself. The essence of piety is creativity, not simply passive submission to inevitability. Nor does creativity mean secular success. Buber's Hassidic creativity embraces the two central areas of Jewish concern, which are, man's duties to God and man's duties to himself. Only from these two expressions of love can despair be transcended. Hassidic creativity is also Promethean, requiring that the skills and knowledge by means of which mankind elevates itself above the rest of God's creation and exercises dominion over nature be used thoughtfully (as suggested by the literal meaning of the Greek words *pro-mathein*) rather than for the mere sake of the power that they make possible.

Following the spirit inherent in the Ba'al Shem Tov's affirmation of Judaism, Fackenheim's 614th commandment can be restated as follows. Auschwitz was an attempt to exterminate Jews. As such it was the symbol of destruction, the end of creation. It was also the glorification of the Faustian intoxication with power and technology, which leads inevitably to a pornographic exercise of power. Therefore, midrashic stubbornness commands not only survival, but survival through creativity and love, and survival by means of the logic of justice rather than of power and domination. Even though all the forces of technology and power were turned against them, Jews have shown themselves to be greater than the forces that sought to destroy them because they comprehend the advantage that power has over innocence. To comprehend and accept the finitude of man is a cause of despair. Yet amid that despair there is joy; the joy of realizing that in spite of the advantage that the forces of evil have over innocence, the human person yet has the freedom to create.

Such a freedom expresses itself on the one hand through the collective sharing of memory and on the other hand through "caring" as opposed to domination. It is through memory and creativity that the survivors of Auschwitz and those of us fortunate enough not to have been incarcerated are able to overcome our guilt and assume instead a shared responsibility to enable the dead to survive through us; in which case, what we do with our lives is no longer simply a matter of individual discretion.[32] If the post-Holocaust world is now characterized by a domination of Faust over Prometheus, then Jews are dedicated to the restoration of the rationality of "caring," or, of listening with the heart, as Buber puts it. The true language of celebration, in response to openness to Being, is not the kind of calculative cleverness or functional rationality that expresses itself in a fascination for "technique," "final solutions," and the organization of means to realize goals regardless of their moral worth. It is rather a rationality in the service of "Mitzvah" and "Simcha."

According to the dialectic of "immediacy after reflection," the challenge of Auschwitz is a test not only of faith but of reason as well. To confront and respond to Auschwitz is thus to confront and respond to the corrupt rationality that it symbolizes and that still infects every aspect of our culture. And this means not only listening to the 614th commandment in the midst of abiding astonishment, which is the source of its *uniqueness* as an event in Jewish history, but to confront the inherent crisis of rationality, which is the source of its *universality*. Midrashic stubbornness begins with a refusal to be terrorized by Auschwitz into adopting a posture of apocalyptic despair and includes as well a refusal to be co-opted by the logic of domination, which is inherently irrational.

But such a protest must begin with a serious effort at social diagnosis. The midrashic response to Auschwitz is not only an affirmation of messianic faith but a renewed attempt to understand the dialectics and dynamics of the relationship between human nature and society. What is it about the human condition that allows events like Auschwitz to occur? The full range of questions to be addressed by contemporary Jews in our mutual attempt at a social diagnosis are well stated by Steven Schwartzchild in his introduction to the symposium "Jewish Values in the Post-Holocaust Future":

> What new knowledge of God has arisen out of the chimneys of Auschwitz? What do we know about man that we did not know before he created Maidanek? By what values shall we try to live that have been seared into our flesh at Bergen-Belsen? What new Jewish actions have been commanded by the loudspeakers in Buchenwald? What new words have been pressed on our lips by the whips and boots of Theresienstadt? In short, what will the world of tomorrow have to look like which we now know to be, to be able to be, and to have been what Rousset called *l'univers concentrationnaire?* . . . Knowing what we do, having become

what we are, seeing the world as it is—by what values are we to act among ourselves and in relationship to the world at large in our future?[33]

It has been my contention throughout that the contemporary authentic Jew speaks of God through the celebration of an existence that refuses to allow itself to be determined by an essence dictated by Auschwitz, and refuses, therefore, to conform either to the logic of domination or to the logic of nihilism. According to the logic of the Midrash, as represented by Fackenheim, a God who is present in history must be present differently than if He were present in the form of pure transcendence. To be present historically means to be subject to the conditions of historicity. This means that God manifests himself differently according to the exigencies of the historical moment. This is the ground of pluralism and thus commands respect for pluralism. I am not speaking here of the kind of radical, idolatrous pluralism that is merely a pluralism of sheer diversity without unity and for which anything goes. I am speaking rather of a pluralism compatible with a belief in objectivity and truth. In order to confront, from the outset, the temptation to believe in the many gods of idolatrous pluralism, the Midrash teaches that while a God manifest in history manifests Himself differently—as mighty hero doing battle, as in the case of the Red Sea, as old man full of mercy, as at Sinai—He is nevertheless manifest in each moment as the one Sole Power of every moment. But—and this is the crucial insight asserted by midrashic logic—the universality of the Sole Power manifested in a unique saving event such as the Exodus demands a correspondingly universal human recognition of its universality, thus inspiring a poetic expression of the universal abolition of pluralism in the form of idolatry: *Shema Yisrael Adonoi Eloheynu Adonoi Echod.* And so it is said, "Who is like unto thee, O' Lord, among the Gods."[34]

Fackenheim points out that when taken as a whole the Midrashic interpretation exposes serious contradictions. The first contradiction is suggested by the fact that a God who, by Himself, was, is, and shall be, yet must be present differently if His presence is to be within history. What is more, the God who is Lord of history was, is, and shall be, sovereign as Sole Power. Yet even in a supreme (albeit premessianic) manifestation of His power, He stands in need of human glorification; and the fact that this glorification is momentarily given by all the nations reveals more poignantly the paradox of a subsequent relapse into pluralistic idolatry by all nations, Israel herself included. Confronting this contradiction and commenting upon the verse, "I will glorify Him,"[35] Rabbi Yishmael asks: "And is it possible for a man of flesh and blood to add to the glory of his creator."[36] For *a parte subjecti,* unless divine presence requires human recognition, man loses all significance and his obedience would seem at best purely abstract; while *a parte objecti,* the power of the divine would seem to depend upon His transcendence—a condition that does not coincide with traditional belief in divine-historical presence.

On the other hand, if human glorification and recognition is required, then even a saving presence, not to speak of a commanding presence, is incomplete without it. The question thus persists: How can human praise and recognition add to the divine glory and yet human failure to give praise not diminish it? Or, how can human failure weaken the power on high? "Ye are my witnesses, saith the Lord, and I am God."[37] According to Midrashic tradition this may be interpreted as meaning: "when ye are my witnesses, I am God, and when ye are not My witnesses, I am, as it were, not God." Or, "When the Israelites do God's will, they add to the power of God on high. When the Israelites do not do God's will, they, as it were, weaken the great power of God."[38]

But once again the question arises, how is human recognition and the freedom thus presupposed to be reconciled with divine power that is affirmed through recognition? As we already have noted, a saving presence requires recognition for a divine act, which conceivably if only momentarily overwhelms human freedom. The paradox is that to affirm the glory of God in this context, which *a parte subjecti* presupposes freedom, comprises as well an affirmation of human powerlessness. At the same time, the commanding presence affirmed requires not simple recognition but *action,* in which case, rather than freedom being overwhelmed by divine presence it must be affirmed. And what is affirmed is thus not simply the freedom to affirm but the freedom and indeed necessity to act. This is how it is both possible and necessary for the Jew to be a witness to the world and why it is necessary, to return to Philip Roth's story, that Jews resist all attempts to force them to take off the black hat.

The paradox of God's presence in history thus lies in the fact that He is both Sole Power and yet dependent upon human recognition, that He both acknowledges man's powerlessness yet affirms human freedom. Fackenheim argues that the contradictions between divine power and human freedom are not resolved, but only expressed. What is clear, however, is that unless obedience and disobedience, recognition or nonrecognition, man's exercise or escape from freedom, made a difference, Divinity could not be historically present as commanding; and unless there was at least some perceptual evidence of salvation, God could not be present as saving.

It may not be possible to *account* for these conditions; yet they must be presupposed. And because they remain unresolved there is the need for a final consummation in the future in the form of a messianic age that can only be achieved by listening to and accepting the injunction of the commanding voice of Auschwitz, and by accepting it in the context of the obligation to perform not only the *mitzvahs* commanded by divine law, but the social diagnosis that alone makes possible the performance of those *mitzvahs* through which the messianic promise will be realized. For this reason, as Fackenheim has insisted, Jews must remember Auschwitz and be its witness to the world. For, to repeat the point already made, not to remember would be blasphemy; not to be a witness would be a betrayal.[39]

Just as midrashic stubbornness commands recognition of divine presence in spite of the fragmentariness of theological speculation, so Jewish social and personal existence is commanded to live by trust, rather than mere argument. That the universe is silent with respect to the resolution of paradox and mystery is no excuse for skeptical paralysis or cynical nihilism. Jewish existence commands an affirmation of values in the midst of tension and despair. What is important, however, is that we continue to exist without illusions. To say, in keeping with midrashic logic, that God's power is diminished by human failure to respond through "caring" is to emphasize the importance of not confusing man's witness through creativity with mere technological progress or even culture. When secular humanists such as George Steiner confront Auschwitz as a failure of culture to protect us from barbarism, their reflections parallel the Jewish theologian's confrontation of the absence of God at Auschwitz.[40] Like the theologian, Steiner focuses attention on the fundamental *hubris* of Western man's idolatry of identifying God's presence as power, technology, technique, and mastery—the very Faustian, satanic temptations prefigured in the myth of Satan. And like the theologian, Steiner too emerges from his encounter with Auschwitz only to reaffirm in his "immediacy after reflection" the fundamental values of humanity so utterly violated by the horrors of Auschwitz.

> The value of being a Jew after Auschwitz is a tremendous one. . . . [It] is the value of being a man who has experienced to the utmost the bestiality of man. We have very few surprises ahead of us. We know in our marrow what men can become when they yield their reason to a flag and put their feet in boots. The value of being a Jew is to try to make truth one's locale and free inquiry one's native tongue. . . . The values of . . . humanity belong

to all men. . . . But the Jew, I think, may have the uncomfortable obligation and privilege of practicing them right now pretty
constantly and at whatever price of discomfort.[41]

What we are asked to remember, then, through the memory of Auschwitz, are not just the idols of the false and corrupt culture in whose name
Jews were slaughtered, but the Jewish soul, as expressed in creativity and
caring. And when we remember the victims of Auschwitz, we pay tribute
not to the glory of man's temple of worldly achievements but to humanity's
capacity to grow through the memory of its past, as well as to the practice of the values for the sake of which we have been commanded to bear
witness.

CONCLUSION

Any meditation upon Auschwitz must be undertaken in a mood of humility
as well as solemnity. I frankly doubt whether the rules normally associated
with the tradition of academic disputation apply to discussions of Auschwitz. Just as Auschwitz is itself an episode in the history of obscenity, so
the attempt to debate and dispute its significance risks becoming an expression of academic pornography. One cannot debate Auschwitz in the
manner in which philosophers are accustomed to debate whether there are
synthetic a priori truths, or whether it is possible to argue from the "is" to
the "ought." The truth about Auschwitz is not a mere prize to be awarded
at the end of a successful competition. The radical uniqueness of Auschwitz lies as much in its refusal to be comprehended in terms of the normal
categories of scientific inquiry as in its effects on the lives of its victims.
Perhaps all that can be said is that each person suffers the event as if it were
part of one's own personal history and then chooses whether to respond
through affirmation in the form of both memory and deed.

The uniqueness of Auschwitz and "the final solution" lies also in its
radical absurdity; in the fact that it is pure, demonic, evil, evil for evil's
sake. This was not evil committed, as it so often is, for the sake of power,
wealth, pleasure, self-interest, or even revenge; although the legitimation
of these values by the culture in which they operated created an atmo-
sphere in which "the final solution" could be more easily implemented. The
structure of evil at Auschwitz thus appears to defy comprehension through
the mediation of any kind of rationale. To face such evil and respond to
it is therefore the greatest test the Jew has ever had to endure. In the case
of all other evils that have been visited upon us throughout history, there

had been at least a reason and an explanation. And it was therefore both possible and reasonable to believe that once the conditions that nourished these reasons were eliminated then evil would disappear as well. But such hopes fled together with faith up the chimneys of Auschwitz.

Faced with the absurdity of Auschwitz can we expect our response to it to be any less absurd? Some, as we have seen, have responded by arguing that after Auschwitz either Jews should give up their Jewishness or else should no longer have children. But this is not an authentic response, because it uses Auschwitz as an excuse to betray not only the victims but the Jewish tradition itself. Yet after Auschwitz even such judgments, no matter how justified, must be made with compassion.

Others have responded by insisting that the best we can do is continue to remember and retell the tale. But consider how poor and inadequate is the language of man when confronted by the horror of Auschwitz. We remember yet we cannot speak, for the essence of Auschwitz—precisely what it is that makes it radically unique—escapes capture by language. Perhaps the only authentic language for expressing the memory of that essence is the language of silence. The Kotzker Rebbe said: "the Oral Torah Tradition that we know is not the real one; the true Torah *she-b'al peh* remained oral and secret."[42]

The poet Kenneth Rexroth once wrote: "Against the ruin of the world there is only one defense, the creative act."[43] In the end this seems to me to be the most that can be expected of those who remember but cannot explain or apologize for what has happened in the past. For me personally, what is decisive in my renewal of the covenant is my determination to live humanly in the world as creatively as I can and refuse to abandon my Jewishness—which consists of a continuous reenactment and affirmation of tradition—no matter how inconvenient. And, whereas survival might once have been regarded as without meaning, in the age of Auschwitz a Jewish commitment to survival is in itself a monumental act of creativity and courage, as well as a monumental, albeit, fragmentary, act of faith. Emil Fackenheim writes:

> Even to do no more than remain a Jew after Auschwitz is to confront the demons of Auschwitz in all their guises, and to bear witness against them. It is to believe that these demons cannot, will not, and must not prevail, and to stake on that belief one's own life and the lives of one's children, and of one's children's children. To be a Jew after Auschwitz is to have wrested hope for the Jew and for the world—from the abyss of total despair. In the

words of a speaker at a recent gathering of Bergen-Belsen survivors, the Jew after Auschwitz has a second Shema Yisrael: no
second Auschwitz, no second Bergen-Belsen, no second Buchen-
wald—anywhere in the world, for anyone in the world.[44]

The commanding voice at Auschwitz thus decrees that Jews may not
respond to Hitler's attempt to destroy totally Judaism by themselves co-
operating in that destruction. In ancient times, the unthinkable Jewish sin
was idolatry. Today, it is to respond to Hitler by doing his work. To this
idolatry Jews in the post-Auschwitz world respond by reaffirming that ancient tradition whereby Jews bind themselves to one another and to the
past through the rituals of commemoration. As Emil Fackenheim reminds
us, foremost among those rituals is the Yizkor, and to be a Jew is thus to be
part of a community woven by memory—the memory whose knots are tied
up by the Yizkor, by the continuity that is summed up in the holy words:
Yizkor Elohim nishman aboh mori—may God remember the name of . . .
Nor can such words be recited, to repeat Michael Lerner's point, without
remembering also the previously cited words of Isaiah, reminding us what
it means to bear witness both to the covenant and to the memory of the
dead: "feed the hungry," "clothe the naked," "fight against oppression!"

NOTES

1. Robert Alter, "The Apocalyptic Temper of Our Time," *Commentary,* June
1966.

2. Ibid., 66.

3. On this point, see Richard H. Popkin's contribution to the symposium "Jewish Values in the Post-Holocaust Future," *Judaism* (Summer 1967): 273–76. Popkin
refers to the sixteenth-century Jewish tradition of presenting catastrophe as the
catalyst that would eventually bring about the triumph of Judaism.

4. Cited by Emil Fackenheim in *God's Presence in History* (New York: New
York University Press, 1970), 67.

5. Ibid., 6.

6. Norman Podhoretz, "My Negro Problem and Yours," *Commentary,* February 1963, 101.

7. Boris Pasternak, *Dr. Zhivago,* translated by Max Hayward and Manya
Harari (London: Collins and Harvill Press, 1958), 22.

8. Ibid.

9. Albert Memmi, *The Pillar of Salt,* translated by Edouard Roditi (New York:
Orion Press, 1962). Cf. also Albert Memmi, "Does the Jew Exist?" *Commentary,*
November 1966; and *The Liberation of the Jew,* translated by Judy Hyun (New
York: Orion Press, 1966).

10. Albert Memmi, *Portrait of a Jew,* translated by Elizabeth Abbot (London: Eyre & Spottiswoode, 1963), 21.

11. Memmi, *Liberation,* 19.

12. Pasternak, *Dr. Zhivago,* 117–18.

13. Emil Fackenheim, *Quest for Past and Future* (Boston: Beacon Press, 1970).

14. Goethe, *Faust,* pt. 1, lines 682–83.

15. Fackenheim, *Quest for Past,* 17.

16. Ibid., 18.

17. Ibid., 20.

18. Michael Lerner, ed., *Tikkun,* 5, no. 6 (1990): 6.

19. Ibid., 7.

20. Fackenheim, *God's Presence,* 49.

21. Ibid., 8; Fackenheim, "Jewish Values," 269.

22. Fackenheim, *God's Presence,* 8; and *Quest for Past,* 4.

23. Carl Becker, *The Heavenly City of the Eighteenth Century Philosophers* (New Haven, Conn.: Yale University Press, 1932), 14–15. Cf. also Bertrand Russell: "That man is the product of causes which had no prevision of the end they were achieving; that his origins, his growth, his hopes and fears, his loves and his beliefs, are but the outcome of accidental collocations of atoms; that no fire, no heroism, no intensity of thought and feeling, can preserve an individual life beyond the grave; that all the labors of the ages, all the devotion, all the inspiration, all the noonday brightness of human genius, are destined to extinction in the vast death of the solar system, and that the whole temple of man's achievements must inevitably be buried beneath the debris of a universe in ruins—all these things, if not quite beyond dispute, are yet so nearly certain, that no philosophy which rejects them can hope to stand. Only within the scaffolding of these truths, only on the firm foundation of unyielding despair, can the soul's habitation be safely built." "A Free Man's Worship," 1902, in *Mysticism and Logic* (New York: Anchor Books, 1957), 14–15.

24. Fackenheim, *God's Presence,* 84. Cf. also Fackenheim, "Jewish Values," 272–73; and "Jewish Faith and the Holocaust," *Commentary,* August 1968.

25. Hegel, *The Philosophy of History,* translated by J. Sibree (New York: Dover, 1956), introduction, 21.

26. Philip Roth, in *Goodbye Columbus* (London: Gorgi Books, 1964, 1973).

27. Ibid., 185–87.

28. Ibid., 189.

29. Ibid., 190.

30. Martin Buber, *Hassidism and Modern Man* (New York: Harper Torch books, 1958), 185.

31. Ibid.

32. Cf. Adele Weisman, *Memoirs of a Book Molesting Childhood* (Toronto: Oxford University Press, 1987) 49.

33. Steven Schwartzchild, in the symposium "Jewish Values," 268.

34. Exod. 15:11; cf., also, *Mekilta de-Rabbi Ishmael,* edited by J. Z. Lauterbach (Philadelphia: Jewish Publication of America, 1933), 2:24ff.

35. Exod. 15:2.

36. *Mekilta de-Rabbi Ishmael,* 2:25–26.

37. Isa. 43:10–12.

38. Fackenheim, *God's Presence,* 23.

39. Fackenheim, *Quest for Past,* 18.

40. See Interview with George Steiner, *Psychology Today,* February 1973, 57; and George Steiner, "Jewish Values," 276–81.

41. Steiner, "Jewish Values," 280–81.

42. Cited by Eli Wiesel in the symposium "Jewish Values," 284.

43. Kenneth Rexroth, "Disengagement: The Art of the Beat Generation," in *The Beat Generation and the Angry Young Men,* edited by Gene Feldman and Max Fartenberg (New York: Dell, 1959), 352.

44. Fackenheim, "Jewish Faith," 32.

10

CHARACTERIZING THE EVIL OF AMERICAN SLAVERY AND THE HOLOCAUST

Laurence Thomas

AMERICAN slavery and the Holocaust were fundamentally different.[1] They were such radically dissimilar institutions that no sense whatsoever can be made of the view that one was more evil than the other.[2] I begin by discussing the two institutions from the standpoint of coercion: the Holocaust was coercive in a way that slavery was not. Then I take up natal alienation, which has to do with having no historical moorings: American slavery was natally alienating, whereas the Holocaust was not. Further, I offer an account of the conception that each institution had of its victims: the Jew was considered irredeemably evil, whereas the black was considered a moral simpleton. Along the way, I consider such important issues as the evil of death itself and the difference between disdain and hate.

From the outset, however, a caveat is in order. Discussions about the Holocaust, during which at least six million Jews were killed, and American slavery, which was responsible for the deaths of approximately twenty million blacks (during the slave trade), become contests in which evil is matched for evil—especially in the light of the heightened tension between Jews and blacks nowadays. But if, as I believe, we have two radically different forms of evil here, then there are evils in the Holocaust that have no parallel in slavery, and conversely. And this truth does not make either any less a horrendous form of evil. It is most unfortunate that our endeavor to understand the Holocaust and American slavery should be clouded by what is surely a most pernicious form of competitive ideology of which no good can possibly come, namely, the view that the evil that one group has suffered is somehow diminished unless the evil visited upon it can be shown to be equal or parallel in all respects to the evil visited upon the other group. An institution need not be evil in any and all ways in order to be profoundly evil. American slavery and the Holocaust were each profoundly evil in their own ways.

The person left paraplegic by a drunken driver and the person left whole but without family by the same drunken driver have both suffered in such radically different ways that it would be foolish, pointless, and just plain wrong for either to insist upon having suffered the most, as if this judgment were indispensable to recognizing the depth of the suffering of either. It is in this spirit that I write about the Holocaust and American slavery.

A final comment: The account that follows is not meant to be an indictment of every German who lived under the Nazi regime or every white who lived in the United States during slavery. It is manifestly false that every such German or American white viewed Jews and blacks, respectively, in any or all of the ways indicated below. Further, in some instances, at least, there was undoubtedly ambivalence on the part of those whose behavior was quite morally reproachable. I hardly wish to deny any of this. Instead, I am interested in capturing the kinds of considerations that were part of the horrendous moral climate of the two oppressive institutions under discussion, although these considerations—as in any moral climate—were embraced to varying degrees by the members of the societies in question.

THE COERCIVE FACTOR

In *The Concept of Law,* H.L.A. Hart conclusively demonstrates that, contra John Austin (*The Province of Jurisprudence Determined*), a legal system does not reduce to simply a set of commands backed up by threats.[3] He distinguishes between the external point of view and the internal point of view, and maintains that essential to the existence of any legal system is that a substantial number of its constituents have the internal point of view toward it: that is, they obey the laws of the legal system because they see such laws as rightly binding upon them. If a substantial number of constituents fail to have the internal point of view, but have only the external point of view, then on Hart's view what we have instead is an extraordinarily coercive system. There can be no doubt that Nazi Germany and American slavery were both coercive institutions. Even so, on this score we have a most important difference between them.

It is wildly implausible to suppose that Jews during the Holocaust had anything remotely resembling the internal point of view toward the extremely anti-Semitic laws of Nazi Germany calling for the death of the

Jews. The Nazis were never under the illusion, nor was it ever remotely their hope, that the Jews would come to see the genocide that the Nazi state was imposing upon them as something to which they should rightly submit. And, of course, the Jews did not come to see the genocide imposed upon them in this way. More generally, there is no respect in which Jews can be said to have extolled the "virtues" of the Holocaust. To be sure, it seems evident that some Jews regarded the Holocaust as in some way a profound judgment of God upon the Jews. But to so view the Holocaust is not at all to look favorably upon any aspect of it—for even the wicked can be pawns in the hands of God—but instead to understand its significance and the possibility of its occurrence in a certain light. The Holocaust was an entirely coercive institution. And it was seen as such by the Jews. The genocide of the Jews was the aim of the Holocaust; and this evil institution was designed to succeed in the complete absence of any cooperation with and trusting of Jews by the Nazis. The moral climate of the Holocaust was intended to insure compliance by destroying the very will of its victims to resist their deaths.

Needless to say, among Jews who had converted to Christianity there were some who saw the Holocaust as giving Jews their just deserts. The remarks in the preceding paragraph, however, are meant to refer to individuals of Jewish birth who identified with being Jewish, and not those so born who explicitly and completely rejected their Jewish origins by converting to Christianity.

More important, no doubt, there were the actions of the leaders of the Jewish councils. It might seem to some that there was a measure of cooperation among the Jewish leaders in selecting individual Jews from the community for Nazi purposes. Allowing that there was such cooperation,[4] the point that I have been concerned to make stands. The success of the Holocaust was hardly contingent upon the cooperation of the Jews. And even if Jews passively walked into the gas chambers, it does not follow from this that they were partners in their own deaths. To lack the will to resist is not thereby to cooperate.

Now, while American slavery was indisputably a coercive institution, slavery being what it is, slavery cannot be coercive in the way that the Holocaust was; on the contrary, slavery works best—that is, it is most stable as an institution—precisely when slaves believe, at least to some extent, that they are rightly subordinate to the will of slave masters. I take this to be a conceptual point. American slavery, as we understand it, simply could not have existed had slaves acted only on pain of death. There was cooperation and trust between blacks and whites, as well as feelings of affection, goodwill, and loyalty. What is more, significant numbers of slaves believed that there were right and wrong—good and bad—ways for slave masters to treat blacks as slaves.[5] That is, normative assessments of the role of slave master were made from the internal point of view of the institution of slavery—or what was very nearly that. Indeed, slaves even were able to see themselves as deserving of some instances of punishment. The sentiments just mentioned, which to varying degrees obtained on the part of blacks and whites toward one another, could have done so only if, to some extent at least, blacks as well as whites viewed slavery from the internal point of view—which is not to maintain that every slave viewed slavery from the internal point of view. None of this makes slavery any less of an evil institution. The evil of an institution is not in any way diminished just because it is to some degree successful in bringing it about that people cooperate in their own victimization.

Consider, for instance, the role of the black nanny. This role simply cannot be understood from an entirely coercive point of view. No role could be more incompatible with pure coercion. One wants the person who cares for one's children to do so with concern for the well-being of the children and, indeed, with affection for them. One wants the person to take a measure of pride in the flourishing of one's children. It must be assumed that things were no different with slaveholders. And there is the simple truth that these favorable attitudes cannot be produced by coercion. Slaveholders no doubt wanted slaves to perform all their tasks with such favorable attitudes toward them. But these attitudes are not thought to be an essential ingredient in the production of such finished products as a well-kept field or floor, say; whereas these attitudes are thought to be part of what proper child care involves. The role of nanny could not have existed had some blacks not been trustworthy caretakers of the children of whites; and this blacks could not have been in the absence of an internal point of view toward the role of nanny.

Naturally, the internal point of view is not an all-or-nothing matter. Many slaves were not viewed as trustworthy. Nor do I claim that black women who were nannies were completely content with their role, or that they never harbored any ill will toward their owners. And so on. And while I do not for a moment want to suggest that black women took such delight in caring for white children that they gave no thought to the conditions of slavery, it is important to realize that such besottedness is not required in order to allow that black women experienced feelings of affection, and so forth, for the white children in their charge. After all, black slaves did not subscribe to a conception of whites that would have been cognitively incompatible with their experiencing feelings of affection for white children that naturally arise in warm adult-child interactions. My claim is simply that the role of the nanny is incompatible with pure coercion, because it is most unreasonable to suppose that slave owners would have allowed their children to be cared for by black women they did not trust at all. The considerations just adduced are part of the explanation for why black women could be trusted as nannies. And if whites could trust slaves as nanny, then an important role in slavery was anchored in a cooperative spirit.

Finally, I should mention that there is no incompatibility in there being trust in an oppressive relationship; for trust is not an all-or-nothing matter. It is possible to believe that those who oppress us will not harm us in certain ways—not simply out of self-interest but out of moral conviction.

Most certainly, the Holocaust had nothing analogous to the role of the black nanny. More generally, Jews did not play an intimate role in the family lives of the Nazis to the extent that black slaves did in the family lives of white slaveholders. Or, to put a finer touch on the point, there were no institutional practices, informal or otherwise, definitive or characteristic of the Holocaust where Jews played this role in the family lives of Nazis, whereas slavery had many such institutional practices where black slaves played an intimate role in the lives of whites.[6] There was the black confidante and the black cook. And while it may seem that the latter role did not involve trust, a moment's reflection should suffice to reveal that it surely did. One is loath to eat food prepared by a person whom one believes is chafing at the bit to poison one. And while a cook's poisoning of the family would surely have brought down the wrath of other whites, this could hardly have given a white family much comfort. For one thing, an avenged death is no substitute for living. For another, and much more important, the threat of death would carry little weight with slaves who would rather run the risk of death than endure the injustices of slavery; and there was no formal way slaveholders could rule out the possibility that the slaves who cooked for them were of this mind. In the absence of some degree of trust, it would have been most imprudent for slaveholders to have slaves cook for them. And in the context of slavery, trusting blacks in this regard makes sense only if the blacks trusted have, to some extent, the internal point of view toward the institution of slavery, as presumably some did; for in the eyes of the slaveholder, there were "good" and "bad" blacks, the former being more trustworthy. In general, it was possible for slaves to play an important role in affirming the self-worth of slave owners.

And this would not have been possible if some slaves did not adopt the internal point of view toward the institution of slavery. Jews simply did not play an affirming role in the lives of the Nazis. Quite the contrary.

The idea that victims of oppression may unwittingly contribute to or participate in their own oppression by accepting, to varying degrees, the very norms of the institutional practices that oppress them is not a new one.[7] And the point being made here is that one fundamentally important difference between the Holocaust and American slavery is this: Jews most certainly did not come to accept the norms of the Holocaust—that is, the view that they were vermin worthy only of death at the hands of the Nazis. There were, of course, Jews who committed suicide during the Holocaust, but certainly not because they believed that the Nazis were right in holding that Jews do not deserve to live, and so wanted to contribute in their own way to the realization of that end. By contrast, the conclusion that blacks to varying degrees accepted some of the norms of the institutional practices of slavery, and so had an internal point of view toward slavery, seems very nearly inescapable.[8]

There is, for instance, the notion of an Uncle Tom, namely, a servile black who is unduly solicitous of the approval of whites. From the standpoint of slaveholders, an Uncle Tom is a "good black" because he knows his place, and his sense of worth is to a significant degree tied to measuring up to the roles as defined for him by the institutional practices of slavery itself or, after slavery, those practices that embodied the belief that blacks are rightly subordinate to whites. One aspect of the evil of slavery lies in the fact that it defined a set of roles to which the self-esteem of blacks could be tied, although such roles were part of an institution that was manifestly oppressive of blacks. As one female slave remarked:

> I hope and prays to git to hebben. Whether I's white or black when I git dere, I'll be satisfied to see my Savior dat my old marster worshipped and my husband preached 'bout. I wants to be in hebben wid all my white folks, just to wait on them and love them and serve them, sorta lak I did in slavery time.
> Dat will be 'nough hebben for Adeline.[9]

Another slave remarked:

> But all and all, white folks, den were de really happy days for us niggers. Course we didn't habe de 'vantages dat we has now, but dere was sump'n back dere dat we ain't got now, an' dat secu'aty. Yassuh, we had somebody to go to when we was in trouble. We had a Massa dat would fight fo' us an' help us an' laugh wid us

an' cry wid us. We had a Mistus dat would nuss us when we was sick, an' comfort us when we hadda be punished).[10]

By contrast, one aspect of the evil of the Holocaust is that it embodied so undesirable a conception of Jews—namely, the Jew as irredeemably evil—as to preclude the very possibility of there being roles to which the self-esteem of Jews could be tied. This gives us a sharp conceptual difference between the Holocaust and American slavery: During the Holocaust, the only good Jew was a dead Jew; but it is simply false that during American slavery, the only good black was a dead black. Blacks, while not considered intrinsically useful, were certainly considered useful, whereas Jews were considered intrinsically detrimental.

This difference lies at the heart of the explanation for why Jews did not come to have the internal point of view toward the Holocaust, whereas numbers of blacks did, to varying degrees, come to have this point of view toward slavery. The psychological makeup of human beings is such that people cannot adopt an internal point of view toward a practice if it is impossible for their self-esteem to be in any way enhanced by acting in accordance with the practice. The sheer physical brutality of the Holocaust made it irrational for any Jew to see the Holocaust as in any way affirming. The Holocaust could not have been described as a form of mass martyrdom.

This picture of the difference between blacks and Jews has been painted in broad strokes. I hardly wish to deny that blacks were often deemed despicable creatures. Nor do I wish to suggest that the Nazis never found any use for Jews. But the character of a moral climate is not determined by the exceptions. Slavery was predicated on the idea that there was a role for blacks to play in the lives of whites. A black who played that role well was a good black. The Holocaust was not predicated on a like idea of Jews, but just the opposite. And this is so even if some Nazis found some useful roles for Jews to play in their lives.

Before moving on, perhaps the most important single piece of evidence available showing that blacks to some degree came to have the internal point of view toward slavery can be found in the linguistic practices of blacks. If the word "nigger" was a derogatory term adopted by whites in referring to blacks, one cannot help but be struck by the extent to which blacks used the term in referring to themselves both negatively and positively.

Dere wuz a lot'ta mean "Niggers" in dem days too. Some "Niggers" so mean dat white fo'ks didn't bodder 'em much.

So white fo'ks have deir service in de mornin' an' "Niggers" have deirs in de evenin'. . . . Ya'see "Niggers" lack'ta shout a whole lot an' wid de white fo'ks al'round 'em, dey couldn't shout jes' lack dey wan to. . . . "Nigger" preachers in dem times wuz mighty-nigh free." [11]

Even after slavery—until very recently, in fact—the term "nigger" continued to have considerable currency in black speech practices. A black could be a good, sweet, or mean "nigger," all admitting of positive connotations. The Holocaust did not yield an analogous linguistic practice among Jews. But this should come as no surprise if, as I claim, one difference between the Holocaust and slavery is that Jews did not at all come to have the internal point of view toward the Holocaust, given its sheer coercive nature, that in significant ways blacks did toward slavery. [12]

THE ISSUE OF NATAL ALIENATION

The concept of natal alienation sheds further light on why blacks came to have the internal point of view toward slavery, whereas Jews did not come to have this attitude toward the Holocaust. [13] We have natal alienation in the lives of an ethnic group when the social practices of the society in which they are born prevent most of the individuals from fully participating in, and thus having a secure knowledge of, their historical-cultural traditions. Natal alienation is not an all-or-nothing matter; and, if stopped early enough, it can be permanently arrested and sometimes reversed.

A factor most relevant to whether the harm of natal alienation occurs and the extent to which it does is time: The longer the members of an ethnic group are exposed to oppressive institutions that are natally alienating, the more likely it is that they will become natally alienated. Substantial natal alienation of an ethnic group requires several generations. The first generation of an ethnic group subjected to natally alienating institutions will have firsthand knowledge of their historical-cultural traditions, since prior to the subjugation this generation will have fully (that is, actively, directly) participated in the historical-cultural traditions of their people—and, let us assume, in an environment that affirms their doing so. Accordingly, individuals belonging to this generation will have a vividness about who they are historically and culturally that can come only in the wake of direct participation in one's historical-cultural traditions. For these reasons, the lives of those belonging to the first generation will bear a full imprimatur, let us say, of their historical-cultural traditions; and the significance of this imprimatur in their lives cannot be eradicated by being subjugated to na-tally alienating institutions, although the individuals are no longer able to particulate fully in their historical-cultural traditions. By contrast, the lives of those in the very next, and thus first, generation born into natally alien-ating institutions will not—indeed, cannot—have a full imprimatur of the cultural-historical traditions that belong to their people. At best they will have firsthand reports from those with a full imprimatur. By the fourth and fifth generations, however, not only will no one among the subjugated people be fully participating in the historical-cultural traditions of their people, but worse yet, there will be few, if any, firsthand reports from those who did. By the seventh generation there will be no surviving members bearing a full imprimatur of their historical-cultural traditions.

After seven generations of having been subjugated to very natally alien-ating institutions, an ethnic group's historical-cultural traditions can no longer be seriously defined in terms of the historical-cultural traditions that were theirs prior to the oppression. Or, at any rate, we have two different historical-cultural traditions, even if one is an offshoot of the other. For historical-cultural traditions survive only insofar as individuals can fully participate in the practices that define them; and precisely what natally alienating institutions do is make such participation impossible by ensur-ing that the practices definitive of the historical-cultural traditions simply do not survive.

By the 1650s, slavery was well under way in the United States. By 1750, there were more slaves in the United States who had been born here than who had been forcibly brought here. And by 1860 virtually all slaves in the United States had been born here, since the slave trade ended around 1808. Taking a generation to be twenty years, the natal alienation of blacks ranged over ten generations and became especially efficacious after 1750 and even more so after 1808.

The concept of natal alienation gives us yet another important insight into the difference between the Holocaust and American slavery. The evil of the former lay in the painfully many deaths of Jews it brutally brought about in the attempt to extinguish the entire Jewish people; the evil of the latter lay in the painful degree of natal alienation it brought about through the enslavement of blacks. It might be tempting to think that these two forms of evil are on a continuum, with death being the worse of the two. But this line of thought should be resisted. One does not wish to offend with too imaginative of an example, but the truth of the matter is that by the present criteria by which a person is deemed a Jew—being born of a Jewish woman or converting—complete natal alienation alone is as much

of a threat to the existence of Jews as is genocide. If over seven generations none of the rituals of Judaism was allowed to be practiced—if there
were no circumcisions, no Bat or Bar Mitzvahs, no synagogues, and no
conversions—and if over seven generations, Jewish women had fewer and
fewer children because as a result of social indoctrination their sense of
worth became ever more tied to caring for the children of others rather
than bearing children; and if children born of Jewish women were separated from their families at birth and raised as non-Jews: If all these things
happened over seven generations, it is not clear if anyone could say with
any confidence that the Jews as an ethnic group still exist—at least not if
the criteria stated above were used. By then it would be almost impossible
for anyone to know who had been born of a Jewish woman, although this
would perhaps be true of some individuals.

It goes without saying that no ethnic group can survive mass murder.
It does not follow, however, that an ethnic group will survive just because
its members are not victims of this sort of evil. For if participating in certain practices is definitive of who the group is and, moreover, there are no
phenotypical features that could be deemed decisive in this regard, then
the elimination of those practices from the lives of the group over seven
generations would suffice to eliminate the group itself; by then it would
no longer be possible to determine with any assurance who belonged to
the group by reference to ancestry, which is the only criterion that would
be available. There is a difference between individual survival and group
survival; and while it is certainly true, as matter of logic, that a group will
not continue to exist if none of the individuals belonging to it survives, it is
nonetheless false that if those who belong to the group survive, then, as a
matter of logic, the group itself will continue to exist.

Individuals who survive successive generations survive as an identifiable
group only if there is some criterion by which it is possible to distinguish
them as a group. And from the fact that a people are not murdered, or
do not have their deaths hastened in other coercive ways, it does not follow that a criterion for distinguishing them as a group obtains. Hitler was
concerned to bring about the end of *a people*—not just people. And while
extermination is the most efficient means of achieving this end, it is not
the only means. Given Hitler's conception of the Jews as irredeemably
evil, however, probably nothing short of their extermination would have
recommended itself to him.

Because skin color is often taken as decisive when it comes to determining ethnic identification, and by that measure it is clear that people of

African descent survived slavery, it is easy for the profoundly natally alien-ating character of slavery to go unappreciated. If it is obvious that people of African descent survived slavery, what is anything but obvious, however, is exactly what they survived as. Only if one trivializes the practices that were definitive of the historical-cultural traditions of Africans prior to their enslavement can one possibly think it obvious what blacks survived as.

In claiming that slavery was natally alienating, what I am not claiming is that nothing from Africa survives in the culture of black America. It is generally held that Africa left its influence on the music and, especially, the religious practices preferred by a great many black Americans, such as the spiritual "shout" in church.[14] While I should not want to trivialize this influence, I think it is a mistake to regard it as the centerpiece of the historical-cultural traditions that blacks inherited from Africa. This influ-ence is primarily style, form, and mode of (self-) expression, not narrative content; and without a narrative a people cannot maintain a sense of their history. Indeed, they are without an interpretation of the very practices said to inform their identity.[15]

Consider the following thought experiment. An oppressor says to a vic-tim "choose—choose, that is, between the physical death of your people or the complete and total natal alienation of your people, as a result of which the ethnic identity of your people is forever lost." The only thing I would like to say here is that I do not see how anyone could rationally choose here. People do die for what they believe in. And death can be preferable to certain forms of degradation. So it is not at all obvious that it is better to live as something than to die, if that something is radically at odds with how one currently and profoundly identifies oneself. If death were indis-putably the worse of these two evils, then the choice should be obvious. It is surely not, however. And this suggests that it is a mistake to suppose that these two are on a continuum with death being indisputably the worse of the two.

We can distinguish between two ways of understanding the claim "X is an ultimate evil": (a) No evil can be more horrible than X; (b) All other evils are less horrible than X. The first is compatible with another evil, say Y, being as horrible as X, whereas the second entails that Y—any Y—must be less horrible than X. I maintain that the Holocaust and American slavery are best understood as ultimate evils in the first sense. Likewise, death should be understood as an ultimate evil only in the first sense. There can be a fate as horrible as death itself. At any rate, it has seemed so to various individuals, which is why people sometimes choose to die rather than to confront certain horrors. This way of understanding the Holocaust and American slavery enables us to avoid the very appearance of invidious comparisons. Only very unsavory motives could explain a person's insisting that one (but not both) of these institutions must be regarded as an ultimate evil in sense (*b*).

My saying that what distinguishes the Holocaust from American slavery is that the Holocaust was not natally alienating in no way diminishes the evil of the Holocaust, any more than affirming that slavery was not about genocide diminishes the evil of slavery. The Holocaust was not natally alienating precisely because its aim was the genocide of the Jews; the natal alienation of a people can occur only if they are not killed off, but the official doctrine of Nazi Germany that held Jews to be irredeemably evil was incompatible with wanting Jews to survive in any way.[16] Further, the brutal events of the Holocaust took place over a single generation. This is not enough time for significant natal alienation to occur, which is hardly to deny that the Holocaust had grave deleterious psychological effects on Jews. But not every grave psychological harm constitutes a form of natal alienation. So, although the Holocaust made it extremely difficult for Jews to participate in the practices definitive of their historical-cultural traditions, and although very many Jewish families were separated, the period in which these events occurred was short enough that neither the historical-cultural traditions of Jews nor the practices definitive of these traditions were lost. The pain of the Holocaust was extraordinary. But that pain was not about a people desperately in search of some thread of their historical-cultural traditions, groping to identify or to relearn the practices definitive of these traditions; it was the pain of a people desperately seeking to reconcile their commitment to their historical-cultural traditions in the face of the extraordinary suffering they had undergone. Had, in fact, the Holocaust been natally alienating, this very profound pain could not have been experienced.[17]

THE CONCEPTION OF THE VICTIMS

No oppression of a people can be fully articulated without an account of how the victims were viewed by those who oppressed them.[18] Here, again, we get a most important difference between the Holocaust and American slavery. Although the oppressors in both institutions considered their respective victims to be morally inferior, they did so in quite different ways. With the Holocaust the only good Jew was a dead Jew—not a subservient Jew but a dead Jew; whereas with American slavery, a good black was indeed a properly subservient black. Slavery's "official" view of blacks was that they were by natural constitution moral simpletons, if you will— creatures not capable of excelling at the high moral and intellectual virtues because of having diminished moral and intellectual capacities.[19] The black was not viewed as essentially evil, though perhaps one who would easily succumb to the ways of evil if not watched.

I do not claim that this view is consistent with all the ways in which slave masters (and whites, generally) interacted with blacks. It clearly was not. This view is consistent, however, with many of the severe forms of treatment that blacks received for not behaving as desired. Assuming a Skinnerian stimulus-response model, one can treat a creature severely in the hopes of eliciting the right behavior without attributing high moral and intellectual powers to the creature. What is more, we sometimes think that creatures incapable of either virtue or vice, strictly speaking, can nonetheless mimic such moral behavior. And on some occasions, their doing so can result in our having genuine moral feelings appropriate to the behavior in question, as if it were in fact characteristic of a virtue or a vice. Observe that whereas one can become outraged at one's dog for having just ruined the garden, one does not become outraged at one's tree for having just lost a branch that fell on one's car and damaged it. Trees are not capable of enough agency to make conceptual sense of rage toward them. Dogs are— or so we seem to believe. I have drawn attention to this point about behavior and displays of moral attitudes because it is important to realize that the slavery conception of blacks as moral simpletons is not discredited by pointing to the truth that some of the slave owners' attitudes and behavior toward blacks can only be described as moral.

Nazi Germany's "official" view of Jews, however, was that they were irredeemably evil—although capable of moral agency, they were so constituted by their very nature that extreme vice was necessarily the dominant expression of their moral agency. As Nazi doctor Fritz Klein responded when asked how he could reconcile killing Jews with the Hippocratic oath: "Of course I am a doctor and I want to preserve life. And out of respect for human life, I would remove a gangrenous appendix from the diseased body. The Jew is the gangrenous appendix in the body of mankind."[20] Jewish infants were deemed no less possessing of this nature than Jewish adults. This nature of vice was not thought to be one that could be diffused if only one got to it early enough. Accordingly, the Nazis viewed Jewish infants with as much disfavor and disdain as they viewed Jewish adults. No social interaction between any Jew of any age and any non-Jew of any age met with approval. This is in sharp contrast to slavery, where it was common for the children of slave owners and the children of slaves to play together. Slave owners were not merely waiting impatiently for black children to become old enough to perform the tasks of slaves; they often condoned the play between black children and white children.

It is most rare for young children to bear the full brunt of hostility directed against the ethnic group to which they belong. As I have indicated, what most often distinguished black children from white children during times of slavery was the difference in what the future held for them—not the amount of suffering that black children experienced in comparison to white children. No such claim can be made about Jewish and non-Jewish children during the Holocaust. Absolutely not. This difference underscores the moral significance of the difference in the way that each of these two institutions conceived of its victims. If a people are held to be irredeemably evil, then the only appropriate moral and psychological attitude to have toward them is complete and utter disassociation. There could be no reason to approve of any form of social interaction with them, because the very existence any of them, at any stage of life, would represent is that which one should oppose at all costs.[21] On this view, children could not be the exception to the rule. And indeed they were not. If, however, a people are held to be moral simpletons, this is not, in and of itself, a reason to oppose their very existence, let alone to do so at all costs. Quite the contrary, one can even have a caring and protective attitude toward moral simpletons. So, it follows, one can have such an attitude toward the children of such a people. Not only that, since children generally do not exhibit great moral and intellectual maturity, the psychological attitude toward the children of a people with truncated moral capacities would not be substantially different from the psychological attitude toward children of people without truncated moral capacities, except insofar as the future would bear upon matters.

The following observations bring into sharper relief the importance of the difference between the ways in which American slavery and the Holocaust each conceived of its victims. The belief that a people are moral simpletons is perfectly compatible with having norms of benevolence toward them—with believing that there are good and bad, appropriate and inappropriate ways of treating them. This is so even if one does not believe that the people fall under the scope of justice itself. After all, the norms of benevolence operate nowadays with respect to animals, although few are inclined to think that animals fall within the purview of justice. And, as the example of animals shows, the norms of benevolence may be anchored in deep moral considerations and thus not stand as optional claims upon our behavior.

If, however, a people are held to be irredeemably evil, then surely norms of benevolence toward them would be out of place. This characterization of a people simply does not support any sustained benevolent psychological attitudes toward them. Indeed, it is not clear what an appropriate practice of kindness toward the irredeemably evil would be. The virtue of forgiveness might come naturally to mind here.[22] I am not even confident of this, though. I believe that the psychology of forgiveness is such that it is extraordinarily difficult to forgive those whom we believe are constitutionally committed to doing wrong, who have a deep and unshakable preference for doing wrong. While I should like to stop short of saying that this is impossible for any individual to do, I doubt that forgiving the irredeemably evil could be a norm among people; for a norm refers to a stable practice; and I do not see that forgiving the irredeemably evil could ever be a stable practice. An irredeemably evil person is too much of an affront to the very act of forgiving.

Whereas American slavery was undoubtedly a nefarious institution, it must nonetheless be conceded that in individual slave households there were norms of benevolence toward slaves, which is what one would expect given the view of the black as a moral simpleton. Although there were vicious slave masters, to be sure, there were also slave masters who felt it their moral duty, in virtue of their role as slave master, to treat their slaves with kindness. And it is precisely because there were such slave masters against the backdrop of an otherwise evil institution that we can make sense of the various instances of strong loyalty that slaves had toward their slave masters. For there is no better way to occasion gratitude on the part of individuals among an oppressed people, and feelings of loyalty too, than to treat them less harshly than one has a right to treat them, according to prevailing institutional practices, and so less harshly than many others actually treat them. It is not necessary that the individuals be treated as they rightly should be treated; it suffices that they can count on being treated by those having power over them better than other similarly situated oppressed individuals can.

This is an extraordinarily deep and important feature of the psychology of persons. We are understandably grateful to the other for whatever relief from evil or suffering that person offers us, even if that person still contributes to our oppression in other ways. If we can be extremely grateful for an isolated instance of relief, then it stands to reason that sustained relief may go beyond just generating increasingly deeper feelings of gratitude. The most natural other feeling to have toward another as a result of sustained feelings of gratitude is loyalty owing to a debt of gratitude.

As one might imagine, norms of benevolence during the Holocaust on the part of Nazis toward Jews were virtually nonexistent, which is what one expects given the view of the Jew as irredeemably evil. There were no Nazis who thought it incumbent upon them, in their role as Nazis, to treat Jews with kindness. And it was with rare exception that Jews could count on any Nazi to treat them with leniency. With slavery, there can be no denying that some slave owners were touched by the humanity of the blacks. With the Holocaust, what is astounding is that so few Nazis were touched by the humanity of the Jews.

Although there were no norms of benevolence, some Nazis were more humane in their treatment of Jews than others. The most outstanding example is Dr. Ernst B., a Nazi doctor at Auschwitz.

> Former prisoner doctors, in both their written and their oral accounts, constantly described Dr. B. as having been a unique Nazi doctor in Auschwitz: a man who treated inmates (especially prisoner doctors) as human beings and who saved many of their lives; who had refused to do selections in Auschwitz; *who had been so appreciated by prisoner doctors that, when tried after the war, their testimony on his behalf brought about his acquittal; who was "a human being in an SS uniform."* . . . Former prisoner doctors rallied behind Dr. B. with impressive testimony on his behalf.[23]

One barely has conceptual space for the idea of Jewish survivors of Auschwitz being so grateful to a committed Nazi doctor in Auschwitz as to rally to win his acquittal at Nuremberg—and Dr. B. was a committed Nazi. But against the backdrop of Nazi evil, and in comparison to the way other Nazi doctors at Auschwitz treated prisoners, Dr. B. consistently offered a humaneness in his treatment of prisoners that no one in the concentration camps could ever have had reason to hope for. So on reflection we can see that there is nothing strange in the enormous gratitude Auschwitz survivors had for Dr. B.: In general, we are very grateful to those who do more than they have to by way of helping us, as determined by expectations anchored in prevailing institutional practices. Dr. B., as it turns out, did considerably more by doing considerably less. The prevailing norm in concentration camps was brutal mercilessness on the part of Nazi doctors. Dr. B.'s behavior fell considerably short of that norm. As one Holocaust survivor so poignantly put it:

> [Dr. B.'s] very first visit to the lab of Block 10 . . . was an extraordinary surprise for us. He came into the lab without force unlike the other SS, without a dog (Weber always came with a dog), locked the doors behind him [so that his behavior could not be observed by other SS], said "Good day" and introduced himself, . . . offering his hand to my colleagues and me. . . . We were . . . long unused to anyone from among the camp authorities treating us as people equal to himself.[24]

Regarding a being as a moral simpleton is quite compatible with having strong norms of benevolence toward it, whereas there is no such compatibility if a being is regarded as irredeemably evil. One could easily believe that it was ordained by God that one should treat moral simpletons with benevolence in a systematic way, whereas one would require quite a feat of imagination to believe that it has been ordained by God that one should so treat the irredeemably evil. What makes Dr. B.'s humane treatment of numerous Jews most incredible is that he so treated Jews without ever rejecting—at least not entirely—Nazi ideology. He never condemned Nazi practices, including the selection of Jews for the gas chambers, although he himself did not perform any selections.

We see here how the ideological conception of a victim makes such a phenomenal difference in terms of social practice. As a slave owner, one could be good to slaves in a systematic way without at all condemning, or calling into question, the practice of slavery itself.[25] This is because the very conception of the victim, although quite compatible with being cruel toward it, is equally compatible with being kind toward it; hence, kind behavior did not require any great psychological feats of reconciliation or compartmentalization. A kind slave master, for instance, in order to make sense of his acceptance of the practice of slavery, was not forced to play down either his own kindness toward slaves or the cruelty of other slave masters toward slaves; for he could perfectly well acknowledge that some (he among them) were better slave masters than others without calling into question the practice, just as it is acknowledged that some parents are better than others without calling into question the practice of parenting. Thus, being a kind slave master did not require psychologically blocking out or downplaying the cruelty of other slave masters, any more than being a kind parent requires blocking out or downplaying the cruelty of other parents.

Finally, the practice of slavery was not something that a slave owner had to continue participating in or supporting. It happened often enough that slaves were willed free upon the death of their slave masters.[26] The logic, if you will, and ideology of slavery is perfectly compatible with granting slaves freedom.

Things were quite different with the Holocaust, however. To be kind toward Jews was to call into question the very conception of the Jew as pronounced by Nazi ideology. Thus, Nazi doctors who did not want to participate in the selection of Jews for the gas chambers had to claim psychological inability on their part rather than voice their objection to the practice itself—if, that is, they wished to avoid punishment.[27] Nazism itself allowed no room for a good Nazi to be kind toward Jews. And Nazi doctors who were consistently or frequently kind did so at great psychic costs. They could not allow themselves to appreciate the implications of their own deeds of kindness. Their being kind was viewed by themselves and others as more like something that *happened* to them rather than a profound expression of their recognition of the humanity in Jews. In this way, the doctors could manage to avoid seeing that their being kind to Jews was a moral condemnation of Nazi ideology. Whereas a slave master could regard his being kind to slaves as a virtue, a Nazi doctor could do no such thing. The Nazi regime was relentless in its demand that its practices meet with public approval.

Perhaps nothing brings out the difference between the way the Holocaust and American slavery each conceived of its victims than the difference in the sexual attitude each held toward its victims. Of course, black women were raped during American slavery,[28] and Jewish women were raped during the Holocaust. But Nazism strictly forbade sexual relations between Jews and non-Jews because Jews were considered too low a form of human life, too evil, for there to be any such interaction between a Jew and a non-Jew even just for mere sexual pleasure. To accuse a Nazi citizen of having sexual relations with a Jew was viewed as a form of grave moral contamination of the citizen. Recall Klein's remark that "the Jew is the gangrenous appendix in the body of mankind." This is exactly what one would expect given the conception of the Jew as irredeemably evil. By contrast, while sexual relations between white slave owners and black slaves were not officially sanctioned by marriage, such relations were certainly common. Indeed, some were long-lasting and exceedingly rich. Miscegenation was common enough that schools were set up for children of "mixed blood" to attend. Given the conception of the black under slavery as a moral simpleton, one would not expect the kind of hostility on the part of whites toward sexual relations with blacks that Nazi Germans exhibited toward Jews.

The difference between hate and disdain illuminates the way the two institutions conceived of their victims. We actively oppose that which we hate; we want it destroyed. But we feel superior to that for which we have disdain. Hate does not entail disdain, since one can hate a person whom one takes to be one's superior. Hate for the Jews was the operative sentiment of the Holocaust, and disdain for blacks was the operative sentiment of American slavery.

The aim of the Holocaust was to destroy the Jews, period. Not just the Jews of Germany or of France. The aim of American slavery was not to destroy blacks. In contrast, a great deal of effort was expended to bring blacks to the United States—not for the purpose of killing them but to use them in subordinate roles. The aim of whites was not so much to disassociate themselves from blacks as it was to associate with blacks in ways intended to remind blacks that they were inferior to whites and to remind whites that they were superior to blacks. Note the pattern after slavery: While blacks were allowed to ride the same bus as whites, blacks were required to sit in the back of the bus; or they were not allowed to sit at all if this meant that a white had to stand. Similarly, blacks could prepare the food in restaurants in which they could not eat. And they could clean houses in neighborhoods in which they could not live. Thus, the moral import of segregation in the old South, which was absent during slavery, was not that blacks were irredeemably evil, and so should be destroyed. No, the South unquestionably had a place for blacks.

By contrast, it was unthinkable to Nazis that Jews should play a similar role in the lives of the citizens of Nazi Germany. Of course, the Nazis took themselves to be superior to the Jews. But we might distinguish between nonaffirming superiority and affirming superiority. The Nazis believed they were superior to the Jews in the same way human beings are superior to worms. Such superiority cannot in any way be a source of pride and therefore is best defined as unflattering. The superiority implicit in the belief of (some) whites that paternalism toward blacks was in order was affirming superiority—it could serve as a source of pride for whites. There was no sense of paternalism in the Nazis' attitude toward the Jews. These remarks accord well with the account that the Jews were regarded as irredeemably evil and blacks as moral simpletons. The very idea of being paternalistic toward an irredeemably evil people is just plain absurd; the idea of going to great lengths, and costs to oneself, to exterminate a people conceived of as mere moral simpletons is equally absurd.

Now, it might be thought that if the aim of hate is to destroy, but not with disdain, then hate is worse than disdain. When taken in the abstract perhaps this is so. But in both cases, we must look at the institutional expression of hate and disdain. There is no in-principle reason why the expression of disdain cannot be on a par with the expression of hate in terms of moral horribleness. Accordingly, the difference between disdain and hate does not yield a difference in nefariousness between the Holocaust and American slavery.

I should like to conclude this section by focusing on a similarity between American slavery and the Holocaust, which is nonetheless owing to an important difference. There can be no denying that both blacks and Jews were victims of extreme injustice. But even here ideology makes a differ- ence. Blacks were deemed not deserving of justice in the way that things or animals are deemed not deserving of justice. A thing or an animal belongs to the wrong category to be deserving of justice. This is not, however, be- cause animals and things have a morally depraved character, but because they lack the requisite moral complexity. Jews were deemed not deserving of justice, but not because they were thought to belong to the category of things lacking the requisite moral complexity, but because they were held to be so morally depraved and thus evil that the restraints of justice no longer applied to the treatment of them.[29] Thus, from the standpoint of the official doctrine of the Holocaust and American slavery, Jews and blacks turn out not to be deserving of justice for radically different reasons. And radically different forms of injustice were meted out.

CONCLUSION

On one hand, we have the horror of brutal natal genocide; on the other hand, we have the horror of brutal alienation. Each horror stands in its own right in that neither is the logical predecessor or successor to the other. Neither horror could have given rise to the other. And if this is so, then there are no clear criteria by which one institution could be deemed more evil than the other. I do not see that there are any considerations by which it would be rational for one group to prefer the suffering of the other to its own, on the grounds that the other group experienced less evil.

I believe that by endeavoring to understand more fully the ways in which the Holocaust and American slavery differ, we can leave aside the invidious comparison of numbers. The magnitude of an evil institution is a function of the number of people harmed, but that is not the only determining factor. Equally relevant is the very character, as revealed by its practices, of the evil institution itself. To lose sight of this truth is to embrace a very narrow-minded view of the nature of evil. And to do this with piety and self-righteousness is to aid and abet evil, if only unwittingly.

NOTES

Acknowledgments: A version of this essay was read at the New York Society for Philosophy and Public Affairs to a most responsive audience. Thanks are also owed to Steven Kepnes, who has listened most patiently to and commented most thoughtfully on the ideas in this essay; to Alan Berger, who wrote extensive comments, not all of which I have been able to accommodate; to Claudia Card, who offered much helpful advice; and to Susan Shapiro, who was extremely encouraging from the start. A special word of thanks goes to Howard McGary, who has so fruitfully disagreed with me. Likewise for Bill E. Lawson. Michael Stocker has been an ever-present sounding board and source of encouragement. Finally, I am delighted to acknowledge the helpful comments of Joshua Cohen, Thomas Digby, Samuel Gorovitz, and Richard Wilkens. A version was given as the 1990 Martin Luther King, Jr., Lecture at Eastern Michigan University. This essay is expanded in Part II of *Vessels of Evil: American Slavery and the Holocaust* (Philadelphia: Temple University Press, 1993).

This is a revision of "American Slavery and the Holocaust: Their Ideologies Compared," which appeared in *Public Affairs Quarterly* 5 (1991). Although the events are listed chronologically in the title, I do not adhere to that order throughout the essay.

1. I can speak in a somewhat informed way to the pain, moral and otherwise, only of blacks and Jews. I wish to record my awareness, however, of the suffering of other peoples: specifically, in this instance, Armenians and Native Americans. Between 1915 and 1923, nearly 1.5 million Armenians were killed by the Turks; and to varying degrees, the attitude of the Turks toward the Armenians was not unlike the attitude of the Nazis toward the Jews. Native Americans, of course, have experienced their share of dehumanization, deception, and marginalization at the hands of Christian whites. While acknowledging the suffering of others is, to be sure, no substitute for understanding their suffering, I should very much hope that acknowledgment is a gesture in the right direction. For an important discussion of the difference between the experience of the Armenians and the Jews, see Berel Lang, *Act and Idea in the Nazi Genocide* (Chicago: University of Chicago Press, 1990), 7–8.

2. Contra Richard L. Rubenstein, *The Cunning of History* (New York: Harper & Row, 1975), chap. 3. He writes: "Slavery in North America was thus an im-

perfectly rationalized institution of nearly total domination under conditions of a shortage of productive labor. The death camp was a fully rationalized institution of total domination under conditions of a population surplus" (p. 41)—Rubenstein's point being that as bad as slavery was, the Holocaust was significantly worse.

3. H.L.A. Hart, *The Concept of Law* (New York: Oxford University Press, 1961).

4. For a discussion of this, see Rubenstein, *The Cunning of History,* chap. 5; and Lang, *Act and Idea,* chap. 3.

5. Frederick Douglass, a former slave who symbolizes the ideal of a self-determining black and who did not hold back his criticisms of slavery, nonetheless wrote: "I had resided but a short time in Baltimore before I observed a marked difference, in the treatment of slaves, from that which I had witnessed in the country. A city slave is almost a freeman, compared with a slave on the plantation. . . . Few [slaveholders] are willing to incur the odium attaching to the reputation of being a cruel master; and above all things, they would not be known as not giving a slave enough to eat. Every city slaveholder is anxious to have it known of him, that he feeds his slaves well" (*Narrative of the Life of Frederick Douglass, an American Slave, Written by Himself,* edited by Benjamin Quarles [Cambridge, Mass.: Harvard University Press, 1988], 59–60). All further references to Douglass are to this edition.

6. The remarks about trust in the text presuppose a sharp distinction between trust and prediction. While trust entails prediction, the converse does not hold. I have attempted a more complete analysis of trust, as it differs from prediction, in "Trust, Affirmation, and Moral Character: A Critique of Kantian Ethics," in *Identity, Character, and Morality: Essays in Moral Psychology,* edited by Owen Flanagan and Amelie Rorty (Cambridge, Mass.: MIT Press, 1990).

7. Cf. Herbert Marcuse, *An Essay on Liberation* (Boston: Beacon Press, 1969). Consider, for instance, the internalization of sexist attitudes on the part of women. I have discussed this in my "Sexism and Racism: Some Conceptual Differences," *Ethics* 90 (1980).

8. Douglass tells of slaves of different masters quarreling, whenever they got together, over which master was richer or smarter. He goes on to say: "They seemed to think that the greatness of their masters was transferable to themselves. It was considered as being bad enough to be a slave; but to be a poor man's slave was deemed a disgrace indeed!" (44).

9. Quoted from Eugene Genovese, *Roll, Jordan, Roll* (New York: Basic Books, 1972), 355. Needless to say, I do not mean to suggest here that there was no slave testimony disparaging slavery. There most certainly was, as Howard McGary has forcibly reminded me. The point is to bring out the kinds of favorable attitudes that slaves were capable of having regarding the interpersonal relationships between themselves and the slavemaster.

10. Ibid., 120.

11. Quoted from John W. Blassingame, ed., *Slave Testimony* (Baton Rouge: Louisiana State University, 1977), 641–42, 643.

12. Sterling Stuckey, *Slave Culture: Nationalist Theory and the Foundations of Black America* (New York: Oxford University Press, 1987), who is concerned to

show that American black culture is basically African at its roots, nonetheless admits that the term "nigger" is evidence of some assimilation on the part of blacks: "The peculiar mixture of Africanity and assimilationism, the latter symbolized by the word nigger, does not hide the fact that the values are African throughout."

13. I borrow the idea of natal alienation from Orlando Patterson, *Slavery and Social Death* (Cambridge, Mass.: Harvard University Press, 1982).

14. Stuckey argues this in *Slave Culture,* chap. 1. On the significance of the shout, see pp. 86–90.

15. Stuckey suggests that the "shout" had great meaning in African contexts (ibid., 88). This I hardly deny; however, I do not see that the "shout" retained that significance in black worship, and if it did not, then the self-identity of black Americans is not as informed by the "shout" from Africa as Stuckey would have us believe.

16. On this way of understanding how Jews were conceived of during the Holocaust, I am indebted to Richard L. Rubenstein and John K. Roth, *Approaches to Auschwitz: The Holocaust and Its Legacy* (Atlanta, Ga.: John Knox Press, 1987), chap. 2.

17. For an important implication regarding natal alienation, see my essays "Liberalism and the Holocaust: An Essay on Trust and Black-Jewish Relationship," in *Echoes from the Holocaust: Philosophical Reflections on a Dark Time,* edited by Alan Rosenberg and Gerald E. Myers (Philadelphia: Temple University Press, 1988); and "Jews, Blacks, and Group Autonomy," *Social Theory and Practice* 14 (1988). I argue in these essays that Jews have more group autonomy than blacks, a claim that does not revolve around invidious comparisons. See pt. III of my *Vessels of Evil.*

18. The failure to be clear about the proper characterization of the way in which Nazis conceived of the Jews presents a difficulty for Berel Lang's otherwise very illuminating discussion of the contributory role of the Enlightenment to the occurrence of the Holocaust (*Act and Idea,* chap. 7). See my "Characterizing and Responding to Nazi Genocide," *Modern Judaism* 11 (1991).

19. Cf. the account of the black as a sambo developed by Stanley M. Elkins, *Slavery: A Problem in American Institutional and Intellectual Life* (Chicago: University of Chicago Press, 1959). I have chosen the expression "moral simpleton" because it has important connotations that the worked "sambo" lacks. True enough, myth would have it that blacks were lazy; however, I do not believe that this does justice to the way in which whites conceived of blacks. The expression "moral simpleton" is compatible with some blacks being lazy, without entailing that any were.

20. Quoted from Robert Jay Lifton, *Nazi Doctors: Medical Killing and the Psychology of Genocide* (New York: Basic Books, 1986), 16. Nazi doctors were affiliated with a concentration camp. Not all had a terminal medical degree or complete genuine medical training.

21. For a masterful discussion in this regard, see Lang, *Act and Idea,* chap. 1, sect. 2 and p. 39. The Nazis were determined to exterminate the Jews even at the risk of losing the wider war they were fighting. Lang writes: "Up until the last

days of the war, in May 1945, the extermination of the Jews continued, with the diversion that this entailed of material resources (trains, supplies) and personnel."

22. Recently, Howard McGary, "Forgiveness," *American Philosophical Quarterly* 26 (1989), has suggested that there could be self-interested reasons for forgiving others. But for reasons mentioned in the text, I do not see that such reasons can operate with respect to the irredeemably evil. For a powerful discussion of forgiveness in connection with the Holocaust, see Martin P. Golding, "Forgiveness and Regret," *Philosophical Forum* 16 (1984–85). In general, the question of whether we should forgive those who have committed acts of egregious evil is a most important one philosophically.

23. Lifton, *Nazi Doctors,* 303, 326 (italics added); for the full account of Ernst B. offered, see chap. 16, "A Human Being in an SS Uniform: Ernst B." See my discussion of Nazi doctors in pt. I of *Vessels of Evil.*

24. Ibid., 303.

25. Of his own slavery in Baltimore, Douglass wrote, "few slaves could boast of a kinder master and mistress than myself" (*Life,* 75).

26. Blassingame, *Slave Testimony,* 480 n. 22, points out that Jefferson provided for the manumission of some of his slaves. Of course, as Blassingame observes (363–64), wills that manumitted slaves were sometimes set aside. But, needless to say, this hardly vitiates the point being made in the text.

27. Lifton, *Nazi Doctors,* 109n., 198.

28. As Bell Hooks so forcibly reminds us in *Ain't I a Woman? Black Women and Feminism* (Boston: Beacon Press, 1982).

29. Whether from a conceptual point a person can be so evil that the restraints of justice no longer apply, I do not know. What I do know, though, is that a person can be deemed so evil that decent people no longer *feel* bound by the dictates of justice in their treatment of the individual. Presumably, Hitler comes readily to mind here.

11

UNIVERSALISM AND PARTICULARISM IN JEWISH LAW
Making Sense of Political Loyalties

Gordon Lafer

For this reason was the world created with one man: so that none may say to his fellow: my ancestry is better than yours.
—Babylonian Talmud, *Sanhedrin 88b*

When a stranger resides with you in your land, you shall not wrong him . . . you shall love him as yourself, for you were strangers in the land of Egypt.
—*Leviticus 19:33–34*

Thou shalt not lend upon interest to thy brother. . . . Unto a foreigner thou may lend upon interest; but unto thy brother thou shalt not lend upon interest.
—*Deuteronomy 23:19–20*

If the ox of a Jew gored the ox of a gentile, the Jew is not required to pay damages; but if the ox of a gentile . . . gored the ox of a Jew, the gentile is required to pay full damages.
—*Mishnah Baba Kama 4:3*

TWO QUESTIONS immediately jump to mind when reading the quotations that introduce this essay: How could the four verses cited possibly fit together as parts of a coherent doctrine? And what type of morality could possibly justify the blatant favoritism of the last two rulings?

This second question in particular points to the recoiling from discrimination that has become almost instinctive for those of us who grew up in liberal polities. A legal code that advocates *in*equality before the law, which explicitly upholds different legal standards for community members and for outsiders, would seem *prima facie* to disqualify itself from consideration as a serious body of political thought. Yet just such a system is advocated by one of the primary historical traditions in which Western thought locates its roots—the Old Testament. In this essay I attempt to explain why such a system made sense to the authors of the Hebrew Bible and the tradition of rabbinic law it spawned and explore the philosophical paths along which this tradition diverges from liberal thinking about universal and particularist ethics of obligation.

While I am interested in presenting an account of Jewish thought that recognizes both centrifugal and centripetal impulses in the tradition, I am particularly interested in articulating the rationale behind Jewish clannishness, separation, and exclusivity. In a liberal culture such as our own, it is the particularistic commitments of ethnic identity that, while frequently enough advocated, seldom seem comprehensible; which are regularly described even by their proponents as nonrational. By examining the philosophical sensibilities that underlie Jewish particularism, I hope to make particularism understandable not as a prerational instinct but as a system of obligation that, while sharply divergent from liberalism, is both highly rational and, in some ways, deeply attractive. As such, I hope both to reinforce particularist loyalties in Jewish and other communities, and—by rendering these intelligible as reasoned principles rather than brute assertions—to suggest ways in which universalist and particularist obligations may be sensibly combined.

I take John Rawls to be describing a deep truth about American political culture when he asserts that our "firmest convictions . . . of social justice" rest on a belief that each individual's demands must be treated with equal concern.[1] For liberal theory, the fundamental unit of political life is the individual, and therefore however justice may be defined, one of its core attributes must be that it is applied to all individuals uniformly; to suggest that we recognize differential obligations to discrete sets of individuals is to violate a primary tenet of fairness. It is because this universalist principle of liberalism is so deeply ingrained in us that we are unable to affirm particularistic commitments in more than a tokenistic manner. The choice between universalism and particularism is commonly understood to mean that embracing a particular identity requires a fundamentally chauvinistic and degrading attitude toward outsiders, and conversely that accepting universalist obligations must entail relegating one's particular identity to a subordinate, and ultimately meaningless role. In this context, mainstream thought has come to view particularist morality as both dangerous and offensive. The ultimate paradigm of modern particularism—that is, of conceiving of one's primary identity as a member of a particular ethnicity, and placing the concerns of that group before those of any broader community—is the Third Reich. An ethnic identity that confines itself to colorful costumes and festive foods may constitute a nostalgia that we can afford to indulge. But any attempt to formulate serious political priorities along these lines seems like it must deteriorate into an ugly assertion of national superiority; there appears to be no logical stopping point between the passions of nationalism and the justification of racist barbarism. Political sanity seems to require that we reject appeals to ethnic loyalty and pledge allegiance instead to a set of universal principles, which bind us to respond equally to all instances of injustice, no matter how we may be related to their victims or perpetrators.

Thus, while many of us acknowledge both an allegiance to a particular nationality and some universal obligation to all human beings, we cannot provide a legitimate rationale for our particularist attachments; they appear rather as a holdover from prerational times. To the extent that we accept Rawls's assertion that social obligations arise only "when a number of persons engage in a mutually advantageous cooperative venture,"[2] it seems that the sole fundamental allegiances we can justify are those arising from either universal moral worth or contractual commitments. But the ties of communal allegiance constitute something more akin to covenant than contract—the obligations that God and Israel assumed at Mount Sinai, for instance, are eternal and not contingent on stipulations of performance. Communities whose cultural roots have their source in such unconditional bonds, but whose intellectual training is based in contract theory, are left with an emotional attachment they cannot rationalize. With no firm philosophical grounding for particularism, we lack an understanding of how it might be combined with universalist principles; we have no sense of how to negotiate the terrain between these two or how to stake out a position that sensibly balances elements of each.

The American Jewish community offers a vivid instance of this problem. For most of its history, American Jewry avoided the conflict between universalism and particularism by identifying its selfish interests with the broader dictates of liberal universalism. Indeed, in the early part of this century, the circumstances of American politics conspired to offer Jews an easy congruence between the general principles of liberalism and their particular economic and social interests. While American Jews were primarily laborers, the pursuit of their own material self-interests was identical with that of the broader goals of labor rights and unionization; when Jews were commonly excluded from educational and social organizations, efforts to advance their own career opportunities meshed seamlessly with the more general struggle for the triumph of meritocracy over chauvinism; and later, when Jews were victims of Nazism, the struggle against fascist anti-Semitism could easily be understood as part of the larger struggle against all assertions of national superiority.

In recent years, however, the easy marriage between liberal universalism and Jewish particularism has unraveled. As Jews have largely moved out of the working class, and as Israel has lost its underdog status in the Middle East, it has become increasingly apparent that the community's selfish interests diverge significantly from the dictates of abstract universalism, leading the Central Conference of American Rabbis to note in 1976 that "until the recent past our obligations to the Jewish people and to all humanity seemed congruent. At times now these two perspectives appear to conflict." [3] Faced with this situation, Jews have been forced to address a fundamental question of identity: are they primarily members of a tribe, Americans, or "citizens of the world"?

Jews continue to feel an emotional allegiance to their coreligionists. But with no philosophical justification for particularism, these bonds take on the form of crude commitments that can be asserted but not explained; and the community therefore faces an apparent choice between assimilation and an ungrounded and unbounded chauvinism. With the choice defined in these terms, Jews have been pushed to either extreme of this issue. On one side, many people have internalized the logic of liberalism and have come to view their national identities as increasingly irrelevant to their political commitments. And on the other, those who have insisted on maintaining ethnocentric priorities have hardened into an increasingly belligerent position; denied any philosophical grounds on which to justify itself, the ethnic right begins to feel that it needs no justification, and deteriorates into a brute assertion of national interest. This is a community that is being rent apart partly out of an inability to solve this conceptual problem, and in the case of those who cannot abandon their universal imperatives and cannot rationalize their particularist attachments, Jews are literally disappearing not for lack of material sustenance but for lack of intellectual categories.

In debates within the Jewish community, both universalists and chauvinists claim to be speaking in the name of traditional Jewish values. Yet not only have both sides practiced the art of selective citation, but by removing principles from their religious context and inserting them into secular arguments, they have frequently distorted even those principles cited. In this essay, I seek to present a more holistic account of this issue's treatment in Jewish law. It is my hope that this account will illuminate a set of intellectual categories that may help Jewish politics to become unstuck by enabling this community to make sense of an aspect of its life that has previously proved opaque.

I believe that the material presented here is of value to political thinkers generally, however, beyond the confines of the Jewish community. Specifically, I believe that the model of thinking about universalism and particularism that emerges from biblical and rabbinic law suggests that the dichotomy posed above is artificial and unnecessary. Rabbinic law describes a hierarchy of political obligation in which universalism and particularism are dialectically entwined, which seeks to formulate a particularist identity without dehumanizing outsiders, and conversely which recognizes limited universalist obligations without being fundamentally compromised by them. My aim here is to render this hierarchy intelligible by unearthing the intellectual assumptions sustaining it. Furthermore, I believe that the sensibilities that underlie Jewish particularism offer lessons from which many communities can draw. In this way, I hope that the essay will prove interesting even to scholars who have no particular interest in Jewish law per se.

Before proceeding with this analysis, however, I must make a short detour to clarify exactly how Jewish communal law may be pertinent to other communities, and to specify exactly what type of lessons may be gained from such a study. To do this, I delve briefly into an overview of the epistemological issues surrounding communitarian critiques of liberalism.

Over the past fifteen years, communitarian theorists have criticized liberal political theory for failing to provide an adequate account of community. Thinkers such as Robert Bellah, Michael Sandel, Michael Walzer, and Alasdair MacIntyre have argued that liberalism's preoccupation with individual autonomy has resulted in a politics of anomie, in which "wholly unencumbered selves" come together in a polity of "strangers," each seeking to maximize his or her personal good.[4] In opposition to this, communitarians have proposed a society whose "basic structure" is defined by communal attachments,[5] in which rather than seeking isolated selfish goods, participants join together on behalf of a "common good."[6] Where Rawls proposed that members of a just society must be "mutually disinterested," MacIntyre insisted that political life could be meaningful only in "communities whose central bond is a shared vision of and understanding of goods."[7]

Initially, what this critique counterposed to liberalism was an account of specific traditions lived out in particular historical contexts (e.g., MacIntyre's evocation of the Athenian polis, Walzer's of medieval Jewry). Indeed, MacIntyre's *After Virtue* is in some ways an argument against the possibility of developing a general theory of politics that stands outside all particular cultures. Similarly, in asserting that individuals are deeply "constituted" by the practices of their cultures—that they are, in fact, much more deeply a product of culture than of nature—Sandel argued against the notion of a transcultural political theory.

But as the debate developed, this is exactly the form that "communitarianism" increasingly took on—not a rejection, but merely an alternative version of universal theory. The very label "communitarianism" implies a set of social principles that hold true for all communities at all times. As theorists began to search for the principles that united Athens and Jerusalem, Aztecs and Amish, the particularistic nature of communitarian critiques faded into the background, to be replaced by generic assertions concerning the importance of strong social ties and a commitment to the common life. What began by insisting on fundamental particularism came to profess a general theory of its own, and hardly a bold one at that. At times it seems that all "communitarianism" has to offer is a lukewarm rehashing of Aristotle's assertion that human beings are social animals; the contention that it's better to live in some community than in none at all. This genericized critique finds its full expression in the conclusion to Bellah's *Habits of the Heart*: "we have committed what to the republican founders of our nation was the cardinal sin: we have put our own good, as individuals, as groups, as a nation, ahead of the common good." [8] At this point "communitarianism" has become indistinguishable from good-neighborliness, a generic commitment to participation in and support for a generic community—a social altruism which could as easily be applied to Sandel's "strangers" as to MacIntyre's Athenians.

I believe that if we are to develop a substantive communitarian alternative to liberal ways of thinking about politics, it must be by returning to an engagement with particular traditions, by rerealizing the specificity of traditions, and by resisting the temptation to jump toward the construction of a general theory.

In this essay I discuss the Jewish tradition's approach to universalism and particularism as such an instance of communitarianism. The issues of universalism and particularism—the construction of group identity, the definition of insiders and outsiders, and the determination of what obligations are owed to each—must be central to any politics that takes the community rather than the individual as its essential unit. Yet the purpose of this presentation is not simply to extract from Judaism those elements that can be usefully incorporated into a general theory of community politics. For a variety of reasons, the relationship between appreciating one tradition and prescribing programs for others is more complex, and less direct, than such a mechanical reconstruction implies. Each culture constructs its relationship to outsiders out of different materials—different terms, tools, and sensibilities—and there is no easy way to translate the attractive aspects of one into the language of another. The temptation to cannibalize social traditions like used cars, in order to build a single ideal theory out of what seem to be the best working parts of, say, the Gita, the Koran, and J. S. Mill, ignores the first essential insight of communitarians: that political life is constructed out of the lived traditions of particular cultures; that there is no extracultural place to stand in when formulating general theory and no "generic" social setting in which to apply it.

But then what is it, exactly, that we learn, when we learn about particular traditions? What do we have when we have a "thick description" of one culture's approach to a political issue? Clearly, I would not have written this essay had I not believed that an examination of Jewish law offered insights to a broader audience beyond the religious Jewish community. If the truths of each culture are solipsistic, there is certainly no reason to publish them in academic journals. Yet the lessons that one culture can provide another constitute not reproducible social blueprints but rather a set of nuanced insights whose potential application can be worked out only gradually and casuistically, in the stumbling steps through which cultures go about remaking themselves. The type of knowledge involved here is similar to that gained in psychotherapy. When a therapist achieves a deep understanding of one patient's motivations and emotional makeup, this is inevitably helpful in anticipating and interpreting the conditions of others. But there is no way to distill the first patient's case history into a predictive schema—much less a prescriptive program—that maps neatly onto the lives of others. The knowledge achieved here is something less than a general theory, yet more than a case study; cultures can "speak" to one another, but the things they say do not lend themselves to operationalized theories.

It is in this spirit that I present the analysis that follows, not as a prescription that seeks to replace liberalism with a general communitarian theory of obligation, but as an example from which other cultures may draw in ways that cannot be specified in advance. The essay is in four sections. After a brief overview of the biblical treatment of universalism and

particularism, I present a fairly detailed account of the differential obligations owed to Jews and to three classes of non-Jews under rabbinic law.
The third part of the essay explores the philosophical bases of these distinctions and seeks to articulate the rationale for Jewish particularism. In
conclusion I consider the potential implications of this tradition for current
thinking about political obligation by American Jews and by Americans
generally.

UNIVERSALISM AND PARTICULARISM IN THE HEBREW BIBLE

Commenting on the first verse of the first chapter of Genesis, the authoritative rabbinic commentator Rashi asks: Why does the Bible start with the
creation of the world? Since this is really a story about the Jewish people,
should it not start with the Exodus, the beginning of Jewish national history? Why do we have to know about what came before Moses?[9] Rashi
answers his own question with the most narrowly nationalistic response
possible: The only purpose served by the Book of Genesis is to establish that
Jews have legitimate title to the Land of Israel as a divine inheritance from
the creator of the world. But this answer is obviously wrong. Apart from
anything else, if the purpose of Genesis were solely to establish a property
right, the book could have been condensed into a brief series of "begats,"
tracing the lineage from Adam to Abraham, and rejecting as irrelevant the
stories of Adam and Eve, Cain and Abel, Babel and Noah, and so on. The
fact that these stories remain, recounted in rich detail, indicates that Genesis is not primarily a document of Jewish claims, but a statement of the
universal condition of human beings that precedes and underlies any particular culture. The character of Adam and Eve—creatures endowed with
tremendous powers and deep weaknesses, with the ability to distinguish
between good and evil and with conflicting inclinations that pull them in
both directions, whose origins are in the dust of the earth and yet who
alone are capable of entering into a real relationship with God—all of this
is a description not of Jews but of all people at all times.[10] The fact that all
human beings are created "in the image of God"[11] establishes their essential moral worth and, for followers of the biblical tradition, dictates the
minimal standards of decency with which all must be accorded. Judaism
agrees with Christianity and opposes, among others, Aristotle, in insisting that that there is no biological hierarchy distinguishing superior and
inferior types of human beings, and moreover that the humanity we have
in common carries with it an essential dignity and demands a fundamental
respect.

Yet, against the hopes of the Enlightenment, Judaism does not believe that this universal core of human beings is a sufficient basis on which to ground a political order. If universalism is indicated by the fact that the Bible begins with Genesis, particularism is mandated by the fact that it does not end there. For the chronology of the first book of the Bible traces the successive failures of a universalist ethic. God's original plan for a harmonious world was shattered by Adam and Eve's rebellion. His subsequent attempt at a relationship with a unified humanity, the effort to give universalism a fresh start in the covenant made with Noah following the great flood, was ended in the hubris of the Tower of Babel, after which the unity of humankind was shattered into multiple fragments. It was only after this that God sought out Abraham to pioneer a new people that would bear the divine message. Particularism—the division of humanity into distinct peoples, and the selection of one of these peoples to be a "model nation"—thus appears in the Bible as a third-best alternative.

The Book of Exodus, then, comes as the natural outgrowth of, and response to, the failures of Genesis. Yet Genesis was not thrown out. The depiction of basic humanity in Adam and Eve was not proved false, but merely insufficient. Thus the Jewish tradition maintains Genesis and Exodus side by side: the belief in an essential dignity common to all human beings, and the belief that life must be lived on a particularistic basis. It is this dialectic that underlies the primary themes of political obligation in Jewish law: a recognition of common humanity coupled with a primary commitment to one's particular community.

DIFFERENTIAL OBLIGATIONS IN JEWISH LAW: JEWS, STRANGERS, HEATHENS, AND NOAHIDES

In order to better understand the dialectical relationship between universalism and particularism in Jewish thought, I want to consider Judaism's attitude toward non-Jews—how it understands them and what political obligations it assumes regarding them. Since the start of the talmudic era, rabbinic law has classified the non-Jewish world into three groups: "strangers," resident aliens or Noahides, and heathens. In what follows, I will outline the legal status of each of these groups and the claims they exercise on the Jewish community, as well as the additional set of obligations Jews owe only to one another. Beyond identifying the contours of these groups, I hope to illuminate the intellectual themes defining these categories, and thereby to reveal the peculiar bases of obligation in rabbinic thought. Specifically, I believe that the legal categories described below embody a theory of obligation based on four aspects of potential claimants: (1) an assessment of moral respectability, (2) a measure of responsibility created by relations of dependence, (3) a measure of the proximity and intimacy of social connections, and (4) the dynamics and requirements of social solidarity. Rabbinic thought's foremost departure from universalism is its insistence that by focusing only on those commitments arising from innate moral worth and isolated individual transactions,[12] liberalism misses critical dimensions of social commitment, and thereby produces an eccentric system of obligations. To understand the thrust of this critique, we must examine in some depth the constitution of and obligations due to each of these classes of non-Jews. These are the categories in which Jewish universalism and particularism get played out in concrete legal form, and it is with them that an investigation of this issue must begin.

The Case of the Stranger

The oft-repeated biblical injunction to "love the stranger as yourself"[13] has been commonly understood as a commitment to universalism. Indeed, these commandments, and particularly the assertion that Jews "know the heart of the stranger," constitute a declaration of eternal sympathy with the marginal based on Jews' own history as dependent aliens.[14] Yet to understand the "stranger" as the generic Other, and the commandments as establishing Jews' obligation to selflessly aid all who are in need, regardless of their relation to oneself, turns out to be mistaken. For the "strangers" here represent not outsiders generally but a very specific and carefully defined class of non-Jews. The Hebrew word that is commonly translated as "stranger" (*ger*) would actually be more accurately rendered as "sojourner" or "one who lives with you." The first people to whom the word is applied is the "mixed multitude" of Egyptians who chose to join the Israelites in their flight from Pharaoh.[15] This group constituted a population of non-Jews who nevertheless lived among the Jewish people, joined its destiny to theirs, and accepted both the leadership of Moses and the authority of the law handed down at Sinai. From the beginning, then, the "stranger" did not refer to the word's intuitive meaning in English—to foreigners in general—but to a very particular type of foreigner who had actively affiliated herself with the Jewish community.

Beyond this population of Egyptians, the vast majority of *gerim*[16] in early Jewish history probably came from among the Canaanite nations that inhabited the land of Israel before the Jewish conquest.[17] Once again, these were not foreigners who continued to live in their own communities and according to their own customs, isolated from the Jewish population. Rather, these were individuals who lived in Jewish society and observed at least some minimum of Jewish law. Most importantly, these were people who were vulnerable to and dependent upon specifically Jewish authority, and it is this characteristic of *gerim* that makes the Bible so insistent that their welfare be protected. Upon entering the land of Israel, the Hebrews were commanded to divide all land among the nation's twelve tribes. Furthermore, the Jubilee law, mandating that property revert to its original owner at the end of each fifty-year period, guaranteed a Jewish monopoly on land in perpetuity.[18] The *gerim*, therefore, were effectively prevented from owning land for more than a temporary period, and in an agricultural society this necessarily relegated them to a position of continuing economic insecurity. It is for this reason that the "stranger" is so often mentioned together with the Levite, the widow, and the orphan[19]—each defines a category of residents incapable of supporting itself and whose needs must therefore be recognized as a special responsibility of the community at large. That the vulnerability of "strangers" stemmed particularly from their landless condition is further evidenced by the fact that the Bible specifically identifies them as eligible to participate in the institutions of agricultural charity— to pick from the fallen fruit of the vineyards and from the "corners" of the fields that farmers were prohibited from harvesting.[20]

It is this dimension of vulnerability that also helps make sense of the Bible's repeated injunction to "love the stranger, for you were strangers in the land of Egypt."[21] What exactly is it about the Jews' experience in Egypt that is supposed to parallel the status of strangers in Israel? I believe the evocation of Egypt once again indicates that "stranger" is not an indiscriminate designation of all non-Jews, but rather a relational term; a description of people who live in a very particular relationship toward Jewish political authority. The Jews in Egypt were permanent residents of Pharaoh's kingdom, conducted themselves in accordance with his law, lived a life that was intimately enmeshed with that of the larger Egyptian society, and occupied a position of extreme political and economic vulnerability.

Philosophically, then, there seem to be three important components to the definition of "strangers." First, *gerim* accept Jewish political authority and embrace at least a modicum of Jewish law. Second, their day-to-day lives are permanently intertwined with those of Jews; the word *ger* is etymologically related to the verb "reside" (*gar*), and the biblical text repeatedly emphasizes this connection by referring to strangers with the phrase *"ger ha-gar"*—"the stranger who lives among you," or more clumsily but more accurately, "the dweller who dwells with you."[22] Finally, despite their affiliation, since "strangers" lack Jewish nationality, they remain vulnerable to political and economic marginalization.[23] "Strangers" are not simply vulnerable but, it is important to note, are specifically dependent upon Jewish authority, and this dependence places the Jewish community in a special relationship of responsibility toward them. This is the meaning of the possessive pronoun in the biblical references to "*your* stranger who is within *your* gates";[24] *gerim* in some sense "belong to" the Jewish community, and it therefore bears a moral obligation toward them that far exceeds the level of assistance normally due to outsiders.

Over the course of the biblical and early rabbinic period, the definition of the *ger* grew increasingly restrictive, eventually coming to be reserved for someone who accepted Jewish law in its entirety and was therefore treated as an equal to Jews in all things—that is, a convert.[25] The concept of conversion was developed alongside with, and as an outgrowth of, the evolution of the *ger,* such that the Hebrew word for convert (*mitgayer*) is a conjugation of the root word "stranger." Thus, by the beginning of the talmudic period (c. third century C.E.),[26] the "*stranger*" had ceased to represent any meaningful class of non-Jews. However, the concepts that gave meaning to the category of *gerim*—a distinction between foreigners in general and those who have marked themselves as morally decent by accepting some basic tenets of the Law, acknowledgment of a special bond with those foreigners whose lives are intertwined with that of the Jewish community, and a recognition of obligations created by one community's dependence on the powers of another—continued to provide the terms through which Jewish law interpreted its relationships with non-Jews.

Heathens and Foreigners

The term "heathen" in Jewish law refers to those non-Jews who do not observe even those fundamental aspects of Law that Jews consider to constitute a minimal code of moral decency.[27] The text of Genesis records that in the generation of Noah, human society became characterized by such pervasive evil that God resolved to entirely destroy the known world,[28] and to begin human society anew, this time with a reduced set of expectations embodied in a short list of seven commandments. Genesis 9:8–17 tells the story of the end of the great flood and the renewal of human society. As Noah and his family settle themselves once again on dry land, God strikes a covenant with them in which He promises that the world will never again be destroyed, and in return obliges them to observe those basic commands that constitute the minimal standards of civilized behavior. According to rabbinic tradition, these include the obligation to establish a legal system and courts of law (eschewing the arbitrary rule of personal will), and the prohibition of murder, robbery, blasphemy, idolatry, sexual perversion, and physical cruelty (literally, "tearing off and eating the limb of an animal while it is still alive").[29] The "heathen," then, is specifically defined as a non-Jew who rejects even the Noahide laws.

Non-Noahide foreigners were therefore considered to represent the lowest form of human society—the chaotic realm of ungrounded super-stition and unrestrained, unpredictable behavior. This category of cul-tures was never considered subhuman—they have the full status of human beings, and Jews are obliged to treat them accordingly—but they have no claims for consideration by Jewish authority or by individual Jews apart from the most minimal claims stemming from a common humanity.[30]

The primary concern of Jewish law regarding non-Noahide foreigners was to insulate Jews from their potentially corrupting influence. This is evident from the initial prohibition on establishing relations with the idola-trous Canaanites: "Thou shalt make no covenant with them . . . neither shalt thou make marriages with them . . . for they will turn away thy son from following me, that they may serve other gods."[31] To avoid both the seductiveness of idolatry and the ritual impurity of heathen cultures, a series of restrictions was mandated to enforce the segregation of Jews from the surrounding peoples. To avoid any semblance of condoning idolatrous worship, Jews were forbidden from conducting business with heathens during any of their religious festivals.[32] Similarly, contracts could not be undertaken that involved a heathen swearing an oath in the name of his or her god.[33] To guarantee the strictness of dietary laws, heathens were forbidden from participating with Jews in slaughtering animals, making wine, or preparing meals.[34]

Furthermore, the lawlessness of non-Noahide foreigners was reflected in their treatment in Jewish courts. Essentially, the only positive obliga-tions that Jewish law recognizes toward non-Noahide foreigners are the prohibitions against murder and physical cruelty. Beyond this, they had no integral property rights. Maimonides explains the fourth law that intro-duces this essay, exempting Jews from liability for their oxen goring gentile oxen, by pointing to the fact that the gentiles themselves do not recognize the Noahide ban on theft and therefore have no property law whatsoever. While Jewish courts may exact payment for damages from such heathens, it would be senseless to make payments to a member of a culture that does not itself recognize the category of property liability. The Talmud is in disagreement over whether Jews may rob gentiles,[35] but even the liberal au-thority Rabbi Menachem HaMeiri agrees that a Jew who finds something that was inadvertently lost by a gentile is not obligated to return it, "since finding gives some title and restoring is an act of solidarity—and we are not obligated to show solidarity with godless barbarians." [36]

The Noahide commands thus serve Judaism as a kind of limited universalism; they identify the bounds within which cultural pluralism is acceptable. While rabbinic law does not demand that the rest of the world be converted to Judaism, Maimonides notes that Jews are obligated, to the extent that their political power allows, "to coerce all the inhabitants of the world to accept the seven Noahide commandments." [37] It is because they fall outside these bounds that heathens are denied any but the most minimal claims on Jewish law. [38]

Resident Aliens and Noahides

As the term *ger* came to denote a convert, rabbinic law developed the status of "resident alien" (*ger toshav*) to designate an individual who lived under Jewish political authority without converting to Judaism. In order to be permitted to live in the Jewish polity, a *ger toshav* was required to obey the seven Noahide commands. [39] In return, resident aliens were granted certain protections under Jewish law, though they were not entitled to the full range of considerations accorded the convert. [40]

Thus, while Jews retained sovereignty over the land of Israel, acceptance of the Noahide laws marked a class of non-Jews who occupied an intermediate position between the "stranger" and the completely untutored foreigner. Following the loss of Jewish independence, however, this term came to lose all practical meaning, as there was neither any possibility of imposing Noahide law on non-Jews nor any substantive legal authority with which to define the rights of such residents. [41] Furthermore, rabbinic authorities largely assumed that no foreign nation would adopt Noahide law of its own volition, without being coerced by Jewish political power. Therefore, as they settled into exile, Jews resigned themselves to living in a variety of cultures that might be more or less hospitable, but all of which were essentially heathen.

This remained true for more than one thousand years, until the early medieval period, when rabbinic authorities began to recognize Moslems and Christians as Noahides. [42] HaMeiri, writing at the turn of the fourteenth century, held that Christians, though differing in the specifics of their faith, essentially worshiped the same God as Judaism: "they believe in God's existence, His unity, and power, although they misconceive some points according to our belief." [43] Since the Noahide prohibition against idolatry requires only that non-Jews accept monotheism but not that they embrace Judaism, this was enough to qualify them as Noahides. HaMeiri thus drew a distinction among non-Jewish cultures, between those "constrained by the ways of religion" and those that "have no religion whatsoever, and . . . did not refrain from any iniquity."[44] The former group, comprised of Christians and Moslems, were declared to be "like a resident alien," and considered to have the same legal status as the *ger toshav*.[45] While HaMeiri's position was largely unknown and therefore uninfluential in his own time, it came to be adopted as the mainstream principle over the next several centuries.[46] Thus, since converts ("strangers") had been collapsed into the same category as Jews, rabbinic law by the eighteenth century had come to divide the political world into three broad categories: Jews, heathens, and Noahides.

In recognition of their moral stature, Noahides are exempt from the restrictions against association with idolators. Thus, following HaMeiri's ruling, Rabbi Isaac permitted business transactions that involved Christians swearing an oath in the name of Jesus, as this was no longer judged to constitute idolatry.[47] Similarly, where the Mishnah forbids Jews hiring gentiles to care for their animals, out of suspicion of bestiality, HaMeiri ruled that this was no longer a concern, as those "constrained by religion" were not suspect on this basis.[48]

Most important, in nearly all cases Noahides are treated as equals with Jews before the law. The permission to rob or deceive heathens, the denial of liability for damages to heathen property, and the permission to retain the lost objects of heathens, all are abolished in the case of the resident alien.[49] In HaMeiri's words, "anytime the law obligates them for the seven Noahide laws their case before us is like our case before us. We do not favor ourselves in the case."[50] Beyond this, Jews bear a responsibility to safeguard the material and emotional well-being of Noahides, which far exceeds that due to heathens.[51]

Yet there remain important differences between resident aliens (the *ger toshav*) and Noahides. Recalling the four attributes of "strangers" outlined above, it is clear that while both these groups accept some portion of Jewish law, and both may live in close daily contact with their Jewish neighbors, only the former stands in a relationship of dependence on the Jewish community. As residents of the land of Israel subject to Jewish authority, resident aliens were vulnerable to and dependent upon specifically Jewish power, and this created an obligation on the part of the Jewish community that is not reproduced in the case of Moslems and Christians living in their own countries. The Bible in several places describes the position of strangers as "the stranger who dwells with you,"[52] or even "your stranger who is within your gates." [53] There is an important difference between non-Jewish Noahides who in some sense "belong to" the Jewish community because they live under Jewish authority, and those who themselves are members of the ruling culture in which Jews are visitors. If anything, in the latter case the position of Jews is closer to being themselves the "stranger," vulnerable to foreign political power and occupying a position of institutionalized insecurity. When Noahides are neither vulnerable to nor dependent upon Jewish authority, there is no concomitant obligation for the Jewish community to guarantee their welfare. Thus for example, while the Talmud disagrees over whether resident aliens may be charged interest,[54] there has been no suggestion that Jews refrain from taking interest from Noahides. In Greenberg's words, the status of the resident alien "was based on the principle that the Jewish community was obliged to provide him with sustenance." [55] By contrast, any obligation to provide for the needs of Noahides could only be on the same basis as that of unschooled foreigners: for the sake of social peace between Jews and their host communities.[56]

Obligations to Fellow Jews: The Imperatives of Social Solidarity

Even when Noahides are considered as equals before the law, they are excluded from those institutions of mutual assistance through which the Jewish community seeks to provide for the needs of its members. While Jews bear an obligation to insure that the emergency needs of the *ger toshav* do not go unmet, they are obliged to participate in a much more extensive set of institutions designed to provide for the ongoing upkeep of the Jewish poor. Thus, the institutions of the interest-free loan and the sabbatical cancellation of debt were designed specifically for fellow Jews.[57] Likewise, the "poor man's tithe," which Jewish farmers were required to set aside from every third year's produce, was reserved exclusively for the poor of Israel.[58] So too, rabbinic law's just-price doctrine, and its restrictions on profiting from trade in subsistence goods, pertained only to trade within the Jewish community.[59] As Moshe Greenberg explains, "these aids to the poor were the expression of solidarity among Israelites; outsiders could neither be expected to share such obligations, nor expect to enjoy their benefits." [60]

Thus, rabbinic law mandates a hierarchy of obligations that distinguishes different classes of claimants on the basis of moral stature, dependence, social intimacy, and communal solidarity. I have hinted at some of the reasoning that lies behind this system of differential obligations. I now turn to a more concentrated analysis of the philosophical sensibilities that provide this system with its deepest rationales.

PHILOSOPHICAL BASES OF JEWISH PARTICULARISM

Distinction and Intelligibility

The insistence on differentiating between Jews and non-Jews is part of a broader hermeneutic within Judaism that equates distinction with intelligibility and conflation with chaos. In Genesis, the world is created not by bringing things together, but by pulling them apart—God divides day from night, the heavens from the earth, dry land from water, and so on.[61] The process of bringing order out of chaos is one of making distinctions within a previously undifferentiated mass. Chaos here is the lack of patterns, the lack of categories, the lack of boundaries; such a world, in Jewish thought, is both dangerously unpredictable and fundamentally unintelligible—there is no way to take hold of, or to operate within, such an undifferentiated world. In Jewish thought, then, the movement from opacity to intelligibility—from darkness to light—is a movement from aggregation to disaggregation and from the general to the particular.

This ethic provides the prime rationale for the categories of membership into which Judaism divides the political world. For Jews, the differentiation of the earth's population into distinct nations is an integral step in making the political world intelligible. Even within the Jewish community, Jews are obligated to recognize differential obligations, to provide for family members ahead of nonrelatives, neighbors ahead of more distant townsmen, and even distant townsmen ahead of the Jewish poor of other jurisdictions.[62] This hierarchy of commitments stems from the conviction that political obligations derive not from abstract principles but from the lived connections forged by shared lives and common identity. Moreover, it is this hierarchy that provides a means by which to make sense of the social world. To suggest that all individuals be thought of without distinction, as standing in equal proximity to me and as making claims that are equally binding on me, is in this scheme to reduce political relations to incomprehensibility. For theorists whose tenets emanate from ideal principles, Jewish social life must appear as a tangled web of irrational favoritisms. But for Jews, the replacement of this texture with abstract universalism leaves a social surface so flat that it precludes any meaningful arrangement.

The understanding of national distinctions as a means for making sense of the political world is well conveyed by Michael Walzer in his *Spheres of Justice*.[63] In imagining what a world without such distinctions might look like, Walzer recounts the story of the Good Samaritan, who offers assistance to a stranger he has met at the side of a road. This act of mercy involves a recognition of the obligations we bear even to strangers; it is a response to the respect demanded by the universal dignity of all human beings. But while this represents a critical moral code, if *all* our relationships were conducted on the same basis as that with a stranger we meet at the roadside, our social lives would be transformed into something *random*. To commit myself to reacting with equal passion to the needs of a neighbor and those of a passing traveler would be to let my life be "shaped and determined by . . . chance encounters." [64] Walzer's description here refers not merely to the impracticality of devoting equal resources to whoever happens to call on me but also to the ways in which such a political commitment would strip one's life of any sensible pattern.

As an instance of this, imagine a liberal-minded college student who completes her B.A. and wants to spend a year working on some socially beneficial project. Imagine further that her choices for employment include counseling AIDS patients in Los Angeles, teaching English on an Indian reservation in North Dakota, digging irrigation ditches in Nicaragua, helping to rehabilitate decrepit housing in the Bronx, or driving an ambulance for the Emergency Medical Services of the city of Phoenix. All of these are worthwhile, and all may in some sense be admirable. But behind any of these choices lurk two disturbing questions. On what basis can this student go about choosing which project to commit herself to? And what will be the nature of her commitment to the population she serves, given the type of choice this project has sprung from?

I imagine that the answer to the first question is that the student's choice will be based on some personal and relatively arbitrary preference: She likes the climate of a particular location or has a friend living nearby, or perhaps she wants to improve her Spanish, or for some reason she cannot quite identify, she has always felt particularly outraged about the housing crisis. And given a choice of this nature, I believe the answer to the second question is that she may or may not form close personal relations with some of the people she works with, but her commitment to the population as a whole will always be a limited one, infused with the consciousness that this is a project that was chosen but might not have been.

Now imagine a Puerto Rican student who grew up in the Bronx, attended the same college, and is returning to work in the same rehabilitation program as her classmate. The difference between these two graduates is not merely that one is connected to the project in a way the other can never hope to replicate. It is also that this connection makes one of their lives more deeply intelligible than the other's. If we met both of these students at a party and listened to their respective plans, there's an important way in which one of these stories would seem to *make sense,* while the other would be marked by a curious arbitrariness. It is not that anything the first student could do might be *wrong*—on the contrary. But it turns out that there's another dimension to political obligation beyond an action's being right or wrong according to some measure of justice. That dimension is the extent to which an action can be *made sense of* in the broader context of a person's life; and this is the part of politics that no universalist theory can address.

It is this belief, that the establishment of distinct categories of political obligation renders social life intelligible, that animates Jewish particularism. Judaism recognizes a minimal set of obligations toward all human beings and a more extensive set toward members of all "civilized" societies. Yet both of these remain largely passive, rather than active, obligations. Jews are bound to respect the lives and property of others, to accord them equal treatment in Jewish courts of law, and to respond to their material needs in cases of emergency. Beyond this level of general consideration lies a deeper commitment that extends only to fellow Jews: the obligation to actively promote their welfare and the acceptance of an ongoing responsibility to guarantee their well-being.

To renounce this distinction is not to extend the intimacy and commitment of communal relations to the world at large, but rather to reduce even familial and communal bonds to the level of our relations with strangers. This is not simply because it is impossible to commit the same level of resources to the world at large as we do to our local communities, but also because the psychic nature of political solidarity is such that it can only be substantively realized on a small scale and as the product of shared identities. Here rabbinic thought echoes Aristotle's critique of communalization of the family in the *Republic.* He viewed the proposal that all members of the guardian class consider themselves brothers, and their collective children as all equally their sons, as a policy that would empty the very concept of family ties of its meaning, concluding that "it is better, indeed, to have a cousin of one's own than a son in the sense indicated." [65] Where Deuteronomy calls for the provision of interest-free loans only to one's "brother," [66] universalist ethics insist that we treat the whole world as our brothers. But in Jewish thought, this is an unworkable proposition. The institution of interest-free loans is an instance of economic solidarity that materially sustains and psychically binds a community. Neither these economic arrangements nor the commitment to mutual support that they express is possible to reproduce on a universal scale. Rather, the result of attempting to take a particularistic institution and apply it universally is to simulate an officially professed but psychically empty brotherhood; to arrive at what Benjamin Nelson has termed "universal otherhood."[67]

This understanding of social solidarity also helps to make sense of the concept of a "chosen people," which will be a "light unto the nations." The example that Jewish law seeks to set is one aimed not at individuals but specifically at other "nations." The institutions of solidarity that mark off Jews' commitments to one another from their more minimal obligations to outsiders are not designed to be applied as universal law governing relations among all people, but rather to be reiterated within each particular nation.[68] This, then, is the universalist mission of Judaism: not to be "a light unto all individuals," not to establish an international system of justice, but rather to teach specific nations how to live *as* a nation.

It is for this reason that even HaMeiri, despite concluding that Christians were not idolators, insisted on maintaining barriers between the two peoples. Katz notes, for instance, that HaMeiri might have ruled Jewish dietary laws superfluous, since their prime rationale was to separate Jews from idolators.[69] But for HaMeiri, segregation remained valuable even among nonidolators, in order to maintain the distinctness of each culture, and to avoid the eventuality that "we would . . . become one people."[70]

This ethic of distinction permeates all aspects of Jewish life. Where philosophers have long argued over whether the distinguishing (*sic*) attribute of human beings is our capacity for speech, for creativity, or for moral reason, Judaism would doubtlessly add that one of the defining attributes of a *civilized* person is the ability to make distinctions between different classes of things and between appropriate and inappropriate behavior. This is what primarily accounts for the prohibition on sexual "perversion," rather than a concern that sex be reserved for procreation. Heathens do not have distinct relations: friends, children, siblings, wives, and farm animals all constitute an undifferentiated universe of potential sexual partners. But in Jewish thought, an essential part of being a civilized person is the capacity to distinguish between different types of relations. Thus Mary Douglas, commenting on Lev. 18:23 ("And you shall not lie with any beast and defile yourself with it, neither shall any woman give herself to a beast to lie with it: it is perversion") notes that the word "perversion" (*tevel*) would be better translated as "confusion" or "mixing up"—the prohibition is not based simply on a revulsion at the thought of bestiality, but more specifically on the sense that to have sex with animals is to deny God's design for the universe, to erase lines of demarcation that are part of the divine plan, and to thereby take a step backward from order into chaos and from sense into nonsense. In Douglas's words, sexual morality in the Bible "is more a matter of separating that which should be separated than of protecting the rights of husbands and brothers." [71]

It is the failure to make such distinctions that centrally characterizes Judaism's perception of non-Noahide cultures. What it means to be barbaric is to be driven by pure will, with no recognition of limitations. At some deep level, Judaism identifies terror with chaos.[72] Brutality here is understood as a species of *randomness,* as something left over from the void that preceded creation. This is the meaning of HaMeiri's designation of Noahides as peoples "constrained by the ways of religion"; the "constraint" here is the acceptance of critical boundaries that must not be crossed.[73] This point is further suggested by some of the alternative versions of the Noahide covenant recorded in the Talmud. One such list adds to the seven laws presented above a prohibition against crossbreeding animals of different species or grafting together trees of different kinds.[74] That these, of all things, would be seen as pedagogical tools to educate heathens in the ways of decency emphasizes again the motif of differentiation as a central feature of Jewish morality.[75]

Antinaturalism

That universalism appears chaotic to Jews reflects the tradition's lack of faith in the reliability or determinacy of human nature. In this sense Judaism's insistence on the importance of maintaining distinct nationalities represents an antinatural political sensibility, emphasizing convention rather than nature as the bearer of political meaning. At least since Hobbes, the search for reliable political theory has been predominantly a search for the natural. In much of Western thought, what is natural has come to be associated with what is true and enduring, and what is conventional with what is arbitrary and fleeting. For Judaism, however, the truths of nature are minimal, and the meaningful arena for political life is that constructed by the mores and life-styles of particular cultures. The fundamental traits common to all humanity, the fact that all people are created "in the image of God," remain intact. Indeed, the very fact that all peoples are included in the Noahide covenant, and are held accountable for these commandments, assumes that they are capable of carrying them out; commands are given only to beings that have the free will and moral intuition necessary to observe them. But this natural intuition turns out to be an insufficient basis for political life. This is most clearly evident in the evil ways of the seven Canaanite peoples, who were marked for expulsion in part due to their failure to adhere to Noahide law (including, for example, the practice of child sacrifice and literally tearing the limbs off living animals), and particularly of Amalek, a nation so thoroughly evil that Israel is commanded to annihilate it completely.[76] The fact that human beings endowed with the same innate moral capacities given to Adam and Eve could devolve nevertheless into such barbaric cultures suggests that the universal aspects of human nature, the moral capacities with which we're endowed at birth, are too tenuous and too easily perverted to serve as the building blocks of a political system. In rabbinic thought, then, a moral society is made moral not through nature but through culture; and Judaism nowhere aspires to achieve a "natural" society or to realize "natural" political relations.

Here Jewish thought departs radically from the Enlightenment faith in innate rationality. For many Enlightenment thinkers, while individuals may come to act evilly, human nature is sufficiently "thick" that society as a whole never loses its understanding of basic moral principles. Kantian notions of morality, for instance, picture evildoers as individuals who are fully conscious of what's right and wrong but choose to act out their lust, jealousy, or selfish interest in violation of this knowledge. Indeed, for Kant, it is because everyone *knows* what's right and wrong that they can be punished. Similarly for Rawls, the process of reflective equilibrium assumes that, while people may be driven to pursue selfish interests at the expense of others, they always retain, and at the deepest level affirm, an underlying recognition of the principles of fairness. But the rabbinic understanding of evil involves much more of a moral abyss, in which members of a barbaric culture may become so accustomed to cruelty and so morally hollowed out by their environment, that they lose any capacity for empathy or any substantive understanding of the limits of moral behavior. It is this fundamental moral void that makes "heathens" undeserving of any but the most minimal obligations.

Yet there are many intellectual traditions that agree that untutored human nature provides an insufficient basis for political life and nevertheless believe that this nature is the most philosophically important aspect of human beings, and therefore that a constructive politics must consist in a strategy for cultivating these universal traits. This, then, is the second sense of political naturalism that Judaism rejects: the belief that political life must be formulated at the level of the species. At least since Plato, philosophers have assumed that whatever the best regime might be, it must be "best" in virtue of traits that are true about human beings qua members of the species—there must be one set of laws that governs all humans. This is a view that regards human nature as morally ambiguous, but still determinate; for Judaism, however, the truths of nature are neither durable nor substantial enough to provide a basis for politics.

The assumption that the proper subject of politics must be the human species is an instance of a broader epistemological hermeneutic that assumes that what is general must be more important, more fundamental, more real. By contrast, David Novak notes that "Judaism [is] much more compatible with the opposite metaphysical assumption, namely, [that] the general is merely a background, that, indeed, the particular and unique is the content of our experience."[77] Thus within the level of generalization specified by nature, Judaism identifies a further layer of distinctions, and *this* is the relevant level for political life—not nature, but convention; not the species, but the national culture.

Selfishness/Selflessness

To medieval Christian eyes, the Deuteronomic law cited in the introduction to this essay, allowing Jews to take interest from non-Jews but not from fellow Jews, must have appeared deeply offensive. For if this is based on the same evaluation of interest that Christianity holds—that is, that this is an ugly act degrading to the borrower—its logic implies that non-Jews are unworthy of the respect demanded by full human beings and therefore are acceptable targets of degradation. This was exactly the view of the Church father Ambrose: "From him demand usury whom you rightly desire to harm, against whom weapons are lawfully carried. . . . From him exact usury whom it would not be a crime to kill. Where there is the right of war there is the right of usury."[78]

But this represents a mistaken understanding of Jewish usury, which turns on the contrasting views of self-interest in Judaism and Christianity. Judaism does not see anything wrong with taking interest per se, even from Jews[79]; usury is rarely portrayed as an intrinsically ugly or degrading act. The laws of usury stem rather from the fact that Jews have an additional obligation of economic solidarity with fellow Jews, which extends beyond the morally acceptable practice of taking interest. This obligation is not to desist from something ugly, but to engage in something integral to the sustenance of the community: the provision of interest-free loans.[80] In the words of the medieval rabbinic commentator Abarbanel:

> There is nothing unworthy about interest per se, because it is proper that people should make profit out of their money. . . . It is an ordinary business transaction and correct. Nobody is under obligation to give his money away to somebody else, unless it be for the sake of charity. Equally, one cannot be compelled to lend one's money free of interest, unless for the sake of charity. God

considered the matter of interest-free loans to be on the same level as the (sabbatical cancellation of debts). Both are applicable only vis-a-vis the brother, i.e., the coreligionist, to whom we owe special kindness and consideration. The case is different with the laws on theft, robbery, murder and adultery, which are of universal validity.[81]

Thus, what to Catholics must inevitably have seemed a bald-faced refusal to recognize the common humanity of non-Jews was, for Jews, something akin to the logic by which one might make great sacrifices to pay for one's child's hospital bills but not for those of all children.

The contrast in Jewish and Christian conceptions of usury is the product of a deeper disagreement concerning the values of selfishness and selflessness. Christianity is deeply wedded to an ethic of self-sacrifice; indeed, the central drama of Christianity is the supreme act of self-sacrifice on behalf of a sinful humanity. The accompanying valorization of poverty and humility in part reflect a fear that self-interest is a slippery slope; that if we allow ourselves to actively embrace our self-interests, we will inevitably deteriorate into complete self-absorption, deaf or indifferent to the needs of others. Self-interest here is one of the evil impulses born within us, part of original sin, which we must struggle to overcome.

By contrast, neither poverty nor humility are Jewish virtues, and the tradition is largely devoid of stories glorifying the virtuous poor man. Rather, like Aristotle and Marx, it sees material well-being as an integral part of the good life. To allow others to go hungry is a sin, as is an obsession with money making that leads to the neglect of familial, communal, or religious obligations. But the laws restricting these behaviors are considered to constitute a sufficient "stopping point" that keeps self-interest from sliding into avarice and egocentrism. And within these bounds, the attainment of material well-being is a good, the product of a healthy will.

I believe that the motivating force of Western universalism is related to Christianity's anxiety regarding self-interest. Much of universalist political theory conceives its project as an effort to overcome self-interest in order to attain moral decency. The transition from the state of nature to civil society in classical liberal theory is a transition from unbridled self-interest to self-interest that has been made safe by redirection into a productive channel. Kant explicitly equated morality with self-denial and immorality with self-interest.[82] Rawls's theory of justice, too, is essentially a polemic that urges us to remain vigilant against the morally obscuring effects of our desires, and to bind ourselves instead to "an impartial judgment not . . . distorted by an excessive attention to our own interests.[83]

As Christianity distrusts an individual's privileging her own interests ahead of others', so universalism distrusts a nation's pursuing its interest to the exclusion of outsiders. A nation should act out on a grand scale the same virtues that bind an individual on the micro level. For Judaism, this is clearly to support oneself, to make a living, and to take care of "one's own." For many Christian thinkers, however, the virtues of an individual life are not of providing for oneself but of denying oneself in order to provide for others. The debate between universalism and particularism is thus partly also a debate between self-interest and self-sacrifice, between the selfish and the selfless. Part of the rationale for universalism is that it embodies a rejection, or at least a suppression of self-interest. To advocate a particularist position is, at least to some extent, to accept an ethic that is comfortable with self-interested behavior.

SUMMARY AND CONTEMPORARY APPLICATIONS

In this essay I provide an account of universal and particularist obligations in Jewish law. The rabbinic treatment of obligation addresses a subject that has been notoriously difficult for liberals and suggests an approach to this issue that is strikingly different from that of ideal liberal theory. At the heart of this disagreement is an argument with theorists such as John Rawls over what constitutes a "morally relevant" factor in formulating political obligations, and whether national bonds should be something we build on or vigilantly disregard in defining obligations.[84]

The liberal insistence on undiluted universalism is, I believe, a natural result of the project to construct a system of obligation on the foundation of individual autonomy. For liberals, the individual is the fundamental, and in some sense the only real, unit of political life. Inevitably, then, liberal formulations of community, tribe, or nation tend to be anemic. If nations are nothing more than the aggregate authority of individuals who have chosen to invest their sovereignty in a collective mechanism—if a society is, in Rawls's words, no more than "a cooperative venture for mutual advantage"[85]—then collectivities may represent useful combinations of individual wills, but they can never take on independent moral significance. The individual's voice remains the only legitimate one that can exercise a claim on social resources. In this sense, it is unsurprising that a neo-Kantian such as Charles Beitz cannot think of a reason "why any moral importance should attach to . . . cultural, racial, tribal, or religious groups."[86] What Beitz proposes will seem logical, perhaps even obvious, to many of us who have grown up with liberal sensibilities: "contractarian principles of social justice . . . ought to apply globally. . . . [We must develop] principles of international distributive justice that establish a fair division of natural resources, income, and wealth among persons situated in diverse national societies."[87] But to adopt this as the sole "morally relevant" determinant of obligations will make sense only if we conceive of politics as an arena of fundamentally unrelated actors.

By contrast, Jewish political thought does not begin from an original individual sovereignty. Neither the nation nor its law derives its meaning from the alienated authority of individuals; on the contrary, the individual in large ways derives his or her identity from membership in the collectivity. Jews are joined together not by a social contract but by a covenantal relationship that binds each one to the law and to one another. And the character of the relations created by these bonds is such that their reinforcement constitutes a legitimate moral goal in itself, beyond the claims of the particular individuals involved. Judaism's disagreement with neo-Kantianism, then, is not over the calculation of universal moral worth. Rather, it points to an additional dimension of morality that liberal theory has ignored—the morality of relations—and insists that this too is a "relevant" aspect of political obligations. The injunction to provide for one's poor neighbors before the more distant poor is not based on the moral superiority of the former, but on the conviction that to do otherwise would be neglectful, degrading, and destructive of lived social ties. In a world composed only of individuals, justice demands that we treat all needs with equal urgency; in a world composed of relationships, justice demands that we treat those bonds with the seriousness they deserve.

In this sense, the account of Jewish particularism fits into the broader communitarian critique of liberalism. Yet this account is not provided with the intention of contributing to a competing general theory of obligation, which other communities can simply apply to their own political lives. Certainly, I would not have presented this material had I not believed that the underlying sensibilities, if not all the specific laws, of Jewish particularism offered a positive approach to this issue from which other communities could learn. Yet I do not believe it is possible to prescribe the exact forms such lessons should take in other communities. Part of what it means to be a people is to live out a particular history, in a particular social context, subject to a unique set of circumstances. The hermeneutics of distinction and solidarity may be appreciated, but their concrete application can only be worked out casuistically as each culture confronts its particular circumstances.

Here I return to a question raised at the start of this essay: What, then, can be learned from a "thick description" of Jewish ethics of obligation? For American Jews, I hope that this presentation may provide some means for making sense of particularistic sensibilities that they have felt but been unable to rationalize in liberal terminology. In the conclusion to his *Whose Justice? Which Rationality?* Alasdair MacIntyre describes the experience of "self-recognition" in which someone endowed with the sensibilities of a particular tradition, but schooled in such a way as to be unable to articulate them, confronts a presentation of these traditional beliefs.

> Upon encountering a coherent presentation of [the] particular tradition . . . a person will often experience a shock of recognition: *this* is not only . . . what I now take to be true but in some measure what I have always taken to be true. What such a person has been presented with is a scheme of overall belief within which many, if not all, of his or her particular established beliefs fall into place, a set of . . . interpretative canons for action which exhibit his or her mode of reasoning about action intelligible and justifiable in a way or to a degree which has not previously been the case.[88]

It is my hope that when confronted with not only the emotions but the rationale of particularism, American Jews will be able to begin making sense of an issue that has previously been inchoate, and to construct a sensible approach to the myriad of political claims that confront them. While the exact forms this will take must be worked out slowly, I would like to suggest a few paths along which these issues may be developed. Clearly, Jewish law seeks to legitimate particularist attachments and to emphasize those commitments that reinforce social solidarity within a community. But it also points to a substantial obligation owed even to outsiders—especially since in the contemporary United States there are no groups considered by Jewish law to be "heathen." Beyond this, I believe that the priority placed on helping those whose lives are intertwined with one's own indicates that even among outsiders, Jewish communities must place the poor of their locale ahead of the more distant poor. Finally, I believe that, given the complex interrelatedness of modern economies, the class of obligations that stem from dependence must be interpreted in a broader light. It is possible that, while Jews do not exercise political sovereignty in America, they are sufficiently integrated into positions of social and economic power that it makes sense to think of them as bearing a special responsibility for those made poor in the course of that system's operation.

For Americans generally, the implications flowing from the example of Jewish particularism are more difficult to draw. Not only do Americans constitute a culture whose historical and intellectual roots are extremely different from those of rabbinic Judaism, but we do not constitute a single coherent culture. Instead, America is made up of a plurality of subcultures, and a large number of citizens who do not feel themselves part of *any* particular tradition in the sense indicated by MacIntyre. For people in this position, the lessons of particularism have no direct application.

Yet I believe that there are at least two dimensions along which the example of particularism may speak to us as Americans. The first concerns our judgment of other nations. In the experience of appreciating an ethic of communal solidarity, we may come to a greater tolerance and even sympathy for nations that revolve around more communal and less individualistic ethics. At the same time, we may come to regard our own liberal individualism as the particular intellectual tradition in which our nation has its roots, rather than something to be celebrated as a prescription for all peoples. Second, I believe that the example of particularism suggests directions for change in our own construction of obligation. There may be a limited form of "self-recognition," which, while not involving the exclusivity of tribal solidarity, suggests new ways of conceptualizing local and global, personal and impersonal obligations. Above all, Jewish particularism suggests that in thinking about obligations, we must pay attention to the "morality of relations" in addition to the abstract morality that adheres in human nature. This may mean that we come to think of subcultural groups as entities whose whole is greater than the sum of their parts; that is, which have a moral significance beyond the aggregate significance of their individual members. We may find a way to conceptualize the distinction between groups constituted by a deeply shared identity and those constituted only by a convergence of interests. And we may come to imagine the country more as an assembly of such identity groups than an aggregation of individuals, and to think of desert and responsibility adhering in such groups rather than solely in individuals. None of this, of course, is to prescribe a concrete plan of implementation. But the nature of the project makes this impossible. The aim of examinations such as this is not to yield immediate prescriptions but to present an intuitive rendering of a particular culture that communicates not the rules but the language, terms, metaphors, and hermeneutics of a social system, which hopefully inspires others but which cannot instruct them.

NOTES

Acknowledgments: I would like to thank Steven Smith, Ian Shapiro, David Mayhew, Michael Walzer, Steven Fraade, David Ruderman, Jim Ponet, Noah Efron, Laura Levitt, Peter Berkowitz, Rogan Kersh, Jonathan Stein, and especially Richard Schuldenfrei for valuable comments on earlier drafts of this essay.

1. John Rawls, *A Theory of Justice* (Cambridge, Mass.: Harvard University Press, 1971), 6. Rawls contends that the process of reflective equilibrium will affirm his two principles of justice as fairness, because in American political culture these principles "are ones that we do in fact accept" (21).

2. Ibid., 112.

3. Cited in Eugene Borowitz, *Reform Judaism Today* (New York: Behrman House, 1977), 101.

4. Michael J. Sandel, *Liberalism and the Limits of Justice* (New York: Cambridge University Press, 1982), 182–83.

5. Ibid., 173.

6. Robert Bellah et al., *Habits of the Heart: Individualism and Commitment in American Life* (New York: Harper & Row, 1985), 285.

7. Rawls, *Theory of Justice,* 13; Alasdair MacIntyre, *After Virtue* (South Bend, Ind.: University of Notre Dame Press, 1984), 258.

8. Bellah, *Habits of the Heart,* 285.

9. Rabbi Abraham Ben Isaiah and Rabbi Benjamin Sharfman, *The Pentateuch and Rashi's Commentary: A Linear Translation into English* (New York: S.S. & R. Publishing, 1949), commentary on Gen. 1:1. "Rashi" is an acronym for Rabbi Shlomo bar Itzhak, 1040–105, France.

10. For a more complete discussion of the conception of human nature developed in the Book of Genesis, see Rabbi Joseph B. Soloveitchick's *Halakhic Man* (Philadelphia: Jewish Publication Society of America, 1983).

11. Gen. 1:27.

12. For representatives of this position, see sec. 18 of Rawls, *Theory of Justice.* See also Judith Lichtenberg, "National Boundaries and Moral Boundaries: A Cosmopolitan View," in *Boundaries: National Autonomy and Its Limits,* edited by Peter G. Brown and Henry Shue (Totowa, N.J.: Rowman and Littlefield, 1981).

13. Lev. 19:34.

14. Jon Levenson suggests that Jewish history from Abraham forward reflects a divine intention to forge a people that would always be close to the margins, which even as a sovereign nation would not quite fit into the normal family of nations. See his excellent short article "Poverty and the State in Biblical Thought," *Judaism* 25, no. 2 (Spring 1976).

15. Exod. 12:38.

16. The "*im*" ending indicates the plural form of a Hebrew noun; i.e., *gerim* means "strangers."

17. See *Encyclopedia Judaica* (1978), s.v. "stranger." Although Israel was com-

manded (Deut. 7:2–4) to annihilate these nations, there is ample evidence that this was never fully carried out. The continued presence of Canaanites in the land of Israel is first described in the biblical books of Joshua and Judges.

18. Lev. 25:23–24.

19. E.g., Deut. 10:17–18. The Levites were Temple priests, supported by agricultural tithes and barred from owning land in Israel.

20. Lev. 19:10 and 23:22.

21. E.g., Lev. 19:33–34; Deut. 10:19.

22. E.g., Num. 15:16.

23. The theme of dependence as an aspect of being "strangers" is recapitulated in the Jewish people's relationship with God. Thus, King David proclaims that "I am a stranger with Thee" (Ps. 39:13), and 1 Chron. 29:15 announces, "For we are strangers before Thee." In some sense, the people's dependence on God parallels that of the *ger* on Jewish authority.

24. E.g., Exod. 20:10, emphasis added.

25. The Bible records at different points that *gerim* are subject to the laws of incest (Lev. 18:26), the dietary laws (Lev. 17:10–16), observance of the Sabbath (Exod. 20:10; Deut. 5:14), and even sacrificing the Paschal lamb (Exod. 12:48–49). But ultimately these particular commandments were superseded by the injunction of Num. 15:16, "One Torah and one legal code shall there be for you and for the stranger that resides with you."

26. Dates in this essay use the secular calendar: C.E. (common era) years correspond to A.D. of the Christian calendar; B.C.E. (before the common era) corresponds to B.C.

27. The term "heathen" is used in this essay as a translation for the Hebrew terms *nochri, zar, goy, umot ha-olam,* and *ovdei kochavim.* The word "heathen" is commonly used to translate a number of phrases in Hebrew, including "foreigner" (*zar* or *nochri*), "nation" (*goy,* or *umot ha-olam*) and "idolators" (*ovdei kochavim*). In this essay it is used interchangeably with "foreigner" and designates those non-Jews who rejected even Noahide law.

28. Gen. 6:5–7: "And the Lord saw that the wickedness of man was great in the earth, and that all the impulse of the thoughts of his heart was only evil continually. And the Lord repented that he had made man on the earth, and it grieved him at his heart. And the Lord said, I will destroy man whom I have created from the face of the earth."

29. The seven Noahide commands are not identified in the biblical text but are established by rabbinic interpretation, first recorded in the Tosephta, c. second century C.E. An extensive discussion of this code can be found in David Novak's *The Image of the Non-Jew in Judaism: An Historical and Constructive Study of the Noahide Laws* (New York: Edwin Mellen Press, 1983).

30. During the period of Jewish sovereignty, "heathens" included the nations surrounding Israel as well as merchants who were temporarily traveling through it. While there were at times both folk customs and royal treaties regulating the relationship between Jews and members of these nations, they were joined by no

permanent bond or obligation other than the minimal recognition of a common humanity.

31. Deut. 7:2–4.

32. Babylonian Talmud, Avodah Zarah 1.1.

33. Babylonian Talmud, Sanhedrin 63b.

34. Mishnah Hullin 1.1. See also Jacob Katz, *Exclusiveness and Tolerance: Studies in Jewish-Gentile Relations, in Medieval and Modern Times* (New York: Oxford University Press), chap. 13.

35. The strongest suggestion that this is allowed is in Sanhedrin 57a: "a gentile robbing a gentile, or a gentile robbing an Israelite—this is forbidden. But an Israelite robbing a gentile—this is permitted." Cf. also Baba Kama 113a. Maimonides, on the other hand, insists that Jews cannot steal from heathens, nor even deceive them in financial transactions, *Mishneh Torah*, Hilchot Mechirah 18:1.

36. Rabbi Menachem HaMeiri (d. 1316, Provençal, France), cited in Moshe Greenberg, "Mankind, Israel and the Nations in the Hebraic Heritage," in *No Man Is Alien: Essays on the Unity of Mankind,* edited by J. Robert Nelson (Leiden, Netherlands: E. J. Brill, 1971), 33. The ruling that Jews are not obligated to return the lost property of foreigners is in Baba Kama 113b.

37. Maimonides, *Mishneh Torah*, Hilchot Melachim 8:10.

38. While this is true according to the letter of the law, throughout the history of the Diaspora, actual Jewish behavior has been guided by three broad principles that have superseded this underlying truth. First, the rabbis of the Talmud laid down a general principle that, in all cases where it does not conflict with core principles of Jewish law, the law of the local government was to be respected as fully obligatory (the principle of *dina demalchuta dina,* Baba Bathra 54b). Thus, though in principle foreigners had no moral claim on Jewish action, actual Jewish behavior followed the law of the secular state. Second, Jews were enjoined to go beyond the letter of Jewish law if obeying it strictly would cause others to blaspheme God. The class instance of such sanctifying behavior is told of the sage Shimon ben Shetach, in the Jerusalem Talmud, Baba Metziah 2.2. The rabbi's students had bought him a donkey from a local Arab, who inadvertently left a valuable jewel hanging on it. Although Jews are not required to return the lost objects of Gentiles, the sage insisted on doing so, declaring, "What do you think, that Shimon ben Shetach is a barbarian? Why, he would rather hear 'Blessed be the God of the Jews' from the mouth of the grateful Arab than have all the rewards of this world." Finally, the Talmud called for vastly expanded obligations toward foreigners in cases where this was necessary to promote peaceful relations. Thus, the rabbis ruled that "the heathen poor are supported along with the Jewish, their sick visited along with the Jewish, their dead buried along with the Jewish, for the sake of peace" (Gittin 61a). It is difficult to know exactly what to make of the requirements that Jews accept obligations toward foreigners in the name of promoting peace or preventing blasphemy. On the one hand, taken at face value these appear to be nothing more than the instrumental calculations of a dependent minority, such that we would expect the law to reject any obligation to foreigners in times when this was not

strictly necessary for Jewish survival. Yet at the same time, there are indications that standards enjoined "for the sake of peace" may reflect intrinsic, and not merely instrumental, motives.

The talmudic passage cited above, in which the obligations to heathens are laid out, is part of a lengthier discussion of things done "for the sake of peace," which begins in Gittin 59a with the phrase, "The following rules were laid down for the sake of peace." The cases that follow include some that are clearly about avoiding conflict in areas where the law is silent (e.g., determining irrigation rights when water is scarce), and some that appear to contain some intrinsic moral content (e.g., not taking things away from deaf-mutes, idiots, or children, although these have no legal property rights). This is further supported by the fact that several of the actions commanded "for the sake of peace" involve relations among Jews, toward which the Talmud would certainly not prescribe an instrumental attitude. Yet even if the ruling does reflect some intrinsic value, this would seem to be the value of peaceful relations among peoples, rather than any particular moral value inherent in heathen cultures. This view is reinforced by the derogatory phrase—"worshippers of stars and zodiacs"—which is used in this passage to denote non-Noahide foreigners. Furthermore, Jewish law is notoriously casuistic, and modifications based on technicalities have often disguised a deeper shift in the basic understandings of rabbinic authorities. The abolition of slavery, for instance, came about through a series of restrictions based on apparently unrelated technicalities, but there can be no doubt that these technicalities served as a vehicle for a more fundamental rabbinic conviction regarding the inhumanity of this institution as a whole. In any case, however, the principles enacted "for the sake of peace" served to impose significant restrictions and obligations on Jews in their interactions with foreigners, without challenging the underlying belief that these foreigners were essentially heathen and without inherent moral claim on Jewish behavior.

39. Exactly which laws were binding on the *ger toshav* was long a subject of dispute among rabbinic authorities, but ultimately these were identified as the seven commandments included in God's covenant with Noah. See Avodah Zarah 64b; also Maimonides, *Mishneh Torah, Hilchot Melachim* 8:10.

40. Significantly, Jews are never commanded to "love" the resident alien.

41. The Talmud indicates that the "resident alien" was a live legal category only for the period during which the Jubilee was observed, which in talmudic thought was taken to be the period before the Babylonian exile of 586 B.C.E. It is unclear whether the "resident alien" was an active legal category after this time, but it was certainly unenforceable after the destruction of the Second Temple and the end of even nominal Jewish sovereignty in the first century C.E.

42. Moslems were widely accepted as Noahides several centuries before Christians, due to the clearly monotheistic nature of Islam and, in Judaism's view, the possibly polytheistic nature of the Trinity; e.g., Maimonides classified Christians as idolators; see his Arabic commentary on the third and fourth Mishnayot of Avodah Zarah, discussed in Sigfried Stein, "Interest Taken by Jews from Gentiles: An Evaluation of Source Material (Fourteenth to Seventeenth Centuries)," in *Journal of Semitic Studies* 1 (1956): 147.

43. HaMeiri, *Beit HaBechirah,* cited in Katz, *Exclusiveness and Tolerance,* 121.

44. HaMeiri's phrase is "umot ha-gedurot bedarchei ha-datot." Cited in Katz, *Exclusiveness and Tolerance,* 115.

45. See Novak, *Image of the Non-Jew,* 354.

46. See Katz, *Exclusiveness and Tolerance,* chap. 8, on this point.

47. Rabbenu Yeruham, Sefer Adam ve-Havah, 17.5, cited in ibid., 35.

48. Discussed in Katz, *Exclusiveness and Tolerance,* 117.

49. Baba Kama 113a–b.

50. Cited in Novak, *Image of the Non-Jew,* 63.

51. Gerim 61a states that the *ger toshav,* but not the heathen, is included in the commands "thou shalt do him no wrong" (Lev. 19:33), "thou shalt not oppress" (Deut. 24:14), and "the wages of a hired servant shall not be kept overnight" (Lev. 19:33).

52. Exod. 13:49; Num. 9:14.

53. Exod. 20:10. The phrase that I have translated "resident alien" is a modification of the word for "stranger"—literally, "resident stranger"—and I therefore believe that the sense of special responsibility implied in the phrase "your stranger" is applicable to the case of the resident alien as well.

54. See Gerim 61a and Baba Metziah 70b–71a. Cf. also Maimonides, *Mishneh Torah,* Hilchot Malve VeLove 5:1.

55. Greenberg, "Mankind, Israel," 31, based on Lev. 25:35 and Pesahim 21b.

56. See n. 37.

57. Deut. 15:3, 32:31.

58. Tosefta Peah 3:3c, cited in Roger Brooks, *Support for the Poor in the Mishnaic Law of Agriculture: Tractate Peah* (Chico, Calif.: Scholars Press, 1983), 96.

59. Baba Bathra 90a; also Maimonides, Mishneh Torah, Hilchot Mechirah, chap. 14. For a broader discussion of this point, see also chap. 7 of Aaron Levine, *Free Enterprise and Jewish Law* (New York: Ktav, 1980).

60. Greenberg, "Mankind, Israel," 31.

61. Among many others who have commented on this point, see Leon Kass, "Evolution and the Bible: Genesis I Revisited," *Commentary,* November 1988.

62. Baba Metziah 71a; cf. also Maimonides, *Mishneh Torah,* Hilchot Matnot Aniyim 7:13.

63. Michael Walzer, *Spheres of Justice* (New York: Basic Books, 1983).

64. Ibid., 33.

65. Aristotle, *Politics,* 2.3.

66. Deut. 23:19–20.

67. Benjamin Nelson, *The Idea of Usury: From Tribal Brotherhood to Universal Otherhood* (Chicago: Chicago University Press, 1949), xvi.

68. The concept of reiterative universalism is from Michael Walzer, "Two Types of Universalism," delivered as The Tanner Lectures at Harvard University, November 1988.

69. Katz, *Exclusiveness and Tolerance,* 127.

70. HaMeiri, Beit HaBechirah on Avodah Zarah, p. 132, cited in ibid.

71. Mary Douglas, *Purity and Danger: An Analysis of Concepts of Pollution*

and Taboo (New York: Praeger, 1966), 53. Douglas also offers an illuminating analysis of the biblical dietary laws, asserting that their function is to draw clear boundaries around the three basic types of land, sea, and air animals, and to prohibit those animals whose characteristics do not fit the paradigm of their class, or which cross the boundaries of classification. Thus, for example, all amphibians are nonkosher, as are flightless birds and marine mammals.

72. It is often said that chaos may lead to terrifying results—i.e., that chaos is one type, or one possible cause, of terror. My point here is the reverse: not that chaos is a type of terror, but that terror is a subcategory of chaos; that all terror is a symptom of chaos; that the *nature* of terror is chaos.

73. This perception of gentile life as indiscriminate has pervaded Jewish culture far beyond the bounds of talmudic law, e.g., in Philip Roth, *My Life as a Man* (New York: Bantam, 1970), 96, the protagonist educates his stepdaughter, who appears in the book as the symbol of gentile thuggery and backwardness, by teaching her "to distinguish between the Atlantic and the Pacific, Washington and Lincoln, a period and a comma, a sentence and a paragraph, the little hand and the big hand." Roth does not say that he simply taught the child to *know,* or to *understand* the meanings of these things, but rather specifically to distinguish between them. This, again, is a view of knowledge that understands ignorance specifically as a form of lumping things together that should be separated.

74. Sanhedrin 56b.

75. Similarly, the commandment to return the lost goods of one's "brother" (but not of foreigners) is immediately followed by prohibitions against men and women wearing each other's clothing, sowing a vineyard with diverse types of seed, plowing fields with an ox and an ass yoked together, and wearing garments that weave wool and linen into a single material (Deut. 22). Noahides occupy an intermediate position in this scheme: They have learned to make the most important forms of distinction and to establish the most critical aspects of a social order, yet their morality remains on a much cruder, more simplistic level than that of Jewish law. The partiality of the Noahide capacity for differentiation is indicated from the start, in the text of Genesis describing the covenant established between God and Noah. Unlike that of Abraham, which bound only the Jewish people, Noah's covenant is made not only with all human beings but also "with every living thing that is with you—birds, cattle, and every wild beast . . . every living thing on earth" (Gen. 9:8–17). This level of generality indicates that Noahides are not expected to perceive the full range of distinctions in the world, but only the broadest categories.

76. The commandment to destroy the seven nations is in Deut. 7:2–4. The injunction to "blot out the memory of Amalek" is in Deut. 25:17–19.

77. Novak, *Image of the Non-Jew,* xiv–xv. See also p. 408 for a very interesting discussion of the nature of talmudic methodology, as a form of rational discourse that is carried out by comparing and contrasting particular cases, rather than deducing general principles from a priori axioms. I believe that where the methodology of rational philosophy handed down to us from Athens focuses on discovering generalizable truths, talmudic method aims at developing an understanding of what accounts for the contrasts between distinct cases.

78. St. Ambrose of Milan (340–97), *De Tobia* 15:15, cited in Nelson, *The Idea of Usury*, 4.

79. In fact, through the innovation of the *heter iska,* rabbinic authorities allowed Jews to effectively charge interest to one another. See Levine, *Free Enterprise and Jewish Law,* 165–72. While the *heter iska* effectively circumvents the ban on interest, the positive commandment enjoining Jews to make interest-free loans available to their poor brethren remains in force.

80. In fact, Jewish law includes both a prohibition on taking interest from Jews and a positive command to make interest-free loans available to needy members of the community. The free-loan society was a standard charitable institution in medieval Jewish communities.

81. Don Isaac Abarbanel, commentary on Deut. 23, *Mirkevet ha-Mishnah* (Sabionetta, Italy, 1551), cited in Stein, "Interest Taken by Jews from Gentiles," 153.

82. Immanuel Kant, *Groundwork of the Metaphysic of Morals,* translated by H. J. Paton (New York: Harper & Row, 1964), chap. 2, p. 75; and elsewhere.

83. Rawls, *Theory of Justice,* 20.

84. Although Rawls states that his theory is not intended to provide a framework for international relations (*Theory of Justice,* 8), fellow neo-Kantians have argued persuasively that there is no reason why his principles of justice should not be applied globally. See especially pt. 3 of Charles Beitz, *Political Theory and International Relations* (Princeton, N.J.: Princeton University Press, 1979).

85. Rawls, *Theory of Justice,* 4.

86. Beitz, *Political Theory,* 111.

87. Ibid., 128, 179.

88. Alasdair MacIntyre, *Whose Justice? Which Rationality?* (South Bend, Ind.: University of Notre Dame Press, 1988), 394.

12

STRUCTURES OF PERSONAL IDENTITY
AND CULTURAL IDENTITY

Alan Montefiore

THE "QUESTION" of cultural identity and its relation to that of personal identity is very much one of the present moment. I do not mean to suggest that it has not, in one form or another, been a question of other moments also, nor that it is not likely to be one of future moments. I simply report it as what certainly appears to be a fact, contingent perhaps to the present moment of writing and to the chances of my own observation and experience. It is a question that tends to present itself with insistence to Jews, whether from Israel or the Diaspora or, as one might say, to Jews *tout court*. But the question is not by any means one of concern to Jews alone; this is *not* one of the ways in which they might (or might not) be a peculiar people.

There are, of course, no sharply clear lines to be drawn between the personal, the cultural, and (for that matter) the political and the religious, but neither are there any sharply clear lines to be drawn between the philosophical and, say, the sociological, the anthropological, and the psychological. Problems concerning the nature of cultural identity and the contributions that it may make to the constitution of (other aspects of) human identity as such do not fall neatly within the institutionally given frontiers of any of these forms of study alone, nor even of all of them taken together as constituting one federal territory. History and literary theory, for example, have also their things to say on these matters; and one way or another there exist endless slightly (or less slightly) different attempted definitions of the terms "culture" and "cultural." In what follows I do not pretend to present any sort of overall survey but simply to reconnoiter one route into the subject—well aware that in following any such route we will inevitably find ourselves passing by many familiar landmarks on the way.[1]

Before embarking on the main argument, however, there are certain preliminary points that should be noted. Within the tradition of analytic philosophy a great deal of the (often extremely ingenious) recent and contemporary literature on persons and personal identity concentrates, on one hand, on questions of personal identification, of identifiable and reidentifiable individuation and its ascertainable stability over time and, on the other, on the ways in which the concept of a person (Locke's forensic term) is bound up with matters of value, self-determination, and the ascription of responsibility. These issues are, certainly, closely connected with those with which I am concerned here. The focus of my present concern, however, is with the cultural (and potentially political) elements that may be found in that sense of personal identity that is in question when someone, to whom it may never occur to ask who he or she is in the sense to which a birth certificate may supply the answer, nevertheless seeks a description or set of descriptions under which he or she may recognize himself or herself as belonging to a certain settled place or group, as rooted in some characteristic tradition or, indeed, as bound to some self-assigned or willy-nilly set of commitments to a given range of purposes or values. Not to know who one is in this sense of "personal identity" is to lack a certain kind of ballast or stability; not to be able "properly" to realize one's sense of whom one feels that one should be if one could is to suffer a certain kind of—sometimes all-consuming—deprivation. Most people, no doubt, are aware of issues of personal identity of this sort only at times when they feel themselves to be somehow adrift from the proper continuities of their own past, or when they are suffering from certain deep uncertainties about where they might be going or why, about how or even whether they can possibly carry their own past identities with them into the future. It is in such circumstances, or, again and most important, when they may feel that they are themselves under threat through their share in the humiliation or dangers experienced by some group to which they are being taken or take themselves to belong, that they may be led into concern with questions of who they are. That they may look in such circumstances for one form of continuity or another, be it understood as continuity of abode, whether locally or more broadly defined, or one form of their relations with particular persons and their customs or one form of some wider racial, national, or cultural allegiance is itself very much a function of the culture to which they belong (or, while not fully belonging, of that in which they may find themselves plunged) or from which they may have come. Moreover, in that sense of identity with which we are here concerned, people may, of course, find themselves effectively landed with a plurality of (perhaps overlapping, perhaps conflicting) identities. At other times, equally, when things are relatively all right with them, these questions may simply not arise; their personal and cultural identities may be so secure as to be simply taken for granted.

It should be noted, however, that a state of insecurity about one's own personal identity is different both from one of rootlessness and from one of being uprooted, states that are themselves importantly different from each other. One may even constitute a very strong, if perhaps negative, sense of one's own identity in terms, precisely, of an apparent absence of roots; such an absence constitutes a very different state from that of someone whose sense of identity through his relation to his own roots may survive even long after his roots have been torn from the soil in which they were first put down, who may remain still quite clear about *who* he is even though wholly cast off from his original anchorage or shut out from what he takes to be his home. Such is the condition of many refugees. But for both the rootless and the uprooted there may be no uncertainty, either in their own minds or in those of anybody else, about who "essentially" they are or about that in which their identity consists. Nevertheless, notwithstanding the importance of these distinctions, there may be times—especially, perhaps, when people's sense of security in the other and the more immediately continuous frameworks of identity is shaken, when these frameworks may be actually broken or destroyed—when they may turn back to seek a restoration of identity in a reestablishment of connections with their remoter roots. (Many people seem to feel a similar sort of need simply as they grow old, and hence further distanced through the time of their life's experience from their own roots as they were first put down.) This urge can be very powerful and may derive in part from the fundamental connections to be found between the general capacity for self-awareness and self-identity and that for self-identification as participant in some form of discourse in which one may be recognizable as having an established role.

"Roots" is yet another of those elusive terms of art that present themselves as apparently indispensable to a discussion such as this. One talks of "roots" and "the soil in which they were first put down." In what, in slightly less metaphorical terms, might such a soil consist? In a geographical location, a community, a "culture," in a form of life—or, most notably and typically, no doubt, in some inextricable interplay of all of these. But it is evident that such talk of roots cannot here have the kind of objectivity or determinacy that one may take for granted when it is a matter of the root systems of one kind of plant or another. I am struck by Michael Krausz's suggestion, made to me after reading an earlier draft of this essay, that it might be worth emphasizing at this point "the peculiarly rootless character of Jews." It is true that Jews have often been seen and even attacked as such by many who have noted, and often resented, a Jewish absence of cultural roots in whatever their local surrounding national communities; and it is true that a certain tradition of exile may have nourished much Jewish self-perception as lacking the kinds of permanent roots by which their surrounding neighbors were attached to wherever they more than merely "happened to be." But there is surely nothing peculiarly rootless about contemporary Israeli-born Jews; nor, I should have thought, about a great many Diaspora Jews, whether they belong or may long ago have belonged to, say, today's Jewish New York or to the now-vanished ghettoes of Lithuania or Poland or, again, as in my own case, to the very English society in which, as both my parents and grandparents would most certainly have thought, I was "also" born, educated, and brought up. The (still metaphorical) truth of the matter is that one may have one's more or less real and more or less ideological or even fantasy roots, that not all of even one's very own roots may be easily compatible with one another, that—just like plants, indeed—some people may be capable in appropriately favorable circumstances of putting down new roots in fresh soil (especially if adequately supplied with the necessary psychological, sociological, and material analogues of rooting powder) while others may not, and that, taken overall, Jews characteristically tend to disagree with one another (in this as in so much else) about where one another's roots do or should lie and about what their nature may or should be. All of which reinforces the point that, while questions of identity and of roots are no doubt strongly interconnected, they should nevertheless be distinguished as having potentially different bearing on one's relationships with oneself and with others.

That said, let me try now to give some brief summary of the main lines of my argument. I argue, first, that it is in some sense an a priori truth that personal identity, or at any rate personal *self*-identity (by which I mean, roughly speaking, that characteristic or group of characteristics that anyone may take to be centrally indispensable to the recognition of who or what he or she is or stands for), must include elements that characterize him or her as belonging to one or more particular culture or cultures. At the same time, such an identity can never be either guaranteed as definitive or given as fully complete, though whether its incompleteness or its incompletability is *felt* as obtrusive or not is a purely contingent matter. It is also an a priori truth that such elements of cultural self-identification may always, in one set of circumstances or another, take on political implications; but whether, in any given set of circumstances, these political potentialities are actually realized or not is *in general* another contingent matter—though in certain types of circumstance such implications may become inescapable. Those cultural characteristics that contribute to the making up of different identities are, as such, just different, providing frameworks for adherence to many different kinds of possible community. They are, however, potentially political inasmuch as they are, of necessity, potentially at least competitive, and possibly more seriously divisive. (Moreover, inasmuch as individual identity may be constituted out of elements drawn from a person's formative belonging to more than one culture, not only the cultural differences but, with them, their potentialities for—even political— conflict may make themselves felt as internal to one and the same person in his or her own very self-identity. This, it need hardly be said, is a situation of painful familiarity to many Diaspora Jews.) Mere difference may already, of course, be resented; but when such resentment gives rise to the planning and undertaking of what must *in principle* be contestable courses of action, cultural feelings start to take on the reality of their always potential political dimension. That personal identity, and one's own grasp of one's own identity, particularizes, and moreover particularizes (at least implicitly) to a particular culture or cultures, is a universal truth about human beings; but the exact constitution and weight of the cultural dimension to what we or others may take to be each our own personal identity depends itself on the never fully determinate interplay between the universal and the particular, between the self-determinable and the ineluctable. Insofar as the cultural elements within each personal identity may always come to take on political significance, and insofar as potentially conflictual political involvements of one sort or another may thus be found to have their roots within the elements of personal identity itself, questions of personal and cultural identity must be of very great interest and importance—if also of considerable difficulty—for political philosophers. They may even take on great importance for politicians themselves.

This argument is concerned in its basic intentions with questions of structure—the cultural (and political) aspects or underpinnings of the structure of personal identity. It is, however, one that can only too naturally ramify in all sorts of not easily controllable directions. I merely try to suggest one way of getting at it.

The subheading that I took for an earlier version of this essay was "Interplays Between the Universal and the Particular." There is, of course, a sense in which every individuatable object, feature, or event, of which, once it has been individuated, some description or another may then be given, might ipso facto be said to exhibit an interplay between the universal and the particular. Insofar as it is individuatable, it must stand, as the particular individual that it is, in its own particular set of relationships to all other individuatable items to be found within their common framework or domain. Equally, insofar as any descriptive characteristics, direct or relational, may be ascribable to it—as opposed to its simply being given an individual name, or its simply being situated in spatio-temporal relations to other equally austerely named or situated individuals—it exhibits itself or is treated as an instance of one or more logically universal classes. Whether in general the individuatable items of our universe contain this interplay of the universal and the particular in themselves, so to speak, or whether they acquire both their individuality and their logically universal characteristics only through being brought into the light of human characterization or language, is an old and infinitely debatable issue, on which there is no present need to take sides. Either way it is clear that human beings instantiate this interplay in additional and more complicated ways than do any of the other individual items that go to make up the incompletable totality of the universe. (It *may* be, in fact, that one should add certain animals to the list, and even perhaps certain extraterrestrials, if there be any such, or again certain types of computer, so advanced as to have acquired a degree and kind of autonomy of their own such as only the most enthusiastic artificial intelligence people would contemplate granting them as yet; but, for simplicity's sake, we may here leave such possibilities aside.)

The universality of the "ordinary" individuatable items of the world may be said to lie, if not in their actually being described, at any rate in their being describable. Human beings, however, are in general capable not only of being described but also of describing (and, of course, of many other linguistic or conceptual activities as well). Moreover, inasmuch as they are themselves producers of language or discourse, they necessarily must be capable of referring in one way or another to themselves as objects of possible description and self-description. They are thus committed, as to a necessary presupposition of their own capacity for self-understanding (of whatever degree and however imperfect), both to an implicit capacity or "vocation" for the universal and each to his or her own self-acknowledgment as an identifiable particular or individual. The peculiarity of this situation lies in the fact that neither the vocation nor the acknowledgment is possible except insofar as each makes at least covert reference to the other.

This, it may be said, constitutes the peculiarity of the human situation in general. The above claims already call for much more exploratory and supporting argument than could possibly be deployed within the confines of one essay alone. I should myself wish to argue, moreover, that the basic argument has been sustained or played out in a great number of often very different ways, different in the associated modes of their playing out— philosophical, religious, mythological, and so on—and often strikingly different within any one such mode. It is hardly very satisfactory to leave this matter as one of mere assertion, but the limitations of present space make it impossible to do more than simply report that my own preferred way of teasing out that basic argument has come to be through a certain reading of the philosophy of Kant, and to present, as if with a kind of brief dogmatism, what I take to be one of the main immediately relevant outcomes of that reading.

In Kantian terms, then, the point to be emphasized is this. The principle of reason within us constitutes at once our own power of self-awareness *and* the objectivity of that spatio-temporal order of which not only are we a part but which itself stands as a necessary condition for the realization of that very power of self-awareness; and this principle of reason is itself, *qua* reason, universal. Our embodiment, on the other hand, that equally necessary condition of our own self-awareness as rational beings, is, as such, a principle of individuation and of particularity. Our reason (or our rationality) is that aspect of ourselves whereby we are led to seek harmony and even unity with all other rational beings—with all other embodiments of that reason which, as such, is logically unsubjectable to such categories as unity or plurality, and which, as such, has accordingly no individual identity; in theological terms, we are all (potentially) one in (the infinity of) God. Our spatio-temporally determined individuality, on the other hand, our human finitude, is that aspect of ourselves by which we are led through (the causal determination of) our bodily given desires, through the loyalties and passions of our socially and historically given situations, to affirm ourselves as distinct from (and, if necessary, as opposed in our own distinctiveness to) all other bodily and historically situated beings. Yet, for all the tensions involved, in neither of these our two competing yet complementary perspectives can we afford in the last resort not to give all proper respect to the other; for the very possibility of our own self-awareness, *whether* as rational *or* as embodied subject of desire, is rooted in our own deeper self-awareness of being both at once.

As human beings, then, as beings capable of reflective self-awareness, we have to recognize ourselves as not only limited by but, equally, as only to be realized through a proper acknowledgment of the bounds of the situations in which we may find ourselves or to which we may aspire. But what does it mean to talk in this way and in this context of a proper acknowledgment of bounds? If this is perhaps the sixty-four-thousand-dollar question, it is not one to which one should hope to be able to return any cheap or off-the-peg answer.

It has become one of the more common of contemporary commonplaces that at whatever point of our lives we may come or be brought to take stock of our situation, we necessarily find ourselves to be "always already there." As the embodied particulars that we are, we are always to be found in just that particular area of space-time where we happen to be and with whatever may be our own particular bodily and other causally determined characteristics. Among the most significant of these causally determined characteristics—not necessarily in every single human case *the* most significant, but in general, certainly, among the most significant—are what may be called our own particular capacities for and adaptations to the universal, that is, our capacities for and adaptations to reflection and communication. By this I mean *both* the particular language (or languages) through which we are enabled to achieve at any rate some part of our potential for conceptualization, communication, and reflexive self-awareness *and,* we must surely presume, the particular genetically determined (even if perhaps not very determinate) extent and limits of that potential in each of our own individual cases. Man, as Charles Taylor, among many others, insists (but he more to the immediate point than most), comes to self-awareness through language—or, at any rate, to the articulation of self-awareness, of his awareness of himself or herself as the particular individual that he or she is. But not, of course, through language in general, of which there evidently neither is nor could be any such thing. We are inducted, each of us, into such self-awareness as we may (or may not) gradually attain and seek to hold onto through the particular patterning of the language or languages of the speech communities of our earliest years. Later on we may learn and internalize other natural languages; we may even come to lose our grip on those that were once our own. But at whatever stage we may find ourselves, the meanings and forces, the associations and silences of the language or languages through which we may express our own identities to ourselves and others inevitably remain (rooted in) those of the particular communities whose languages they are and to whom we thus in part or whole belong.

Such languages, we should remember, in that by-now-so-familiar phrase, are also forms of life, or, at any rate, constitute an indispensable and indissociable contribution to the shaping of such forms. And though we may not all easily agree on whether the actualization of the human potential for language can of theoretical necessity occur only in the context of living social and rule-following interchange, or whether, as I would argue, language is theoretically public or social only in the sense that whatever the particular primary meanings of any given language, they must of necessity be at least in principle teachable to and learnable by any other being similarly endowed with the capacity for language, this is not a question that need detain us here. (It is through this necessary open teachability and learnability, however, that each particular language nevertheless opens out onto the universal.) For the plain empirical fact is that people never actually invent their language altogether on their own; nor, by the same token, are they free simply to invent themselves all by themselves, to determine as if by some act of divine self-creation both the forms and contents of their own self and personal identities even as they may represent them to themselves.

Inasmuch as human beings are themselves producers of language or discourse, they must of necessity be capable of referring in one way or another to themselves as objects of possible recognition and description by both themselves and others. This may be regarded as a so-to-speak linguistic version of the Kantian argument that self-awareness (awareness of self *as* subject) and awareness or knowledge of objects are correlatively dependent on each other. But it may also be seen as arising out of Wittgensteinian-type considerations about the impossibility of a purely private language. For if the meaningfulness of any linguistic or conceptual move depends on the condition that the mover—the speaker or producer of meaning—be in principle capable of recognizing a move made by *another* participant in the same discursive or linguistic practice as constituting an at least prima facie check on his own, it follows straightforwardly enough that each speaker must be in principle capable—must in principle have the necessary conceptual forms at his or her disposal—of distinguishing himself or herself from any other. Distinguishing oneself from others involves referring to oneself. But another of the Wittgensteinian lessons is that mere bare pointing at an item can never suffice to secure meaningful reference to it. For such pointing to be meaningful it has to take place in an at least implicit context, a context that can itself only be constituted by further possibilities of meaningful reference. In brief, the "self-pointer" must be ready—that is, must be in principle capable—to go on to say something more about himself by way of situating himself within a meaningfully recognizable universe of discourse.

But, as I have retraced the argument, we can come to such a state of conceptualizing awareness of ourselves and others only through our gradually acquired grasp of whatever happens to be our own particular native language (or languages), the language, or sublanguage, in which we first learn to point meaningfully at ourselves and others, and to recognize others as pointing meaningfully at themselves and us—pointing and doing more than pointing, that is, saying things to and about one another. But, of course, we gradually acquire our grasp of such terms in contexts of active interchange, where—to borrow the language of relatively early speech act theory—the acquisition of language involves coming to understand and to participate in exchanges not only of meaning but also of illocutionary and perlocutionary forces, with, no doubt, a considerable effective blur on the margins of distinction between them, particularly on those between the forces of recognizable convention and those of merely contingent causal impact. So inasmuch as the conceptualizing of our own self-identifications must thus necessarily extend some indeterminate and variable, but nevertheless substantive, distance into the networks of meanings and forces of the languages of the particular speech communities to which we may identify ourselves as belonging, it is no wonder that there is likely to be more to be found in our self-identities than may meet anyone's first unsuspecting eye. (One can hardly overemphasize the importance of the point that language learning involves the acquisition not only of its meanings but also, and inseparably, of an awareness of its infinitely varied "conventional" and other customary forces as well; one acquires one's own personal identity, one might say, as the self-aware occupant of a certain position within a complex, multidimensional, and shifting field of force.) One's own reflexivity, one's own capacity for self-recognition and for the ascription to oneself of a particular identity, is thus inescapably and from even before the beginning an aspect of the relationships through which one is bound willy-nilly to others of one's own community or communities; that is, insofar as one's own capacity for conceptualized or meaningful awareness of anything at all is, from that prebeginning, indissociable from one's capacity for awareness of oneself as distinct from everything and anybody else of which one might be aware, both are rooted in the language and culture through which these constitutive conceptualizations are gradually articulated.

But what, someone might here interject by way of speculative objection, if just one of these languages—English, Chinese, Esperanto, or whatever— came to supplant all others; and if, moreover, all such local variations in forms of life as might naturally give rise to different subdialects of that one world language were themselves to be ironed out by the ever-increasing pressures toward standardization of an ever more "modern" world? Can we not imagine a situation in which the world's plurality of communities, whatever the criteria by which they might then be individuated, was in no way matched by any major diversity of culture? After all, even in present-day England, indeed in the present-day city of Liverpool, one man may convey much of his own sense of who he is by identifying himself as a supporter of the Liverpool football club and another by identifying him-self as a supporter of Everton, without anyone having to suppose that they do not share the broader common cultures of Liverpool and, beyond that very particular city, of England. No doubt, certain very distinctively spe-cific cultural elements would in fact enter into the self-identities of such committed followers of football; but that is because its cult is peculiar to certain communities (and does not even take exactly the same form in all of them). But what, one may further ask, if everyone, wherever they lived and of whatever community they were a member, came to identify them-selves as supporters of one football club or another, and in virtually the same ritualized ways as one another, differing only in the identity of the particular club that they supported? If indeed, as some fear may one day happen, the whole world comes to share one culture in this way, would there still be any point in my would-be insistence that it is an a priori truth that certain cultural elements are bound to enter into anyone's personal self-identity?

As things stand, the world is as yet very far from any such cultural uni-formity, and it is by no means clear that it is not entering a phase of moving even further away from it again. Nevertheless, there is a point to such an objection. It reminds us that the particularity of a culture does not in the last logical resort lie in the de facto existence, at any given stage of history or as far as anyone's actual knowledge or concern may go, of a plurality of other different cultures. For one thing, even in the hypothetical case that there should actually exist but one broad world culture, for many purposes not even usefully differentiable into such diverse subcultures as those that might in other contexts be distinguished as being peculiar to, say, teenage, senior citizen, feminist, or city-dwelling groups, the possibility of a broad cultural redifferentiation must always remain as a further envisageable historical development. This is no mere hair-splitting caveat. This openness and uncertainty of future development is inherent in the essential temporality of human life. So there is point in the reminder that, even if at a particular stage everyone in fact shares in one and the same overall culture, that culture and its perspectives would still be particular among other particular possibilities, possibilities that had perhaps ceased to exist and others that might yet emerge. (We may recall the argument that even in a society in which everyone agrees on the basic forms of the state, and where in consequence the state can indeed function as an in effect neutral framework for the interplays of different interest groups, the possibility must always remain that this basic agreement break down; and toward this possibility the state as it exists at present evidently cannot be neutral. There is, indeed, no more conceptual space for a thesis of absolute neutrality than there is for one of an in principle—as opposed to a de facto—universal culture.)

Even more important, however, it may also remind us that we should misunderstand the terms of our own argument if we were to take those (sometimes slightly rough) boundaries that separate one natural language, or at a lower level one subdialect, from another to be straightforwardly identical with those that mark off different cultures or subcultures. Worries (or fantasies) over the possible development of one world language apart, it is clear that on any viable definition of culture whatsoever, the English-speaking world, to take one example, makes room for a remarkable variety of different cultures—cultures that, along one axis, may be associated with different regions, along another with different (for instance, urban or agricultural) modes of life, along another with different social classes, along yet another with different age groups, and so on. Conversely, certain dominant cultural characteristics, along, no doubt, with a number of more minor variations, may be held in common by groups speaking different natural languages but sharing the same broad modes of life. However exactly the term "culture" may be defined, many different elements as well as those of language are going to enter into the formation and characterization of a culture. At the same time, language is inextricably interlinked with all those other elements, in that they could not be what they are if they were not reflected and articulatable within the languages of their participants; and these languages are in their turn bound to reflect the main cultural characteristics of the speech communities whose languages they are. How these reciprocal relations are played out in the diverse major and minor details of one case or another will, however, be anything but a simple matter. The main points remain that the acquisition of the elements of self-identity is inseparable from the acquisition of language; that the acquisition of language is always the acquisition of a particular language (or languages) and through it the acquisition of a particular culture (or cultures); and that elements of one particular culture or another are thus always and necessarily to be found within the structures of personal self-identity.

All this said, it also has to be remembered that language has to be understood as rooted in its own temporality. This point can be and, in recent times, has been made in a number of widely different ways. Language is normative or essentially rule-governed, and its meaning can never be restricted to just one possible instance alone; it is public and hence of necessity open to the possibility of later response or check by a second and always yet another participant; a meaningful term is essentially iterable and reiterable on successive occasions; human understanding is essentially narrative in its placing of all states of affairs and events in relations of before and after yet others; or, as Kant might have said, if the order of reason is as such atemporal, the indissociable other side of the coin, the order of reasoning, is inescapably successive. And if, as I argue, our very capacity for thought presupposes a capacity for self-identification, and if such self-identification of necessity involves a certain placing of ourselves in relation to others, as they may or may not be encountered, over a certain (however indeterminate) span of our and their own histories, then the languages of our self-identifications, and with them our self-identifications themselves, must likewise carry with them embedded reference to these diverse, and always particular, histories. The descriptions and characterizations, whether of self or others, that any given language may make available to its speakers are universal in their logical import; but the ways in which, and the forces with which, they together make articulable the conceptualizable world are peculiar to the particular speech community whose language it is.

But if a language (in whatever its local variation), that inescapable vehicle of the self-identifications of its native speakers, may be said to be a form of life, that does not mean that anyone can simply read off from its surface rules and forms just what other and perhaps more obviously central aspects of a person's life and history may be deemed central and indispensable to his or her self-identity. Nor, for that matter, should it be too easily assumed that a person must always remain content to recognize himself or herself primarily in those aspects of his or her self-identity that are most naturally implicit in or explicitly accessible through the language of his or her first speech community. This, no doubt, is where self-identifications and even self-identities must always start. But, as we have already noted, they remain always liable to ongoing change; and there are, in any case, many different both established and individual ways of belonging to what is nevertheless clearly recognizable as one and the same community.

From this point on these themes admit of inevitably endless variation. It may help, then, in getting a better focus on some of the possibilities if one starts by trying to look at them out in the light of a particular (and in this case Jewish) example. So let me now quote a passage from a short article by Eva Szita-Morris, a Hungarian economist who came to England in 1989, that appeared in the 1990 spring issue of *European Judaism.*

> I am thirty-eight. At this mid-life point, it is the first time I am really able to look back, and it now seems possible to envision a future. The Holocaust has had its delayed effects; it caused, and is causing, irreparable damage to those people and their children who decided to try silent coexistence in a society which had previously betrayed and rejected them and later sentenced them to death. . . . The war and post-war history of Hungarian Jews is, *par excellence,* that of the outsider: the expelled, the left out, and of those who had internalised this alienation. Assimilation, because it deprived us of memory and self-understanding, made us outsiders to ourselves. Our parents and, until now, ourselves excluded ourselves or were excluded from our real selves, from a possible social, cultural, historical experience.
>
> We are now gaining back our parents. They are at last speaking with us. The internalised denial of their Jewish identity, the burden which they took on their shoulders after the war, that is, the decision to pursue the path of assimilation as though nothing had happened, is slowly being lightened.
>
> We are also gaining back our parents and ancestors symbolically. With the new democratisation, we—Jews or specifically Hungarian Jews, whether religious or nonreligious Jews—are now permitted to read widely and thus step into the long chain of history, to search and find our identity.

There is much that is worthy of note in this passage. There is the reference to history, the history of her parents, which is ipso facto the history of the community to which they belonged, despite their long drawn-out but in the end passing silence on the facts and nature of their belonging. There is the tacit reciprocity of self-identification in the "we" of that reference to her fellow Hungarian Jews, whom in the earlier phases of her life she would not even have recognized, and who would not have recognized themselves, as her Jewish fellows. There is that always problematic but recurrent distinction between the self as one may seem to encounter it in one phase of one's life or another and the "real self." And yet if her first reference to her "real" self seems to be to her newly discovered identity as Jewish, she immediately corrects that reference to one to "specifically Hungarian Jews." And with the reference to the "long chain of history" we have, in immediate juxtaposition, one to a very particular (and complex) social and cultural experience.

What, so to speak, is the status of these different references? Let us return to the somewhat entangled question of what is to be taken as a priori and what as contingent in relation to these matters of personal identity or personal self-identification. It is a necessary truth, so I have claimed, that any participant in discourse must in principle be able to distinguish himself or herself from other actual or potential participants; that he or she must be able in one way or another to identify himself or herself as being *this* particular participant rather than any other; and that in so identifying oneself, one does so, implicitly or explicitly, as belonging to a particular speech community with its own particular past history and, so it is normally to be assumed, with its own more or less probable projection into its own particular future. While it is a necessary truth, however, that any such community must have a certain history behind it, this history might in certain exceptional or extreme cases be an extraordinarily dispersed or disparate one. One may recall, for example, the possibility of a quite new community being suddenly or arbitrarily formed out of a collection of individuals having no previous relations with one another, but all somehow brought together with the means and abilities and the strengths necessary to form a new community *ab initio*, as it were. Of course, they would already have to be language users, and they would have to have brought their language or languages from somewhere; it is thus that they would be bringing with them into the making of their new community—and its history—their several hitherto disparate histories. A community of the uprooted, of refugees or of prisoners, maybe; in which case one might expect their collectively disparate history to bear particularly heavily on them and their partly new and now overlapping identities.

It is also an almost necessary truth—that is, one that would need only a few more fairly indisputable premises to be fully establishable as such—that, language being what it is, the terms of anyone's self-identification in relation to his or her other actual and possible interlocutors are bound to bear traces of the intertwined meanings and forces of many aspects of the histories of the speech communities in which their identities were formed. But the degree of felt or operative importance in any given case of any or all of these aspects to any self-identifying individual or group, and the question of which aspect, if any, be it ethnic, regional, tribal, national, religious, or whatever, be regarded as making a contribution of decisive importance to their self-characterization, as it is or as it seems to them to demand self-realization—these are matters that cannot be determined on any purely a priori grounds.

It is again a necessary truth, however, that any self-identification must, as one might say, be universal in its potential communicability, including that of whatever the particularizing element or elements among its contents. One way of spelling out this point would be by way of some further elaboration of the broadly Kantian characterization of the human being. Less elaborately it may be put thus: The basic moves toward self-identification whereby each participant in discourse comes to establish and reestablish his or her own characteristic position are ones through which he (or she) signals that which marks him out as the particular participant that he is in relation to any other actual or potential participant. The natural point of such a signal is that it should be recognizable (understandable) by those to whom it may be directed. (We may once again recall the fundamental, quasi-transcendental necessity of the in principle recognizability to one another of other speakers *as* other.) In conscious explicit fact such signals are no doubt typically directed to just a handful of addressees alone—if, indeed, as many as that. But in establishing one's own position as speaker, in identifying oneself as holding the place of the first person of speech, one is implicitly signaling one's position to *any* other speaker (or learner) of the language who may find himself or herself concerned. And though once again this signal is in fact typically only likely to be picked up and understood by fellow members of one's own speech community, since the speaker of any natural language must in principle be deemed capable of learning to speak and to understand any other, the implicit audience for one's signal must be the universe of all other learners of the language at large. To identify oneself as oneself is in this sense to offer oneself for recognition as the particular individual that one is by the universe of all other identifiable particular self-identifiers.

So much, then, is of the order of necessity—that, in brief, self-identifications as *particular* participants in discourse are among the necessary conditions of the existence of discourse at all, that the particularity of such self-identifications lies not only in the individuality of each participant but also in that of the culture of the speech community through the forms of whose language and codes any given self-identification may be made, but that the very formulation of one's own self-identification commits one to membership of the universal class of all actual or potential participants in discourse—or, if one prefers, of all rational beings. In general, these points may strike us as almost startlingly familiar. But let us now look back to see how they may help us in reading that passage from the article by Eva Szita-Morris.

"Assimilation, because it deprived us of memory and self-understanding, made us outsiders to ourselves . . . excluded from our real selves, from a possible social, cultural, historical experience." It is clearly implied in this *cri de coeur* that in her case, in the case of all those for whom she spoke, or claimed to speak, in the first person plural, assimilation had somehow failed. But in general it is *not* a necessary truth that assimilation is bound to fail. There are those, indeed, who find the most important elements of their own self-identity in what they deem, precisely, to be the success of a cultural assimilation, their own or that of their parents or of some remoter forebears. But it must remain always and (almost) of necessity a possibility that one may be called upon to acknowledge and take account of how one stands, at any given stage of one's journey, in relation to one's own personal and ancestral cultural history, including whatever stages of cultural assimilation it may have included, and of whether they may be judged or felt to have been a failure or a success; and also, of course, a possibility that even the most apparently successful and long-standing of assimilations *may* one day be called back into question.

Why is this so? Because, to put it at its briefest, if to recognize oneself and to make oneself recognizable as the particular participant in discourse that one is, is in the first instance to identify oneself by reference to one's own particular spatio-temporal embodiment, it is also ipso facto to situate oneself, perhaps explicitly, but at all events very largely implicitly, in relation to a whole endless series of other spatio-temporally embodied individuals—most notably in relation to those with whom one has oneself more or less closely, more or less remotely, interacted (and is, in many cases, still interacting) *and* to those from whom one's own existence proceeds—and through them to all those with whom they may have interacted and from whom they in turn will have proceeded. That I have such a past and that everything that may truly or appropriately be said about my relations to all these other inhabitants of that past, goes toward making up my own history is a necessary universal truth that holds of (almost) necessity about everyone capable of using the first person, singular or plural, in this way.

(The parenthetical "almost" creeps back into the argument at this point by virtue of the fact that it is, when all is said and done, a logically contingent matter that the facts about the ongoing creation of new human beings and of the ways in which they may—and must—undergo the processes of upbringing and socialization, are, broadly speaking, what they are.) My history, like that of everyone else, will always be open to interpretation and in principle endless reinterpretation. But that is not at all to say that I can think of myself as free to invent and to reinvent it as I may wish. Our histories, whatever they may be and to however many rival interpretations they may be subject, nevertheless confront us as facts. They belong to us— and we, in our turn, to them. In the last resort, indeed, we are all part of one another's larger histories; in the nearer and more relevant resort we are more intimately part of the histories of all those who are to be accounted fellow members of those speech and cultural communities whose languages and codes, with their time-accumulated networks of meaning and force, have as a matter of now "always already" unrenounceable fact provided us with the in one way or another indispensable forms of our own self-identifications.

Whether or not we are in fact concerned or forced to concern ourselves with, or whether we are even aware of, any given aspect of our history or another is itself a complex but contingent matter of interest, temperament, upbringing, and circumstance. But, facts being what they are (that is, while always open to further reinterpretation, as facts nevertheless confronting us and demanding acknowledgment in one form or another), it is not a contingent matter that we cannot simply *deny* the basic facts of our history when they are put to us, or if circumstances urge or force them upon us, without risk of serious disturbance to our own relationship with the truth—in such a case to our relationship with a truth or truths touching most closely upon our own self-recognitional relationship to ourselves.[2] Assimilation had, according to Eva Szita-Morris, deprived her and others like her of memory; they knew themselves, if at all, only very dimly as Jews—and *if* they knew of their Jewishness at all, it had no more recognized bearing upon their existence as the people they now were than does my own conscious knowledge that in the eighteenth century one part of my family came from Leghorn (or Livorno) to England. As things are, there is nothing in the circumstances of my life to compel or, indeed, even to incite me to incorporate that aspect of my remoter origins, or any reference to the culture of eighteenth-century Italy, into my sense of my own self-identity. I can, certainly, imagine circumstances in which it might perhaps have been otherwise, in which, for instance, I might have sought to create and sustain some very active society, amounting even to a community, of the Livornese of London, in the life and concerns of which I might have invested a very considerable part of what I might then have regarded as my own "real self." This is of course, a hypothesis of pure imagination. Whatever my personal concerns, however, I cannot properly deny that particular Italian aspect of my own history. And if circumstances were to confront me with it in certain ways, if I came to find that my own immediate forebears had been persecuted simply because of their Italian origins, if I was compelled to the discovery that my own present situation and state of being could themselves only be understood in the light of the part that my Italian ancestry had played in the formation of my own attitudes and of those that society at large had adopted toward me and others in like situation, then I should indeed find myself forced to a choice of how now to readapt to "my" Italian past. Such a choice, though it would still leave much of crucial importance to my own choosing, could not but bring my relation to that past, whether in positive or in negative fashion, much closer to the heart of whatever I should then be able to count as my own self-identity.

There is thus no necessary fatality involved in Eva Szita-Morris's reaction to her recovery of the memories of family and community origin, of which she had perhaps been so deprived that they had never in previous conscious fact been fully hers, but of which she was able to take repossession once her parents had started speaking with her. She might, for instance, have come now to look upon herself as a Hungarian of remote Jewish descent, much in the way that I should have to agree, if asked, that I was an Englishman of remote Italian origin, but without attaching any particular personal importance to the fact. But though she *might* have reacted in that way, we have to recognize that there is something seriously (and perhaps not merely contingently) misleading involved in the suggestion that she might have done so. In my own case there are, as far as I know, no serious social pressures upon me either to adopt or to refuse to adopt any noticeable attitude toward my Livornese ancestry, or the, no doubt, in large part Italian culture of my remoter ancestors. Given the facts of what has happened to the Jews of Europe in the last fifty or sixty years, however, and more specifically to the Jews of Hungary, it is almost inconceivable that anyone in the position of Eva Szita-Morris could have adopted whatever attitude she might have adopted toward the (re-)discovery of her own Jewish background "without attaching any particular importance to the fact." Or if she had herself attached no importance to it, as she contingently might just have done, this fact alone would surely have been very significant in any estimation of her personal and cultural identity—and *in view of all the relevant facts* perhaps necessarily so.

"Our parents and, until now, ourselves excluded ourselves or were excluded from our real selves . . ." There is, no doubt, very good reason for skepticism about whether one can really attach any determinate sense to the notion of a wholly given "real self," a self of which one may be only imperfectly or even maybe totally unaware, from which one might be alienated, but on whose ultimate realization one somehow depends if one is ever to overcome one's own separation from oneself, if ever one is to be made whole. There are well-known empiricist reasons for such skepticism; as far as individual human selves are concerned there are also very powerful Kantian-type reasons. But that does not mean that the notion of a "real self" consists of nothing but illusion and mystification. Even if the facts of our present situation and of our origins can never be given to or by us free of one always disputable interpretation or another, we have still to accept an element of the ineluctable about them, that *as facts* they just are whatever they "really" are. Even if there always exists some ineliminable margin of choice wherein, whether actively or by default, we have to make our own contribution to the determination of whatever we may take to be our own self-identity, the particularities of our situation and of our origins—through which alone we are able to identify ourselves as the individuals and not merely the kind of individuals that we are—confront us, with whatever their threat or promise, as the "real," if never fully determinable, limits of all possible choice. Again, even if the varying interpretations to be given of the facts of our situation as well as the differing weights of relevance to be accorded to one aspect of them or another are in a sense up to us, the available forms of those interpretations are basically given to us through the determination of our linguistic and cultural inheritance— though once again, how we may develop or add to that inheritance is, so to speak, up to us. As when in Kantian mood we might be tempted to put it, the spatio-temporal particularities of our situation confront us as causally determinate, but how we may conceptualize them is a matter of our own meaning-giving creativity; and the possibilities and constraints of all our self-identifications lie in the interplay between them.

Another Eva Szita-Morris, then, finding herself in virtually the same situation, might, one may coherently suppose, have reacted by identifying herself not so much as a Hungarian *Jew* as a Hungarian of contingently Jewish origin. I, as I find myself, am both a Jew and an Englishman of contingently Italian origin. But there is nothing in my cultural situation that would either explicitly or implicitly compel or commit me to taking up any noticeable attitude at all toward that by now very marginal fact—noticeable as an attitude either by myself or anybody else. In her situation, however, while there is and can be nothing to compel her to take up any *particular* attitude, it is far from clear that she would have had the option of not taking up any noticeable attitude at all, nor indeed that the characteristic range of available attitudes was not in significant part determined by her historical and cultural situation. There are situations where, if one is not prepared to stand up and be counted, whether among what one side or another might regard as the sheep or the goats, one is simply going to be counted sitting or even lying down. There are negative as well as positive ways of positing one's own self-identity; but either way there is no escape from *some* sort of cultural alignment.

Either way there is no escape from *some* sort of cultural alignment: this is surely another "almost necessary" truth of some sort. But it would, no doubt, be very misleading to suggest that whenever people find themselves faced with different possible resolutions of the issue of self-identity, it is a matter of their simply choosing how to count and to present themselves to others for counting. Here I am not intending to allude to the infinitely complex problems of ultimate free will or free choice, though I have little doubt that they are not ultimately avoidable; I am thinking rather of the fact that pressures on choice of this sort may be as much internal as external, that they may in either case be very great and that there may indeed be no clear line between the two. Moreover, although one may choose to identify oneself with a cause by throwing oneself into it by way of overnight conversion as it were, or to identify oneself with a country or a community that was not originally one's own by a sudden act of, say, marriage into it, one cannot in such a sense choose to transform the cultural elements in one's own identity from one day to the next. There are, no doubt, those who choose (not necessarily by overnight conversion) so to identify themselves in terms of (at any rate nearly) all evaluative and practical commitment with some other country than "their own" that in times of conflict between the two they are prepared to take the side of their deliberate choice against that of their origins; but even they would not normally think of themselves in their own personal identity, so to speak, or be thought of or treated by others, as anything else than the Englishmen, Frenchmen, Americans, or Russians that they had "always" been by virtue of their "original" self-constitutions. Philby, whether "traitor" or hero or both, remained to the end an Englishman in Moscow.

We must be careful here, however, to try to avoid such confusion as may be avoidable in any move from explicit reference to cultures and communities to implicit reference to nations and even nation-states. It is just as possible to be both a Catholic and an Irishman as it is to be both a Catholic and a Portuguese. It is just as possible to be brought up bilingual and bicultural (or even multilingual and multicultural), and, in fact, to possess a political/administrative as well as cultural dual (or more than dual) nationality in such a way that in general neither takes noticeable priority over the other by virtue of earlier origins or anything else. But for an Englishman, say, to renounce his British citizenship and to become a Soviet citizen, for him to change the nationality of the passport under which he may travel and even, where appropriate, his National Identity Card, is evidently not at all the same thing as for him to change those aspects of his own personal self-identity whose sensitivities and insensitivities, attitudes, tastes, and "involvements" derive from the culture(s) and discourse(s) within which that identity was constituted. One can choose, no doubt and within certain limits, what attitude to adopt toward one's own at present given attitudes and dispositions; one can choose whether to "identify oneself" with them or, on the contrary, to seek to deny them, to modify them, or to live them down. But there can be no ultimately determinate distinction, either in "reality" or even in principle (either here or anywhere else) between attitude and meta-attitude. As things are, it would demand a very deliberate, and altogether unlikely, decision and effort on my part to make anything, in terms of my own self-identity, of my remote Italian background; it would, conversely, demand a very deliberate, and just about equally improbable, decision and effort for me effectively to disentangle myself from the Jewish component in that same self-identity. But although I certainly might manage to arrange to acquire the citizenship of some other state and to renounce my British nationality, there is, as things stand and by this stage of my life, really no sense at all in the suggestion that I might somehow succeed in an effort no longer to be the sort of Englishman that I am and to become, in my particular personal identity, something identifiably else.

For others of different constitution and finding themselves in different circumstances, the Jewish component in their, say, both Hungarian and Jewish identity might present itself as the ineluctably indissociable one. Or both may be so deeply entangled in the double discourses of one's formative constitution that no effective choice can be made to dissociate oneself from either, though one may also adopt, no doubt, many different negative as well as positive ways of living either or both. Some people may, of course, find themselves indissociably tied to disparate components of their own identities, through their constitutive (or sometimes even adoptive) belonging to more than one disparate community, even far beyond the point at which these communities have entered into major conflict with one another. There is nothing in the logic of that concept of personal self-identity with which we are here concerned to ensure that identity must always be felt or even practically livable as a coherent unity—though there must also, and this time of logical necessity no doubt, be a sense in which even the most conflictual elements of such an identity must be containable within the one Transcendental Unity of Apperception. This, incidentally, is as much as to say that, in the vast majority of cases at any rate, there need be no ultimate purely logical contradiction between the different descriptions that may be appropriately (or perhaps unavoidably) applicable to a given person in virtue of their identity, whatever the differences or conflicts that may exist between the different discourses from which the descriptions may be drawn or the different communities to which he or she belongs. One and the same personal identity may, however uncomfortably, accommodate different or conflicting points of view; and any initial appearance of strictly logical contradiction may always be smoothed away by explicit reference to the particular discourses or points of view from which the apparently conflicting descriptions may be derived—though such logical reconciliation typically contributes nothing to the resolution of practical conflict of feeling and commitment. The paradox of apparently indissoluble full logical contradiction would emerge only in such cases as those in which the particularity of a community and its culture lay in crucial part in some characteristic claim to universality. Arguably such a claim does indeed constitute one of the peculiar particularities of the components of Jewish identity. But I return briefly to this point a little farther on.

This said, let us return for the moment, however, to my claim that the cultural characteristics that contribute to the making up of different identities may provide frameworks for adherence to many different kinds of possible community. These characteristics and these differences are inevitably of potential political significance in as much as they are, of necessity, potentially competitive and possibly much more seriously divisive. When this potential becomes a reality, that is to say when the cultural components of people's personal self-identities actually take on their always potential or latent political significance, then political elements and commitments may themselves become a part of those self-identities. It may also sometimes be that such political elements may be embraced and taken up into people's self-identities, or may function as such, in some more directly individual manner, without their necessarily having come to form part of any identifiable culture, at any rate in any usefully specific sense of that key term.

But this would seem to be a purely contingent matter. The more usual and more fundamentally significant cases would still seem to be those in which it is the cultural elements that, in one way and in one form or another, are bound to enter into the constitution of an identity, that come to take on a political significance. For when cultural elements of identity become politically involved in this way, we will *ex hypothesi* have to deal with whole communities whose identities as such, and not only the personal self-identities of their individual members, will have acquired political dimensions. Life being what it is, moreover, we may take it to be yet another almost necessary truth that the great majority of members of such communities will experience no particular internal conflict of identity when their communities are caught up in political conflict in this way, but instead that enhancement of community (or national) unity that involvement in common conflict tends to generate. Only those who live at the intersection of two or more communities will experience such conflict as internal to their own selves. This, no doubt, is one of the great differences in the experiences of a very great number of contemporary Israeli and Diaspora Jews.

Any detailed study of the indefinitely many different ways and circumstances in which such a fusing of the personal, the cultural, and the political may *actually* occur would take me well beyond the bounds of this essay and, indeed, beyond those of "merely" philosophical reflection as such. All I try to do here is gain some preliminary understanding of the conceptual underpinning of the necessarily ever-present possibility of such a fusing; and this is evidently close to the limits of what one can sensibly hope to do within the confines of one essay. Still, it would be frustrating simply to stop without even mentioning at least the following areas of closely related further enquiry.

1. There are, many other kinds of occasion for political conflict than those in which people on one side or the other or both feel that their very identities are somehow at stake; nor, when they *are* at stake, are they at all likely to constitute all that is at stake in the struggle. Still, there is often a peculiar sort of intractability to conflicts where identities are at stake in this way. One may quite rationally bargain over the distribution of wealth, resources, and power; but one cannot so easily bargain over parts or aspects of one's own identity.

For all those who need to understand and perhaps to manage—whether with a view to resolution, containment, or even sharpening—conflicts of this sort, and especially and most poignantly perhaps if they are themselves engaged as one of the conflicting parties, it will be at least helpful, but maybe even essential, to gain some understanding of how the different elements of universality and particularity enter into the identities in question. In seeking to lay open the elements of universality, one moves toward the establishment of a terrain, if not necessarily of agreement, at any rate of possible greater mutual comprehension and reciprocal respect; in identifying the elements of irreducible and ultimately unshareable particularity, one identifies that which each party must hold onto if it is to continue in its existence at all. That there will always be some such elements of particularity in any self-identity is itself an element of (higher order) universality, and as such a further ground of possible mutual comprehension and reciprocal respect. It is in fact characteristic of the human situation that many of the most significant universal features of any given self-identity or self-identification will be of a higher-order level, of a reflective/reflexive nature and thus, one may very well think, be peculiarly suited to or demanding of philosophical attention and illumination.

All that any understanding gained in this way can provide, however, is a greater sense of these possibilities. It is, unfortunately, always also possible that greater understanding should, as a matter of (causally determinate) empirical fact, lead to even greater contempt and even more active hostility. Thus we need also to come to understand as well as we may the conditions and occasions for seeking better understanding and to recognize those where it may belong more properly to human wisdom to acknowledge the given particular limits to its own urge to render its understanding universal.

2. All self-identities, whether personal, cultural, or political, must carry their particularizing elements within them, but, as I suggest above, certain identities seem to form themselves around the claim that among their most important features is precisely their own peculiar insistence on their own universality. Let us just briefly note two well-known cases, that of Jewish identity and that of the political liberal.

The case of the political liberal may at first sight seem to be only a very marginal one as far as issues of self-identity are concerned. Just as one is only too accustomed to debates, worries, and claims concerning or based on considerations of, say, Jewish identity, European identity, Welsh identity, Kurdish, Islamic, Chinese identity or whatever, so one is probably relatively *un*accustomed to hearing anyone speak of their own or anyone else's identity in terms of a commitment to the presuppositions, values, and practices of political liberalism. But there is here room for second thoughts. There is after all nothing particularly strange in the thought of a commitment to, say, communism and the Communist Party as having become something like an extended family commitment, and as having become in this way virtually indissociable from a proper characterization of oneself. This sort of case is perhaps more readily intelligible in view of the all-encompassing nature of the claims that such an ideology and such a party commonly make on their partisans' lives. Where the commitment that is given is total, a near totality of satisfactions may be provided in exchange; together commitments and concomitant satisfactions may quite understandably come to constitute a framework for the constitution of particular self-identities. Something like this is true of certain supporters of the Labour movement or of the Conservative and Liberal parties in Great Britain, for example; or of the Socialist party in France; and so on.

It is noteworthy that when identities are formed in this way, typically over more than one generation and in a particular area, it may be easier to change one's actual views and even, perhaps, one's voting habits than one's sense of identity itself. There are those, for instance, who may continue to think of themselves as being essentially "Labour supporters" at heart, who will nevertheless vote Conservative at one election after another; and where their "Labour identity" is psychologically real enough, this lived ambivalence can in fact give rise to great discomfort. In similar fashion, I think, though in a less party-specific way, people can come to so internalize their habituation and commitment to the forms and language of liberal democracy that this language and these forms can come to affect, to be caught up among the implications of, the language and forms through which they may formulate their own self-identifications. This is more likely to be noticeable where they find themselves wrenched out of the habitat of their native political culture and brought, by way of perhaps acutely uncomfortable contrast, to an enforced self-recognition of the political elements of their own self-identity. Be it for better or for worse, people may simply feel themselves to be separated, as it were, from themselves in sufficiently nonliberal societies; and vice versa, no doubt. One finds oneself just breathing differently, when one is able to get back to the society of one's own self-identity.

It is, however, a well-known central feature of the liberal credo that a liberal society must regard itself as strictly nonsectarian, as universal in its refusal to make any distinction of principle among its individual members. It is an ideology of the state as political framework, a framework that should in principle be capable of accommodating all shades of opinion and variety of interest within it. In practice this may give rise to all sorts of problems concerning such issues as immigration and internal cultural diversity. But these are not problems of practice alone. There are—as is by now at last very well understood—certain types of culture, political or religious or some indistinguishable mixture of both, that, if they become strong and proportionately important enough, become ipso facto a threat to the continued existence of the liberal polity as such. It is at such points that the universality of the liberal principle can only survive by recognition and acceptance of the limits set by its own particularity. Or, if in fact all such radically inassimilable subcultures came to disappear, at any rate for the foreseeable future, political liberalism would indeed survive, but it would cease to function as a principle of individuation or distinctive identity. Conversely, if it insists on its own particularity to the point of disallowing any and every attempt to express and propagate views of a nonliberal character, or to create institutions or other organizations of an internally nonliberal structure, it will lose its own liberal character. It is at such points that it can maintain its own particularity only by recognition and acceptance of the limits set by its own universality.

The case of Jewish identity is arguably even more directly problematic in this way, to the point, I should myself be inclined to argue, of presenting a full-blooded paradox. On one side of the matter it is hard, arguably impossible, to deny the contribution that is made to Jewish identity as we know it by Judaism, the religion of the Jews—the religion of all Jews. There are many scarcely deniable Jews who profess no religion at all. There are even those, or so many would say, who, while they may rightly be considered Jews, adhere to some other religion. It remains the case that Judaism lies within the background structures of their identity. As religion, Judaism lays claim to universal truth; it calls for the recognition and worship of the God of all humankind. But Judaism is also the religion of a very particular people; historically speaking, it constitutes a scarcely extricable part of their culture—or, to put it the other way, their culture contains within it a whole tangled ensemble of religiously charged and potentially significant practices and customs. To be a Jew is to belong to one people among many others, one peculiarly peculiar people; but then what distinctive people is not peculiar in its own way? Among the peculiarities of *this* peculiar people, however, lies the built-in possibility of seeing its distinguishing mark not so much in its common peoplehood as in its shared (if notoriously fissiparous) religion, a religion that, moreover, is committed by its own deepest self-understanding to offering itself as an at least possible universal religion for all humankind.

3. Finally, there is the major issue of whether or not references to personal or cultural identity can properly be construed as providing a basis

for the rational evaluation of choice among alternative policies. That the preservation of identity, however exactly it may be understood, is in fact typically taken to be a major value and a major motivating factor is hardly disputable. But can one provide *reasons* to justify this stance? There may naturally be a certain tendency to take this question to be bound up with that of whether or not one can make any seriously viable distinction between a man's "apparent" and "real" identities. Though they may be interconnected, however, these two questions are by no means exactly the same. One could, for instance, construe the notion of a "real identity" in strictly factual or nonevaluative terms as being, perhaps, rather like a Lockean real essence, whose nature depended on the given organization of the minute parts of the underlying character. Alternatively, it is not at first sight obviously impossible that one should seek to found one's evaluations or the determination of policy on considerations of given identities without making any reference to putative distinctions between those that might be "real" and those that might be merely false, fictitious, imposed, or whatever.

It may be possible, however, to find another starting point for a rational justification for the defense of a continuing identity, both of individual persons and of the communities to which they belong, as at least one very major value among others, if one returns to the basic necessities of meaningful discourse and to the constitutive conditions of self-identification of its bearers and participants. Very briefly, an argument for such a justification might run as follows. The meaningfulness of any gesture, verbal or other, its capacity, that is to function as a symbol, depends on its checkable reiterability by speakers in principle recognizable as being indeed reiteraters—recognizable, that is, as being the same speakers on more than one occasion of repeated utterance. From this it follows, so the argument would run, that the very possibility of meaningful thought, even that of an in fact solitary self-reflecting individual, is tied to such an individual's preservation, throughout the time of what he may recognize as his own thinking, of such basic personal and particularizing characteristics as may assure his recognizability and rerecognizability, not only by himself, but also by such other actual or at least possible participants in his discourse as might present themselves as interlocutors and as providing prima facie checks on the appropriateness of his own usage. Moreover, inasmuch as the meaningfulness of any one speaker's discourse is dependent on its in principle checkability, it is ipso facto dependent on the presumable persistence through time of the universe of that discourse, that is of the world in which members of the relevant community of discourse might (at least in principle) appear as themselves recognizable and rerecognizable speakers.

It is true, I should myself argue, that the last remaining member of a given speech community would not himself lose the meaningfulness of his own speech should all the rest of his community in fact disappear in some catastrophe; the last remaining Jew, as one might put it, could still recite a meaningful Kaddish, even if he were the *only* survivor of some even more terrible Holocaust. But it is a matter of necessity to meaningfulness that the conditions for mutual recognizability remain; and the only ultimate practical assurance that they do so must lie in the persistence of a community in which such recognition may occur.

If the argument works thus far, it still does no more than establish—so it may very well be objected—certain fundamental conditions of meaningfulness; but this—it may be further objected—does nothing to show that meaningfulness and, with it, its preconditions, are to be taken as values. The taking of food and water are among the fundamental conditions of human life; but this does not mean that a man may not choose to starve himself to death in the name of (what he at any rate takes to be) some higher principle or value. What is more, a man may accept or even bring about his own death, his own definitive disappearance from his own speech community, without in any way threatening the ongoing persistence of that community and the meaningfulness of its discourse. So where is the promised justification for the defense of a continuing identity, whether of individual or of community, as one major value among others?

Two further strands seem to be necessary to the elaboration of an argument for such a justification. First, it has to be reemphasized that to establish a value as one major value among others is not to establish it as in all circumstances overriding. (As Sir David Ross might have put it long ago, one may hope by argument to establish a provisional list of prima facie duties, but the determination in any given circumstances of "duty proper" or "duty *sans phrase*" must always remain a matter of essentially revisable judgment.) Second, it has to be shown that the concept of value cannot readily or without serious conceptual loss be identified with those of individual preference, liking or choice. Individual likes and dislikes, individual preference and choice, are, as it might be said, brute facts, and as such can never be strictly deducible from those of the states of affairs or events that may be the object of such individual likes or preferences. Concepts of value, on the other hand, concepts of duty and obligation, of what is right or wrong, good, bad, or indifferent, are always introduced to new individual learners of language as resting on something at least in part independent of their own particular will. Of the nature of what this something may be, the history of different languages and systems of belief provides us with a bewildering and for the most part incompatible series of answers. For my-self, I should wish to argue that it is best understood as residing in some as-pect or another of the community itself, or, perhaps, in some aspect of the conditions that render possible its existence as a community; and that this reference to the community, however disguised, is rendered ultimately in-dispensable by virtue of that inseparable interplay between normativity and checkability by fellow participants that lies at the basis of all meaningful discourse. The defense of interlinked identities of individuals and commu-nity alike thus represents a value that is constitutive of the possibility of meaningfulness itself, and, as such, of the formulation of any other values whatsoever. This does not make of it a value that is absolute. Individuals may not only prefer their own death or the destruction of their own com-munity, but they may prefer it in the name of some value that they set even higher. Cultures may themselves secrete as an even higher value that of an ultimate transcendence of all particularity and identity and the emptying away of all sense (or meaning) of self. But, so the argument would run, the normative maintenance of identities must remain immanent, as one major value among others, in the formulation of any value whatsoever and for so long as values find formulation.

The above is but the hopeful sketch of what must, in detailed elabo-ration, turn out to be a very complex argument. For the moment it must now suffice to say that, if the argument is successful, it will show also how the value of the maintenance of one's own identity and of that of whatever one finds to be one's community or communities must carry with it a basic respect for the demands both of a certain kind of particularism and of a certain kind of universalism, each setting its own definite if indeterminate limits on the other. Some particularisms are, of course, in their own self-understanding so hostile to universalism as such that proper respect for universalism may be seen to rule them out completely. There is, neverthe-less, a prima facie universal commitment to respect for particularisms in their turn. How these mutually conflicting and yet mutually implying de-mands may or should both find satisfaction has always to be worked out afresh—*this* is the meta-message of their paradoxically entwined relation-ship. It may also be read as a call to the recognition of a nonidentical but common humanity, a community not only despite all differences but one to which the existence of difference is indispensable. (And if anyone should wish to argue that Hegel has said just this, but much better, before me, I should not here wish to make that a matter of great dispute.)

I may perhaps be allowed to stop (rather than to conclude), however, by way of a more or less Kantian postscriptorial note. Kant in effect defines the sphere of morality as the "natural" state of the human subject, a precarious and paradoxical state. In effect I may be understood as having simply tried to extend that conception of the moral to show how it is necessarily continuous, by way of the cultural, with the political as well; and how, while, *pace* a good deal of Kant himself, there can be established no definitive answers, recipes, or codes, it may nevertheless be possible to formulate appropriate counsels of general attitude.

NOTES

1. For one very good compilation of discussions turning around *The Category of the Person* by philosophers, sociologists, anthropologists, and historians, one may refer to the collection edited under that title by Michael Carrithers, Stephen Collins, and Steven Lukes. There exist likewise many interesting discussions of the psychological and sociological conditions of interplay between culture and personal identity; see, for one good example, *Texts of Identity,* edited by John Shotter and Kenneth J. Gerger (London: Sage Publications, 1989).

2. For a discussion of the ultimately disastrous effects any systematic but still more or less conscious evasion of the truth, and in particular of truths touching closely upon one's own life, may have on both individuals and societies involved in such evasions, see Vaclav Havel's remarkable essay, "The Power of the Powerless," in Vaclav Havel et al., *Power of the Powerless: Citizens Against the State in Central Eastern Europe*, edited by John Keane (New York: M. E. Sharpe, Inc., 1990).

III

JEWISH IDENTITY AND
POSTMODERNISM

13

A WAY OF BEING A JEW;
A WAY OF BEING A PERSON

Garry M. Brodsky

IN THE course of formulating one of the large problems of contemporary philosophy, Wilfrid Sellars claims that having a conception of what
it is to be human is an essential rather than an incidental feature of the
human being.[1] According to Sellars it is paradoxical but nevertheless true
that "man couldn't be man until he encountered himself."[2] This encounter,
he believes, first took place within and by means of an image or broad categorical scheme, "the manifest image of man-in-the-world," in which all
objects are construed as persons.[3] While Sellars makes a number of points
about this image, for our purposes what is most interesting is his contention
that at first the scheme distinguished between generically different kinds of
persons. So, as he puts it, "*originally* to be a tree was *a way of being a person,* as to use a close analogy, to be a woman is a way of being a person, or
to be a triangle is a way of being a plane figure."[4] Sellars's analogy suggests
that the differences between human beings, whether grounded in their respective genders or in the images of being human by means of which they
encounter and understand themselves and live their lives, can be so deep
and broad as *almost* to warrant the conclusion that there are generically
different ways of being a human person. Consequently it seems appropriate to use the phrase "ways of being a person," with the implication that
we can talk not only about different persons and their different properties
and characters but about properties had in common by a number of people
that are broad and deep enough to be construed as the relatively distinctive
avenues by which these people realize and express their humanity.

This is the idea that underlies my essay. I hope that identifying and exploring a certain common way of being a Jew will cast some light on a way

of being a person and vice versa and that this in turn will help us better understand some of the questions under discussion in the arguments between liberals and their communitarian critics. Of course, the links between modes of experience and philosophical convictions that I try to uncover can be no more than loose and suggestive, and nothing in my argument is intended to support the conclusion that all Jews or only Jews or only Jews like me will be able to grasp, pursue, and appreciate the philosophical points I try to make here. It is enough for my purposes to show that a certain line of philosophical argument makes reasonably good sense of a certain way of being a person or being-in-the world and that a certain way of being a person is something of a concrete instantiation of a line of philosophical argument. I proceed by sketching my biography to indicate the kind of Jew I am or take myself to be. Then I discuss some questions that arise when we consider this way of being a Jew, and, finally, I connect this way of being a Jew with a way of being a person.

I was born in 1932, the first child of Jewish immigrants who arrived in the United States in 1919 and 1921. My home was clearly and unmistakably Jewish. My parents often spoke Yiddish. We observed the dietary laws, and I believe that it was not until I was in my teens that I ate any nonkosher food. Above all, issues of significance to Jews were of central concern to my family. Consequently, during my childhood I was aware of the problems facing Jews in the United States and, to some extent, of the monstrous tragedy befalling European Jewry. But my parents were not observant, religious Jews. For while my father had received an excellent Jewish education and was a believing Jew, he earned his livelihood in a way that made it virtually impossible for him to attend synagogue except on the high holidays and to say Kaddish for his parents.

My Jewish education was typical in being quite limited. I attended the Hebrew school run by our local synagogue where I received some instruction in Jewish history and Hebrew. I was bar mitzvah, and my parents made the more or less obligatory (even for those who could *barely* afford to do so) party. This, by and large, ended my Jewish religious and nonreligious education, though not my identification of myself as a Jew. A large part of my attitude toward my Jewishness is to be explained on the grounds that being Jewish was one of my most obvious and inescapable traits as a child and adolescent. I lived in a Gentile neighborhood and went to a grammar school in which Jews were a very small and obvious minority. As a child surrounded by a none too friendly and at times clearly hostile Gentile world it would have been impossible for me to think of myself as anything but a Jew, and later on I could have done this only by making it a major project of my life. This, of course, would also have involved the explicit rejection of my parents and family. Fortunately, I never had any wish or reason to do this, in part because my parents sensibly made very few demands on me in regard to my Jewishness. They were not troubled by the fact that at roughly the age of fifteen I became an atheist and a nonobservant Jew. Nor did they urge me to interest myself in Jewish culture. Whether for this reason or because of the bent of my mind or because I felt a need to, as it were, escape from the ghetto, I was not drawn to things Jewish. What my parents asked of me was little more than that I not explicitly and offensively deny being Jewish, that I marry a Jewish woman, that I be sympathetic to the plight of Jews and enthusiastic in my support of the State of Israel. Since what was wanted of me made eminently good sense on its own terms, it was not difficult for me to grow up as this kind of Jew and to live my adult Jewish life in this kind of way. But what kind of way is it? I do not subscribe to any of the religious tenets of Judaism or practice the rituals of Judaism, thinking that in this way I can, despite my atheism, affirm my identity and live as a Jew. I am not a member of a synagogue. I have not studied Jewish history and culture, thereby helping to preserve and enhance it. While I wanted my daughter to be aware of her Jewish heritage, the community where she was raised had no school in which Hebrew and Jewish history and culture were taught and I made no substantial efforts to compensate for this. Finally, while I am a Zionist, I have not lived in or visited Israel or done more for it and Jewry than make a few small contributions to Jewish charities. So it would appear that with one qualification the differences between me and my non-Jewish colleagues and friends traceable to my Jewishness amount to little more than that I pay more attention to American-Jewish culture and to the Holocaust than they do.

The qualification to which I just alluded is that I feel a deep sense of Jewish identity and they, of course, do not. But what should be made of this? In the lives of theistic and even nonbelieving secular Jews, these feelings are indicative of bonds that are a source of sociomoral or metaphysico-theological meaning and comfort. For they betoken a connection with something "bigger than oneself" (perhaps a Chosen People, whether singled out by God or its own historical experiences) that serves a life- and history-justifying role. Equally important, those who believe their connection to the Jewish people is of this character can identify themselves with it and by doing so arrive at a somewhat concretely universal answer to the question, "Who am I?" But the felt bond of identity cannot function in this way for someone who is not only an atheist but also a postmodernist and thus finds all grand metanarratives, religious or secular, devoid of credibility.[5] So the question remains: What is the secular, intellectual, postmodern, American Jew (henceforth, simply the postmodern Jew) to make of his or her deeply felt sense of Jewish identity?[6]

One answer to this question is suggested by Alasdair MacIntyre, who claims that because people like this do not subscribe to a metanarrative or "scheme of overall belief which extends beyond the realm of pragmatic necessity,"[7] they

> tend to live betwixt and between, accepting usually unquestion-ingly the assumptions of the dominant liberal individualist forms of public life, but drawing in different areas of their lives upon a variety of tradition-generated resources of thought and action, transmitted from a variety of familial, religious, educational, and other social and cultural sources. This type of self which has too many half-convictions and too few settled coherent convictions, too many partly formulated alternatives and too few opportuni-ties to evaluate them systematically, brings to its encounters with the claims of rival traditions a fundamental incoherence which is too disturbing to be admitted to self-conscious awareness except on the rarest of occasions.[8]

What this suggests is that the way in which the postmodern Jew re-sponds to and copes with his or her sense of Jewish identity is symptomatic of an inherently unsatisfactory way of being a self and that the claim to have and nurture this sense reflects an indulgence in self-deceptive, senti-mental, inauthentic ethnicity of a piece with the sort of thing middle-aged people do when they visit the neighborhoods in which they or their parents lived, eat ethnic foods, drink a bit too much, and reminisce in maudlin ways about how things were when they were young. For, their felt bonds of identity are not connected to a "scheme of overall belief" and embodied in a way of life. But this, as MacIntyre would insist, implies that these felt bonds can only be isolated, self-contained items, parts of a self that lacks unity, coherence, and self-understanding. If this is so then the postmodern Jew whose self is of this nature must be insensitive to and alienated from important aspects of his or her life.[9]

To make clearer some of the things that trouble MacIntyre, we can turn to Cora Diamond's essay "Losing Your Concepts,"[10] in which the Kantian point that concepts make experiences possible is developed along exis-tential lines in an effort to show that there are empirical concepts whose possession "is not a matter just of knowing how to group things under that concept; it is being able to participate in life-with-the-concept" (266). So, it will not do, following Diamond's shift in focus from conception to language, to treat learning a language as simply learning the rules governing the use(s) of terms (268) or to maintain that when a term has a descriptive content "that content can be expressed by an evaluatively neutral term" (267). For according to Diamond, "the most essential thing about language is that it is not fixed in that way. Learning to use a term is coming into life with that term, whose possibilities are to a great extent to be made" (268). Consequently, we go seriously wrong if we attempt to spell out so basic a concept as "human being" as equivalent to "member of the biological species *Homo sapiens*" or even the latter along with some evaluative components. Instead, according to Diamond, "It is part of the concept of a human being that an immense amount of what being human is for us can be present in a look that passes between two people; it is part of the concept that all that can equally be denied in a look" (264). This is the kind of knowledge made available to us by novelists such as Tolstoy and Primo Levi, who reveal the significance of the "sense of the sharedness of human life" as well, of course, as the significance of the "denial of that solidarity"; for this, as Diamond points out, reveals to us "the shape of certain possibilities of human life" (265).

Diamond suggests that one explanation for our failure to pay greater attention to these phenomena is connected to "the tendency of philosophers to focus on concepts like rational moral agent rather than human being," which, she thinks, is at least as much a matter of "conceptual amnesia" as of the use of powerful, nonparochial methods and concepts.[11] Presumably, as a result of this "amnesia" we have "forgotten" what is involved in understanding ourselves and living according to an understanding of ourselves as embodied human beings. Diamond illustrates this in a discussion of the proposal favored by some feminists that we give up the idea that "a person is essentially characterized as a man or a woman" and instead treat sex like hair or eye color (268). Alison M. Jaggar does this and consequently, "What is invisible to her is the structure of the story of her own life and the relation it has—given our concepts—to life's coming into the world through sexual difference. She does not see as a human good our having a range of concepts through which the characterizing facts of human life enter our sense of who we are and what we experience" (269).

Were Jaggar to reply that it is not unreasonable to want not to be burdened throughout one's life by what is not of one's own choosing, Diamond could respond by claiming that matters appear in a much different guise when one is dealing with the very fabric of one's self and identity. Since human beings come to life with sexual differences that manifest themselves in pervasive ways throughout their lives, it is virtually impossible to treat these differences as no more significant than hair or eye color. This, Diamond insists, is the reason we should come to grips with our selves and our experiences by using concepts like "human being," which direct our attention to what is given to us as biological entities and thus apprise us of what we can be, do, and experience in our lives.

Now to come to what is of interest to us, one is not only born a male or female, one is born a Jew or Gentile. Not only does one enter the world as a determinate kind of sexual being, one also enters the world, or rather, one enters a particular world at a particular time and place, as the child of a certain set of parents who themselves have biographies, speak one or more languages, understand their historical situations in various ways, have fears and values all of which they at least partially pass on to or, perhaps, imprint upon their children. So whatever value the notion of the mind or consciousness as originally a tabula rasa might still have for purposes of the reconstruction of knowledge and the elucidation of the meanings of concepts, it clearly will not do to attempt to discuss the questions we are now considering by employing it. To the contrary, they are best dealt with by exploiting hermeneutical ideas and principles that underscore the ways in which human understanding and being in the world are, as Heidegger puts it, "grounded in *something we have in advance—in a fore-having*." [12] Putting this more prosaically, we become conscious of ourselves and our surroundings through preconceptions, prejudices, and predispositions that can be traced to the life-worlds into which we are born and that not only partially predetermine the contents of our minds but are part of the raw materials out of which our lives and selves are fashioned.

These observations along with such equally obvious ones as that human beings are profoundly dependent on their fellow human beings make amply clear why such phenomena as human solidarity and the sharedness of life are as important as they are to us. They also help explain why we feel deep bonds of identity with the groups with which we are identified and of which we are members and thus account for why almost any Jew feels deep bonds of identity with the Jewish people. He knows that like it or not he will be identified as a Jew, which, in turn, may be a matter of life or death for him. In addition, the Jew will probably have learned from the Holocaust that for vast numbers of Jews, including those who made as little as possible of the fact that they were Jews, this fact was the most important one in their lives. Further, because of what she "has in advance," the Jew will have inherited by way of socialization and acculturation conscious as well as preconscious characteristics, attitudes, and values that can be accounted for on the basis of the distinctive experience of the Jewish people. And since traits of character tend to overlap and partially determine one another, what has come to the Jew as a result of birth and upbringing by people whose characters and horizons are also partially determined by their respective Jewish backgrounds, will color his or her entire life and character.[13]

Roughly the same phenomena explain the way the Jew feels and lives his or her ties to a historical people. For one has directly encountered some part of the ongoing history of the Jewish people in the lives, values, and traits of character of one's family and friends. Thus, one knows (indeed, one is *acquainted* with the fact) that one is an immigrant or the child or grandchild of immigrants who fled one or another persecutor or left a homeland to which Jews came fleeing persecution and in which they could live only as second- or third-class citizens. For these reasons Jewish history makes itself felt in one's life as something much more personal and concrete than a body of knowledge about what happened in the past to people other than oneself. For these reasons also, the concept "Jew" is not for the Jew something "to group things under." It is, instead, as Diamond puts it, a concept with which one comes into life. In this respect, also, thinking of oneself as a Jew is like thinking of oneself as a woman. For it enables us to uncover "the characterizing facts of human life [which] enter our sense of who we are and what we experience" and much as the woman reflecting upon her self and life has to concern herself with the way she lives her femininity,[14] a Jew reflecting upon his self and identity has to concern himself with how he lives his Jewishness.

Intellectual and postmodern Jews will also be well aware of the intellectual and political history of nineteenth- and twentieth-century Europe. They will know that during this period many secular Jews were attracted to modernist metanarratives that pictured the inevitable triumphs of Reason, the growth of Progress, and, of course, the results forthcoming from the workings of History and The Dialectic, in part because they longed for Jewish liberation and believed that it and a more general and more pervasive human liberation are interconnected. And the Jew will know that for him as for the non-Jew, it was largely the tragic events of twentieth-century history that led to the abandonment of such narratives. Of course, it would be a mistake to claim that this history teaches the Jew some clear lessons readily applicable in her experience just as it would be a mistake to claim that this history has produced something, "a Jewish character." But something weaker can surely be argued, namely, that people who have lived this history will be disposed to view the world with a good deal of realism, suspicion, wariness, and, probably, cynicism. Since the Jew also realizes that it has been virtually impossible for the Jewish people to escape the effects of politics, he will not conclude that he should abandon political action. But he can be expected to enter the political arena with a deep awareness of the intrinsically corrupting nature of power and the limited nature of political achievements.

Thus far I have emphasized the importance of what the Jew (and, of course, not only the Jew but the human being) inherits with birth in order to show that the postmodern Jew who affirms and nurtures his or her Jewishness is not indulging in a self-deceptive form of ethnicity but expressing an awareness of some of the factors that play vital roles in the constitution of his or her identity. In making this case I have called attention to the workings of what people "have in advance" and what binds them to their communities and families. Now these phenomena play major roles in the efforts of communitarians to demonstrate the inadequacies of liberalism. For example, in a particularly clear statement of the communitarian view, Michael J. Sandel asserts that the most powerful version of liberalism, that is, John Rawls's deontological liberalism, goes wrong precisely because it requires us to view ourselves as "independent selves, independent in the sense that our identity is never tied to our aims and attachments." [15] According to him (and to MacIntyre) this is particularly undesirable because we can only achieve this vision at "great cost to those loyalties and convictions whose moral force consists partly in the fact that living by them is inseparable from understanding ourselves as the particular persons we are—as members of this family or community or nation or people." [16] And Sandel goes on to contend that because these loyalties and attachments are partially constitutive of a person's identity, it will not do to treat them as mere values or goals voluntarily assumed or to ignore the fact that in view of these self-constituting attachments "to some I owe more than justice requires or even permits, and not by reason of agreements." [17] He also claims that once we recognize this we will also see that "we cannot be wholly unencumbered subjects of possession, individuated in advance and given prior to our ends, but must be subjects constituted in part by our central aspirations and attachments, always open, indeed vulnerable, to growth and transformation in the light of revised self-understandings." [18] So, Sandel thinks, we must agree with the ancients who believe that man discovers his ends rather than the modern liberals who believe that the unity of the self is to be traced to a "human subject as a sovereign agent of choice" who wills or chooses rather than discovers his or her ends.[19]

Before attempting to determine whether the conclusions Sandel derives from a recognition of what the human being "has in advance" do, in fact, follow from it, I want to take brief note of MacIntyre's attack on liberalism. In the text quoted earlier, he describes the liberal self as lacking a "scheme of overall belief," a critical understanding of the "dominant liberal individualist forms of life," and a conscious awareness of its own views and those of other traditions. In one explanation MacIntyre offers for the sorry state of the liberal self, Aristotle's conviction that there is a supreme good for human beings is contrasted with the view favored by modern philosophers that the good is the object of desire, that such objects are various, heterogeneous, and incommensurable, and that "there can be no uniquely rational way of ordering goods within a scheme of life."[20] According to MacIntyre, the modern liberal is attracted to the latter view because he is unlike a member of a *polis* as described by Aristotle in not being "already a participant within a form of community which presupposes that there is a supreme, albeit perhaps complex, human good."[21] So the society in which the modern liberal finds herself provides her with an impoverished body of experiences and consequently she faces alternative ways of life from a "standpoint external to them all" and, lacking commitments, has no grounds for choosing between the desires she should develop and the ones she should inhibit.[22]

A second explanation MacIntyre offers for this is that modern philosophers find these ideas attractive because they accept the Enlightenment dogma that the rational justification of beliefs can proceed only on the basis of neutral, impartial principles available to all people and fashion a disembodied, asocial, ahistorical subject to apprehend such principles.[23] Nor is this project the exclusive property of philosophers. To the contrary, the goal of

> founding a form of social order in which individuals could emancipate themselves from the contingency and particularity of tradition by appealing to genuinely universal, tradition-independent norms was and is . . . the project of modern liberal, individualist society, and the most cogent reasons that we have for believing that the hope of a tradition-independent rational universality was and is an illusion derived from the history of that project.[24]

Should the postmodern Jew object to these communitarian views of the self and should she want to reside in a political community in which a "single albeit complex conception of the human good" is presupposed? The first step in the direction of an answer to these questions consists in recognizing the complex character of the life and allegiances of the postmodern, assimilated American Jew. Of particular interest is the fact that she lives her Jewishness and its history as a member of a group whose relations to the dominant, mainstream culture are intrinsically complex. On one hand, she lives as American a life as her Gentile counterparts, practicing the same professions, living in the same kind of dwellings in the same neighborhoods, reading the same books and newspapers, earning a comparable living, attending the same plays, films, and football games, voting for the same political candidates, benefiting in roughly the same ways from the democratic character and economic wealth of the American republic; and, if she is fortunate though not especially so, experiencing no overt and little covert anti-Semitism. So, she has deep ties to her profession, her non-Jewish friends, the institutions where she was educated, her political and cultural ideals, all of which are not connected to her Jewishness. Further, she will be fully sensitive to the liberating effects that she or her parents or grandparents experienced when they no longer had to live in ghettos but could live and participate in the broader sociocultural world around them.

On the other hand, no matter how assimilated the American Jew may be, how comfortable he feels in the mainstream culture, to what extent he identifies with and situates himself within the American version of Western civilization rather than with Jewish culture (for there are no Jewish Mozarts or Cezannes), he knows that there is a significant part of that culture to which he, as a Jew, does not belong, despite talk of "our Judeo-Christian heritage." So he will feel his otherness if not his estrangement from the dominant group and culture and will, in all probability, feel more comfortable with his Jewish than his non-Jewish friends, be a member of a Jewish country club, and find deeply offensive the quasi-secular celebration of Christmas that takes place in towns, businesses, and schools in the United States every year from roughly the second week in November until the first of January. If, in addition, he knows Yiddish, he will also have firsthand awareness of a language many of whose idioms can be translated into English only through glosses, which explain the significance of the idiom by showing how it embodies the experiences that gave rise to it. And even if he knows no Yiddish he will be privy to a style and body of humor that expresses the complicated emotions of a group of people who know that they are a minority, feel somewhat vulnerable and threatened by the majority, are aware of the various undignified things they have, of necessity, done to succeed, and are, at the least, somewhat angry at the mainstream culture and its representatives and not completely happy with the situation in which they find themselves. So, to conclude a story that can go on much longer, the postmodern assimilated American Jew may wish at times to live a simpler, unbifurcated life. He may wish to live or have lived as a believing Jew in a Jewish community or as an American WASP and not a member of a people whose life has always been difficult. What may bring him back from such wishes to reality is the awareness of who and what he is and of the numerous benefits of being who and what he is.

The postmodern Jew, as sketched here, will not be persuaded by MacIntyre's communitarian view that people living in a state that is not structured by a single, complex view of the good are deprived of something quite important. Nor will Jews with any knowledge of history find such a position attractive. For they know that when Jews lived as outsiders in such states they found the experience profoundly unsatisfactory and that even living in its own homeland the Jewish people have found it impossible to agree upon a single conception of the good under which to live. Still, the postmodern Jew who embodies complexity and diversity perhaps may have even deeper grounds to reject MacIntyre's position and want to live in a society that instead of imposing its conception of the good upon its members affords them the opportunity to fashion their own conceptions of the good and is reasonably tolerant of diversity and novelty.

Nor will it do to reply on MacIntyre's behalf that the reason we are unsympathetic to his view is that communities that pursued single conceptions of the human good were invariably devoted to unsatisfactory ideas of the good in which such values of liberty of conscience, free scientific inquiry, social and political justice and mobility, privacy and material wealth are not given due recognition. For any conception of the human good in which the latter values have prominence will be indistinguishable from the liberal view of the state as, so to speak, the place in which different individuals and groups peacefully and competitively pursue their own goods and ideas of the good while sharing the same political rights and advantages but not a common idea of the good.

It might be observed that one reason we are so willing to dispense with what the *polis* made available is that unlike MacIntyre we don't think the kind of self we have ascribed to the postmodern Jew has serious shortcomings. MacIntyre claimed that it does because it has no "scheme of belief which extends beyond the realm of pragmatic necessity" and has "too many half-convictions and too few settled coherent convictions." Presumably, to escape from this condition the postmodern Jew must formulate such a scheme, something MacIntyre thinks can be done rationally only within a community providing him with support and criticism. But the postmodern Jew will not be troubled by these contentions since he has no wish to escape from this condition. He prides himself on his catholic tastes, his ability to take himself and his own ideas with a grain of salt, and his urbanity and cosmopolitanism. Of course he realizes that some of his values and some facets of his life are of vastly greater significance to him than others and that others of them such, perhaps, as his egalitarianism and his elitism, can come into conflict with one another. But he sees no reason to order his values, commitments, and priorities in a clear and explicit manner until and unless circumstances require him to do so. And when this does take place, he believes that no ordering he arrives at can be other than serviceable and temporary and thus far too modest to be labeled a "scheme of overall belief." Nor will he be impressed by talk of the problem of the unity of the self until he is provided with some adequate explanation of what, concretely, a unified self is. So, he will be a pragmatist not only because of his liking for plurality and change but also because he holds both that the function of theory is to serve the needs of experience and that at best theories have limited ranges and provide us with beliefs that are less than certain.

The next points we wish to make answer the question, How can an account of the self that acknowledges the importance of what we "have in advance" and which justifies the postmodern Jew's view of the importance of his Jewishness on the grounds that thinking of himself in this way is how he comes into life, support such liberal views as that people are and ought to be independent of one another and that the self discovers rather than chooses the ends that determine its identity?

Our answer begins with the observation that what we need in regard to the disagreement between the ancients and the moderns concerning whether the self discovers or chooses its ends and identity it is, not proof that one or the other of the extreme positions is correct, but a means of understanding the roles of both choice and discovery in the fashioning of the self. People living in modern rather than traditional societies confront conflicts about their careers, places of residence, friends, marriage partners, and so on, and make choices resolving these conflicts.[25] The choices available to a person are delimited by, among other things, the sociohistorical circumstances in which she lives, her family and her native physical, psychological, and mental capabilities.[26] But if the circumstances are favorable, then she has choices to make, and, if these choices concern relatively deep and important matters, then in making them she is partially responsible for fashioning her identity. Further, while she is not, in Sandel's words, "a sovereign agent of choice," she is a partially sovereign agent of choice, and when she exercises this capacity and makes these choices she also exercises and develops her relative independence from the communities that nurture her.

While these points seem commonsensical if not banal, the texts we quoted earlier along with the general tenor of the communitarian position indicate that Sandel thinks that when subjected to philosophical scrutiny they turn out to be untenable. Perhaps his argument would proceed by reminding us of the ways selves are encumbered and then asking how we envisage someone making such important choices under even the most favorable of circumstances, thus suggesting that unless the aims and ends the person chooses are selected in a wholly arbitrary manner, they are chosen because they appeal to him or because he has good reasons for choosing them. But a subject that chooses something for reasons or because it appeals to her cannot be a *tabula rasa*. It must be an already existing self with ends, values, connections to other human beings and communities. So the much-vaunted independent self of liberalism that chooses its ends and is brought into existence by acts of choice (how, by whom or what? the communitarian will ask) is replaced by an entity that is able to make nonarbitrary choices worthy of rational persons only because it already exists as encumbered by its ends and identity. Because the self has reasons for his choices he (or his biographer) will discover that behind them there is something there to be discovered and understood rather than authored or chosen, namely, the self making the choices.

But a close look at Sandel's position reveals that on his view the self and its ends can, at times and in part, be objects of volition, for after he insists that the self cannot be a "wholly unencumbered subject," he asserts that it is constituted "in part" (but if "in part" then only "in part") by its "central aspirations and attachments" and that it and they are "always open, indeed vulnerable, to growth and transformation in the light of revised self-understandings." Admittedly, how we are to describe and understand what takes place in such circumstances is by no means clear, and perhaps this is why it is tempting to think that when a subject faces an important life- and self-determining choice either his already-existing values and preferences fully determine his choice or he is so unencumbered as to lack the resources to make any rational decision. But there is an alternative to this, for we can exploit a point Charles Sanders Peirce made against Descartes, namely, that while it is not possible to escape dogmatism by engaging in the kind of radical doubt Descartes requires (because to be genuine doubt requires reasons that must themselves be believed and, we may add, the body of linguistic or conceptual materials necessary to identify what is doubted and what is believed), it is possible to do so by holding that all our beliefs are fallible and thus subject to doubt and revision when this is called for.[27] So to think of ourselves (or our selves) as somewhat independent of our deep ties and attachments is not to deny the existence or significance of these items. Nor is it to picture a human subject as an immaculate item that is situated in the self but somehow separate from and free of the various "fore-havings" and prejudices had in advance of and along with the decisions and choices that are the subject's part in the making of itself. Instead, it is to understand the subject as the sort of thing that, as we indicated earlier, cherishes its diverse attachments and can employ and exploit some of them in order to free itself from others of them.[28] Again, it is to think of the self as, like the Jew, having the capacity to resist being completely absorbed in its environing social and natural world. And this will be a matter of great importance to the postmodern Jew. For no matter how much she values her moral and emotional attachments to the larger groups of which she is a part, she knows of numerous cases in which it was extremely difficult and painful for people to break free of stultifying ties to their families and communities and so she is wary of loud and unqualified praise of communities and traditions. She is also aware of such general points as that traditions and communities can be conservative and provincial and that telling someone that her identity is bound up with a family, nation, religion, or tradition often can be a means not of revealing a fact but of fashioning one, thus persuading someone to bind herself to a group, accept a belief, and, perhaps, support an action such as a war, for no good reason.

These points also provide the basis of our reply to MacIntyre's antiliberal position. MacIntyre is correct in holding that the modern liberal does not live in a community presupposing a single complex human good and hence can't appeal to this kind of item to rationally order all available goods within a scheme of life. But MacIntyre also claims that the liberal necessarily faces alternative ways of life from a standpoint external to all of them and is therefore without the resources for choosing between these ways of life and heterogeneous objects of desire. Why should this be the case? Why does it follow from the fact that a society resembles the democratic city Plato describes,[29] by virtue of containing a number of conflicting ways of life, diverse objects of desire, and so on, that its members cannot sympathetically grasp a number of the ways of life and gratifications available within it? If the society is relatively open, then it would seem that information about these matters will be readily available and that sensitive, intelligent individuals will be able to grasp some and perhaps many of these matters from standpoints internal to them.

MacIntyre might reply that this is not enough. For even if a woman has a sympathetic grasp of, for example, the gratifications found in a life devoted to the single-minded pursuit of higher mathematics and in a life devoted to traditional marriage, without a scheme ranking ways of life and gratifications she will have no rational basis for choosing between her options. But what the woman does not have is an antecedently existing scheme that is presupposed by her society and thus sanctioned sociopolitically, religiously, or, perhaps, philosophically. That is, she does not have someone else's conception of the good. From the liberal's standpoint this is a good rather than a bad thing; for the liberal believes that people should have every opportunity to work out their own conceptions of the good and plans of life. Nor is she at a loss when asked what the woman is to do in this situation or the more common one in which her antecedently existing scheme of values, loose though it is, ceases to do the work required of it. For the liberal will exploit Peirce's ideas and point out that even in this kind of situation people are not completely lacking in values.[30] So, if some of their values have "come unstuck," others remain in place and it is on the basis of these values and their own creative and critical abilities that people do for themselves what they should do for themselves.

Before concluding I point out that my efforts to show that the postmodern Jew can affirm and cherish his ties to the Jewish people and its history and, the communitarians notwithstanding, also accept the basic tenets of liberalism have stopped short of discussing the deontological foundations of liberalism. It might be claimed that had I discussed these foundations, I would have been forced to concede that liberalism posits and requires the kind of subject that I and the communitarians find utterly bizarre, namely one "wholly unencumbered . . . individuated in advance" and given prior to its ends.[31] I believe that the communitarians who base this contention on the kind of subject they think John Rawls posits in *A Theory of Justice* have misinterpreted this work and that, in any event, it is possible to follow the later Rawls and defend liberalism on grounds that do not require foundations.[32] But these are questions well beyond the limits of this essay. My purposes will have been served if I have succeeded in showing that the postmodern Jew, as I picture her, has every reason to affirm her Jewishness and her liberalism. Of course, it can be argued that I have not shown that the values of the postmodern Jew have universal validity. My reply to this is to concede the point and insist that the postmodern, liberal Jew will find it acceptable.[33] For while he cares deeply for his way of life and what makes it possible, he has abandoned the hope of finding something other than finite historical human experience to show that it is a good way of life. So he will have a deep suspicion of claims to know what is right on the basis of reason, revelation, tradition, and so on; for, he knows that people like himself suffered greatly at the hands of those making such claims. And while he presents such reasons as he has for valuing what he does and strives to view other ways of life sympathetically, he bears in mind that postmodernity amounts to the abandonment of all grand schemes and that one of the chief goals of a liberal politics is to enable people who disagree about deep matters to live together peacefully. Consequently, he is tolerant of his own inability to prove that his is the only correct way to live.

In summary, let me draw the three strands of this essay together. One strand consists in sketching a certain kind of Jew. Like myself, this Jew is an assimilated, atheistic, nonobservant, postmodern American who neverthe-less feels deep attachments to Jewry and Judaism. A second strand responds to and rebuts the critical suggestion that the postmodern Jew's claim to feel a deep attachment to Jewry and Judaism should not be taken seriously and that his way of being a person is unsatisfactory. The third strand of the essay is devoted to showing that the postmodern Jew is (or ought to be) a liberal and that the kind of analysis of the postmodern Jew I present is consistent with his being a liberal.

No one will be surprised to learn that many Jews are liberals and have very good reasons for being liberals. In this essay I try to make something of this fact by showing that being a liberal is grounded in a complex way of experiencing the world and being a self that coheres with the historical experience of Jews, especially postmodern ones. While I do not argue the case, I think it can be shown that the liberal and the Jew share the ex-perience of being members of minority groups who are often viewed with suspicion and hostility by the dominant majority of their country people, which, in turn, disposes them to view the world in critical, intellectual terms. It can also be argued that members of both groups have good rea-sons to recognize the crucial importance of politics, while being wary of what it can achieve. So the consciousness of both the liberal and the post-modern Jew will be informed with an anti-utopian worldliness. Further, we may expect that both the Jew and the liberal will, because of their re-spective situations as outsiders or quasi-outsiders, value their own private lives and consciences while viewing with particular favor those cases where people with different, competing values and "life-styles" identify their com-mon interests and cooperate in public even though they may disagree and perhaps dislike one another in private.

These points are of some importance, because taken together they offer some solution to the problem faced by the postmodern Jew who wants to be a Jew and affirm his Jewishness while knowing that in the absence of

bad faith he cannot do so as his traditional ancestors or even as his more recent nineteenth-century modernist predecessors did. This Jew knows that
even if he attends services and fasts on the Yom Kippur, the prayers he
chants do not and cannot mean to him what they mean and have meant to
other Jews. He knows that this means of appropriating his Jewish culture
is finally a failure. I have tried to show that there is another aspect of the
Jewish experience with which he can be and probably is connected. Now
it can be pointed out that this, like the Jewishness of the traditional Jew,
is a central and intimate part of a person's identity rather than one of his
superficial characteristics. So, if I am right, then much as being a Jew was
a way of being a person for the traditional Jew, being a liberal can be and
is a way of being both a Jew and a person for the postmodern Jew.

NOTES

1. Wilfrid Sellars, *Science, Perception and Reality* (New York: Humanities
Press, 1963), 6. The problem in question is how to fit together our scientific view of
the world in which persons are not found and our moral view, which requires the
existence of persons.

2. Ibid.

3. Ibid.

4. Ibid., 10.

5. For the identification of postmodernity with the rejection of the belief in
all grand or meta-narratives, see Jean-François Lyotard, *The Postmodern Condition: A Report on Knowledge,* translated by Geoff Bennington and Brian Massumi
(Minneapolis: University of Minnesota Press, 1984), xxiv.

6. I think the position I sketch holds true for postmodern Jews living in Western
countries other than the United States and perhaps for such Jews who live in Israel.
But this is left an open question in this essay. In addition, while the Jew I sketch
is clearly an intellectual by virtue of being able to describe himself or herself and
defend his or her views, I do not believe it is necessary to be an intellectual to be
a postmodern Jew. So I think that nonintellectual, postmodern Jews should recognize problems they face and facets of themselves of which they are dimly aware
illuminated in this essay.

7. Alasdair MacIntyre, *Whose Justice? Which Rationality?* (Notre Dame, Ind.:
University of Notre Dame Press, 1988), 393.

8. Ibid., 397.

9. No doubt the phenomenon under discussion is not restricted to postmodern Jews.

10. Cora Diamond, "Losing Your Concepts," *Ethics* 98, no. 2 (January 1988).
Where convenient, page references to this essay are included in the text.

11. Ibid., 266. I point out that the claim I have ascribed to Diamond is found in

her essay as a question and that Diamond claims that her intention is not so much to answer the question "as to show the difficulties in any attempt to do so." Ibid. I admit that I fail to see how the concluding ten pages of Diamond's essay can be interpreted as other than the answer to the question I summarize.

12. Martin Heidegger, *Being and Time,* translated by John Macquarrie and Edward Robinson (New York: Harper & Row, 1962), 191.

13. I hope it is obvious that I am following Aristotle's observation in *Nicomachean Ethics,* bk. I, chap. 3, 1094b12–1095a1, that discussions of human affairs do not admit of the kind of clarity and precision that can be attained in mathematics. If what I have said rings true and makes sense of what a number of Jews have experienced and provides some indications of how they may continue to appropriate their Jewishness, then I will have done all I hope to do even if it should turn out that there are, here and there, Jews who had no difficulty whatsoever in treating the fact of their Jewish birth as of little or no significance.

14. Of course, these claims hold true *mutatis mutandis* for the male and masculinity. The fact that Diamond uses the example she does to illustrate her claims may call for some explanation, but that matter is beyond the scope of this essay.

15. Michael J. Sandel, *Liberalism and the Limits of Justice* (Cambridge: Cambridge University Press, 1982), 179.

16. Ibid. This text is consistent with and reminiscent of the views MacIntyre advances in *After Virtue* (Notre Dame, Ind.: University of Notre Dame Press, 1981), 203–6.

17. Sandel, *Liberalism,* 179.

18. Ibid., 172.

19. Ibid., 22, and for MacIntyre's formulation of the same points, see MacIntyre, *After Virtue,* 201–6.

20. MacIntyre, *Whose Justice?* 133.

21. Ibid., 134.

22. Ibid., 133.

23. Ibid., 4–6.

24. Ibid., 335. MacIntyre nowhere attempts to show that the failure of this project to be realized is a function of its theoretical deficiencies rather than of the power of entrenched socioeconomic forces to defend their own particular interests.

25. I would think that Jews would be particularly sensitive to the fact that they are such people precisely because they can be expected to know that in very many places and for a very long time such options were not available to Jews.

26. According to Ian Hacking, Sartre, while allowing that historicocultural circumstances delimit possibilities, nevertheless believes that "for every person, in every era, the world is a plentitude of possibilities." Ian Hacking, "Making Up People," in *Reconstructing Individualism,* edited by Thomas C. Healer, Morton Sosna, and David E. Wellbery (Stanford, Calif.: Stanford University Press, 1986), 232. Hacking does not explain how Sartre demonstrates this, and while I do not argue the case, the view I favor is the more obviously commonsensical one, which holds both that different people have different possibilities available to them and that some people have more possibilities available to them than other people.

27. Charles Sanders Peirce, "Some Consequences of Four Incapacities," in *Collected Papers of Charles Sanders Peirce,* edited by Charles Hartshorne and Paul Weiss (Cambridge, Mass.: Harvard University Press, 1960), vol. 5, para. 265.

28. A similar point is made by Nietzsche. In the course of discussing what is necessary to achieve independence, he claims that one must not remain "stuck" to the people one loves, one's fatherland, one's favored sciences, one's virtues, and even one's detachment. Obviously, what he is doing is not positing or setting a premium upon a self utterly without bonds. Rather, his claim is that the various bonds of the self (generally called "roots" by conservatives) that have been praised can all too often imprison the self. But this is not to say that we can free ourselves from all of these bonds once and for all, and Nietzsche makes no such claim. Friedrich Nietzsche, *Beyond Good and Evil,* translated by Walter Kaufmann (New York: Vintage Books, 1966), #41.

29. Plato, *Republic* 557c-e.

30. The liberal can also exploit the description of inquiry that Dewey formulates in a number of places, most clearly and comprehensively, perhaps, in John Dewey, *Logic: The Theory of Inquiry* (New York: Henry Holt, 1938), chap. 6.

31. These are by no means the only questions to which the communitarian critique of liberalism gives rise. As Allen E. Buchanan argues in "Assessing the Communitarian Critique of Liberalism," *Ethics* 99, no. 4 (July 1989): 852–82, liberalism is essentially a political doctrine, and even if early formulations of the doctrine appealed to excessively rationalistic, asocial, and ahistorical conceptions of the self, there seems to be no reason why one needs to subscribe to such views in order to defend traditional liberal values. While I think Buchanan's point is well taken, I do think that a certain way of being a self disposes one to liberalism, and part of the point of my essay is to spell this out.

32. See in particular, John Rawls, "Justice as Fairness: Political Not Metaphysical," *Philosophy and Public Affairs* 14 (1985): 223–51.

33. So, of course, will other postmodern liberals. But the essay is intended to deal with a way of being a Jew.

14

ON BEING JEWISH

Michael Krausz

I DISTINGUISH between two sorts of questions: How are we to *identify* someone as a Jew as opposed to a non-Jew? And how are we to *characterize* someone's Jewishness? The first question concerns Jewish *descent* (sometimes thought of as identity), and the second concerns Jewish *assent*.

These are distinct questions. Distinguishing descent from assent will allow us to say such intuitively plausible things as "so-and-so is a Jew but not very Jewish." Or, "so-and-so is a non-Jew but really is quite Jewish." It makes sense, however ironic, of Jonathan Miller's remark (Bennett et al. 1987, 84): "In fact, I'm not really a *Jew*. Just Jew-*ish*. Not the whole hog, you know." (It's *Miller*'s metaphor!)

PHILOSOPHICAL ASSUMPTIONS

But before taking up these questions, we should indicate the general philosophical landscape in which they should be situated.

I embrace the nonessentialist or the nonfoundational view that self-definition is ineliminably tied to cultural or historical circumstances and that a transcendental grounding beyond such circumstances is, if intelligible, unavailable. Characteristic transcendental doctrines are rejected, as are assumptions about *inherent* obligations that putatively follow from ahistorical or acultural construals of principles or persons. Such nonfoundationalism disallows claims of knowledge about God, transcendental

This essay is dedicated to the memories of my grandparents, Simon and Franciska Krausz, who perished in Auschwitz, and to the memories of my father, Laszlo Krausz, and my brother, Peter Krausz. I extend my thanks to David Goldberg, Bernard Harrison, Jerrold Levinson, Simon Mein, Sidney Morgenbesser, David Novitz, Hans Oberdiek, and Eddy Zemach for their helpful suggestions.

morality, or traditionally construed views of Zionism that hold that, in virtue of an *essentialist* (i.e., a kind of foundationalist) understanding of being a Jew or being Jewish, it is one's objective moral obligation to live in or to support the State of Israel. Obviously, though, support for Israel may well be defended on other grounds.

To the extent that they share a *theistic* belief in God, the three major branches of religious Judaism (Orthodox, Conservative, and Reform) are disallowed. In turn, if Reconstructionism is understood in an essentialist way, it too is disallowed. But it may well be understood in a nonessentialist way, in which case it could be embraced. When founder Mordechai Kaplan declared that the Torah is the constitution of the Jewish people and disavowed his belief that it was given by a transcendental God to the Jewish people, he attempted to place his understanding of Jewishness within a naturalistic landscape. He located the Torah fully within the matrix of Jewish community, history, tradition, or, in his word, within the matrix of "civilization." Yet it is unclear whether Kaplan construed Jewish civilization "or its distinctive vocation" as a category itself independent of cultural or historical variability, that is, as foundationally privileged. If so, then his reconstructionism would be essentialist or foundationalist. Under these conditions he would have replaced one foundationalism for another. If not, his reconstructionism would be compatible with the historicist view here assumed.

I resist essentialist conceptions of human nature that hold that who a person is is embodied in an enduring and invariant essence that is not historically and culturally emergent. On this view persons have ahistorical, asocial "natures": one just *is* a Jew, or not. Rather I understand persons as social, that is, historical or linguistic constructions. By rejecting transcendental theorizing, persons are seen as positions in culturally and historically conditioned discourses.

I follow Bronwyn Davies and Rom Harré (1990) in their general account of the discursive production of the self. Specifically, they say:

> An individual emerges through the processes of social interaction, not as a relatively fixed end product but as one who is constituted and reconstituted through the various discursive practices in which they participate. Accordingly, who one is is always an open question with a shifting answer depending upon the positions made available within one's own and others' discursive practices and within those practices, the stories through which we make sense of our and others' lives. Stories are located

within a number of different discourses, and thus vary dramati-
cally in terms of the language used, the concepts, issues, and
moral judgements made relevant and the subject positions made
available within them. (46)

This discursive view is in contrast to an older ontology that understands
persons in terms of fixed essences, be they individual or collective. Laurence
Thomas provides useful examples, in Chapter 10, for such a new ontological approach. American masters saw their slaves as inferior persons,
and Nazis saw Jews as inherently evil. On the discursive view, it is not
that slaveholders or Nazis *misdescribed the essence* of American blacks or
Jews. It is rather that no essences are to be described at all.

Accordingly, there is no essence of the Jewish people as such. Rather,
there are people in Jewish positions, or positions that are bestowed as Jewish. Jewishness is understood as *a set of characteristic positions in which
certain people are cast or ascribed—by themselves and by others.*

Here arises the interesting question whether such casting or ascribing is
required of oneself or of others. I follow Asa Kasher (Chapter 4) in holding
that Jewishness requires both. This helps to make sense of such perverse
cases as those in which Nazis ascribed Jewishness to those who denied
their Jewishness. Of course, the Nazis' concern was to annihilate Jews by
descent, and they were unconcerned with whether such Jews did or did not
understand themselves as Jewish by assent.

So, according to the presently embraced ontology, Jewish history is not
of reified entities but of positions or situations. And positions and situations are socially constructed. Thus, the questions, What is a Jew? or What
is Jewishness? are misconceived if they are understood essentialistically and
should be recast as, What characterizes one's being positioned as a Jew or
Jewish in various historical circumstances? Being a Jew or Jewish should
be understood in such terms that relate an unfolding story, the salient
episodes of which are *taken* in variously described historical moments as
characteristically Jewish.

Clearly, such a view can help make sense of the way anti-Semitism has
shaped the nature and destiny of the Jewish people. Whatever the historical
facts of the matter, a significant portion of the Christian world assumes as
part of its organizing narrative that the Jews killed their Messiah Christ,
and so anti-Jewishness is an entrenched feature of Christian culture. Jews
are positioned accordingly. Consequently, it is an enduring (at least discursive) burden of Jews in a Christian culture. Now, this we may understand as
"normal" anti-Semitism, as Isaiah Berlin has put it to me. But with the

winds, the embers of anti-Semitism may enflame to "abnormal" proportions. And anti-Semitism takes different forms in different cultures. In Islam, a "competing" religion for whose prophet the question of death by the Jews does not even arise, anti-Semitism takes an altogether different form. In turn, its organizing narrative takes a different form. (Of course, this is no full explanation of anti-Semitism. That would require a separate treatment in its own right. But it does serve to illustrate the general discursive approach here favored.)

It follows from such a general view that there is nothing *inherently* wrong about a Jew's assimilating into the Diaspora, in the sense that by assimilating some essentialized property is being violated. Indeed, given the extraordinary history of the suffering of the Jewish people, one might argue, all other things being equal—which they are not—that on utilitarian grounds alone assimilation might be desirable. Whether assimilation *is* undesirable requires a separate and nonessentialist argument.

One might remark that there might be a tension in my avoiding essentialism and in my affirming that there are Jewish positions. One might ask if the positions labeled as Jewish have any essential traits. Here we should distinguish essentialism—the doctrine that there are ahistorically fixed conditions for a thing to be that thing—from what, at particular moments in historical evolution, are taken to be necessary conditions for a thing to be that thing. For example, just as requirements for membership in a community may change over historical time, it remains that at any given time there are requirements for membership. It is in that vein that I speak of a necessary condition for Jewishness, although—given my anti-essentialism—such a condition cannot be mandated as historically invariant or grounded in some ahistorical foundation. Correspondingly, one might say that there are essences without essentialism, although it would be best if we not speak of essences at all.

Such is my anti-essentialism and antifoundationalism, which provides the landscape in which the notions of Jewish descent and Jewish assent should be understood. Let us turn, then, to those notions.

JEWS BY DESCENT

The question of Jewish descent addresses the question, How are we to *identify* someone as a Jew as opposed to a non-Jew? The question of Jewishness by assent addresses the question, How are we to *characterize* someone's *Jewishness?*

Distinguishing a Jew from a non-Jew is understood in terms of descent or conversion, and, as we will see, it is independent of any particular beliefs a Jew may have. On the other hand, Jewishness by assent involves *identifying* oneself with a history of a people, heritage, tradition, or culture. And this is not a matter independent of belief.

According to the *halakhah,* the Jewish law, either one of two conditions is sufficient for one to be a Jew. One sufficient condition is to be the child of a Jewish mother, no matter how assimilated into the Diaspora one may be. Indeed, a Jew who actually rejects religious Judaism does not on that account cease to be a Jew by descent. Such a condition is belief-independent.

A second sufficient condition for being a Jew by descent, according to the *halakhah,* is conversion to Judaism. Perhaps surprisingly, conversion to Judaism is characteristically practice-centered, and not belief-centered. There is no religious canon whose belief is a precondition for conversion into Judaism. To be sure, there have been many attempts to formulate such a canon in the history of the Jews, but none has been taken on as halakhically significant. In this respect the idea of conversion to Judaism differs from the idea of conversion to Christianity, for example.

Correspondingly, the *halakhah* holds that if a Jew converts to another religion, he or she continues to be a Jew. Again, conversion away from Judaism need not be a matter of belief either. Indeed, one may have converted to Christianity, say, without in fact believing that Christ was the Messiah. That is, one may convert to a non-Jewish religion out of convenience or political self-interest or the like, having nothing at all to do with religious belief. From the halakhic point of view, the credal beliefs one holds in such a case are irrelevant. Conversion to another religion does not cease identity as a Jew.

In a revealing article, Samuel Lachs shows that being a Jew is not definable in terms of a creed (1989, 32–43). Yet in the course of Jewish history, in order to put Judaism on a religious par with other credal religions (characteristically, Christianity and Islam, which understand religion in terms of creeds), Jews were pressed, in turn, to identify their "religion" in such terms. But, as Lachs says, prior to the Middle Ages when Judaism was "compared, contrasted and juxtaposed with Christianity and with Islam," there was no Hebrew term for "religion" because there was no need. More fully, he says:

> The Hebrew *dat* was selected as the word for "religion." In the Bible it means law, and in rabbinic usage it means correct practice or behavior. What is significant is the Hebrew *emunah*, faith or belief, was not the chosen term. The word was *dat* because

it reflects the centrality of Law and behavior in the structure of Judaism. Had *emunah* been selected it would have given primacy to some specific creed and to a belief that faith is essential to salvation. Neither concept describes biblical or rabbinic Judaism. (32)

So, insofar as descent obtains, one cannot cease to be a Jew. Lachs reminds us of the well-known talmudic statement, "A Jew, although he has sinned [meaning, become an apostate] is still [nominally] a Jew." In this respect it is interesting to note that the early history of the Christians was marked by controversy over whether Gentiles had to be Jews as a *precondition* for their being Christians. (See, for example, the *Book of Acts.*)

Now, one might ask whether the idea of correct practice or behavior can be properly understood independently of beliefs. That is, doesn't practice (keeping kosher, for example) presuppose a network of beliefs? But here we should distinguish between there being *some* network of beliefs from there being in place *certain* specific beliefs. For example, one might make sense of the practice of keeping kosher by holding that not doing so is a sin; or, alternatively, by holding that in doing so one is affirming one's solidarity with the Jewish people; or in doing so one is preserving one's health; or in doing so one is expressing an aesthetic preference; or in doing so one is expressing a received form of life, and so on. The point is that the disjunct of possible beliefs in this regard is indefinitely long, and *no one such specific belief is necessary* to make sense of the practice as such. At the same time, it is not the case that just any beliefs will do. Eating in accord with the rules of kashrut for reasons totally divorced from or opposed to Jewish belief and tradition—for example, because an Indian guru might instruct a disciple to do so, or because one wished to infiltrate into the Jewish religious community—would not amount to keeping kosher in a fully intentional sense.

Now, the halakhic view that Jewish identity is a matter of matrilineal descent is one of a number of possible belief-independent views. Other belief-independent views may not conceive of descent so narrowly. For example, one might hold that being a Jew by descent is belief-independent, but construe descent in a way wider than matrilineage.

There are those who think of themselves in such a wider sense of Jewish descent. For example, the mother of Ludwig Wittgenstein's mother was not a Jew, but the father of Wittgenstein's mother was a Jew. And, on the other side, both parents of Wittgenstein's father were ("originally") Jews and converted to Christianity. So, according to the *halakhah,* Wittgenstein's mother was not a Jew, nor was his father. Still, Wittgenstein thought of himself, if divided, in terms of Jewish descent.

This issue is especially pointed in present-day Israel whose Law of Return holds that all Jews have a right to emigrate to Israel. By not clearly specifying the criteria for what constitutes a Jew, the Israeli law allows that a Jew may be one by virtue of matrilineal *or* patrilineal descent. The Orthodox in Israel have repeatedly tried and failed to have the Israeli law changed in order to define a Jew according to the *halakhah*. But it has failed, because, in part, of resistance from the American Jewish community. In any event, being a Jew by descent, however widely construed, is largely a belief-independent matter.

While not all belief-independent views are halakhic, the halakhic view cannot be simply equated with *the Jewish view*. There is no one univocal answer that the Jewish view provides to the question, Who counts as a Jew? This is no surprise, however, since, as I will suggest, the very idea of a culture—and consequently the very idea of a Jewish culture and its membership—is essentially contestable.

JEWISHNESS BY ASSENT

Now let us turn to our second question, that of Jewishness by assent, which, while related to the question of descent, is distinct from it. Jewishness by assent involves certain beliefs, as well as sentiments and dispositions. It involves *identification* with a historical group. The idea of identification is illusive, though well articulated by Nathan Rotenstreich in Chapter 3. At least it involves the beliefs that there are coherent histories of the Jews and Jewish culture, that these are valuable, and that they provide salient and humanly enhancing terms with which to describe and situate oneself in one's present and historically projectable discursive situation. It involves the belief that self-constitution is thereby humanly edified.

To avoid confusion, this sense of "identify" does not amount to a condition for being a Jew or, as one might say misleadingly, an identity condition of being a Jew. According to the sense of identification favored here, a non-Jew may well be Jewish, and, conversely, a Jew may be non-Jewish. There is no doubt that the phenomenology of a Jew identifying himself or herself as Jewish is different from that of a non-Jew identifying himself or herself as Jewish. While the details of such a difference can be pursued on another occasion, they should not affect the underlying distinction urged here between Jews by descent and Jewishness by assent.

Further, the history with which one may identify, though constructed, should not be understood as a subjective invention. That is, it is not for a single person on a given occasion to invent a Jewish narrative in which to place himself or herself. Rather, such narratives are socially constructed, whether they be of a traditional or of a revisionist sort. Thus, such a communitarian achievement provides the grounds for speaking of one's appropriately or inappropriately identifying with one or another history.

As suggested, non-Jews may be Jewish by assent. Indeed, Christian scripture and liturgy, for example, identifies Abraham as "our" father. Jewishness by assent does not presuppose being a Jew by descent, although historically these are closely tied. A non-Jew may identify himself or herself with the history of Jews and Jewish culture. But such a concession is a matter of degree. For when Christians appropriate histories of Jews and Jewish culture, they may do so in highly selective ways for perhaps divergent theological purposes. They may do so in ways that bifurcate Jewish history with the coming of Jesus. *Characteristically,* Christian identification with Jewish history is not with the life and history of the Jews and Jewish culture to the present and beyond, with their trials and tribulations as well as with their challenges and accomplishments. But we should emphasize that this is a characteristic and not a necessary stance, for to hold that such a stance is necessary runs the risk of essentializing non-Jews.

On the other hand, one may find a corresponding temptation to essentialize Jews in the thought that only Jews are capable of identifying with Jewish history. But such an essentialized view of Jews and non-Jews ignores the facts, first, that (perhaps too many) Jews do not identify with Jewish history and nothing from that can be inferred about their ability or inability to do so; and, second, that mass conversion to Judaism—most notably in the case of those under the Russian khazar (for whom Judah Hallevi [1906] wrote so eloquently)—suggests that non-Jews in the first instance are quite capable of identifying with Jewish history.

Of course, there are degrees to which one might identify with a history of the Jews and Jewish culture. In this regard we may distinguish those who do from those who do not, on the basis of certain beliefs, assume responsibility and engage in actions that bear on their rights and privileges as members of a community. For example, an engaged Jew may take some political actions when Israel faces military assaults, or when it encounters problems or opportunities with the Palestinians, or when he or she encounters anti-Semitism in the former Soviet Union or the United States, or when he or she encounters an attempt further to theocratize or nationalize the Jewish community by Hassidim or Zionists, or the like.

Generally, then, Jewishness by assent should be understood in terms of

identification with a constellation of features that may slide over historical time and cultural circumstance. It should be understood rather along
Wittgensteinian lines of cluster concepts, which are "open." This approach
opposes any temptation to enumerate ahistorically conceived features. The
fabric may be patched in many ways over time. And there are a number
of possible threads to such a fabric, for example: believing in a Jewish
God, embracing certain moral or social precepts, pursuing certain Jewish
practices, pursuing Zionist activities, adopting a certain kind of persona
or lexicon, embracing certain practices in terms of which one makes intelligible and facilitates life passages, and so on.

I have suggested that one is Jewish by assent if one identifies with and
positions oneself in Jewish historical narratives. One is Jewish if one identifies with Jewish history as one's own. This involves positioning oneself in
relation to Jewish history, however central or tangential. The point to be
stressed here is that such a view is itself historically and culturally variable.
We should be careful not to elide "identifying with Jewish history as one's
own" with "positioning oneself in relation to Jewish history." Hitler did
the latter and not the former. Clearly, my suggestion that Jewishness should
be understood in terms of identification with Jewish history as one's own
is substantially stronger than only positioning oneself in relation to Jewish
history. The former involves the latter, but not vice versa.

While we may choose the historical narratives with which we identify,
to a considerable degree, our narratives choose and position us. Indeed, it
is being positioned as the Jews were by the Nazis that enforced a common
narrative for twentieth-century Jews. And, that common narrative makes
Jews common characters in a shared narrative.

It should be noted that the presently offered view of Jewish assent is de-
cidedly not halakhic. For example, the *halakhah* would attach no special
Jewish significance to the Holocaust; it would be understood as one people
attempting to kill off another. Yet, the Holocaust is an integral part of
Jewish history—*indeed the most salient episode in contemporary Jewish
history*—and, according to the view urged here, identification with its narrative can hardly not be constitutive of being Jewish. Contemporary Jewish
assent cannot be made intelligible independently of that narrative datum.

Of course, as with all historical narratives, there is no single correct
Jewish history. Both at a particular moment in history and across historical
periods, what should count as the domain of Jewish history is essentially
contestable, depending upon a multiplicity of eligible grounds for Jewish
descent and assent. Jewish historical narratives are written and rewritten
according to what is taken by each generation as salient. There can be no

singular and historically enduring fact of the matter about Jewish history. That is as it should be, if the Jewish community will not become reified. Indeed, such a hermeneutic turn is characteristically talmudic or midrashic. In this respect it is instructive to bear in mind the remarks of Thomas Altizer (1989):

> Judaism as a religious system is a social and not a literary construction, its true origin residing in history and not in the canonical texts. . . . If there is a community of texts in the canon of Judaism, this is not intrinsically present in the texts themselves, but rather lies in an extrinsic quality that has been imputed into the texts from without. Judaism itself is that extrinsic quality, a Judaism that itself creates or defines the canon.

No one discourse can be priviledged as *the* one that captures the singularly right construal of Jewish identity and assent. There is no single fact of the matter as to what Jewishness is. We should resist the temptation—which religious fundamentalists characteristically do not—to identify one construal of Jewishness as *the* construal of Jewishness, one that obtains in virtue of one privileged interpretive moment. Thus, Jewish history cannot be equated with the observance of certain practices, understood in the singularist way that fundamentalists do, be they assenting to certain canons as sacred, praying in certain ways, observing holidays in certain ways, respecting certain leaders as definitive, associating with certain people, refraining from eating and marrying nonkosher, and on and on and on and on. To be kept alive, Jewish history should allow that postmodern Jews may recognize themselves in that history, that they *may* claim and recognize themselves as characters in its evolving history. And, while there can be no single correct Jewish history, there may be incorrect Jewish histories, for, as I have allowed, any twentieth-century history of the Jews that ignores or minimizes the Holocaust is incorrect.

Religious fundamentalists might be tempted to deal with the multiplicity of Jewish historical narratives by disallowing that such a multiplicity is about the *same* group, and, thereby, to privilege one subgroup as the only bona fide group. I have elsewhere called this (1993) a "pluralizing maneuver," which here takes the form of saying that there are many different *disconnected* groups, and there is no organic connection among them. All but one subgroup are disenfranchised as illegitimate, on the totalizing presumption that the preferred group has the license (guaranteed through its own self-certifying strategies) to do so. Such a pluralizing maneuver results in a Babel-like situation in which interpreters about Jews and Jewishness talk past each other, where they don't agree *enough* with each other even to be able to generate the possibility of disagreement between them. But this undercuts the talmudic or midrashic tradition of perpetual interpretation and reinterpretation. It inhibits the very tradition that fundamentalists so vehemently claim they defend.

We may subdivide the issue of Jewishness-by-assent into two varieties: one that involves acceptance of a certain creed connected with the oneness of God or other beliefs connected with certain practices and observances—in short, what goes into "being religious"; and the other, which involves identification with Jewish history. These are distinct modes of assenting to Jewishness. While one may embrace the latter without the former—and clearly this has been the main focus of my attention—it would seem most implausible to embrace the former without the latter.

The very idea of a culture is essentially contestable in that whichever features of a given culture one takes to be salient are motivated by values that are themselves contestable. Correspondingly, there is no determinate singular thing that is the Jewish culture. Rather, over time certain of its features are taken as more or less entrenched conditions of its identity. The Jewish heritage of the prophets was different from that of Maimonides, and his was different from that of the kabbalists, which was different from that of Rabbi Finkelstein, which was different from that of Rabbi Kaplan, and so on.

Consequently, while the account of a culture initially may appear to be descriptive, in truth it is normative. And, practically, this is reflected in such everyday decisions as to whether one should associate with a Jewish community, and if so which one; whether to send one's children to a Hebrew school, and if so, which one; whether one should support the State of Israel, and if so in which respects and in which ways, and so on.

Insofar as there is no one historically fixed thing that a Jew has to *be* to be a Jew or to be Jewish, according to this suggestion, there are no fixed antecedent requirements that have to be satisfied. This attitude departs from others exemplified in Jewish history. For example, up until the Zionist revolution there was a more or less unified view that a necessary component of Jewish consciousness was religious practice. Then Zionism rejected religiosity as a necessary condition of Jewishness, and in its early stages even *required* that Jewishness exclude religiosity. In its place the Zionists substituted nationality. Either religiosity or nationality constituted the antecedent conditions in the sense just suggested. In turn, other antecedent conditions in the pertinent sense have been offered. For example, Emil Fackenheim holds that an antecedent condition of Jewishness is the reckoning with the Holocaust as an episode in the history of the Jews understood in terms of the original covenant with Abraham. This eschatological view holds that there is a point to waiting for the providential realization of the covenant. Thus, Fackenheim tells us, what is characteristically Jewish is a certain kind of *listening* to Jewish history as it unfolds (see Chapter 9). Rather, in holding that there are no transhistorical or transcultural antecendent conditions for being a Jew or for being Jewish, I allow that such conditions are emergent *within,* and do not precede, the unfolding of Jewish history.

At this juncture we should at least register the question of bad faith, whose answer deserves a separate treatment in its own right. That is, how should one understand the phenomena of not identifying with a certain history but saying or believing one is identifying with it; or, alternatively, of identifying with a certain history but saying or believing one is not identifying with it. How can one determine whether one's identifications are authentic, and if they are not authentic what is to be done? These questions are especially pointed for one who embraces an anti-essentialist view of history, which resists the idea that history itself should be understood as autonomous of its interpretations. This is an instance of the more general problem of bad faith, and whether there is something distinctive about these questions as they arise within the Jewish context is an open question.

JEWISH OBLIGATION

The question arises whether the fact of one's being a Jew by descent or Jewish by assent implies any obligations about the furtherance of Jewish history and culture, leaving open what specific form such obligations might take. Notice that this question concerns obligations in contradistinction to duties and responsibilities (as a Kantian, say, might sketch the conceptual terrain). But a discussion of whether an obligation/duty/responsibility trichotomy should be drawn would take us beyond the scope of this essay. In any event, I confine myself to the question of obligations.

There seems to be no obligation that is entailed by the fact of Jewish descent. Yet Jewishness by assent does seem to entail such obligation. Jewishness by assent is already to see oneself as part of a valued Jewish historical narrative, and as such it is to place oneself under an obligation to foster the integrity of that narrative itself.

Eddy Zemach argues in Chapter 8 that Jews have an objective moral obligation to preserve and foster Jewish history and culture. As he says, "we are not free not to right those wrongs that history has put in our laps."

On Zemach's view, the obligation derives from a more general view that holds that, other things being equal, there is a prima facie obligation for anyone to preserve and foster the history and culture of his or her kin. (We should note that recognizing that a history *has* been put in our laps is a function not of descent but of assent.) For example, whatever one may believe or feel about one's parents, he holds, one has a prima facie objective obligation to care for them when they are ill, just because they are one's parents. Such obligation does not depend on their worthiness or the quality of one's relationship with them, or the like. Of course, there may well be considerations that override such a prima facie obligation.

Zemach's general claim is meant to hold for fully fledged cultures— which enrich its members, satisfying deep human needs and desires. Indeed, a fully fledged culture needs to endure over time, providing its members means for satisfying such deep human needs and desires, including the enrichment of human discourse, notably through the development and elaboration of language and symbol systems generally, its cognitive achievements, art, music, and the like. What qualifies a culture as such is that it must embody values that contribute to what is human. Thus, on Zemach's account, Nazism is no culture. It is a barbarous ideology. Their practice of book burning, at the least, was an emblem of their own disqualification as a culture.

When Zemach says that one has a prima facie obligation to care for one's parents, we should understand "parents" not in the biological sense of descent (which entails no obligations as such) but in the fuller more historical sense of a (presumably caring) history. Put otherwise, "parents" and "prima facie" should, contra Zemach, be historicized. So seen, we may agree with Zemach's remark that "we are not free not to right those wrongs that history has put in our laps." This is tantamount to embracing the view that whatever obligations do obtain follow from assent rather than descent. And this is part and parcel of what is involved in the idea of Jewishness by assent.

So the case for the obligation to parents follows upon one's already having recognized them as more than mere biological parents. Such obligation requires more than the concession that certain persons preceded one in a line of descent. Instead, obligation obtains upon the recognition of parents within the context of assent in the sense indicated. Correspondingly, a Jew by descent and not by assent may have no obligation to further Jewish history, while a Jew by assent has just such an obligation that he or she has already implicitly or explicitly accepted.

A further argument for the obligation to nurture Jewish history is a general argument against cultural suicide. It applies to those who already identify themselves in terms of the history of their culture. It holds that without some Jewish historical narrative in which a Jew is positioned, he or she will effectively suicide as a cultural being and cease to be the sort of cultural being that he or she is. His or her cultural and historical narrative would have dropped out of his or her self-conception. To the extent to which this is impoverishing, it is objectionable not to keep one's culture and its history alive. Again, this holds for those who already understand themselves in terms of the pertinent culture. Clearly, for the Jew who does not already identify himself or herself in terms of Jewish culture, such an obligation would not obtain. The argument against cultural suicide holds for one already immersed in a given culture, for whom the intelligibility of oneself as a cultural being is already significant. It does not hold for the person for whom cultural suiciding in the pertinent sense makes no difference.

SUMMARY

In sum, my approach is anti-essentialist, antifoundational, and social constructionist. I distinguish being a Jew by descent from Jewishness by assent, and I suggest that Jewishness by assent should be understood in terms of identification with a Jewish history. That involves embracing certain beliefs and seeing oneself as a character in a valued Jewish narrative that one both occupies and fashions. One who assents to his or her Jewishness at least partly understands himself or herself in terms of the historically emergent threads of the fabrics of Jewish histories.

POSTSCRIPT

Parenthetically, we should note that the thesis that Jewishness should be understood in terms of identification with Jewish history will be resisted by Zionists and by poststructuralists. On one hand, the Zionists will hold that the very question of Jewishness does not arise for it is fully replaceable by becoming an Israeli national; Israeli nationality dissolves or makes otiose the question of Jewishness. On that view, the question of Jewishness is outmoded and remains a curious lingering preoccupation among Diaspora Jews. On the other hand, my thesis will be resisted by poststructuralists who hold that there is no such thing as history; therefore there is no such thing as Jewish history; therefore the suggestion that Jewishness should be understood in terms of identification with Jewish history is a nonstarter.

Given space limitations my responses to these challenges must be sketchy. As for the Zionist position, the Zionist idea itself cannot be made intelligible independently of the idea of Jewishness, and reducing the latter to the former undercuts the possibility of justifying Zionism to start with. As for the poststructuralist, the denial of the idea of history undercuts the possibility of making our own lives intelligible to ourselves, since that requires the idea of history. It should be evident that I embrace neither of these views. Both the question of Jewishness and its understanding in terms of identification with Jewish history remain live for me. A fuller development of this parenthetical sketch must await another occasion.

BIBLIOGRAPHY

Altizer, Thomas J. J. 1989. "In Search of That Which Binds the Tradition." Review of *Canon and Connection: Intertextuality in Judaism,* by Jacob Neusner. *The Reconstructionist* 55 (September–October/Tishrei–Heshvan, 5750): 34.

Bennett, Alan, Peter Cook, Jonathan Miller, and Dudley Moore. 1987. *Beyond the Fringe.* London: Methuen.

Butler, Judith. 1990. "Feminism and the Question of Post-Modernism." Paper presented at the Conference on the Philosophy of the Human Studies, Greater Philadelphia Philosophy Consortium, Haverford College, September 22.

Coggen, Donald. 1990. "Jews and Christians." *Theology,* July/August, 261–66.

Davies, Bronwyn, and Rom Harré. 1990. "Positioning: The Discursive Production of Selves." *Journal for the Theory of Social Behaviour* 20, no. 1 (March): 43–63.

Hallevi, Judah. 1906. *Kitab Al Khazari.* Translated by Hartwig Hirschfield. London: George Routledge & Sons.

Handelman, Susan. 1986. " 'Everything Is in It': Rabbinic Interpretation and Modern Literary Theory." *Judaism: A Quarterly Journal of Jewish Life and Thought* 35, no. 4 (Fall): 429–40.

Harré, Rom. 1979. *Social Being.* Oxford: Basil Blackwell.

Krausz, Michael. 1993. *Rightness and Reasons: Interpretation in Cultural Practices.* Ithaca, N.Y.: Cornell University Press.

Lachs, Samuel T. 1989. "Jews and Judaeo-Christians in the First Century: Confronting Heterodoxy." *Proceedings of the Institute for Distinguished Leaders.* Waltham, Mass.: Brandeis University, July 30–August 1.

Lurie, Yuval. 1989. "Jews as a Metaphysical Species." *Philosophy* 64, no. 249 (July): 323–47.

Sollors, Werner. 1986. *Beyond Ethnicity: Consent and Descent in American Culture.* Oxford: Oxford University Press.

15

THE PHENOMENAL-NOUMENAL JEW
Three Antinomies of Jewish Identity

Berel Lang

T HE ART form of the pastiche has become an emblem of postmodernism, and there is an obvious parallel between the discontinuities
and anticentrism of that form and the theoretical claims of postmodernism.
On this same basis—adding to it the irony of a long, unmodern past—
the question "What is Jewish identity?" also appears now as postmodern. Not because of the many discordant answers given to the question (in
this, postmodernism has no distinctive claims), but because the question
itself seems inconsistent, directed at a subject that is at once one and many.
Put more exactly, the question would ask, "What *are* Jewish identity?"—
the grammatical implausibility reflecting the incongruous assembly subsumed under a single rubric. Here religion and culture, history and politics,
psychology and morality, faith and common sense elbow each other for
place, each of them confident of its own claims but vague or even indifferent about what is due the others. And yet, of course, this collective
improbability has not silenced the question itself, which emerges then as
unlikely but unavoidable, not unintelligible but overdetermined: It makes
too much sense.

Philosophy has typically resisted such questions, shunting them to its
margins in the cause of disciplinary rigor or simple economy. But one tac-
tic of philosophical discourse is directed at assertions that converge in
just such a superficially incoherent structure; this is the figure of the "antinomy," where opposed but equally compelling claims are somehow—
each of them—to be sustained. In this figure, an ostensive contradiction
is overridden by a more inclusive claim of compatibility—the latter being
necessary because *its* denial exacts a higher price than the original contra-

diction. Resolution of such antinomies (Kant refers to them as "dynamic") comes, then, not by discrediting one of their two sides but by finding a means of affirming them both.

For Kant, the resolution of whatever qualifies as an antinomy is theoretical and universal. For reasons I hope to make clear, no such general resolution is possible for the "Antinomies of Jewish Identity" elaborated here. Yet the opposed assertions in these (as in any) antinomies are not "merely" contradictory; the means of reconciling them, then, will be practical rather than theoretical, involving self-definition for a particular self, not a general rule for all selves or for all identity. Resolution of the antinomies is thus not universalizable; although the terms of the argument leading to the resolution *can be* formulated as having general reference, that generality only sets limits within which a practical inference then directs itself to one particular "I." This does not mean that Jewish identity is subject to *no* general rules (prescriptions or proscriptions), much less that Jewish identity or individual identity more generally is a matter of only personal taste or will. It does mean, however, that any general conditions that impinge on this self-identity are by themselves insufficient to determine it. Theoretical overdetermination, in other words, turns into practical underdetermination, with the self then located in the unpredictable space—on the cusp—between what is actual and what is possible. That is, no doubt, an uncertain and uncomfortable place, but since what is at stake here is the discovery or establishment of an identity—including, as it may happen, one's own—there should be nothing surprising about this.

ANTINOMY I

  a. Jewish identity is a matter of fact—determined on the basis of objective criteria to which the person whose identity is at issue has no privileged access.

  b. Jewish identity is a matter of choice—to be made by the person whose identity is in question, and by subjective criteria (if any).

  1a. *Jewish identity is a matter of fact—determined on the basis of objective criteria to which the person whose identity is at issue has no privileged access.*

An exemplary formulation of this thesis appears in Jewish history itself. Notwithstanding their other disagreements, both critics and advocates of normative Judaism acknowledge that, historically, the conditions of Jewish identity have been defined in objective terms. Those and only those persons have been held to be Jews for whom matrilineal Jewish descent was demonstrable or who had undergone conversion in accordance with requirements objectively specified. On this account, there is no other ground for ascribing or assuming Jewish identity; furthermore, nothing else is required—neither doctrinal knowledge nor confession, not faith or affirmation. Nor is renunciation or escape possible: Jewish identity is not only objectively determined but, if applicable at all, permanent. Sin, heresy, apostasy—all carry stigmas and often warrant punishment. But even on the most severe of these verdicts, Jewish identity nonetheless remains fixed: once Jewish, always Jewish.

Where within this context a question of Jewish identity occurs, then, an answer to the question requires no more than a determination of fact. That this determination may be difficult to make on practical grounds or that its conclusion may be unwanted and perhaps rejected by the person whose identity is in question does not bear on the principle. Like other more obviously objective features of identity (the date and place of a person's birth, genetic coding, etc.), here, too, the individual whose identity is determined has no say in the matter. On this account, Jewish identity does not require affirmation or even acquiescence; historical and/or social identification, based on external and objective features, is the one necessary and sufficient means.

To be sure, not only normative Judaism has conceived of Jewish identity in the terms of matter of fact. Analogous formulations have appeared in other legal or quasi-legal codes, often as a preface to persecution that has *that* reason for seeking objective identification. The most notorious instance of this remains the "racial" definition of Jewish identity stipulated by the Nazis' Nuremberg Laws, according to which (in its last formulation) three Jewish grandparents and/or identification with the Jewish community sufficed for inclusion in the category that was later marked for the "final solution." The harsh analogy between this objectivist definition of Jewish identity and that found in Jewish law is obviously no more than formal; what is crucial in the view is the priority it assigns to historically objective features.

> 1b. *Jewish identity is a matter of choice, made by the person whose identity is in question, and by subjective criteria (if any).*

But, this contradictory thesis goes, individual identity involves more than only physical or material characteristics and thus requires more than only an external finding. Reference to personal identity, whatever else it entails, addresses the character of the self—not only its identification *by others* but its own self-definition. And this in turn assumes affirmation or choice, with the knowledge and self-consciousness—thus also the freedom to dissent or to change—that these entail. Moreover, to the extent that personal identity involves affiliation with a group (invoking, for example, religious or ethical norms), assent by the self becomes a stronger requirement still. Even on the objectivist prescriptions of Jewish law, this need is acknowledged; so, for example, the authoritative formula of Maimonides' "Thirteen Principles" with each of the thirteen prefaced by an avowal of belief. Outside the normative tradition, of course, the features of subjective affirmation are even more prominent and emphatic—as in Ben Gurion's assertion, related to the connection he claimed between Judaism and Zionism, that Jewish identity requires no more than an affirmation that one *is* a Jew.

The force of the counterthesis in this first antinomy is not simply to posit a competing definition of Jewish identity. Because of their institutional and public character, legal stipulations commonly tend to be objectivist, minimizing the role of individual or subjective intention. Thus, unless (begging the question) the possibility of contesting the "legal" definition is denied a priori, a place will remain for individual choice or decision. Even beyond this merely logical possibility, however, the counterthesis here makes a claim of plausibility. How much *sense* is there in identifying someone as a Jew who, although meeting the "objective" criteria stated, is removed (possibly as an inheritance of generations) from all consciousness or practice associated with that identity? Or to designate a person as Jewish who has formally undergone conversion away from it and thus has embraced a different community, a different group of practices and values—all of them distinct from, perhaps opposed to, Jewish identity? And yet—to rehearse the antinomy—does it make more sense to have the matter of Jewish identity depend *only* on a feeling, even one that ensues in an avowal? A retraction only a few moments later might also be based on reasons equally deeply felt.

ANTINOMY 2

a. Jewish identity, like all other determinations of personal identity, is a function of the individual's historical and social past.

b. Jewish identity, like all other determinations of personal identity, is a function of the individual's immediate present (including present interpretation of his historical and social past).

2a. *Jewish identity, like all other determinations of personal identity, is a function of the individual's historical and social past.*

Even if one rejects legal or quasi-legal criteria as definitive, personal identity depends—psychologically, culturally, morally—on the historical setting (*also* objective) into which individuals are born and which then, wittingly and willingly or not, is constitutive. The family and the other communities of which the individual is part shape personal identity; indeed, they are required if it is to *have* a shape. Values, language, customs, the sense of self in a context: These all compose a "surround," which the individual, even when reacting against it, depends on and then embodies.

In this respect Jewish identity reflects a past designated (whether in its own terms or in others) as Jewish. And neither the circularity in this process of identification nor the variety in its detail, not even the attempt to deny them, suffices to blunt or nullify this source. Such historical conditions may not be sufficient for defining Jewish identity, but they are necessary to it; it is impossible to imagine personal—human—identity without them. Even to reject an inheritance does not erase the fact of the inheritance itself; and where the present is possible *only* with an inheritance from the past, the latter's role is confirmed even more strongly.

In this sense historical constraints affect every moment of personal identity, remaining always a step ahead of it and to that extent outside the control of the individual. Such historical grounds affect personal identity generally; they thus hold also for Jewish identity in particular and, given the longevity and self-consciousness of Jewish history, with more than usual force. Admittedly, the historical foundation of Jewish identity at any one moment may be problematic. (Recall as an example here Gershom Scholem's account of the childhood gift that he received of a picture of Theodore Herzl: his family's Christmas present to him.) But such marginal instances only underscore the many others where the factors of historical (and Jewish) identity are evident and unequivocal.

2b. *Jewish identity, like all other determinations of personal identity, is a function of the individual's immediate present (including a present interpretation of his historical and social past).*

History undoubtedly has something to say about personal identity, but what it says is not necessarily—more exactly, not *ever*—the last word: The person or individual self in the present always must confirm or deny the past. If human freedom or autonomy has any claim at all, it will be evident in the assertion of personal identity. The choice of a spouse, a career, friends—all undoubtedly have anticipations in a personal and social past; but it is present judgment—"present" because judgment would not otherwise be judgment—that pronounces on the past and finds a role for it in the present. Even the historical aspects of individual identity that are irrevocable—biological or cultural or linguistic "givens"—remain subordinate and defeasible at least in one sense. What they *mean* for personal identity is a matter of the present moment, not of the past—and this holds for Jewish identity as well, notwithstanding the strong claim it asserts for authority over the present through its distinctively cohesive past.

ANTINOMY 3

    a. Jewish identity is particularistic and exclusionary.

    b. Jewish identity is universalistic and inclusive.

3a. *Jewish identity is particularistic and exclusionary.*

However broadly conceived, Jewish identity revolves around a center that excludes others—not only because such exclusion holds for all determination of individual identity but because Jewish identity openly defines itself as particularistic and exclusionary. In the normative tradition of Judaism, this contention is unmistakable, entailing a commitment to separation and difference between the Jewish community and others and thus between the individual Jew and the non-Jew. Such commitment amounts to a denial of "others," even if at the same moment it anticipates a time when "God will be one and His name one," when the harmony and reconciliation of a messianic age are envisaged. In fact, also the latter ideals (which have at best an *occasional* history in comparison to the history of particularity) first require the realization of a particular (Jewish) identity—beginning with one, not *all* communities or codes of law, and thus starting with the individual family and the particular self. Values or preferences that hope to transcend these limits cannot avoid deferring them at some point. To "love one's fellow as oneself," for example, is a religious commandment (not only within Judaism) that otherwise serves also as a secular ideal. But the improbability of love being "commanded" at all becomes more tenuous still as the object of the imperative is generalized to humanity or creatures as such. Only its origin in *particular* attachments gives the inclusive ideal its force; only this makes the latter at all possible. "The particular," the cosmopolitan Goethe conceded, "is always more than a match for the universal."

3b. *Jewish identity is universalistic and inclusive.*

The claim that Jewish identity, like any other individuating quality, is particularistic is—the *counterthesis* asserts—tautological: How could it *not* be particularistic? On the other hand, this restrictive allegiance, however necessary, need not be an end in itself; it might well be—and in fact is—a means toward a quite different end. Indeed, for neither the letter nor spirit of normative Judaism is exclusion itself a goal; the Prophets unendingly chide those who make this mistake. Certainly in the cultural inheritance left by the encounter between Judaism and the Enlightenment, the press for universalization dominates on both sides; particularism is at most a means—with the universal end it is intended to serve constantly in view. Particularism in these terms may be a psychological or physical requirement, but then, too, it is an instrumental consideration, not one of principle. And Jewish identity did not have to wait for the Enlightenment to acquire the ideal of universality: The Noahite code binds Jews and non-Jews alike, thus asserting a basic—biblical—claim of human commonality. The sometime charge of "cosmopolitanism" against Jewish identity, malicious though it has been in motivation, is at least as accurate as the charge of "clannishness" or "separatism" that from Roman times has often accompanied it (contradictorily).

THE THREE ANTINOMIES of Jewish identity have been cited without attribution, but each of their respective sides recurs historically in both Jewish and non-Jewish sources. (Statements for almost all of them appear elsewhere in the present volume—sometimes separately, sometimes as antinomies, sometimes even as contradictions.) I have claimed both reason and history for each of the sides, inferring from this that the relation between them in each antinomy, accurately construed, is more than only a contradiction. This leaves open the question, however, of how a reconciliation between thesis and counterthesis in the several antinomies is possible. About this I have suggested that whatever form such resolution takes, it will not be "universal": the determination of personal identity is least of all a general or theoretical issue. An alternative option is for a "practical" resolution, in something close to Aristotle's conception of practical judgment where the outcome embodies the combined effect of two conflicting extremes rather than the denial of one (or perhaps of both). Neither side of the antinomies, in other words, is to be left out.

What this requirement amounts to can be seen *by contrast* in certain "thwarted" versions of the antinomies: "thwarted" insofar as only one side of the antinomy is preserved, the other, rejected. Perhaps the most familiar of these thwarted antinomies is in the dispute between the claim that historical names or categories determine identity and the opposed contention that the *self* is (by itself) responsible for engendering such names or categories. In the first alternative, the self is an external construct; the second conceives of identity as spun by the self out of whole cloth. An all too common version of Jewish identity enlarges on the first of these, construing that identity exclusively as the result of external imposition. The historian Salo Baron wrote disparagingly of this "lachrymose" conception of Jewish history: Jewish history viewed as a history of suffering, with Jewish identity constantly sustained by the threat of repression. Sartre's extreme formulation of this view, in *The Anti-Semite and the Jew,* asserts that if Jews were not designated "Jews" by others—"dirty Jews," in the full force of his argument—Jewish identity would in effect disappear. (Presumably, it would also not have arisen in the first place, although Sartre leaves the question of origins—how denial can bring something *into* existence—untouched.) A variation on this view associates Jewish identity with an alienated or divided self, also the result of external displacement: The "wandering Jew" wanders not by choice but under duress.

This "other-directed" conception of Jewish identity is, however—even in its own terms—historically misleading. It ignores substantial evidence of the persistence of Jewish identity in the absence of external threat; it is equally implausible (if not unfalsifiable as a whole) in psychological and cultural terms. So, for example, prior to the linking of "biological" racism to genocide by the Nazis, persecution of the Jews (for example, by the Church) invariably included the options for escape by conversion or assimilation. Unless one also ascribes to Jewish identity an innate masochistic impulse, persecution or repression would presumably have led as readily to assimilation as to affirmation and thus the persistence of that identity (which was, after all, the ostensive occasion of persecution). In other words, the causal role ascribed to persecution in *behalf of* Jewish identity would do equally well to explain the relation between persecution and the *disappearance* of Jewish identity (through assimilation), not only as a possibility but also, since assimilation *has* occurred, in fact. And explanations that apply whatever outcome transpires are hardly explanations at all.

A different but equally conclusive objection affects the opposing claim that Jewish identity may draw exclusively on subjective grounds, sustained by the individual self's assertion or affirmation. In its religiously orthodox version, this view invokes a founding role for faith or confession; in a more moderate and secularized version, the view entails commitment either to a "religion of reason" or to an existential "self-creation." Each of these alternatives, however, begs a crucial part of the question. To claim that the phenomenon of Jewish identity began or has been sustained historically by rational discovery alone almost certainly entails a tendentious definition of reason: How could reason, indifferent to all proper names, imagine a *Jewish* identity? (That is, without transgressing its own bounds.) The corrective to a conception of Jewish identity in which history has the last word is not a subjective conception in which history is displaced either by reason spinning abstractions out of whole cloth *or* by the personal will or sensibility (as history itself has demonstrated what may be expected from *them*).

The necessity on each side of the antinomies cited suggests, as I have mentioned, a similarity to the Kantian Antinomies, which at once reflect and entail the distinction Kant drew between phenomena and noumena. But Kant's "two-worlds" theory brought coexistence to the opposing sides in the antinomies at the price of a substantive dualism. And such a solution for the antinomies of Jewish identity—separating the "phenomenal" Jew of history and particularity from the "noumenal" Jew of subjectivity and universalism—would only further confound the issue of Jewish identity, which is not a general problem, but a practical one, applying in the end to individual persons. The two sides of *these* antinomies, in contrast to Kant's, not only must be sustained side by side but are mutually implicated, the one unintelligible in respect to the individual person without the other. And lastly, like the frameworks for all practical judgments, the issue of Jewish identity is directed to the future—impelling the individual to what he or she *will* be, with the antinomies by themselves providing no ground for moving in one direction rather than another.

Individual decisions or affirmations—required on one side of each of the antinomies—are thus only one and a limited part of the determination of Jewish identity. This does not mean that choice does not figure in that determination, but that the choice or construction of a self is contextual, set in a historical frame that affects the process with or without the concurrence of the agent and in any event always beyond the agent's awareness of its full role. Because of this, others are at times able to judge or "determine" the self-identity of a person more accurately than the latter can himself.

This limitation does not simply hinder or impede, since there is reason to view the historical ground of personal identity as providing a necessary basis for it. Identity in the present, in other words, requires the conditions of the past; an "immaculate" self without some such ground hardly can be imagined. The history incorporated in a self is in this sense accidental in detail but necessary *as* history. (The very questions of personal identity or of Jewish identity in particular are themselves historical phenomena; both are modern and in a sense antihistorical developments—if not unintelligible, largely irrelevant for ancient and medieval thought, and tangential, in the second case, to Jewish history at least up to the Emancipation at the end of the eighteenth century.)

There is not, then—because there *cannot* be—any general basis for answering the question of what Jewish identity is, and this is most evident as that question turns to the future—the immediate future, it has to be said, since for the question of identity there are no postponements or deferrals, and the "long-term" is only the short-term repeated again and again. Certainly where Jewish identity is the issue, no *general* basis is available for deciding between even the extreme alternatives of affirmation or denial. The Enlightenment and post-Enlightenment arguments against difference, against the practice or identity of cults, remain at best high-level abstractions, at worst, tendentious versions of particularism in the guise of universalism. Even such an apparently historically rooted claim as Emil Fackenheim's post-Holocaust "614th Commandment," which argues for the affirmation of Jewish identity in order not to provide Hitler with a posthumous victory by the "voluntary" disappearance of the Jewish people, fails finally in its presupposition of general applicability; directed to whatever such affirmation would be *against,* it avoids the question of what such affirmation could be affirmation *for.*

Any general resolution or resolution in principle proposed for the antinomies thus disqualifies itself: the determination of personal identity and so also of Jewish identity is immediate, individual, and above all practical. Even if we admit the moral requirement of universalizability, that hardly pertains here, since it remains an issue for individual identity as to what extent this is exclusively a moral issue (whatever such exclusivity might in fact mean). One version of universalizability that bears on the determination of Jewish self-identity does so, in fact, because of and not despite a particularistic ground. This ground is the relation between present and future—specifically, the consequences that follow from the determination of one's own identity for the identities of others who are likely to take *theirs* from it, most immediately (for obvious reasons) for one's children. To be sure, no one fully "chooses" identities for their children—but the determination of one's own identity is, almost invariably and to some extent (in fact if not in intent), also a choice for them—and in a way that may disclose aspects of that identity more clearly than it does in one's self.

At the very least, a view emerges from this bequest of the present as seen from the future, with something in it that resembles the mirroring or doubling effect that the Kantian Categorical Imperative has through its implication of one's own self in the selves of others. Thus, a corresponding, albeit limited imperative for personal and then for Jewish identity: "Act as though you were choosing also for your children." Because, in a substantive sense, you are. Thus Jewish identity—because personal identity does this more generally—constitutes a choice for more than the one self with which its determination might otherwise seem to begin and to end. Leslie Fiedler's self-portrait of a "terminal Jew" sets the issue directly and severely: his own identity, Fiedler recognizes in encouraging and directing his children away from its particularity, is—successfully—without a future.

That even the formal imperative just cited entails no specific prescription does not mean that the question of personal or, more narrowly, Jewish identity remains a matter only for the will or taste (or still less than these, for chance) to resolve. Idolatry is commonly associated with "gods" outside the self, made of a different and larger stuff. But there is no reason to exempt from that violation idolatry *within* the self—where the rival "gods," although perhaps subtler or less obtrusive, are no less alien. Jewish identity enters, then, when history and the self meet, with only an approximate guide available to the geography or logic of that improbable place. Perhaps the one certainty about this determination is that it does not emerge from either of its two sources alone: For personal—and Jewish— identity, history without self-affirmation is empty, self-affirmation without history is blind. The Yiddish saying, "S'iz shver tsu zein a yid" ("It's difficult to be a Jew") is usually understood to refer to the burden of Jewish identity for those who have no doubt about their own acceptance of it. A simpler gloss would associate the statement with what is difficult in the *first place,* that is, in the movement of the self into the future from the present. The difficulty here, once formulated, is evident—although Kafka's witty exaggeration of it suggests, inversely, the possibility of living also with that hardship. "What do I have in common with the Jews?" Kafka asked of himself—and then undid the question: "I have hardly anything in common with myself." For anyone who gets past *that* point, it will not be surprising that the difficulty of establishing an identity for oneself diminishes as the options available to the self become less and less abstract and closer and closer to life-size.

16

NEXT YEAR IN JERUSALEM?

Postmodern Jewish Identity
and the Myth of Return

Richard Shusterman

I

How does one realize one's Jewish identity? We don't need a Socrates to tell us that this depends on how Jewish identity is to be defined, and we don't need an ordinary language philosopher or a sociolinguist to tell us that there are a number of divergent definitions that present themselves as candidates. Fortunately, we cannot help but have reached the recognition that the definition of this concept (like that of more openly honorific concepts as "justice," "democracy," "art") is essentially contested; for (perhaps less fortunately) it has long been the focus of intense debate and struggle in the legislature and courts of Israel. Clearly, any attempted neutral definition of Jewish identity will be virtually void of meaningful content. How, then, given the concept's essentially complex and contested character, is one to choose how to realize one's Jewish identity among the very many ways of being Jewish? (And we should remember that these may include some rather perverse ways, like trying to deny or escape one's Jewish identity.)

Part of the answer to this question of choice surely has to depend on the contingencies of who you are, how you were raised, and what has happened to you. To use a notion of William James, some choices of Jewish self-realization are not live options for every Jew. The son of the Admor of Sedogora has not the opportunity to express his Jewishness in the manner of Woody Allen or of an atheist kibbutznik, nor vice versa. Although there are numerable exceptions involving dramatic conversion to devout religious orthodoxy, generally speaking it is not a live option for secularly reared Jews in America to realize their Jewish identity through an orthodox

Jewish life. Indeed, to express one's Jewishness primarily through religious practice of any sort is not an attractive option for secular Jews. Nor is the notion of participation in "the Jewish community" very appealing, since this is always somehow tied to the synagogue and thus by extension to religion. What meaningful mode of Jewish self-expression remains for the secular Jew in the secular yet clearly Christian culture of America except to regale himself with Jewish soul food and Jewish jokes? But this will satisfy only superficial appetites and clearly will not answer the needs of a spirit seeking substantive secular fulfillment as a Jew. The hungering or simply confused secular Jewish spirit thus turns to Israel.[1]

For quite a time, and especially in the sixties and seventies (when it was a promisingly socialist state and in many other ways a more hopeful and just society than it is today), Israel represented perhaps the only real chance for secular Jewish fulfillment. Particularly for secular Jews in the Diaspora, it offered a unique opportunity for a radical and romantic re-definition of themselves as Jews, an opportunity to be meaningfully and committedly Jewish without being religious, and with the added bonus of no longer belonging to a cultural or religious minority. *Aliyah* to Israel be-came a popular project among secular Jewish youth who were looking to "find themselves" or define themselves as individuals and as Jews. "Next year in Jerusalem" was transformed from a mythic dream of return into a concrete immigration proposal and a promising plan for creating a new self in a new land. In this essay I wish to suggest why the promise proved largely illusory, why Zionism and immigration to Israel cannot be an un-problematic solution to the problem of secular Jewish identity, and how the myth of return needs to be reinterpreted in the spirit of postmodernity. But first I must raise a methodological matter of some metaphilosophical significance for the issues of identity discussed here.

II

It is perhaps not necessary in every discourse to know where the author is coming from in order to gain a proper understanding of his message and perspective. But in discussions of Jewish identity and Zionism, such locating of authorial standpoint is indeed essential; and the injunction to declare where you are coming from can even be taken in a literal, geo-graphical sense. I therefore feel compelled to begin by some account of my own Jewish and Zionist background. But I also feel an awkward reluctance to do so, as if such autobiographical remarks were tastelessly out of place in a philosophical essay, as if the personal was philosophically taboo, even in an essay dealing with personal identity and its relation to such cultural and ideological tags as "Jewish" and "Zionist."

This reluctance and its generating assumption that even the issue of personal identity demands an impersonal perspective, are both, I believe, unfortunate consequences of philosophy's ancient and deeply rooted prejudice for universality and necessity. Philosophy in inquiring into personal identity is supposed to seek a universal formula for individuating each of us as a different person; it is supposed to do this by looking deep into the alleged essence of human kind to find the common and necessary core on which our individual personhood is based, to find the general principle of human personhood in something like a soul or (incarnated) mind. The presumption has always been that there must be some general and necessary principle for individuating human persons and selves.[2] The apparent reason for this presumption is the still more implicit and invidious presumption that if the criteria and constitution of personal identity and selfhood were a matter of contingency rather than ontological or rational necessity, something deep and sublime would disappear from human personhood, that all self-dignity would be lost if the self was not foundationally fixed by the nature of things or by the law of reason.

This view of the human self and of philosophy is beginning to weaken under the weight of postmodernist polemics.[3] There is growing recognition that the self is socially constituted rather than foundationally given and that it consequently varies with the different societies that inform it. As these societies are the product of historical contingencies, so the socially produced self is a contingently produced web. Moreover, the attempt to go deeper than the social to find the true self seems to afford no escape from the contingent. For, in the first place, even our most private thoughts and wishes are and must be structured by a particular language that is itself a contingent sociohistorical product. And secondly, even that deeper more personal self alleged to lie behind the public, social self we inhabit, seems still more radically contingent, revealed by Freud as a web woven from chance occurrences and idiosyncratic perceptions, misperceptions, and associations. If the self is indeed a contingent product, its proper understanding will involve taking these contingencies seriously; and this means that inquiry into the self demands an autobiographical moment that has so far been repressed in standard philosophical treatments (though it no doubt motivates many of them).

Apart from contingency, there is another currently salient theme in the philosophy of self, which seems to dictate a more personal approach to this issue. I refer to the idea of self-constitution through self-narrative and self-projection that informs both the radical aesthetic ideal of self-creation advocated by Richard Rorty, Alexander Nehamas, and Michel Foucault, and the more conservative and socially responsible view of the self as a strongly "self-interpreting" agent advocated by Charles Taylor and Alasdair MacIntyre.[4] If to some extent we can, do, and should determine what selves we have by redescribing and renarrating ourselves, one is surely entitled to speak of one's self and its constitutional dilemmas in one's own voice and from one's own experience. I am therefore unperturbed by the thought that what emerges from my more personal reflections may not be valid or even interesting for every Jew, let alone every human being. For neither is most allegedly universal philosophizing. But I trust my story and philosophical commentary will be illuminating to some of the many who are vexed with similar difficulties of Jewish self-understanding and self-definition. Let me then provide the relevant biographical background.

I was born to a middle-class American Jewish family that was neither religiously observant (prayer being confined to High Holidays) nor politically Zionist (its Jewish activities being focused on the American Jewish community). As a youth my strongly secular and rebellious instincts led to my expulsion from Hebrew school. But not very much later, at the age of sixteen, I found myself in Israel, since that same spirit of rebellion (probably reinforced by typical adolescent alienation and certainly fueled by the spirit of the sixties) made me leave home and country. Israel promised the excitement of a Jewish-socialist adventure and self-definition, as well as a warm, welcoming sense of belonging to an organic and supportive community, which was also expressed in attractive concrete terms (through the Jewish Agency) of financial support and university scholarships. I remained in Israel for twenty years, studying and teaching in its universities, serving as an officer in its army, and making it my new home and country. There is no doubt that in thus fulfilling the Zionist imperative of *aliyah* to Israel, I became clearer and more comfortable about being Jewish, or, more precisely, I found a way of being Jewish that I could be clear and comfortable about—the life of a secular Jewish Israeli. As a Jew, I was automatically naturalized through the "Law of Return," perhaps the most fundamental statute of the State of Israel, which basically guarantees the rights of residency and citizenship to all Jews returning to the homeland. Of course, in a more literal sense, neither I nor any other immigrants so naturalized were really returning to Israel, having never been there before. When I first arrived, it was only my homeland in a very dubious and mythic sense. To return there truly I had to go elsewhere, a fact suggesting the deep conceptual link between return and departure, which I develop below. And my departure involved a return to my more literal American homeland.

In 1985 I returned to the United States for a year's visiting appointment, and through a complex constellation of personal and institutional contingencies and (I hope) rational choice, I decided to give up my tenured position in Israel and remain for a time in the States. From the Israeli census bureau's point of view, I am no longer an immigrant but an émígre, from the Zionist perspective no longer one of the redeemed ascenders to full Jewish national identity (*olim*) but one of the fallen (*yordim*) who lives in what is termed "exile" (*Galut*).[5] However, I'm not yet sure whether I should be finally written off as a *yored*. For not merely do I maintain a love for Israel, whose experience and way of life have structured so much of my own that it is an inalienable part of me; but I have not renounced the option of going back to resettle there and thus to reenact the myth of return that, I argue, is quintessential to Jewish identity. But such a return, in contrast to my official *aliyah*, will indeed be an actual return as well as a mythic one, for I will have already been there before.

III

1. Three points of philosophical interest emerge from my story and current situation. The first concerns the deep connections between action, narrative, and personal identity. Once we abandon a foundationalist essentialism about the self, we can only constitute the self in terms of a narrative about it. Even if we try to constitute the self in terms of its actions, we find that the meaning (or even proper description) of any action is not atomistically given in itself but is a function of the narrative context in which it appears. It is largely for this reason that even a conservative philosopher like MacIntyre insists on "a concept of self whose unity resides in the unity of a narrative,"[6] for there seems to be no other unity on which to ground it that does not itself rely on narrative unity, since even stories of bodily and mental continuity do.

The problem with narrative as constituting identity is that for any series of narrative events, given an indeterminate future in terms of which these events can be interpreted and further given the future revisability of past narrative interpretations, there will be more than one narrative unity that can fit the individual. This plurality of self-narratives, of course, suggests the presence of more than one self. More acutely, the actual awareness of very divergent futures, hence divergent narratives, not only undermines any fixed sense of self identity but denies any univocal sense of the meaning of any action.

For example, the radical and conscious uncertainty of my own future Israeli-American narrative renders my sense of identity in *either* case as extremely problematic. I can see myself as having returned to my American home after a youthful exploration of an essentially foreign culture, or I can see my current stay in America (as I had originally planned it) as an excursion for professional development so that I could better serve a less developed Israeli society to which I shall return. The meaning of my actions and the definition of myself as agent change significantly according to the story told: Is my involvement in the American philosophical community a serious and lasting project or but a temporary convenience until I return to that of Israel? It's not merely that I don't know the answer with Cartesian certainty because I don't know the future. The point is rather the clear and painfully divided consciousness of simultaneously living two radically divergent self-defining narratives, because there is no way of knowing which is the true one; for indeed there is no true one. How, then, can I know how to realize my Jewish identity unless I know who I am? But how can I know who I am unless I know how I will (or won't) realize my Jewish identity?

It is tempting to take the idea of self-constitution by narrative still further to argue that if there is no one true narrative, then there is no one true self. We thus reach the postmodern dissolution and fragmentation of the self or subject. Of course, on the primitive logical level we can assert that a single self must be presupposed as the referent needed to talk at all about self-narrative and especially divergent self-narratives. But such a minimal logical notion of self as the subject for predication is virtually empty of substance; and it neither can assure us that a true self-narrative or substantive self must exist, nor does it preclude the existence of multiple substantive selves identified with the same logical self or individual for predication.

Since my aim here is to speak less about the general logical possibilities of selfhood than about the particular problems of Jewish identity as I have lived them, let me state candidly that I do experience myself as a multiplicity of selves with regard to the Jewish question. Basically, I have an Israeli self (with an American background or penumbra) whose Jewish identity is strongly and obviously defined through Israeli nationality; and then I also have a (more recently acquired or reclaimed) American self (with an Israeli background or penumbra), whose consciously Jewish identity is virtually nonexistent or neglected, and is only avowed or expressed indirectly through its Israeli background when that background occasionally gets foregrounded in my American life. In short, though I feel, even now in America, more sure of my Jewish identity having made *aliyah*, it has not really resolved my problem of being a secular American Jew; it has only circumvented it by allowing Jewishness to be expressed through Israeliness.

2. In fact, *aliyah* has made it much more difficult to see myself as an American Jew and to relate to that Jewish community, since the American Jewish experience is inevitably perceived by my Israeli eyes as superficial, alienated, and inauthentic. For example, when I attended Yom Kippur services at a progressive synagogue in order to try to express my Jewishness and also my solidarity with the American Jewry I should feel closest to, I could not help but be distressed by the fact that English rather than Hebrew was the dominant language of prayer. Though I am not religious, because of my experience of the Hebrew language and its liturgical use (with which even secular Israelis are quite familiar through public education, national events, and the mass media), I felt the translated prayers to be hollow and unauthentic. I was still further dismayed that traditional and poetically powerful phrases like *Avinu, Malkenu* ("Our Father, Our King") were transformed pathetically into the likes of "Our Parent, Our Sovereign" to suit current American sensibility about gendered language, a sensibility I greatly appreciate in English. (This might suggest that my Israeli self is more sexist than its American counterpart; and I think this is true, though it in no way invalidates my sense of the translation's inauthenticity.)

It might be argued that the fact that American Jews share a deep love of Israel should provide me a way of identifying myself with them and *as* an American Jew. But again I find their experience and understanding of Israel so superficial and artificial that I am generally annoyed and alienated by attempts to bring me into the American Jewish community through my Israeliness. My experience and identity as an Israeli constitutes a real obstacle to achieving American Jewish identity. I have no reason to think this is a personal aberration, because it is a well-known fact that the *yordim* from Israel have not been assimilated into the American Jewish community but have preferred to form and remain in their own little communities of exile. The only apparent exceptions appear to be the "professional Israelis" engaged in Jewish education or Jewish community "business." But they tend to be more religious rather than secular; their motives for interaction with American Jewry tend to be professional rather than social; and the interaction is indeed confined mainly to professional frameworks.

This, then, is the second lesson I wanted to draw from my own history: that defining one's Jewish identity secularly through Israel is largely incompatible with being an American Jew in any fulfilling, substantial sense; and this is not because of any similar and subsuming incompatibility between being Israeli and being American, for I feel no incompatibility about being both the latter. The perceived incompatibility between Israeli and American Jewish identity not only indicates that the concept of Jewish identity is overdetermined and that its determinations can be in conflict. It also suggests the two major and conflictual determinants of Jewishness: nationality and religion. The tension between them is painfully obvious in the continuing strife between national and religious interests that stridently divides Israeli society as a whole, and it is not surprising to find it reflected in the individual Jew.[7]

The Israeli author A. B. Yehoshua argues that this fundamental conflict between the national and religious definitions (or "systems") of Jewish identity provides the prime reason why life in the *golah* has been so attractive to the Jewish people, even though it "was the source of the most terrible disasters to befall the Jewish people" and still constitutes today a dreadful "neurotic condition."[8] Exile from Israel, though originally imposed on the Jewish people, became the preferred choice for its survival, by blunting the conflict that since biblical times threatened to divide and destroy it. In exile there was no need to resolve unequivocally the religious/national debate, to determine whether the Jewish nation had to be devout or compliant worshipers of the Jewish religion. For there was no organized state to provide the apparatus to enforce such a decision. "The Jewish framework in the *golah* is essentially voluntary. The Jew is, in essence, free to direct the fervor of his Judaism in any way he desires," and (I would add) he is also free to have no fervor at all. "The golah freed the national and religious systems from the need to disavow each other," not only because it made definitive conflict resolution unenforceable but also because it made all such conflict unwelcome and unwise. Since Jewish unity was needed to face the threat of a politically stronger and potentially hostile host nation, "disputes over the content of Jewish identity were of secondary importance."

I have introduced Yehoshua's theory of the *golah* because it relates most interestingly to this essay's concern with defining a firm and healthy Jewish identity through Zionism and secular life in Israel. Though he recognizes the *golah*'s attractions and its very deep roots in Jewish identity, Yehoshua condemns it as a "neurotic, painful, and compulsive choice," a pathetic state of "schizophrenia." He insists that Jewish identity should be realized univocally by national (and essentially secular) life in Israel, hoping eventually "to eliminate the *golah* as a viable possibility" for Jewish life.[9] To achieve these ends he urges that Israel assert a scornfully superior attitude of independence from the *golah*, insisting on the necessity of *aliyah* and refusing to go on legitimating the *golah* by gratefully accepting its financial support and smiling so fondly on its economic, political, and cultural achievements.

Yehoshua's powerful case against the neurosis of the *golah* and for Zionism as the only key to healthy Jewish identity relies on a number of insufficiently examined oppositional contrasts. The first is that the *golah* is necessarily perceived by all "authentic" Jewish thinking as an "abnormal," deficient, and fallen situation, as opposed to the "sovereign, normal life in *Eretz Yisrael*," which is always perceived as redemption. From this follows the neurotic tension of *golah*—that though spiritually we repudiate it, practically we seek to preserve it.[10] Second, while (rightly) castigating the religious Israeli philosopher Yishayahu Leibowitz for the view that Jews do things (e.g., eat, dress, copulate) essentially "differently from other peoples," Yehoshua himself posits without argument his own differentiating essentialism: "The essence of our life in Israel is different from that of *golah* life, and the differences should not be obscured."[11]

Unfortunately, these essential differences are not itemized or clarified by Yehoshua; and though I am eminently aware how Israeli life is different from American Jewish life or English or French Jewish life, I cannot, after twenty years of life in Israel and an equal amount of years spent in America and Europe, identify an essence of Israeli life that can be opposed to an essence of *golah* life. The particular qualitative contrast that Yehoshua seems to identify as the source of the essential difference between Israel and the *golah* represents the third oppositional premise on which his argument depends. Life in Israel is one of independence, while exile is neurotic bondage. "Zionism is a process of self-liberation from the fears of independence," and the *golah* represents the refusal of the Jews to accept independence and normalcy.[12]

We find in all these premises a modernist faith and privileging of the normal, the autonomous, the essential, and the authentic. Not surprisingly, the radical Zionism these premises support—that only life in Israel can be fully and authentically Jewish, and can definitively and decisively resolve our problems of Jewish identity and unity—is a very modernist view. It is one guided by a goal of stable unity and definitive closure with the final return of all Jews to Israel. In what follows, I question this view and its premises from a postmodern perspective and offer an alternative account of the Zionist ideal of return. I begin with the third point that my biographical sketch raises: the conceptual interdependency of *aliyah* with *golah,* which undermines any relentless privileging of the former.

3. It is a seemingly trivial but nonetheless crucial point that there can

be no return without departure, hence no *aliyah* without a *golah*. If *aliyah* is an essential defining myth for Jewish identity, then not only the presence of a *golah* but actual life in the Diaspora is a precondition of the enactment and very meaning of that myth. Part of this argument, of course, relies on the general poststructuralist logic of supplementarity that I think Jacques Derrida adapted from the Hegelian principle of organic unity.[13] The idea is that there can be no sense to the notion of origin or homeland without the contrasting (and seemingly gratuitously supplemental) ideas of sequel and of foreign parts, and hence no meaning to national presence or homecoming without some distance or departure from that land.

But, I think, with respect to *aliyah* and *golah,* there is more than this merely logical point of conceptual interdependence through differential definition. For the idea that Jewish identity is realized in *aliyah,* and hence in a movement from *golah* to Israel, is perhaps the most formative myth of the Jewish people. We must remember that Abraham, the very first Jew and founder of the Jewish nation, was born outside of Israel; and his *aliyah* to Israel was part of his covenant with God. Yet Abraham was also the first *yored,* leaving for Egypt when there was famine, only to return again to Israel. This pattern was repeated with Jacob and his sons; and it was only in Egypt that the Jews became a numerous (albeit) enslaved people.

The story of the exodus shows that it was in exile that the Jews first demographically achieved nationhood and also established their religion. The law was given to them in the wilderness of Sinai, that same wilderness where they wandered for forty years until they were sufficiently unified as a nation. It is significant that the important national-religious holidays of Sukkot, Pesach, and Shavuot (as distinguished from the purely religious ones like Rosh Hashanah and Yom Kippur) deal with the Jews' experience in the wilderness rather than in Israel proper, and they are designated as the three holidays of pilgrimage to Jerusalem or Zion. It is further significant that Moses, the essential founder of the Jewish religion and rehabilitator of its enslaved people, was not allowed to enter the Promised Land of Israel but only to approach it.

Thus, from the very beginning, the *golah* is a formative part of Jewish identity, and it is the very explicit precondition from which Jewish self-realization through *aliyah* is made possible. Though already evident in early biblical times, the *golah*'s role in defining Jewish life and giving it spiritual direction (even if only negatively as the desire to return to Zion) became increasingly dominant in the two-thousand-year exile. Even Yehoshua recognizes "how closely woven the *golah* is to the essence of a Jew," though he insists that this condition is "abnormal" and "neurotic." [14] But in actual fact, through most of Jewish history the *golah* is the rule rather than the abnormal exception. Moreover, its role has been clearly more than pragmatic survival, for it has contributed centrally to the spiritual substance of Judaism, as well as providing the ground for the Jewish regenerative myth of return. The *golah* cannot be dismissed as inauthentic, because it is precisely what helps form the notion of the authenticity of *aliyah* and life in Israel.

The second premise that motivates Yehoshua's case against the *golah* is the essential difference between Israeli and "*golah* life." Obviously, there are important differences between life in Israel and life in other countries, just as there are such differences between life in America and life in all other countries. But apart from the Hebrew language, the only "essential" (in postmodern scare quotes) cultural difference between secular Jewish life in Israel and the *golah* is the nationally enforced and oppressive religious authority that Israel suffers from and that Yehoshua himself would like to undermine.

In the history of Israeli cultural politics, it has been a very vexed issue whether Israel has achieved (and even whether it can or should achieve) a satisfyingly substantial secular culture that is sufficiently independent both of traditional Jewish religious culture and of foreign cultures. I need not rehearse this debate to make my point against the presumption of a pure Israeli culture or authentic "essence of life" that can be opposed as essentially different from and privileged over all other ways a Jew can live. For the undeniable fact is that the secular Israeli culture (which both Yehoshua and I support) is very strongly influenced by foreign cultures. Israeli folk songs and dances are derived largely from the folk art that immigrants to Israel brought from the *golah,* particularly from Eastern European and Arab cultures. The past dependence of Israeli high art on European culture (e.g., the Moscow theater and Parisian painting) is certainly just as striking. And today's Israeli culture (for which socialism has become mere nostalgia) is enormously dependent on American culture, not only in the arts and mass-media culture but in consumer culture and in everyday life. For most secular Israelis, America represents not only the paradigm of quality goods but the very model of the good life.

Thus, in a paradoxical way, to assimilate oneself into secular Israeli culture one must live like an American. Israeli academics are no exception to this. To get tenure in an Israeli university, one must publish in the English language and in journals housed for the most part in America. It is a matter of prestige for Israeli academics to land a job in America for their sabbatical year (which is almost never spent in Israel) or for postdoctoral research.

The quest for America is so strong and universal that there is a joke about a new degree sought by Israelis to follow the B.A., M.A., and Ph.D. It's called a G.T.A., and it stands for "Going to America." I must admit to having lived this paradox myself, religiously watching "Dallas" in Israel because it was the Israeli thing to do, though never glancing at it in America. Indeed, my search for a temporary job in America (which resulted in my apparent *yeridah*) was prompted primarily by Israeli peer pressure. My most admired colleagues were seeking American jobs for their sabbaticals, and I felt the need to emulate and measure myself against them.

The argumentative thrust of these remarks should be obvious. Israeli life is so completely pervaded with American and other foreign culture (and moreover with the desire for such culture) that there can be no appeal to a pure, authentic Israeli "essence of life" that could stand wholly autonomous of the *golah* and make it altogether gratuitous, and thus even theoretically "eliminate the *golah* as a viable possibility" for life as a Jew. There is no essential and fully autonomous Israeli culture. But perhaps our postmodern experience would argue that this may be true for almost all national cultures, and that what I have been designating American culture is not a truly national one but more an international culture with some distinctively American roots. Jean François Lyotard attests to postmodernism's dissolution of authentically national cultural life into a multinational eclecticism: "one listens to reggae, watches a western, eats McDonald's food for lunch and local cuisine for dinner, wears Paris perfume in Tokyo and 'retro' clothes in Hong Kong"; and Fredric Jameson explains the multinational postmodern style as a function of our current phase of multinational capitalism (the successor of capitalism's classical and national-imperialist phases).[15] Thus, though American culture pervades Israel, we should also recognize that the cultural life of America includes pita and falafel, not to mention the hora.

This postmodern blurring of national cultural lines virtually vitiates the cultural argument for Zionism, and it is probably why Yehoshua strikes out against the *golah*'s growing absorption of Israeli culture and insists on maintaining a firm distance and division between the two. "Recently Israel has become a too-familiar presence in the *golah,* especially in the United States. Paradoxically, it is no longer necessary to immigrate to Israel, and it is possible to acquire scraps of significant Israeli reality in the *golah* itself. The aura of distance and mystery surrounding Israel has become blurred. . . . We must at all costs reestablish a certain feeling of alienation between the *golah* and Israel—a controlled disengagement."[16] The large number of American Jewish (and expatriate Israeli) tourists who vacation regularly in Israel, and the perhaps larger and more painful number of Israelis who descend upon America, clearly suggest that no controlled disengagement is possible, that Israel and *golah* not only conceptually depend on each other but culturally interpenetrate one another.

Defenders of the integrity and essential distinctiveness of Israeli culture might try to explain the deep attraction of *golah* life for Israelis not in terms of its pervasive presence in Israeli culture but precisely in terms of the attraction of foreignness. Such an explanation seems flawed by the inability to explain why Israelis prefer to go to America rather than to some more culturally remote region, but it still has an important insight. Self-discovery and self-expansion, which are essential to self-realization, typically involve an exploration into the unfamiliar. Israelis quite often only realize themselves as Israelis, achieve a cultural self-understanding, by defining themselves against a foreign land and people. The voyage out into the unknown, the exploratory quest and experience of the alien, is a familiar myth of self-discovery that is embedded into a myth of return. But this would constitute no argument against the importance of the *golah*. Quite the contrary. For, as a necessary moment in the Zionist myth of return, the *golah* remains an essential part of the apparatus for defining Jewish identity even in the most Zionistic terms.

Our discussion of the dubious essentialism and integrity of Israeli cultural life already should have indicated the difficulty with Yehoshua's third Zionistic presumption: that Israeli life best realizes "the things for which we [Jews, humans?] are fighting: freedom and independence." [17] The Israeli population is in fact one of the most constrained and beleaguered not only in terms of punitive taxes and military constraints on one's liberty but more shockingly with respect to religious freedom for Jews. There is virtually no such freedom, since religious orthodoxy enjoys unchallengeable authority. Marriages (and divorces) by Reform or Conservative rabbis are not recognized, nor is there an apparatus for civil marriage and divorce. Nor is there choice for Jews about burial or alternative funeral arrangements. In contrast, Jews in America have these forms of religious freedom but more importantly can also enjoy a freedom *from* religion, which in Israel would be unthinkable. And if we move from personal to national life, we see how Israel's own independence is seriously constrained by economic, political, and cultural dependencies on the *golah*. It might be argued that in these days of multinational capitalism, the whole idea of national independence becomes questionable. But one needs no such general arguments to challenge the specific claim that only in Israel are the Jews truly free and independent.

IV

My resistance to Yehoshua's repudiation of the *golah* should not be taken as a rejection of *aliyah* and of the view that it provides the best way for a secular Jew to realize her Jewish identity. Rather I have been arguing that the *golah* is essential to Jewish identity precisely because *aliyah* is, since *golah* is a precondition of the latter and gives it its special point. If one best realizes one's Jewish identity through *aliyah,* and if to define and realize oneself as a Jew is not something to be performed by a single act but by a life of activity, an intriguing possibility arises: a life of continued Jewish self-expression and self-realization through cycles of *yeridah* and *aliyah,* departure and return to Israel.

This, in fact, is a possibility that many Israelis practice, though perhaps not consciously and programmatically; and it is a project with which I greatly sympathize for a number of reasons. First, it incorporates the *golah* (which has been so central to Jewish history and experience) as a necessary and contributory moment in the determination of Jewish identity, thus allowing for a richer notion of Jewish identity than Yehoshua's rigidly Zionistic line can tolerate. Second, its circular structure provides for flexibility and openness, which is most necessary in dealing with life's contingencies. Rather than making *aliyah* "a once and for all" affair whereby any temporary turning back is seen as despicable backsliding, recognition of the cyclical movement of departure and return to Israel enables us to integrate the periods of Israeli and *golah* living that life may thrust upon us into a coherent narrative of continued Jewish commitment.

It thus allows for the narrative constitution of a reasonably unified and stable Jewish self who repeatedly moves between the *golah* and Israel, where each phase of life and movement can enrich those and the developing self that follow it. If we accept this circular view of *aliyah,* we are not forced to condemn a life divided between Israel and the States as necessarily one of seesawing schizoid split between redeemed Israeli and fallen *yored.* These different quasi selves can be seen as deeply interpenetrated by narrative unification and experiential funding, just as Israeli and *golah* culture can be seen as interpenetrated by each other. This circular narrative of Jewish identity could provide the only form of unity of self that postmodernism might tolerate—an open, fragile narrative unity embracing a confusing multiplicity and division of subnarratives that are (like the overarching narrative itself) open, at any moment, to divergent interpretations and future reconstructions. Finally, however, if we instead wish to go radically postmodern and celebrate the individual's plurality of selves, the circular movement between Israel and the *golah* can quite easily supply us with two different, nonconverging life narratives and selves. My own experience, as I earlier confessed, testifies to this; and I live alternatively (sometimes spasmodically) as Israeli or American, where Jewish identity is expressed only through the former.

It seems to follow from this that the best way for me to realize my Jewish identity would be to live life as an Israeli, even if it be only as a "circular" Israeli. I wish to end this essay not by resisting this conclusion, which I find unimpeachable, but by challenging its implied practical injunction to return to Israel. To do this I must return to my opening question and query its motivating assumption. The question, "How does one realize one's Jewish identity?" gets its force from the presumption that this is something one *should* realize. But we might just as well ask, "Why should one realize one's Jewish identity at all?" This question is not easily answered.

I can hardly argue that one's Jewish identity should be realized and expressed so that one can be true to what one really, really, ontologically is. For my antifoundationalist skepticism about the presence of a given true self makes me doubt whether there is anything originally and immutably there to be true to. And even if I thought there was something like an essential self, I surely would not consider that Jewishness could be a necessary part of it. But if being born Jewish is a contingency, why then should one have to live one's life in accordance with such an arbitrary fact?

One fairly common but painfully misguided answer is the appeal to what we could call "the Hitler principle": Though your Jewishness is insignificant to you, it is essential to rabid anti-Semites; and you should therefore see yourself and live your life according to their benighted outlook, since in the very unlikely yet still possible event that they again take power, it could become the determining outlook. But to this we should surely object that one's choice of life should be guided by actualities and probabilities, rather than extremely unlikely possibilities; and one should not live madly because of the possibility that madmen will come to rule the world.

A better and more original answer to the question why one should realize one's Jewishness if it is merely contingent may be developed from the postmodern advocacy of the self's radical contingency. Since, as Rorty argues, the self is contingency "all the way down," we have no choice but to build and govern our lives on the contingent. The secret of successful living is not to escape contingency by philosophically discovering the true and necessary essence of human selfhood and then living by that. There is nothing like that to discover, and there is no escaping contingency. The only mastery of contingency we can achieve is by recognizing it and then constructing from it an appealing life narrative we can choose and affirm as our own, in a Nietzschean act of "becoming what we are" by narratively creating and affirming ourselves as works of art.[18] In other words, the only way we can free ourselves of the oppressive meaninglessness of the contingent facts of our birth and history is by molding them (or at least some of them) into something meaningful that one deliberately chooses.

This idea of transforming the meaninglessly contingent and imposed into the meaningfully created and willingly chosen is, I believe, the source of *aliyah*'s enormous appeal to secular Jews like myself. One's Jewishness, which is originally experienced as a senseless and imposed contingency of *filiation* through the accident of being born to Jewish parents, is transfigured through *aliyah* into a conscious and meaningful choice of *affiliation* with a long struggling people and continuing national project one can now claim as one's own. One's own self-narrative and hence one's self become greatly enriched by being embedded into this larger and historically momentous story.

This attractively noble idea of self-creation still does not entail, however, an injunction for secular American Jews to make *aliyah*. For even if there are no equally fruitful ways for them to make their Jewishness meaningful (and there may be, say, through the model of the rootless Jewish intellectual), they have other contingencies besides being Jewish on which to build their life narratives as works of art; and only a "unity fetishist" would require an adequate life narrative to contain and fully integrate every contingency of the individual. In short, we can just as well choose not to make anything of our Jewish identity without being guilty of trying to escape or deny it. Being born a Jew can (under certain circumstances) remain an unredeemed contingent fact that is neither explicitly rejected nor endorsed but is simply not incorporated into one's life project. This is the phenomenon of assimilation. There is no moral imperative for one born Jewish to make himself a Jewish work of art.

But I think we can go farther and argue, against the likes of Nietzsche and Rorty, that there is similarly no compelling reason to create ourselves as original and distinctive works of art at all. Artistic self-creation is a fine project, if one wants to pursue it. But I see no moral imperative to do so; and even if there is an aesthetic imperative, I think the freedom to live as one chooses, to live inartistically if one wishes, overrides it. Finally, there is also cause to question the specific nature of this aesthetic imperative. Implicit in the Nietzschean-Rortian view that one should make one's life a work of art is a residual high modernist aesthetic of originality, depth, and distinction, which postmoderns like Rorty claim to disavow. If we really go postmodern and accept its blurring of the high/low art distinction, then we no longer need to construe aesthetic living as self-creation into original art; one can see one's life not as a unique well-wrought work of art but as multichanneled entertainment, not as masterpiece theater but as ordinary popular TV.[19] Next year in Jerusalem, or tonight on "Dallas" and "L.A. Law"? The aesthetic choice is as contingent and as variable as our (Jewish?) selves.

NOTES

1. This difficulty of secular Jewish self-expression in America is recognized by many. Bernard Berofsky, for example, explains "the disappointing condition of American Jewish life" as resulting from the fact that the dominant secular Jewish community "no longer discerns the eternal verities of the Jewish faith and is not prepared to uproot itself from its native land in order to redefine this faith in national terms." Hence, "there is no positive goal or meaning in continued Jewish existence." Not surprisingly, Berofsky recommends *aliyah* to Israel as the best solution for expressing Jewish identity. See Bernard Berofsky, "Jewish Spirituality in the Diaspora," in *Diaspora: Exile and the Jewish Condition,* edited by Etan Levine (New York: Scribner, 1983), 123–33. The quotations are from p. 128.

2. The concepts of person and self may be usefully distinguished for a variety of contexts and issues. We can use them, for example, to allow for the existence of a single person's having many selves, or for a radical transformation of self that would still not entail the assignment of a different personal identity. For more on the distinction between persons and selves, see Rom Harré, *Personal Being* (Cambridge, Mass.: Harvard University Press, 1984).

3. For an account of this phenomenon and its effect on ethical theory even within the more conservative Anglo-American philosophical community, see my "Postmodern Aestheticism: A New Moral Philosophy?" *Theory, Culture and Society* 5 (1988): 337–55.

4. See Richard Rorty, *Contingency, Irony and Solidarity* (Cambridge: Cambridge University Press, 1989); Alexander Nehamas, *Nietzsche: Life as Literature* (Cambridge, Mass.: Harvard University Press, 1985); Michel Foucault, "On the Genealogy of Ethics: An Overview of Work in Progress," in Paul Rabinow, ed., *The Foucault Reader* (New York: Pantheon, 1984), 340–72; Charles Taylor, "What is Human Agency?" and "Self-interpreting Animals," in *Human Agency and Language: Philosophical Papers* (Cambridge: Cambridge University Press, 1985), 1: 15–76; Alasdair MacIntyre, *After Virtue* (London: Duckworth, 1982).

5. The term's primary sense of forced expulsion and prolonged separation from one's native land is arguably no longer applicable, since with respect to most Jews (at least since the demise of the Soviet Union) there is no political power or even force of circumstances that enforces their separation from Israel.

6. MacIntyre, *After Virtue,* 191.

7. I should note that devout American Jews who make *aliyah* for religious rea-

sons do not typically suffer the same problem and can move very easily between their Israeli and American Jewish identities, because religion is the foremost determinant of both. The same goes for devout Israeli Jews, who feel much more at home in Orthodox communities in America than secular Israelis do in progressive and essentially secular American Jewish communities.

8. A. B. Yehoshua, "Exile as a Neurotic Condition," in Levine, ed., *Diaspora,* 15, 16. The other quotations in the paragraph are from pages 24–25. The second main reason Yehoshua gives for the attraction of *golah* is that it provides an easy solution for the felt Jewish injunction "to be different" as a special "chosen people." As a distinct minority living in a foreign land rather than their own homeland, it was easy to be different.

9. Ibid., 22, 31, 33. Yehoshua recognizes that the religious element cannot be completely expunged from Jewish identity, but he means to give it a very subordinate role in Jewish experience, by having it radically reformed by secular thought and experience. He wants orthodox religious authority (but not Israeli national authority) to be decentered "through the creation of additional centers of authority" in religion. To this purpose, "secular Jews . . . must become involved in religious affairs . . . as daring reformers" (ibid., 30, 31).

10. Ibid., 22–23.

11. Ibid., 26, 34.

12. Ibid., 28.

13. For the details on this, see Richard Shusterman, "Organic Unity: Analysis and Deconstruction," in *Redrawing the Lines: Literary Theory, Analytic Philosophy, and Deconstruction,* edited by R. W. Dasenbrock (Minneapolis: University of Minnesota Press, 1989), 92–115.

14. Yehoshua, "Exile," 16.

15. See Jean-François Lyotard, *The Postmodern Condition: A Report on Knowledge* (Minneapolis: University of Minnesota Press, 1984), 76; and Fredric Jameson, "Postmodernism; or, The Cultural Logic of Late Capitalism," *New Left Review* 146 (1984): 53–93.

16. Yehoshua, "Exile," 32.

17. Ibid., 34.

18. For more details on this project of self-creation from contingency and on its Nietzschean source, see n. 4 for the works of Nehamas (141–49) and Rorty (23–43, 96–121). For criticism of their particular versions of aesthetic, self-creation, see Richard Shusterman, "Nietzsche and Nehamas on Organic Unity," *Southern Journal of Philosophy* 26 (1988): 379–92, and *Pragmatist Aesthetics: Living Beauty, Rethinking Art* (Oxford: Basil Blackwell, 1992), 246–61.

19. I develop these points in considerable detail in Richard Shusterman, "Postmodern Ethics and the Art of Living" in *Pragmatist Aesthetics,* chap. 9.

17

GOING AND RESTING

Gabriel Josipovici

I HAVE often asked myself what it is that makes me a Jew. Since I am not circumcised, have not taken my bar mitzvah, do not attend synagogue or celebrate any of the feasts (unless as the guest of friends who do), the answer ought to be simple: nothing. Yet all my ancestors were Jews, and, as I grow older, I feel more and more affinity with Jews and their (our) past. I may not be much of a Jew, but I am more of a Jew than anything else.

What then is a Jew? As soon as I try to answer that question I feel my mind clouding over and panic rising in my chest. Exactly the same thing happens when I ask myself, What is a man? Perhaps that is why I am a writer and not a philosopher. As a writer I feel the panic subside and the clouds lift as soon as I move away from such large general questions and start to tell a story. Nor does this mean that I feel I am shelving important questions for the sake of trivia. The narrative writers I love—Homer and Dante and Proust and Kafka and Muriel Spark—do not seem to me to be doing something more trivial than the philosophers. On the contrary, when I start to read them I feel myself to be much more closely in touch with things that are central to life than when I start to read Plato or Descartes. It is as though the food they provide were more nourishing to me than that of the philosophers. And in my own writing of fiction, when things are going well, I also get the feeling that this is what is important and truly nourishing for me, and that the doubts that often arise about the value of what I am doing must be seen as temptations to which I must not succumb.

When things are going well. That is the operative phrase. And when do things go well with my writing? "The idea you and George Balanchine have of doing a 'ballet to end all ballet,'" Stravinsky wrote to Lincoln Kirstein when they were discussing what was later to become *Agon*[1]—well, limits are precisely what I need and am looking for above all in everything I compose. The limits generate the form. Every modern artist knows just what he means. Other people may talk in grandiose terms of a ballet to end all ballet, but what Stravinsky wants is a precise set of limits: so many minutes, so many musicians, so many dancers. Every modern artist also knows, however, that three-quarters of the problem lies in finding those limits. It may be easier for the composer, who does still, after all, get precise commissions (unless he is as famous as Stravinsky!) and thus knows in advance what is required of him, at least in terms of length and size of orchestra. Even then, for the modern composer, who does not have a single patron, the problem will still be what commissions to accept and what to reject. For writers it is even worse, and one could say that what every serious writer has had to do is establish for himself or herself the parameters within which to work for each separate project. One can see Proust groping for ten years for the right parameters for a long novel, as he starts it in the third person and then drops it, starts a critical onslaught on the method of Sainte-Beuve and then drops it, and finally understands what it is he is really after. Even then the search continues, and the new Pleiade edition of *A la Recherche du temps perdu* gives us nine separate versions of the opening page in its section of variants. Virginia Woolf's *A Writer's Diary* gives a marvelous account of the agony and excitement of the process by which *The Waves* came into being. More recent writers, like Robert Pinget, have talked about the terrible period between novels, when one gropes in the dark for a voice, never knowing if one will find it. What Pinget means by voice is in effect a mode of telling: *this* way, not *that*.

In my own work I have found that what I always need is for two kinds of pressure to come together. These could be described as an existential and a formal pressure, or as the need to explore and understand something about the world and its inhabitants (myself included) and the desire to solve a particular formal problem through the making of something out of words. I have found over the years that when the one pressure exists without the other, no matter how powerful that single pressure, I can never bring the work to a satisfactory conclusion. The desire to speak about something without the corresponding desire to make something, or the desire to make without the desire to speak about—this can keep me going for several weeks, but sooner or later I discover that nothing genuine is emerging and I lose interest.

On the other hand, when the two do come together I find that the work races ahead and there are just not enough hours in the day. This happened to me with my first novel, where it was the title, *The Inventory*, that generated both the plot and the form. I had been wanting for a long time to write about people and their possessions, about the fact that we humans are the only creatures who hoard and yet what good does that do us when we die, as die we must? And when a person dies the possessions he leaves behind both mock those who loved him and act as triggers for their memory. I was drawn to the idea of objects holding the traces of their previous owners. When the title came to me I felt my heart beating faster, and when I asked myself why, I realized it was because the word seemed to go in two directions at once, to hold within itself the traces of the word *invent,* with its connotations of subjectivity, and of that most objective thing, inventory. It came to me that the book would deal with the relatives of a man who has just died gathering at his house to make an inventory of his belongings, and that in the course of doing this we would find them trying to make sense of their relations to the deceased, their memory or invention triggered off by the objects in the house. At the same time I realized that my book would do without a narrative voice but would move forward by means only of dialogue and inventory lists. As soon as I had made these decisions, the writing of the book became a challenge rather than an imposition. As I worked I found that the challenge of the form helped me to find the meaning, and by the time I had finished I had said more than I knew and made something where before there had been nothing.

Three novels later it was again a title that showed me the way. In *Migrations* I wanted to explore what it means to belong nowhere, to be constantly on the move, with nowhere to settle and nowhere to return to. Before writing the book I read quite a lot about nomads and about modern migrant workers today. At the same time I wanted to explore the way in which, in the telling of any story, the elements that make up that story have difficulty in staying in place, want to migrate from one area to another, and usually are held in place only by the writer's firm commitment to some form of realism. This may be difficult to understand for someone who has not tried writing a story, so an example from the visual arts may help. It was Ernest Gombrich, I think, who pointed out that doodling is a much more primitive form of art than realistic representation. It takes a great deal of study to be able to draw a realistic representation, but it also takes a great deal of repression. The desire of the hand and spirit have to be subdued in the interests of realism. One way of looking at modernism would be to say that the repression was removed—but then of course the problem of the limits to freedom arose with a new intensity.

In my own writing I found myself struggling with the desire to let go and the need to keep order, and what I wanted was a subject that would allow me to let go, make this part of what the novel was about. In *Migrations* this became possible: The sense of having nowhere to settle and nowhere to go, but of having to be always on the move, became a condition both of the hero *and* of the narrative.

As I worked an image emerged and became central: that of Lazarus rising from the grave, wrapped in his grave clothes, as I had seen it in Epstein's great sculpture of the subject in New College Chapel in Oxford. But for me Lazarus did not have the connotations he had for St. John and the later Christian tradition. I imagined a Lazarus who rises from the dead and starts to unwind the grave clothes from his body; he unwinds and unwinds, more and more cloth falls to the ground around him, but when all has been unwound there is no glorious resurrected body but only a little heap of dust beside the folds of cloth.

This image did not seem to me depressing, and I did not use it ironically or satirically. Rather, it represented for me a triumphal insight, what all the slow unwinding of the narrative had been driving toward from the start. For the first time since I had begun work on the book I grasped clearly what it was I was trying to say: Our lives and our art exist between the fully hidden and the fully revealed; there is the need to bring what is hidden out into the open, but a full revelation means the arrival of the end.

I had been reading the minor prophets and came upon a phrase of Micah's that seemed so close to my sense of what I was trying to say that I immediately appropriated it as an epigraph: "Arise and go now," the prophet tells the Israelites, "for this is not your rest" (2:10). This word *rest, menuchah,* is, I discovered, one that occurs frequently in the Hebrew Bible: The dove sent from the ark finds no rest for her feet, for example, and in the Book of Ruth Naomi tells her daughters-in-law: "Go, return each to her mother's house. . . . The Lord grant you that ye may find rest, each of you in the house of her husband" (1:9). The word *go, lekhu,* is also a key one in Scripture. It is after all the primal injunction to Abraham: "Get thee out of thy country," God tells him, "and from thy kindred, and from thy father's house, unto a land that I will show thee" (Gen. 19:1). *Lekh lekha,* God says to him, get up and go. And Abraham obeys, thus starting the long march of the Hebrew people, which is still going on and of which, willy-nilly, I am a part.

So, is the emphasis in the Bible on going or on resting? Jon Levenson, in a fascinating book entitled *Sinai and Zion,* argued that the two mountains form two alternative centers to the Hebrew Scriptures, each exerting its pull over the surrounding material.[2] The first, the Mountain of the Law, is associated with Wandering, the Wilderness, and the Covenant; the second, the Mountain at the Center, is associated with sacral kingship, David, and the Messiah.

Both, it seems to me, still exert their pull, on Christians as well as Jews. Some will see themselves and their history in terms of desert and wandering, or its Christian analogue of pilgrimage—"we are pilgrims even as you are," Virgil tells the souls he and Dante meet at the foot of Mt. Purgatory; and Kafka, in a late diary entry, writes: "Moses fails to enter Canaan not because his life is too short but because it is a human life."[3] But others will stress the goal, either the Heavenly Jerusalem or the actual city of Jerusalem as the capital of a Greater Israel, Judaia, and Samaria. Naturally my own sympathies are with Sinai rather than with Zion, for I can see the fanaticism and hatred engendered by the latter, but I have to ask myself whether my total lack of feeling for any kind of Zion or the advent of any Messiah is only the sign of my unredeemable secularity.

Be that as it may, I felt, when I came across that sentence of Micah's in the midst of my work on *Migrations,* that here, if anywhere, was the heart of a kind of Jewishness I myself could understand and imaginatively identify with. Micah does not say where rest is, only that *this* is not it, and *this,* I wanted to say in my book, is never going to be your rest; while the belief that somewhere, sometime, there will be such a place of rest, is misguided and misleading, only brought into being by a nostalgia similar to that for fleshpots of Egypt, which Moses, to his sorrow, found so prevalent among the generation he had led out from the bondage to Pharaoh.

Not only could I understand Micah's remark, or God's command to Abraham, but I found comfort and strength in the thought that something that was so central to my own experience and so alien to those among whom I found myself should also be so central to the Bible. It brought that book alive for me across the centuries and made me feel that if Judaism was somehow related to this then it was less foreign to me than I had hitherto imagined.

Central not only to my experience but also to everything I had been told about my family, for as far back as it can be traced my family has been doing what Jews have always done: leaving one place to go to another. My father's grandfather left his Romanian village to seek his fortune, first in Constantinople, where he married, and then in Egypt. My mother's great-grandfather must have left his native Ferrara a little earlier in the last century and, with the help of a whip-around organized by the local rabbi, sailed across the sea, also to Egypt. My mother's father, having been wounded in the Russo-Japanese war, left his native Odessa and himself settled in Egypt, where he set up his medical practice. My parents in their turn left Egypt, where they had been born, to study in France; and it was in France that I was born, in October 1940, on the last day on which my parents could have escaped from war-torn Europe. It was to Egypt that my mother returned with me after surviving the war in France, and from Egypt that we both came to England in the summer of 1956, so that I in turn could pursue my studies.

I do not feel myself an exile, for an exile has a home to which he longs to return. (But then neither did Abraham consider himself an exile.) My home is not France, where I was born, or Egypt, where I spent my childhood, or yet England, where I have lived for two-thirds of my life. The feeling of a Stravinsky or a Nabokov for the Russia of their youth is quite alien to me. There is no land or language of which I feel I have been deprived by historical circumstances, nowhere to which I dream one day of returning.

If that leaves me without the bitterness of the exile, it also leaves me without his sense of a lost paradise or of a native language. This is not a comfortable state to be in. What made it worse was my discovery that what I wanted above all was to write, for a painter or a composer can more or less choose his language today, but that privilege is not given to the writer. I write in English because that is the language I am most accustomed to by now, but of course I have none of that inwardness with English and its various registers that a native speaker would have. Even worse, I have none of that inwardness with English culture (in the anthropological sense) that a native Englishman would have.

When one is young one is easily discouraged. How can I ever write as I had hoped to do when the cards are so stacked against me? I thought. What saved me from despair was the discovery that my case was not unique, that other people had had to face similar difficulties. Thus I read with a quickening pulse Kafka's diary entry for October 24, 1911, in which he examines why the German language, which is the only one he really knows, is incapable of expressing in the word *Mutter* his own (Jewish) sense of his mother; or Proust's description of Marcel's despair at not being able to express his sense of joy at the way the sunlight strikes the river and being reduced to banging his umbrella on the ground and crying "Zut zut zut!"

It was Stravinsky once again who most perfectly summed up the paradox. He remarks somewhere that had Beethoven had Mozart's lyric gift, he would never have developed his own remarkable rhythmic talents. In other words, what is required is that we make the most of what we have and do not mourn the absence of what we do not have. Because circumstances have caused certain roads to be blocked to you, you are forced to discover others, which might never have been discovered had it not been for you and your circumstances. For what do Kafka's and Proust's remarkable fictions, Eliot's remarkable poems, emerge from, if not the profound sense that all the known ways were blocked to them?

I had to accept that I was not and never would be an English writer. Nor was I a French or an Egyptian writer who happened to write in English, as Julian Green is an American writer who writes in French. But was I then a Jewish writer? The answer, it seems to me, is a little complicated. Balzac is a French writer and Dostoevsky is a Russian writer, but is Kafka a German writer? The word clearly covers two quite different meanings. Balzac writes in French and he is French; Dostoevsky writes in Russian and he is Russian. Kafka writes in German but he is not German. Nor is he, like Rilke, simply a native of the Austro-Hungarian Empire who, coming from an educated family, would, until 1918, have naturally had German as his first language. But if Kafka is not German, he is not Czech either. Is he then a Jewish writer?

There are, I think, two categories to which the term can be applied. There are Jews who write about Jews and Jewish culture as they have grown up with it, as Balzac and Dostoevsky wrote about French and Russian culture. The most distinguished representatives of this category in our century are I. B. Singer and Shmuel Yosef Agnon, who wrote in Yiddish and Hebrew, respectively, about a world and a tradition that were as familiar to them as nineteenth-century France and Russia were to Balzac and Dostoevsky. To me all these writers, though they may move and interest me, seem equally alien. For I am as unfamiliar with the worlds Singer and Agnon write about as I am with the worlds of Balzac and Dostoevsky.

But Kafka seems to be different. When he writes: "What have I in common with Jews? I have hardly anything in common with myself" and talks about "the impossibility of not writing, the impossibility of writing German, the impossibility of writing differently. One might also add a fourth impossibility, the impossibility of writing,"[4] I feel I know exactly what he is talking about. And the same is true of Paul Celan when he says: "Perhaps poetry, like art, moves with the oblivious self into the uncanny and strange to free itself. Though where? in which place? how? as what? This would mean art is the distance poetry must cover, no less and no more." His translator, Rosemary Waldrop, elaborates: "He always finds himself face to face with the incomprehensible, inaccessible, the 'language of the store.' And his only recourse is talking. This cannot be 'literature.' Literature belongs to those who are at home in the world."[5]

By this token Singer and Agnon write "literature," Kafka and Celan do not. Singer and Agnon are at home in their world, or at least as much at home in it as Dostoevsky and Graham Greene are in theirs—and that world includes assumptions about what constitutes art, novels, and so on. Kafka and Celan are in flight from all such assumptions. But the paradoxes multiply, for their remarks could be paralleled by those of many modern writers from Mallarmé to Beckett. Does this suggest that we should abandon my division of Jewish writers into two categories? That we should think of Singer and Agnon as Jewish writers and Kafka and Celan as international modernists? That, I feel, would be a mistake, for there is no doubt that their Jewishness is somehow central to Kafka and Celan.

It may be that in a strange way the condition of modernism meshes with the condition of Jewishness, just as the condition of romanticism meshed with the condition of being a rooted denizen of the English Lakes. This I think is what the painter R. B. Kitaj was getting at in the fascinating series of jottings he has called *First Diasporic Manifesto*. Kitaj feels able to talk about Jews and modernists in the same breath, because he finds in both the marks of displacement. He sets modernism against romanticism as the art of rootlessness against the art of rootedness: "To my mind," he writes, "the very deeply rooted Provençal Cezanne . . . had baked Impressionism into the final synthesis of his great southern baking machines, to which Picasso replied as a young relocated Spaniard in the *Demoiselles d'Avignon*."[6]

I am sure there is something in this, but I can also see how such formulations can lead to misunderstanding; for it might look as though the terms "rooted" and "rootless" were purely descriptive and thus miss the tension (desperation might be a better word in some cases) in modernism and in such Jewish writers as Kafka, Walter Benjamin, and Paul Celan. It would be an understatement to assert that Kafka was not happy with the thought that he had "nothing in common" either with himself or with Jews. If he was profoundly critical of his father's Judaism, which he saw as a religion of mere external conformity, he was also profoundly aware of the fact that his father might just be right and that his own inability to accept the externals of Judaism cut him off not only from others but from Judaism itself. Similarly his longing to settle in Palestine was perfectly genuine, and if he could not finally bring himself to do so it was himself he blamed and not Palestine. In a moving letter to Else Bergmann, who, as late as 1923, was trying to arrange his passage there, he confessed: "I know that now I shall certainly not sail. . . . Even assuming that I could carry out anything of the sort, it would not have turned out to be a real voyage to Palestine at this time, not at all . . . but in a spiritual sense something like a voyage to

America by a cashier who has embezzled a large sum of money. . . . No, I could not go that way, even if I had been able. . . . That is how it is, and what a pity, but in the final analysis quite right."[7]

We could say that what we find in Kafka is a continuing and powerful desire for rest, whether it be rest in marriage, in the religion of his fathers, or in the land of Palestine, along with an equally powerful sense that such rest was simply not an option *for him.* "Nothing is given me," he writes to Milena (admitting, in his usual way, that he may be exaggerating), "I have to acquire everything, not only the present and the future, but even the past, that which is given to all men as of right, that too I have to acquire. It is perhaps the hardest task."[8]

Each destiny is unique and it would be foolish to pretend that one can generalize from Kafka's life and his anguished twistings and turnings. Nevertheless it is striking that we find many of the same ambivalences in the lives of Walter Benjamin and Paul Celan. Both flirted with the idea of settling in Palestine/Israel and neither could in the end bring himself to do so. Yet their tragic ends suggest that staying in Europe was no solution either.

I sense that Kafka, Benjamin, and Celan all recognized that the idea that the true role of the Jew was to be a wanderer could itself be seen as a sort of nostalgia, a clinging to what one knows and a refusal to take the decisive step that would lead one out of the wilderness and into true community. Not for them Richard Shusterman's blithe remark in Chapter 16 that one would live as one chooses, that "we can just as well choose not to make anything of our Jewish identity without being guilty of trying to escape or deny it." The idea that we can make ourselves in any way we want, which Shusterman ascribes to Nietzsche and labels "postmodern," would have made no sense at all to them. All of them had a longing for rest, for an end to wandering, which was as much a part of themselves as their impulse to refuse *this* rest or that. Shusterman would say that this was because they were still clinging to "modernist" notions of unity and the realization of the self. I wonder.

At the same time there is no shortage of voices, mainly in Israel, claiming that Kafka, far from being representative of Jewry, was representative only of the kind of impotent Jewish self-hatred bred out of centuries of ghetto life and now finally put behind them by those Jews who have had the courage to return to the Promised Land. After all, God's injunction to Abraham does not stop with his telling him to get up and go. Go, says God, "unto a land that I will show thee, And I will make thee a great nation, and I will bless thee and make thy name great" (Gen. 12:1–2). Is it not irresponsible to take the first part of the injunction to heart and not the second? Is not the condition of exile bound up with the notion of homecoming?[9]

That Kafka would have agreed with this criticism is no proof that it is right. I am aware of the element of masochism in Kafka, but I am aware too that to try to "place" him by the use of terms like "masochist," "neurotic," simply will not do. There is something too profound, too generous, too pure in his life and writings. It judges us, and it is a failure of our own imagination to think we can judge him by the use of terms drawn from any narrow discipline, psychoanalysis or theology or philosophy.

What both the postmodernist and the Zionist position fail to register is the strength and richness of the tension that we find in both Kafka and in modernism. What both the postmodernist and the Zionist imply is that the feeling of "having nothing in common with myself" can be simply overcome. But can it? Should it? Is that not itself a romantic myth?

In an early letter Kafka recounts something that has happened recently to him: "When I opened my eyes after a short afternoon nap, still not quite certain that I was alive, I heard my mother calling down from the balcony in a natural tone, 'What are you up to?' A woman answered from below, 'I'm having tea in the garden.' I was amazed at the ease with which some people live their lives."[10] Kafka was so affected by this scene that he included it in one of his early, unfinished stories, "Description of a Struggle." It begins as *Metamorphosis* and *The Trial* begin, with the narrator waking up from sleep, unsure of who or what he is. It goes on, like those other stories, to show us the narrator as outsider, listening and watching but forever debarred from "the natural." Yet here the reader has no difficulty in identifying with the narrator. We have all undergone similar experiences. At the same time we can be certain that if others seem at times rooted and natural to us, it is doubtful that they feel that way to themselves. Most novels, though, in the very way they are told, even if they are in the first person, present life to us as if it was natural. But Kafka's tormented narratives—including the narrative of his own life as it is expressed in letters and diary entries—feel liberating rather than constricting precisely because they speak of what we normally have no words for: the sense of disorientation that results from the sudden sense that nothing is given one, that it is only others who seem to lead their lives "naturally." At the same time it makes him—and his reader—recognize the wonder of life itself: Even having tea in the garden is a kind of miracle.

Kafka's sense of his life as a state of "in betweenness"—between tradition and secularity, between East and West, between childhood and adulthood—this gives him his sense of his own unnaturalness, but also of the wonder of the natural. And though of course it springs from his own unique temperament and circumstances, it is also perhaps closer to the mainstream of Jewish tradition than the unitary views of his critics. For if, in the Bible, certain absolutes are presented to us, such as strict adherence to the law on the one hand and whoring after strange gods on the other, the Israelites themselves are shown as wavering uneasily between the one and the other, as the Jews of the Diaspora will later waver between an impossible adherence to the letter of the law and the ever-tempting embrace of assimilation. And if the prophets are the mouthpieces of the one view and certain kings emblematic of the other, those to whom the Bible gives most space—Jacob and David, for example—also hover between the two.

"In-betweenness" also seems characteristic of the lessons that the feasts of the Jewish calendar seek to inculcate. On Passover night Jews are enjoined to eat unleavened bread to remind them of their former captivity: "This is the bread of affliction which our fathers ate in Egypt." It is as if the celebration of true freedom must start with a remembering of bondage, not a denial of it. At the same time the Passover service is designed to elicit the question from the child, "Why is this night different from all other nights?" It is meant to make the child understand that what he had simply taken for granted, his own existence, is the product of a miracle: Had that not happened then, you would not be here now.

Again, on Sukkot, Jews are enjoined to build booths to remind them of their wanderings, but also of the fact that life itself is fragile, that we cannot ever build walls that will protect us completely. And the Sabbath is seen as a day of rest not simply because on that day all labor stops, but because on that day will be celebrated God's own rest from his self-imposed labors. The institution of that day suggests the difference between God's making of the world and the ceaseless toil of the Israelites in Egypt. The daily prayer book, by insisting that this day is given by God and that it is a celebration of that "perfect rest wherein thou delightest," transforms the notion of rest from being merely the ceasing of work to being a day of active renewal in communal recognition and praise.[11]

What all these feasts suggest is that we can understand something only by understanding what it is not. In Aharon Appelfeld's wonderful novel, *The Age of Wonders,* the hero, whose childhood in an assimilated Jewish home in the thirties we have followed in the first part, returns after the war to his native town somewhere in central Europe. He wanders in a sort of ghostly underworld not because so little of the town has survived but on the contrary because so much of it is still there, looking as though nothing had happened. And in the town he comes across the ghosts of men, too, for the Jews who have survived have done so through another sort of death, by converting, denying their Jewishness. They are, in one sense, alive, but in one sense only. They are no better than Achilles would have been had he escaped his destiny at Troy and fled back to Greece. That, of course, is not a choice Achilles would contemplate, for a man's life in Homer's epics does not depend on length of years but rather on the *kleos andron,* the fame of men, how he will be spoken about in aftertime. Bruno's hometown may seem far indeed from Homer's Troy, but that is perhaps an illusion. For by contrast with the ghosts Bruno meets is his memory of four brothers who, though converts already, chose to join the deportees when the moment came: "The way they stood by themselves in the locked temple stirred the hearts of the beaten people with wonder for the last time. There were four of them and all the way to Minsk they did not remove their caps. . . . All night long Bruno continued to see the converts standing at attention in the temple like reprimanded soldiers. And afterwards, too, in the cold and close to death, they did not utter a sound." [12]

The brothers had to choose. Not for them the delightful postmodern freedom advocated by Shusterman. (One is tempted to say that in their choice they found themselves, as Achilles would find himself in his. But that is too positive, suggesting as it does the triumphant overcoming of suffering. None of us is permitted to say that of them and for them. All one can say is that in their choice they did not lose themselves forever, as the survivors Bruno meets lost themselves.)

Most of us, fortunately, do not have to make such choices. But, as the example of Kafka shows, there is such a thing as coming closer to oneself or the contrary, falling away from oneself. Interestingly, though Kafka insists again and again on his inability to find true rest, there are two places in his diary where something of the sense of Sabbath renewal comes through strongly. The first is when he reads aloud to a small gathering a speech he had written on the Yiddish language; the second is when, in one night, he writes the first story he truly acknowledged as his own, "The Judgement": "The fearful strain and joy, how the story developed before me," he writes, "as if I were advancing over water. . . . How everything can be said, how for everything, even the strangest fancies, there waits a great fir in which they perish and rise up again. The weariness that disappeared in the middle of the night." [13]

What I find, then, in Kafka, in Celan, in Appelfeld, in certain parts of the Bible and the liturgy,[14] is the articulation of something that I myself have felt, but that I would not have been able to recognize and accept had

I not seen it expressed in the words of another. Their words speak to me across the centuries and the miles, helping me to understand what I feel about not belonging, having no language, always being on the move; they make me realize that these are not things to be denied or overcome but are part and parcel of what I am, to be lived with and put into the service of that creativity that I recognize as a gift even if I cannot bring myself to believe in a Giver.

NOTES

1. Igor Stravinsky, *Selected Correspondence,* vol. 1, edited by Robert Craft (London: Faber, 1982), 287.

2. Jon Levenson, *Sinai and Zion: An Entry into the Jewish Bible* (Minneapolis: University of Minnesota Press, 1985).

3. Dante, *Purgatorio II,* 63; Franz Kafka, *Diaries,* Max Brod, ed. (Harmondsworth, England: Penguin, 1964), 394.

4. Kafka, *Diaries,* 252; *Letters to Friends, Family, and Editors,* translated by Richard Winston and Clara Winston (London: John Calder, 1978), 289.

5. Paul Celan, *Collected Prose,* translated by Rosemary Waldrop (Manchester, England: Carcanet, 1986), 44–45; vii–viii.

6. R. B. Kitaj, *First Diasporic Manifesto* (London: Thames and Hudson, 1989), 87.

7. Kafka, *Letters,* 373–74.

8. Kafka, *Letters to Milena,* edited by Willy Haas, and translated by Tania Stern and James Stern (London: Minerva, n.d.).

9. For a forceful assertion of this point of view, see Jonathan Sacks, "A Challenge to Jewish Secularism," *Jewish Quarterly,* 36, no. 2 (Summer 1989): 30–37.

10. Kafka, *Letters,* 17.

11. See the comments of Irving Greenberg, *The Jewish Way: Living the Holidays* (New York: Summit Books, 1988).

12. Aharon Appelfeld, *The Age of Wonders,* translated by Dalya Bilu (Boston, Godine, 1981), 246–47.

13. Kafka, *Diaries,* 181–82; 212–13. Peter Handke, in his beautiful poem *Gedicht an die Dauer* (Frankfurt: Suhr Kamp 1986), brings out well the difference between the kind of rest given by a glorious holiday and by working regularly at what satisfies one in one's normal environment. He calls this "true duration," but I think we are talking about the same things.

14. And in Hilary Putnam's essay in Chapter 7.

18

TALKING TO MYSELF

Joseph Margolis

I

I am immensely curious to find out what I shall *say*. I shall explain why in a moment. But I find it very difficult to begin, because there are a great many memories jostling in my mind for pride of place. They are all anecdotal, which seems fair enough, since autobiographical order is properly narrative. Allow me, then, to mention a few memories that have never left me, that have a certain insistent freshness that I would be dishonest to deny. Admitting them, however, betrays a complication that I cannot yet assign a quiet place in the skillful narrative I should like to form but am not sure I can.

There are two particular memories that give shape to my own sense of Jewish identity and the puzzle of not being able to shake it off. The first concerns my childhood; the second, my experience as a soldier in World War II. My father was a dentist practicing in Newark, New Jersey, at one time in the Vailsburg section of the city, the most important neighborhood of pro-Nazi Bundist activities during the early and middle thirties. He was really a poet, a translator in every direction between Hebrew, German, Yiddish, and English, a storyteller in the Yiddish tradition, one of that small number of immigrants from Eastern Europe around the turn of the century who actually went to high school in the United States and achieved a high level of literacy. I recall that the door of his office was often marked in chalk with a swastika; and I, with absolutely no understanding of the issues at stake, once found myself in a terrible fistfight with some ferocious kid from my school (in the lower grades) who identified me as a Jew. I no longer remember the details, but I do remember being questioned very closely by my father when I finally returned home. I obviously had not grasped the implications of the fight. The sense of the world's irrationality and danger has never left me since and hangs by one tenuous thread at least from that first episode. I have the impression that I could not have been more than eleven or twelve, possibly younger. In any case, these details are not the heart of the memory, only its necessary backdrop. What I do remember most clearly is my father's marvelously gay humor, a first cousin to gallows humor of course, in telling the story, again and again, of a German patient of his who came by one day quite deliberately to check out the "rumor" that my father was indeed a Jew. They spoke in German; and the man, who obviously esteemed my father, finally rendered the lovely judgment—after an extended conversation (which must have had some charm of its own)— that "it is impossible that anyone who speaks German so well could be a Jew." The verdict, doubtless carried back to the Bundists, seems to have ended the most serious forms of harassment. But what I remember best was my father's appreciation of the elegance of that short verdict. I believe I saw there, very dimly I admit, something of the world's best instruction.

The other memory is somehow linked to the first by a kind of farcical seriousness that only wars have ever managed to perfect. I recall that when I was inducted into the army I was asked what my religion was. I answered truthfully that I was an atheist. My interrogator paused a little too long, I could see, to impress me with the fact that he was not amused. He asked me, then, quite deliberately, what my father's and mother's religion was. I answered that *they* were Jewish—replying to what I took to be a precise question. He obviously wrote down that *I* was Jewish. A little later I received my official dog tags marked with an "H" in the corner. So I learned at once that adhering to the Jewish religion was, in the United States army, designated by an "H" on one's dog tags—for "Hebrew" of course; that one's religion was, for professed nonbelievers at least, the religion of one's parents; that religion was not always clearly separable from ethnic background; and, perhaps most important, that the army had not the foggiest idea of the point of the war it was supposed to be involved in or the history of Nazism. I recall, much later, in actual battle and in approaching the German border with every prospect of engaging the enemy on his own soil, that I needed to get rid of my own dog tags, that I couldn't do so without endlessly complicating my life in the U.S. Army, and that the ruse could be recognized at once by the Germans if I were captured. The madness of the whole thing is what I remember best, the supercalm assessment of the utter pointlessness of risking my life among my fellows, who were nearly to a man completely illiterate politically, who had absolutely no sense of what Hitler signified, and who were themselves quite comfortably (sometimes, amusingly) anti-Semitic. I recall for example that I was (with a mixture then of a certain pride and prejudice of my own) the only "Jew" of my battalion who volunteered for and actually completed paratrooper training. There's no question that I became acceptable to my army mates for that reason—and I was smugly grateful to be able to enjoy the fruits of my labor—whereas a number of other "Jewish" recruits were always thereafter (as before) treated with complete contempt. I must say that I made no move to soften their shame and isolation. I coopted myself in that dirty little game and accepted the terms of play of the dominant population I could not influence or fully understand or even trust. I think I have always had the sense, from Vailsburg to wherever the army happened to be to the present moment, of being an alien among humans. I have always joked about being a Martian rather than an earthling. But what I think that must have meant and must mean still (it is deeper than I can penetrate) is at least that, among "non-Jews," I was certainly not one of them, and, among "Jews," I was certainly not one of them.

Let me risk extending this sort of story a little longer. I taught for about five years, at the beginning of the sixties, at the University of Cincinnati. I recall a very nice dinner hosted by a professor from the Reformed Jewish seminary of the city, a friend of mine at the time, whose name I have lost. He was a very deliberate and thoughtful person, and the dinner was rather wonderfully stylish and tactful at the same time. But somewhere in the conversation after dinner, when we were all still at the table, he chided me in the most carefully contrived way for not having ever acted to identify myself with the Jewish community in Cincinnati. It *was* an impressive "community," and it surely regarded itself as a community. I certainly had a great many friends among its number, and I never had the slightest impulse to align myself with "it" or other available "communities." My host's complaint was the confession of one who liked and respected me both as a man and a professional—but who could not fathom my defect. I must confess that, for my own part, I was quite unprepared for this sort of frontal remark, particularly from a man of serious professional credentials. I was taken completely by surprise. The question struck me as an intrusion. I was in fact instantly reminded that when I took a post at the University of South Carolina, in Columbia, South Carolina, about two years after the Supreme Court's decision on racial discrimination, the man I expected to be my colleague there (he had just secured a post at Yale) mentioned very casually that he and his wife were pondering "which community" I and my (then-) wife "intended" to join: the Greek or the Jewish (my wife being of Greek origin). Apparently, both were distinctly powerful groups in Columbia. In effect they were congratulating me. They thought, it seems, that I was in an enviable position of being able to choose between two such fortunate options; and they obviously concluded that I must be an idiot—since I answered, without guile or hesitation, that I had no intention of joining either one. Now, I think both of these small episodes draw attention to the obvious benefits of different forms of social solidarity. To be frank, I see no difference in this regard between joining the Rotary Club or the Knights of Columbus or any number of genteel religiously denominated communities that would never dream of imposing a heavy doctrinal obligation from day to day on their members but that keep an implicit, accurate account never- theless of relevant credits and debits. Also, as I now realize, both episodes afford good evidence of a certain lack of ethnic prudence on my part.

Once again, these bits and pieces do not get to the heart of the story. The issue lies a little deeper. During my stay in Cincinnati, I was approached by a rather elusive personality who identified himself as a "grants broker." I had never heard of him or of his specialty. I was both annoyed and in- trigued by his proposal. He insisted on treating me to an expensive lunch and had enlisted the aid of one of the municipal judges in Cincinnati, a friend of mine, also Jewish, to confirm his bona fides in person. It turned out, later, that Bettman, my friend, did not actually know the man and was himself co-opted for the purpose. In any case, the stranger, a certain Birnbaum, if I remember correctly, tried to get me to be the contact man and local organizer for a group of German educators that were to visit the United States fairly soon. Birnbaum, it seems, was affiliated with an important national Jewish organization and had somehow intercepted a governmentally sponsored trip by these German educators—had actually arranged for them to travel to selected cities and to meet the "best" of the Jewish communities of the United States—in the process of making an informal survey of American social and educational life (of "American democracy," in short). He had some grant money and could sweeten the offer somewhat—how much I cannot remember. It makes no difference, although my salary at that time made every penny seem worth considering. Our German visitors had all been members of the Hitler Jugend, were all now Socialists; at least one or two were professed Communists; one was a member of a state parliamentary house; one proved to be an ardent (rather convincing) Judeophile; and (as I discovered) all were extremely appeal- ing, knowledgeable, attentive to the implications of the war; none was very expert in English. My own German was almost nonexistent.

I borrowed a Volkswagen bus from a friend, thinking they would find that amusing. I located a bar or two that served acceptable German beer; and then I discovered that prominent people in the city (well-to-do Jewish businessmen) had already been alerted to their visit and were anxious to make arrangements to host them during their stay. The whole thing was rather pushy on the side of Cincinnati's would-be hosts, but irresistible in terms of my being able to meet men of my own age or slightly younger who had been active in the German world. I never heard from Birnbaum again, that is, after the visit.

The important point of the story depends on the sheer contingency that, during their stay in Cincinnati, the Berlin airlift was suddenly organized as America's response to Russian threats to cut Berlin off from the West. Our German visitors were terribly upset. They thought war might break out at once. One of their number actually lived in West Berlin, was married to a Slavic woman (I believe) who, besides being pregnant and about to deliver, had once been confined in a Russian concentration camp and might therefore be picked up again. We were awaiting the arrival, from Germany, of the last of their number. If *he* did not come on the flight announced, then (they felt) it was certain that war would follow. We went in the Volkswagen to the airport and proceeded to get drunk at the restaurant as we waited. All the cautions of formal etiquette were pretty quickly discarded, and someone asked me point-blank what sort of a name "Margolis" was. I sensed at once that the question was not a casual one; everyone seemed suddenly alert, though we were all pretty nervous and pretty drunk. Now, in that Augenblick, I realized that I could not detach myself from what they might infer from my name's origin, that is, from my merely acknowledging that it was a Hebrew name. I could not afford to give our visitors any impression of the fine-tooled distinctions I had worked on so carefully and would ordinarily have found quite adequate—for instance, that I was an atheist, opposed to my father's Zionism, unwilling to identify myself as adhering to Jewish practices, and the like. I could not allow them any relief from their own nervous sense of involvement—or from *my* perception of the seriousness of my having accepted the commission to receive them as the professed representatives of postwar Germany. I felt I had no right to make things easy for them or for myself. I had to give a proper sense of our being implicated together—they and I alike—in the terrible history we shared (and knew we shared without mentioning). But I had to act without explicit accusation or judgment, without any presumption that I was somehow entitled to set the record straight then and there in our small republic of the airport bar.

All this is hindsight, of course. But I sensed—I am glad to say I did not identify myself as the "aggrieved party"—that the logic of the situation could have made it impossible for our German visitors to have done anything else but to have "suffered" in silence the testimony of such a witness and the verdict of such a judge rolled into one in the voice of their chauffeur and friendly neighborhood guide. I must have struck the right chord in signaling my unwillingness to ignore *their* part (whatever it was) in the war years that were still so well remembered by all of us and my own unwillingness to soften in advance whatever might be their guess about what was meant by my simply announcing that my name *was* indeed a Jewish name. Because, immediately after, when the plane finally arrived and the last of their number did join us, we understood at once our new-found openness. The relief conveyed, the even greater relief we felt because we now had found ourselves in a moment of total but unspoken candor, produced a camaraderie that cannot be described.

The point of the story, of course, is that I was caught up in the contingent history of my own time and life and could not extricate myself— dared not in fact. I was angry, at risk, distinctly careful. Accordingly, I could not reconstruct any particular rationale I pleased regarding the war and my Jewish origins—as if I would never have had to answer to others who would have been doing the same thing and testing me all the while. I shared with our visitors certain constraints of relevance, seriousness, responsibility, tact, fairness, plausibility, manliness that no solo response could possibly satisfy. What was wanted (we all knew at once) was a series of small, matched, carefully linked public acts—dance steps almost, if that will not seem too frivolous—by which a supervenient protocol could be formed, there and then, by all of us to catch up all that remained so mercifully inchoate. Inchoate but still present.

It is in this rather complicated sense that I have always managed so unsuccessfully to identify myself as an alien being—neither one of those nor one of these; or, as an alien bound to both and, therefore, perhaps a member of both. That is to say, a member of the same human race that is forever disposed to divide itself in privilege and is forever obliged to undo that mischief.

II

You will see that I have come around to theorizing in spite of myself. I have thought about these memories a long time. I have shaped them. I have tried to make them emblems of my life, tried to bring my life into line with their instruction. All somewhat secretly, of course, never programmatically. They are more a matter of style than of substance, except that, ultimately, style is also substance.

I mistrust people of principle, I must say. For me, the Nazis were a people of principle. All fanatics are. You will say, but we must have principles—good ones, of course. I say there are none. They are all powermongering strategies meant to hold onto the old order or to impose a new one. Every form of corporate life is committed to gathering more and more power to ensure its own apparent principles. I don't say we can do without them—the profession of principles or the conspiracy of collective power. And I do not suppose I have any right to tell *you* what to believe or how to act. There is a terrible anarchy risked all the time, and there is a terrible order risked as well. We move between those limits, while all the evils of the human world need to be made known and remembered. There *are* great evils, I don't deny. The Jewish world is obsessed with the fact and with its own remarkable history of misfortune. But that hardly means that there *are* true principles to live by, or "communities" that live correctly. There are none.

If you now ask me: Well, and what exactly is your view of what it is to "be a Jew?" How do you comport yourself in terms of your "origins?" How shall I answer? Certainly, one thing I say is that I live with the perpetual caution that reminds me that the remarkable calamities of Jewish history *are mine* and that future calamities of the same sort *may claim me* some bright sunny morning when I get out of bed. But that is prudence; that is not principle. I cannot ignore my history—and I'm not exactly stupid. But it is *also* our history, not really "mine" as opposed to "thine."

I remember, in my army days, a rather nice chaplain offered once to get me a Bible if I could care to have it to read. Great, I said (it's a pretty good book). But, you know, he brought me only the Old Testament. With that extraordinary tact for which it is justly famous, the U.S. Army had managed to divide the Bible into the Old and New Testaments—so as not to offend anyone, you see—and had naturally given the Jewish chaplains a stack of Old Testaments to distribute and the Christians, a stack of the New. An absolutely superb piece of wit—and thrift, of course. He was a bit nonplussed, my Protestant chaplain, when I drew his attention to what was missing. To make a long story short, he had a helluva time finding a complete Bible, in one volume. He did, finally, and I have that very book (army issue) still in my collection, cheerfully signed by C. C. Chaffee—that is, the very same book that, already in ancient times, had managed to exclude what did not rightly belong to the canon. That's fine. I don't really fault the original authors for that. We all do it.

But what I want to say is that there is no principled preeminence to the history of Jewish calamity. It is a remarkable history, of course, very likely unique. No doubt a preeminent indictment of man's inhumanity to man. Well, "Man's inhumanity to man" *can* be a whitewash, I don't deny—as it seems to have become just recently in the Polish flap regarding the Carmelite nuns at Auschwitz. One can never ignore the salient perceptions of evil. The extermination of the Jews at Auschwitz was not merely an instance of man's inhumanity to man, it *was* the extermination of the *Jews*. But it is also a Jewish mistake to disallow the warning that it was a case of man's inhumanity to man—meaning by that that there were and always will be similarly remembered calamities involving other peoples (*at* Auschwitz and elsewhere) that cannot be delayed or separated from one another or ranked. The Holocaust does *not* represent the single most important, the only, the indispensable, the paradigmatic, or the greatest collective calamity of mankind. It is not even a proprietary evil for Jewish custodians or "professional" Jews; or, for that matter, an adequate calling *for anyone*. There is no such thing. It's a history that needs to be remembered—by everyone. In my opinion, it is remembered best when it is remembered in every other large and small evil that we now or soon will confront—and may, therefore, act to defeat. The point of remembering is to be ready to act against anything comparable. *Anything else is a fraud, construed on a principle.*

I must say that I have been fascinated by Elie Wiesel's great skill in functioning as an effective custodian of the Holocaust. But I *watch* him like a hawk (when I can, on television). I do not trust his role, though I see the man's humanity. And his smoothness. And the good he does. In my mind, he occupies a place comparable to that of Mother Teresa. I don't trust her either, frankly; she has a mad woman's monophilia. I suppose I am asking the impossible of both. I doubt Mother Teresa could organize her care of the humanity she's collected without the fire of her faith. But I also doubt she can bring to that sustained care a Christian love that never intrudes the least improper zeal. In a word, I doubt she acts to relieve human suffering *simpliciter:* She acts, in serving those she serves (of whatever history or persuasion), with the perfect optimism of one who would bring them all in good time (and for their own good) to the *greater* benefit of knowing the same Christian faith that inspires her own effort.

It is a matter of some delicacy: I doubt she ever forces the question. I only say she probably cannot separate in principle her care of the suffering and her grave concern for the salvation of their immortal souls. Similarly, Wiesel is certainly much affected by the calamities of *peoples* other than the Jews; but as the public witness for the latter, he cannot permit *any* absorption in the sheer suffering of other peoples that threatens to eclipse the permanent privilege of the other. Both are compromised, I feel, though in the most human of ways. They are affected through the filter of their respective collective loyalties; and, I say, every such loyalty is an artifact hostage to power.

I am prepared to be corrected. But in either case, my point is secure: There is no *principled* reason to assign a privileged position to the suffering of the Jews, and there is no *principled* reason for Jews to assign it such a position. There are natural reasons for doing so—instincts of affiliation, the profound infectiousness of perceived suffering, for instance, and prudence. There is also no *principled* reason, no *prior* legitimating reason, for tending to those who suffer, are dying, are neglected, shunned, cast aside, diseased. There is only the deep but by no means ubiquitous impulse of humanity *on which* we may construct whatever rationale we please. To make these matters matters of principle is, as many shrewd voices have remarked, to "intrude one clause too many." Allow the point, I say: Elie Wiesel and Mother Teresa become entirely admirable. Their own conceptual linkages—their principles and collectivities—become merely personal idioms or styles that attract us without danger. Certainly both "produce more good" than I could ever claim. *But they know what I know they cannot know.* They are ruthlessly principled people. They are self-effacing figures of immense moral power, gathering a community of souls around them. But their most endearing trait *is subsumed under an exclusionary principle that each has universalized.* I would rather have them than Hitler, of course. But *they* define the danger I see, every bit as much as Hitler— more clearly in fact because of the power of their agreeable seduction. I am not one of those. I remember meeting a Scottish television evangelist in a sleeping compartment on the train from Brussels to Rome, who said triumphantly (on the point of leaving me—that is, after a long harangue between us about atheism and Christianity) that I would surely see the force of his message as I approached the end of my life. I shot back, equally disagreeably, that I had hoped his best claims did not depend on the growing enfeeblement of his opponents.

We produce monsters of principled evil because we produce titans of principle whose own exclusionary good we refuse to see *as* a distinct kind of evil. We imagine *we* must also be committed to some similar exclusionary principle; and so we divide humanity into the habituating collective groups we find ourselves born into, or which we can join by easy projection from the other. Having done that, *we* become the custodians of our own exclusive principles.

Just last October I had dinner with some friends during a conference in Vancouver. At the table an Israeli colleague of mine, a very dear friend, became absolutely furious at another guest because—as far as I could make out—that man had somehow conveyed the idea that the Holocaust was *comparable* to other political or ethnic calamities, not even *primum inter pares* among the world's famous genocides. The Holocaust *was* indeed a unique slaughter, possibly the greatest single crime of its kind. But I see no principle at stake in assigning it first place. My own ignorance keeps me from fully comprehending the Khmer Rouge's murder of the Cambodians, the Turks' murder of the Armenians, or, more ambiguously, the starvation of a whole side of Africa. There are also crimes of compelling evil but of smaller scope and "small" significance—due to little more than technical ineptitude (on the part of the perpetrators), narrowness of vision (on our part), geographical inaccessibility, and the sheer indifference of Western journalists. I think of the Brazilians' clearing the land by machine gunning Indians.

These *collective* evils afford a distinctive lesson. Understanding them defines what is so uneasy about the would-be instruction of one's role "as a Jew." First of all, collective entities are fictions: "peoples," "races," "nations," "churches." They are all divisions of aggregated human persons drawn from the same species according to some exclusionary principle. If they were not that they would not survive in the reflexive zeal of their own adherents. Second, we are all caught up willy-nilly in the life of some such perceived collectivity; and we permit ourselves, by our inertia, at least, to slip from the intimacy of that history to the loyalty of its contrived principle. Third, the worst or the best of us cleverly invent a rationale for believing that one or another of those principles is really the expression of a superior rule uniquely suited to the whole of mankind. There, I dare say, you have the essential structure of the political and moral and religious ecstasy of every remembered "movement." There is no such discovery to be made—transforming exclusion into true inclusion.

I am rather fond of pointing out that atheism *is* a religion, a whole flock of religions, in fact, not the mere opponent of religion as such—though, certainly, the opponent of all "organized" religions, the opponent of all exclusionary universal religions. The decline of a vigorous atheism in this sense is almost medically indicated by the pathology of the other. (Pathology and power are the same thing.) By analogy, to "be" a "proper" Jew in our time is, I am suggesting, to be a Martian, an alien on earth, one who refuses to honor the Jewish claim to have suffered more than any other people, one who opposes the right to exact the present's tribute to the past, one who opposes all *principled* exclusions or exclusions transformed into privileged inclusions. No more tax collectors, please, no matter how endearing they may be. It's what in a very small way I resisted in Cincinnati and Columbia. I could have joined, I suppose—I could have "passed." I'm still resisting. I've been a loner too long. I'm hypersensitive to the collusions of power—the small collusions, of course, the lesser obscenities, you might say.

Life is hieratic in a good sense. What I mean is that at some point of maturity we bring to full flower the exemplary images (not the principles) of life we most admire; and, by declension, we study how to bring the meanest level of our own life into accord with those. At the lowest conceptual limit, we hold onto our best intuitions of how the members of Homo sapiens are bound to suffer—in a bodily way at first, and then, by extension, in the struggles of the spirit. We live between those limits and, between them, *anything goes,* anything *may* be as reasonable as anything else, on someone's say-so—except of course in the eyes of those fanatics who insist on the exclusive (or inclusive) principles of one privileged life or another, the vanguard of the entire *race,* of the "human family" that finds its instruction in the history of a privileged *society.* The non sequitur stares you in the face. I'll have none of it.

At the risk of pedantry, try this out: Socrates was baffled by the simple fact that although a pilot, a physician, a shepherd all have a distinct function—and therefore a proper "good" to aim at—the human person as such *has none.* Unable to accept that stunning truth, he or Plato invented a world of eternal norms. So he managed after all to find a function for man. You will not, I trust, think it bizarre of me to suggest that the "professional" role of the Jew (substitute whatever admirable wizard you please) is the direct beneficiary of the kind of thinking that produced that sort of solution. *Man has no natural norm—and no revealed norms either.* But he cannot, it seems, live with that fact alone. He would rather recognize the potential legitimacy of his enemy's principle in order to ensure an audience for his own. There is the key to the prudence of Jewish identity.

There is no way to earn the right to instruct mankind. Every human being has the gift to see when people suffer greatly. There is no morality, no politics, no law, no art, no religion, no instruction ultimately saner than that. To go beyond it is to risk a false prophecy and a falser principle. No doubt there are practical regularities every complex society requires. But that is not a basis for universal principles that cut off all those who endanger the universality of principled claims. No doubt there are contests of power we cannot evade in securing our own rules. But why pretend they are more than that—except to match the dangerous pretensions of others? In that sense, the history of Jewish suffering mocks us with the truth. It focuses by deflection all the histories of suffering mankind. It cheats the theme, therefore, being proprietary, principled, privileged. It has even been known to acquire a self-congratulatory voice, in the sense that this particular people knows itself to have been marked as a people for a truly distinguished career of misery.

It would be wrong to think that it would be wrong for Jews to take whatever steps they imagine might minimize another such world-class disaster as the Holocaust. But in that very passion it is altogether too easy to take on airs. Envy the dead, for they are beyond suffering, goes the saying. I say, memories be damned if they cannot be made to serve those who live. *And anything goes if it can do that.* The Holocaust risks becoming a commodity. I'll have none of that—at any cost. But I do remember, I do remember, the mounds of bones. We need to see the evidence again and again. But not to blind us to the suffering under our noses. Who knows what our own Vietnam accomplished? Our Guatemala? Our South Africa? Our Israel? How can the Holocaust be separated from these? And how can one respond to them as a mere "Jew"?

III

The irony is that I have actually begun to define a role for the "Jew." It is not a Jewish role, however. It involves no principles, no assumptions of power, no exclusiveness, no norms, no rewards or punishments ("on earth as it is in Heaven"), no reference to corporate Jewish life, though it does draw on the themes of Jewish experience: *Bear witness to great suffering everywhere;* relieve it in whatever way you are moved to do. It is a role responding to an invitation, not to a rule or principle. There is no relevant principle. It is a role that is not concerned with monitoring conformity with the settled criteria of right and wrong. It is no more than a focused response to the temptation to enlarge our sensibilities. But it does have a touch of daring about it, a simplicity that defies the habits of familiar power. The Jew has the distinction of having defined his own history dialectically—as the history of an entire people marked for suffering and marked for a loyalty tested through that suffering. Elie Wiesel is the compelling virtuoso of the practice. Singly, each Jew is tempted to make himself the public witness of that same suffering. But by that very obsession, he risks the natural generosity of the role. He ranks the suffering of others, certainly of his enemies. I do not say it's possible to be the kind of saint required—or, possible for many. But to be the self-appointed custodians of the Holocaust, to seize the role as the test of Jewish distinction, is to invite a counterexclusion. What is the use, after all, of such a role in today's Israel? What is the point of being a Christian among Christians in the West? Why be a Communist in Tiananmen Square? Or a Muslim caught up in the war between Iraq and Iran?

I say the experiment is an utter failure. We cannot afford to stand on principles any longer. We must invent another mode of life. Jews, therefore, *are* in an enviable position. They have made a glorious calling of their accusation against the world. They have marked themselves as the victims of the Egyptians, the Assyrians, the Catholics, the Christians, the Muslims, the Nazis, the Soviets, the Europeans, the ancient and the modern world. And who can deny the justice of it? They have an acquired skill that could be of considerable use. But they have committed it to a collective fate. They have mystified a conspiracy of deadly partners in order to elevate their own history. And that is a self-defeating maneuver. What, after all, is My Lai in comparison to the Holocaust, or "retaliation" in Lebanon, or the fate of the Gypsies? The Jews have "only" to divest themselves of their special pleading. *They need to be everyone:* Poles, Biafrans, Laotians, Bangladeshi, who knows what. To make a joke of it: They must be Martians to become themselves. I should like to believe that, wherever I was born, that theme would have captured me. But I'm not at all sure.

I have had to work out for myself the meaning of that unique history—the history the Jews are so proud of and impose so unconditionally on their children. But there must be a better way of employing its distinction. There must be a way that does not ensure its repetition. Call that an Old Testament prophecy if you wish. It has no need, however, of revelations, no need of doctrines, no principles, no gods, no supernatural contracts—except, of course, for whatever in a subordinate sense particular peoples require in order to keep their resolve intact. But that is not news. The answer, I suggest, is that they (*we:* I and thou and everyone similarly fated) disown the special privilege of their (our) remembered history. We need to think of the planetary Holocaust. Being a Jew (being a Martian Jew, if the joke be allowed) is knowing that the memory of that history is too much and not enough—in our time. It is time to move on.

About myself: I am an atheist, as I say, although I do admire parts of the Old and New Testaments, parts of the Koran, parts of the Vedas and Upanishads, parts of even more exotic books. I would admire them, I suppose, if I were orphaned at birth in Antarctica. But what of it? The Old Testament belongs to the Jews only in the thinnest sense. I am pleased to be a Jew because I am not one; and I am not one because I really am one. Why, otherwise, could I think and talk this way? It is a style as natural to me as anything I do. I remember a compelling remark made in a book review of an autobiography I never read, by an author I can no longer re-call. He was apparently a gifted and neurotic young man in that strained way New York Jews pride themselves so much on being. He converted to Catholicism because he was dissatisfied with Judaism; and of course he eventually abandoned Catholicism because he came to see that there was no greater gain to be had in it of the sort he had imagined he needed. Let him be, therefore: He may even have suicided. The reviewer observes, in passing, that Jews and Catholics suffer related but opposed disorders. Jews, he says, are distressed by the notion that there may be something of great importance about the world remaining to be discovered, that they will be deprived of ever finding out; Catholics, on the other hand, are dis-tressed by the notion that whatever they do discover may subvert whatever it is right for them to believe; and both pursue their heated inquiries with the force of a devotional. I find the contrast apt, though I admit the options are not equally attractive in my eyes. But I *am* a Jew on that double count. Now, what is the doctrinal significance of that?

I must remind you that my Martian option is only the option of a Jewish Martian. Remember that. There are other Martians around, not even of European origin. There are lots of Japanese and Chinese and Indian Mar-tians, African Martians and the Martians of other native peoples. And they may well hit on a better way of making the same point. I shouldn't be a bit surprised.

As for Jewish identity: Ignore the religious and ethnic professions of parents, allow for voluntary nonadherence to the Jewish religion, acknowl-edge nonconformity with regard to the interests of self-styled Jewish com-munities, concede the absence of "racial" traits—then either there are no defining traits of "Jewish identity" or there are none that preclude such identity. For example, hatred of Jews could be a Jewish trait. My own sense is that "Jews" just are those who dwell, however slightly, on the question of *what* is the implication of their having been born from stock that, *some-where* along the line, professed to adhere to the Jewish religion or to live in accord with Jewish custom. Or, they are those whom others wonder about in the same way. From there, *anything* else may be a "Jewish" trait.

But Jewish identity may be made to have normative force as well. If it does, it signifies either membership in a spiritual corporation that claims legitimate moral priority (the "Jewish people") or it signifies an ineluctable obligation of some sort under exclusionary rules (the code of "Jewish life") or both. Otherwise, "Jewish" is a descriptive predicate of any sort depend-ing on the vacuous predicate mentioned, applicable by divided reference to any pertinent aggregate of individuals. Its distinction is that it accommodates a limitless range of attributes—notably incompatible ones—for instance, adherence to the Jewish religion or to atheism (or to Christianity, for that matter); adherence to Zionism or resistance to Zionism (or indifference). There you have the point of the worry about Elie Wiesel and Mother Teresa. And there you have the sense of the carnivalesque notion of the "Jew."

Nevertheless, against myself, I freely acknowledge also that, regarding crimes against collective Jewry (I admit that there have been such crimes), I would always wish to act on behalf of that collectivity; that to preserve Jewish lives in the Second World War, many Europeans, many Christian Europeans, behaved heroically out of their own principled convictions; and that such monuments as Auschwitz correctly testify to the conscious effort of the Nazis to exterminate the Jews. I say only that my own testimony is not meant to be incompatible with making room for the testimony of others who would condemn my own.

ABOUT THE CONTRIBUTORS

BERNARD BEROFSKY is a professor of philosophy at Columbia University. He has written on a variety of topics in metaphysics and the philosophy of mind. The area of his special interest is freedom, autonomy, and moral responsibility and his principal work is *Freedom from Necessity: The Metaphysical Basis of Responsibility* (1988).

GARRY M. BRODKSY is a professor of philosophy at the University of Connecticut. He has published articles on John Dewey and pragmatism and is currently working on a study of Nietzsche's immoralism.

CORA DIAMOND is a professor of philosophy at the University of Virginia. She is the author of *The Realistic Spirit: Wittgenstein, Philosophy, and the Mind* (1991) and the editor of *Wittgenstein's Lectures on the Foundations of Mathematics Cambridge, 1939.*

DAVID THEO GOLDBERG is an associate professor in the School of Justice Studies at Arizona State University. He is the author of *Racist Culture: Philosophy and the Politics of Meaning* (1993); editor of *Anatomy of Racism* (1990), *Ethical Theories and Social Issues* (1989), and *Multiculturalism: A Reader* (forthcoming); and co-editor of the new journal *Social Identities.*

LEON J. GOLDSTEIN is a professor of philosophy at the State University of New York at Binghamton. He is the editor of *International Studies in Philosophy* and the author, with Lucy S. Dawidawicz, of *Politics in a Pluralist Democracy* (1963), and of *Historical Knowing* (1976). A book on conceptual tension is in progress.

GABRIEL JOSIPOVICI is Professor of English in the School of European Studies, University of Sussex. He is a novelist, playwright, and critic. His most recent novel is *The Big Glass* (1992) and his most recent critical book is *The Book of God* (1990).

ASA KASHER is Horodisch Professor of Philosophy of Language at Tel-Aviv University, the editor of *Philosophia: Philosophical Quarterly of Israel,* and the author of numerous papers in philosophy of language and in philosophy of religion, as well as on moral aspects of public affairs in Israel.

MICHAEL KRAUSZ is the Milton C. Nahm Professor and chair of the Department of Philosophy at Bryn Mawr College. He is also the founding chair of the Greater Philadelphia Philosophy Consortium. He is the author of *Right and Reasons: Interpretation in Cultural Practices* (1993) and editor of *The Interpretation of Music: Philosophical Essays* (1993), *Relativism: Interpretation and Confrontation* (1989), and *Critical Essays on the Philosophy of R. G. Collingwood* (1972). He is also co-editor of *Rationality and Relativism in the Human Sciences* (1986), *Relativism: Cognitive and Moral* (1982), and *The Concept of Creativity in Science and Art* (1981).

GORDON LAFER is a doctoral candidate in political science at Yale University, where he is a fellow at the Institute for Social and Policy Studies. He has worked as a union organizer and served as a policy analyst in the New York City Mayor's Office for Economic Development. He is interested in political theory, contemporary Jewish politics, and urban policy.

BEREL LANG is a professor of philosophy and humanistic studies at the State University of New York at Albany. Recent books of his include *Writing and the Moral Self* (1991), *The Anatomy of Philosophical Style* (1990), and *Act and Idea in the Nazi Genocide* (1990).

JOSEPH MARGOLIS is Laura H. Carnell Professor of Philosophy at Temple University and past president of the American Society of Aesthetics. He has recently published *The Truth about Relativism* (1991) and will be publishing shortly *The New Puzzle of Interpretation* and *The Flux of History and the Flux of Science.*

DIANA TIETJENS MEYERS is a professor of philosophy at the University of Connecticut, Storrs. She is the author of *Inalienable Rights: A Defense* (1986) and *Self, Society, and Personal Choice* (1989), and she is at work on a book about psychoanalytic feminism and moral philosophy—*The Multiplex Self.*

ALAN MONTEFIORE is a fellow and tutor in philosophy at Balliol College,

Oxford. He has published works on, among other subjects, moral philosophy, political philosophy, philosophy of education, contemporary French philosophy, and the description and explanation of goal-directive behavior. He is currently working on questions raised by the interplay of personal and cultural identity.

HILARY PUTNAM is Walter Beverly Pearson Professor of Modern Mathematics and Mathematical Logic and a professor of philosophy at Harvard University. His books include *Reason, Truth, and History* (1981), *The Many Faces of Realism* (1988), *Representation and Reality* (1988), and *Realism with a Human Face* (1992), and his Gifford Lectures, *Renewing Philosophy*, is forthcoming.

NATHAN ROTENSTREICH is Ahad Ha'am Professor of Philosophy emeritus, the Hebrew University of Jerusalem, and is also a member of the Israel Academy of Sciences and Humanities, International Institute of Philosophy. His recent books include *Order and Might* (1988), *Alienation: The Concept and Its Reflection* (1989), *Immediacy and Its Limits: A Study in Martin Buber's Thought* (1991), and, in Hebrew, *From Presuppositions to Reality* (1991).

LIONEL RUBINOFF is a professor of philosophy and environmental studies and chair of the Department of Philosophy at Trent University, Peterborough, Ontario, Canada. His publications include *The Pornography of Power* (1968), *Faith and Reason* (1968), *Collingwood and the Reform of Metaphysics* (1970), and *Objectivity, Method, and Point of View* (1991), which he has recently edited with Jan van der Dussen.

RICHARD SHUSTERMAN, editor of *Analytic Aesthetics* (1989) and coeditor of *The Interpretive Turn: Philosophy, Science, Culture* (1991), is the author of *The Object of Literary Criticism* (1984), *T. S. Eliot and the Philosophy of Criticism* (1988), and *Pragmatist Aesthetics: Living Beauty, Rethinking Art* (1992). Educated at Hebrew University of Jerusalem and Oxford University, he is currently a professor of philosophy at Temple University.

LAURENCE THOMAS teaches in the Philosophy, Political Science, and Judaic Studies departments at Syracuse University. He is the author of *Living Morally* (1989) and *Vessels of Evil: A Psychology of Slavery and the Holocaust* (1993).

EDDY M. ZEMACH is the Ahad Ha'am Professor of Philosophy at the Hebrew University of Jerusalem. His books in philosophy include: *Aesthetics* (1976); *The Reality of Meaning and the Meaning of "Reality"* (1992); *Types: Essays in Metaphysics, 1992.* His books on Hebrew literature include *Kshoresh Etz* (on S. Ibn Gabirol), 1962; *Halavie Hamistater* (on H. N. Bialik), 1966; *Yetzira Mehukama* (on Shmuel Hanagid), 1983; and *Kriah Tamah* (Hebrew literature of the twentieth century), 1990.

INDEX OF NAMES